This book is an analysis of two major resource allocation mechanisms which function in the modern economy. One is the market mechanism, which has been subject to extensive examination by neoclassical economists. The other is a mechanism instituted by a firm, which has been given relatively little attention. Professor Ichiishi presents a groundbreaking theory of the firm which views the firm as an organization characterized by (1) diversity of (and most likely, conflict among) the interests of its members, and (2) in spite of such diversity, the members' acceptance of a coordinated choice of activities. A firm is a coalition formed when people play a cooperative game, and this descriptive cooperative game is the firm-specific resource allocation mechanism.

The author first constructs a formal framework which embodies both the neoclassical market mechanism and the descriptive cooperative game. Among the basic results he obtains in this setup are: definition of a new descriptive equilibrium concept that can be interpreted as an outcome of simultaneous workings of the two resource allocation mechanisms, existence results for this concept which synthesize the existence theorems of the neoclassical paradigm and of the core theory (a traditional descriptive cooperative game theory), Pareto non-optimality of the equilibrium, and a welfare comparison of the present-day capitalism and market-cooperative socialism. He then develops a normative mechanism theory to implement Pareto optimality in the presence of increasing returns to scale. He closes the book with his partial equilibrium analysis, which characterizes the coalitionally stable hierarchical structures in a firm.

This book is thus a major contribution to the theory of the firm, cooperative game theory, general equilibrium analysis, and fixed-point theory.

The cooperative nature of the firm

The cooperative nature of the firm

TATSURO ICHIISHI

Department of Economics,
The Ohio State University

CAMBRIDGE
UNIVERSITY PRESS

Published by the Press Syndicate of the University of Cambridge
The Pitt Building, Trumpington Street, Cambridge CB2 1RP
40 West 20th Street, New York, NY 10011–4211, USA
10 Stamford Road, Oakleigh, Victoria 3166, Australia

First published 1993

Printed in Great Britain at the University Press, Cambridge

A catalogue record for this book is available from the British Library

Library of Congress cataloguing in publication data

Ichiishi, Tatsuro.
Cooperative nature of the firm / Tatsuro Ichiishi.
p. cm.
Includes bibliographical references and index.
ISBN 0 521 41444 X (hardback)
1. Industrial organization. 2. Game theory. 3. Equilibrium (Economics) 4. Welfare economics. I. Title.
HD2326.I24 1993
338.5–dc20 92-2708 CIP

ISBN 0 521 41444 X hardback

SE

To Barbara and the memory of my Mother

Contents

Preface

This monograph presents my view on the essential workings of the modern economy – the view that I have developed over almost two decades. The presentation here is formal, that is, axiomatic. Axiomatic treatment conveys ideas clearly, and avoids any influence on analysis of a particular interpretation of the model and a specific ideology. Using the axiomatic method, I hope I have expressed my economic view clearly here, both its scope and limits. I could not find any existing economic model that would provide a formal framework within which to express my view consistently, so I had to develop a new formal theory that would do the job.

My basic view is summarized as follows: A modern economy embodies two major resource allocation mechanisms. One is the market mechanism, sometimes called the price mechanism. The other is a mechanism instituted by an organization of people called a firm. To realize coexistence of two mechanisms is not new; it goes back at least as far as Max Weber early in this century. Since then, the development of the neoclassical paradigm has greatly clarified the workings of the market mechanism. The neoclassical paradigm has indeed played an essential role in shaping my own thinking. On the other hand, not much consensus has been obtained in regard to the nature of the firm-specific mechanism, nor have many attempts been made to formalize any view. My view in this respect is quite different from that of Max Weber, and also from that of several recent schools of the theory of the firm which have gained some popularity, such as the behavioral model approach to the firm (Herbert A. Simon), the new institutional economics (Oliver E. Williamson), and the principal-agent theory. I view a firm as an organization characterized by (1) diversity of (and most likely, conflict among) the interests of its members, and (2) in spite of such diversity, the members' acceptance of a coordinated choice of activities. A firm understood in this way is precisely a coalition which is formed when people play a cooperative game, and this descriptive cooperative game is the firm-specific resource allocation mechanism. (The definition of the term "cooperative game" differs even among the contemporary researchers in game theory. My definition is spelled out in Section 2.1 of this monograph; in short, I define a cooperative game according to a behavioral principle, that is, according to whether or not players coordinate their strategy choice, rather than according to a specific game-theoretical model.)

The formal general equilibrium framework I provide in this monograph embodies both the neoclassical market mechanism and the descriptive cooperative game. The theory I develop here may be considered a synthesis of the neoclassical paradigm and the classical descriptive cooperative game theory. When I started my research in the theory of the firm more than eighteen years ago, the formal analysis of cooperative behavior at an appropriate degree of generality for economic application was not readily available. I have developed the cooperative game theory to the extent that my results can be applied for this purpose. Among the basic results I have obtained in this general equilibrium setup are: definition of a new descriptive equilibrium concept that can be interpreted as an outcome of simultaneous workings of the two resource allocation mechanisms; existence results for this concept; Pareto non-optimality of the equilibrium; and a welfare comparison of the present-day capitalism and market-cooperative socialism.

My further results on the cooperative decision-making in a firm are: developing a normative mechanism theory to implement Pareto optimality in the presence of increasing returns to scale; and providing a partial equilibrium analysis, which characterizes the coalitionally stable hierarchical structures in a firm.

This monograph presents the aforementioned work in a systematic and readable way. Chapters 1 and 2 are expository. Chapters 3–6 constitute the main body of the work, and are based on my original articles, most of which were published in various journals or in edited books.

Chapter 1 reviews some of the basic elements discussed in the theory of the firm literature, and indicates that the neoclassical theory is too simple to treat them. Many criticisms of the existing literature presented here reflect my own view.

Chapter 2 reviews the elements of descriptive cooperative game theory that are related to my approach to the theory of the firm. The Appendix to Chapter 2 consists of several simple economic examples which illustrate some of the theorems of Sections 2.1–2.4. Many of these examples capture diverse aspects of the main models of Chapters 3–6.

Chapter 3 is the basic part of my work: It presents my general equilibrium model which embodies both the neoclassical market mechanism (for allocation of non-human resources) and the cooperative resource allocation mechanism within the firm (for allocation of human resources). The equilibrium concept I propose here is a hybrid of the neoclassical competitive equilibrium (a typical descriptive noncooperative solution concept) and the core (a typical descriptive cooperative solution concept). There are two specific versions of my model: (1) the modern capitalistic economy as observed by Adolf A. Berle, Jr. and Gardiner C. Means (1932), in which ownership (stockholding) and control (management) of a firm are separated, and (2) the post-war market-cooperative socialism as observed by Jan Vanek (1972), in which the market mechanism is introduced into the socialist regime. An equilibrium existence theorem is established for the general model, which clarifies conditions on the data under which the present general-equilibrium method is valid. I remark on the technical matter that this existence theorem includes as special cases: Kenneth J. Arrow and Gerard Debreu's (1954) neoclassical competitive equilibrium existence theorem; John F. Nash, Jr.'s (1951) noncooperative equilibrium existence theorem; Herbert E. Scarf's (1967a) theorem for nonemptiness of the core; and my own strong equilibrium existence theorem. These existence theorems are properly located in the fixed-point theorem literature.

Chapter 4 continues the study of the descriptive economic model of Chapter 3. It first reports the simple fact that the two fundamental theorems of welfare economics, which establish relationship between the neoclassical competitive equilibrium and the Pareto optimum, are no longer true for the equilibrium concept I introduced. It then addresses a different welfare problem. The macro versions of the capitalistic economy and the associated socialistic economy are defined, and in this macro context, the following theorem is established: If the socialistic economy can be decomposed into subeconomies, each satisfying increasing returns with respect to the firm size, then for each equilibrium of the capitalistic economy there exists an equilibrium of the socialistic economy such that the former is Pareto superior to the latter. It is also suggested that given the generality of the assumptions, this welfare implication is likely to be the only result one can hope for in comparing the performance of the two systems.

Chapter 5 reports the result of the work that Martine Quinzii and I did jointly (1983), in which a new normative resource allocation mechanism (a new constitution) for a production economy with increasing returns to scale is proposed, so that if the people follow this rule while pursuing their self-interests, then the Pareto optimum will be achieved in equilibrium.

Chapter 6 reports my results that characterize the class of all hierarchical structures within a firm that have a nonempty core regardless of the preference relation of each member.

For more developed philosophical and conceptual discussions of the work in this monograph, see Tatsuro Ichiishi (forthcoming).

The most important ingredient of this monograph, in fact, in any monograph in descriptive economic theory, is the author's view about the essential workings of the economy under study. Once such a view is formulated in a formal economic model, analysis is frequently facilitated by looking at the underlying game-theoretical structure; this is indeed the case in the work reported in this monograph. I had my first systematic exposure to game theory when I was a visiting research fellow at the Center for Operations Research and Econometrics (CORE), Université Catholique de Louvain, Belgium in the academic year 1974–75. CORE provided me with an ideal environment for absorbing the updated highbrow game theory.

Throughout the long period of research the results of which are summarized in this monograph, my association with many economists, game theorists and mathematicians influenced and helped my thinking in a fundamental way: Ky Fan, Richard P. McLean, Bezalel Peleg, Martine Quinzii, Roy Radner, Joachim Rosenmüller, Juan J. Schäffer, Murat R. Sertel, Lloyd S. Shapley, and the late Ryuichi Watanabe (my teacher in Japan), to name only a few.

I started deliberating on how to organize and write this monograph, when I was visiting the Institut für Mathematische Wirtschaftsforschung and the Fakultät für Wirtschaftswissenschaften, Universität Bielefeld, Germany in September–October 1988. The experience of giving a series of lectures at Bielefeld at that time presenting the materials that I planned to include in this monograph, and another round of lectures during my visit to the Departamento de Análisis Económico, Universidad del País Vasco/EHU, Spain in November–December 1988 were very helpful for the actual writing.

I completed the first draft of the monograph in April 1990. Since then I have made many revisions, largely upon the suggestions, information, and encouragement provided by a number of people, in particular José María Aizpurua, Pradeep Dubey, Jiguang Fang, Bogomil Ferfila, Jonathan C. Glover, Robert A. Hart, Adam Idzik, Van W. Kolpin, Mordecai Kurz, Michael Magill, Boris Mityagin, David Schmeidler, Jan Svejnar, Jean L. Waelbroeck, and anonymous referees. To all the individuals and the institutions mentioned in the last four paragraphs of this Preface, I would like to express my deep gratitude. Needless to say, I am solely responsible for any possible deficiencies in this monograph.

TATSURO ICHIISHI
The Ohio State University

1 Elements of the theory of the firm

This chapter reviews several basic issues in the theory of the firm, and indicates how they are addressed in subsequent chapters. Section 1.1 provides a critical review of thought on the *raison d'être* of the firm as an organization. An organization is a coalition of people characterized by diversity of (and most likely, conflict among) their interests and by coordination of their activities. Among the works presented are Coase's (1937) seminal view on the nature of the firm, Arrow's (1969) concept of transaction cost, Alchian and Demsetz's (1972) monitoring problem, and Williamson's (1975, 1985) various more specific types of transaction cost. It is concluded that at least two issues should be addressed in order to analyze the firm's activities: modelling the effective incentives of each economic agent, and postulating the cooperative behavioral principle. The remark on pp. 11–12 briefly compares the cooperative approach of this monograph (analysis of the situation in which economic agents interact based on the cooperative behavioral principle) with the principal-agent approach. Section 1.2 reviews empirical observations of the separation of ownership (stockholding) and control (management) of a firm in the modern capitalistic economy. The pioneering work by Berle and Means (1932), and the more recent observations by Larner (1966) are presented. The managerial utility hypotheses by Baumol (1959), by Marris (1964) and by Williamson (1964) are briefly discussed. The need for developing a theory which gets to the heart of the basic theory of the firm, in particular the thought on the *raison d'être* of the firm, and at the same time can describe the separation of ownership and control is emphasized. Section 1.3 first points out that there are many modes of socialistic economies that have actually prevailed in this century. The market-cooperative socialism is one of them. It has attracted much attention from economic theorists, due to the initial work by Ward (1958). Institutional studies by Jan Vanek (1972) and by Prasnikar and Svejnar (1988) are presented. Their findings are fundamentally important in developing a theory of market-cooperative socialism. It is concluded that the essential difference between the manager-controlled firm in the capitalistic economy and the firm in the idealized market-cooperative socialism is that while the former can take advantage of financial markets, in particular the stock market, the latter has no access to such markets. Section 1.4 shows that the cooperative approach resolves many difficulties inherent in the classical definitions of the entrepreneur. Section 1.5 discusses two further issues related to Section 1.1: the internal labor "market" of Kerr (1954) and Doeringer and Piore (1971), and the Keynesian unemployment problem. This chapter is based on Ichiishi (1985), itself a revised version of a part of the paper, Ichiishi, "Management Versus Ownership," GSIA Working Paper No. 46–76–77 (revised: August 1979), Carnegie-Mellon University, which had been circulated since 1979.

1.1 The firm as a cooperative resource allocation mechanism

A firm is an organization of human-resource holders which engages in production activities. This section provides a critical review of thought on the *raison d'être* of the firm given by basic literature in the theory of the firm.

Before proceeding to such a review, clarification of the term "organization" is in order. A customary definition of organization given in organizational science is that it is a system of activities of two or more persons, consciously coordinated and controlled by the executive in order to achieve a set of objectives. Empowered with authority, the executive enforces coordinated activities. Barnard (1938) argued that there is a gap between the organizational objectives pursued by the executive and the personal objectives held by the individual members, so that successful organizational performance would require both effectiveness of activities and satisfaction of individual motives. Underlying Barnard's argument is his perception that an organization consists of people having diverse and conflicting interests, yet each person gains from interacting with others, in particular through their coordinated activities. Throughout the present monograph, an *organization* is characterized simply by (1) diversity of (and most likely, conflict among) the interests of its members, and (2) coordination of the members' activities. How coordination is agreed upon and enforced depends upon a decision-making rule in each organization. The top-down decision-making rule based on the authority of the executive, that is characteristic in most of the organizational science literature (such as Max Weber (1922), Barnard (1938), March and Simon (1958), Radner (1975)), is actually one of many rules. Unwritten practice in a partnership is another rule. Other rules include the unanimity or majority decision rules in workers' idealized profit-sharing cooperatives without a hierarchy. The present organization concept does not depend upon specificities of these rules, so the economic theory to be developed in Chapters 3–5 has broad applicability. See Remark 3.1.8.

In the neoclassical economics a firm is not conceived as an organization, but is merely identified with its production set (Definition 3.3.3). The only organization is a nation-wide market system in which, guided by the prices observed in the markets, individuals unconsciously coordinate their consumption activities and production activities. Suppose economic agent *A* has a plant as his initial endowment and wants to use it for his production activity. All he has to do is, for example, go to the perfectly competitive labor market, ask laborer *X* to supply labor in his factory at 8:00 a.m. at the wage rate established in the market, ask laborer *Y* to come to the factory at 9:00 a.m. to take over *X*'s work and perform another task, again at the established market wage rate, and so on. Since agent *A* can find any type and any quantity of human resources in the perfectly competitive labor market at any moment, there is no need for him to organize a firm; he has only to purchase all the necessary labor on a freelance basis.

In his seminal paper, Coase (1937) asked why there is a firm as an organization. In the presence of the market system, some of the neoclassical hypotheses on the system have to be replaced by an alternative hypothesis which would explain the formation of firms. Coase argued first that the neoclassical hypothesis of free complete information on the labor market has to be replaced by the hypothesis of the costliness of obtaining information on the labor market. Economic agent *A* in the example of the preceding paragraph does not know whether the wage rate he settles at after negotiation with laborer *X* is really the market rate, or whether *X* actually has the intention or ability to supply as high quality labor as promised in the contract. In reality, agent *A* finds it costly to identify the right labor and relevant wage rate each time he tries to use the labor market. Based on this hypothesis of incomplete information on the labor market, Coase then argued that an entrepreneur (like agent *A* of the example) does not fully rely on the labor market when assigning labor for his production activity, as such labor allocation would be costly if done properly, but instead forms an organization of human-resource holders, called a firm, and within this organization dictates labor assignment each time he undertakes production planning. Rather than detailed specification of labor, obedience up to certain limits, or more generally, willingness to coordinate labor supply to specific instances during the laborer's tenure, is the object of the contract between the entrepreneur and a laborer. Thus, a firm is formed as a human-resource allocation mechanism which is a superior alternative to the market mechanism in default of complete information. In Max Weber's (1922) view, the market as a place of exchange and the firm (organization) as a place of conscious coordination provide two of the basic complementary functions in the modern society. Coase (1937), on the other hand, attributed the formation of firms to a market failure.

At this point, it is necessary to fix the following terminology, in order to facilitate further discussion in this chapter: A *resource allocation mechanism* is a set of specified forces in a society which together transform *a priori* given initial resources of the society, and allocate the transformed resources among its members. The *social outcome* of a resource allocation mechanism is the final allocation of the transformed resources. The market mechanism is a particular resource allocation mechanism that works in the organization called the market system, and the competitive equilibrium is its social outcome.

Arrow (1969) classified the possible causes for Pareto non-optimality of social outcome into (1) purely technological conditions (such as increasing returns to scale) and (2) specific modes of economic organization (such as the market failure), and discussed the latter causes. He viewed the market failure as the situation in which instituting the perfect market system to achieve Pareto optimum at its competitive equilibrium is not worthwhile, as it would be too costly. In the presence of externalities (specifically, in the presence of a public good), for example, the exclusion principle and hence Pareto optimality of the equilibrium could be restored, if [the good held by agent *i* and enjoyed by *i*] and [the same good held by *i* and enjoyed by another agent *j* due to the externality] were distinguished as different commodities, that is, if sufficiently many markets were introduced. To introduce such an abundance of markets and to enforce the price-taking behavior as opposed to the free-riding behavior would be too costly, however, so in reality there are fewer markets than necessary at the sacrifice of the exclusion principle, hence Pareto non-optimality of the social outcome of the resulting imperfect market system. Another example of market failure, in the presence of uncertainty, is a situation caused by asymmetric information among the agents. The competitive equilibrium realized in the complete set of state-contingent markets given the *ex ante* information structures is Pareto optimal relative to the same information structures, but it is in general not Pareto optimal relative to the *ex post* information structures obtained by each agent's observing the other agents' behavior (Radner, 1968). Arrow then defined the generalized concept of *transaction cost* as the cost of using a resource allocation mechanism for achieving Pareto optimality of its social outcome. The market failure, in his view, is the extreme case in which the market mechanism involves too high transaction cost to justify its use. In this case, Arrow argued, there will arise pressure in the society to overcome it by introducing additional resource allocation mechanisms that possibly have lower transaction costs. He was aware of the nature of the firm *à la* Coase as an alternative resource allocation mechanism (Arrow, 1969, p. 20), but he mainly (1) discussed problems inherent in another mechanism, decision-making in the government, and (2) proposed one force that can be internalized in the market system, norms of social behavior.

Arrow's concept of transaction cost is a general notion: It means whatever cost of using an organization for allocation of resources, and includes specifically Coase's notion of the cost of obtaining information on the imperfect labor market. To be precise, the *transaction cost* concept should be re-defined (as done implicitly in the literature) relative to the set of agents who would bear it. In the preceding paragraph it is defined relative to all members of the society, so achieving a Pareto optimal social outcome is the natural criterion. To choose a resource allocation mechanism that has lower transaction cost then becomes an issue of normative economics. In the example of the third and fourth paragraphs of this section, the transaction cost is borne solely by agent *A* (at least, that is how Coase formulated his model), and is defined as the cost of achieving his optimal state in this context, i.e., the cost of identifying the right labor and the right wage rate in the imperfect labor market. Agent *A* will go ahead to create an alternative resource allocation mechanism (firm), in an attempt to replace the so-defined transaction cost by the lower transaction cost of using the firm. To study how these firms are formed and how their mechanisms work in conjunction with the market mechanism is an issue of descriptive economics.

Malmgren (1961) emphasized the advantages to a firm of controlling (in particular, of processing) information, and of monopolizing better information. Arrow (1974) pointed out several issues pertaining to the information processing within a firm.

The subsequent development of thought on the *raison d'être* of the firm took place basically (1) by making precise the contents of the transaction cost associated with any organization, the imperfect market system or another form of organization; (2) by clarifying the specific mode (i.e., specific internal organization) of the firm as an organization; (3) by comparing firms having different specific modes (e.g., Chandler's (1962) unitary structure versus multidivisional structure); and (4) by studying the workings of these resource allocation mechanisms by specifying the behavioral principle and (conflicting) motives of the members of an organization. To appreciate this development, it is necessary to see the precise contents of the transaction cost that Coase originally had in mind. Recall again the example of entrepreneur *A* in the third and fourth paragraphs of this section. The Coasian transaction cost is best expressed in the following passage:

In order to carry out a market transaction it is necessary to discover who it is that one wishes to deal with, to inform people that one wishes to deal and on what terms, to conduct negotiations leading up to a bargain, to draw up the contract, to undertake the inspection needed to make sure that the terms of the contract are being observed, and so on (Coase, 1960, p. 15).

Coase contended that the firm is created in order to reduce these specific costs (provided that the transaction cost of using the firm is lower); specifically, the firm (1) internalizes the cost of obtaining information on the available labor, and (2) replaces a succession of short-term complete contracts by a single long-term incomplete contract which essentially stipulates only the limits to *A*'s authoritative power, thereby avoiding the costs of bargaining and concluding too many short-term contracts. Here is a minor logical gap: It does not follow from his specification of the transaction cost (listed above) why the organization with this specific mode and this specific hierarchical structure has the lowest transaction cost and satisfies *A* the most. There might be another mode such that some of the costs listed above may not be minimal, yet the overall transaction cost is minimal because other costs not listed above are sufficiently cut down. Agent *A* might choose yet another mode which does not minimize the total transaction cost, because it brings in sufficiently large revenue and hence the maximal utility. As possible other modes, it suffices to think of use of a subcontractor rather than an employee, and formation of a partnership rather than a strict hierarchy. Even if this logical gap is somehow filled, there still remain unsolved more serious and fundamental problems; these are the issues introduced in the next paragraph.

The central thesis of Coase (1937) is that a firm is formed as a human-resource allocation mechanism which is a superior alternative to the market mechanism in default of complete information. The central drawback of Coase (1937, 1988) is that he has not clarified what precisely this alternative human-resource allocation mechanism is. Economists want to capture the laws prevailing in the economy as properties of a social outcome, indeed Coase wants to "understand the working of the economic system, to analyze many of its problems in a useful way, or to have a basis for determining policy" (Coase, 1988, p. 6, final three lines), but the very mechanism that gives rise to the social outcome is not pinpointed here. There are at least two issues that one has to address (and Coase did not) in formulating the required resource allocation mechanism. The first issue is the effective incentives of each economic agent. Even in the authoritative organization that Coase suggested as a firm, entrepreneur *A* cannot make a successful decision without having a good sense of what interest laborer *X* may pursue or under what constraint *X* may try to realize his best interest. One may postulate, as in the neoclassical economics, that the ultimate interest of *X* is represented by the utility level of his consumption bundle. The constraint of *X* is, on the other hand, influenced by other economic variables, like the willingness of another entrepreneur B to make a new employment contract with X, so it should be endogenously determined as a part of the social outcome. The second issue is the behavioral principle of the economic agents. Coase was aware that the concept of organization is something new to the neoclassical economics. He brought in without questioning, however, the neoclassical noncooperative behavioral principle as the behavioral principle of the members in an organization. Coase's error in this respect is illustrated in the following discussion, again using the example of the third and fourth paragraphs of this section: It is a one-sided view to assume that the transaction cost is borne solely by entrepreneur A. Just as A finds it costly to identify the right labor and wage rate, laborer X also finds it costly to identify the right capital to work with and the right wage rate to request. There is a host of literature in the search theory; see, e.g., Lippman and McCall (1976a, 1976b). Rather than fully relying on the labor market to obtain information on its demand side each time he wants to supply labor (say, once every day), agent X joins a firm and accepts his daily work assignment, or better still (in case his labor is sufficiently differentiated from the others'), makes every effort to have the assignment made to his best interest. Without joiners, like X, a firm cannot be formed. The firm's ownership is a separate issue. Thus, an organization of agents $\{A, X, Y, \ldots\}$ is formed as a firm to minimize the transaction cost borne by the coalition $\{A, X, Y, \ldots\}$. Here, the concept of organization should be understood broadly as defined in the second paragraph of this section. Formation of a firm should be viewed as a consequence of cooperative rather than of noncooperative behavior.

For a clear understanding of the difference between the two types of behavior, cooperative versus noncooperative, a brief digression is in order. The distinction lies in the very definitions of the behavioral principles: *Cooperative behavior* takes into account joint decisions made by more than one agent about their strategy choice, while *noncooperative behavior* does not. Consider a manufacturer as an organization of agents $\{A, X, Y, Z, \ldots\}$, in which A is the sole executive, and suppose that a specific coordination of activities is to be enforced according to the top-down decision-making rule. If A's order is too harsh for worker Z to take, Z will quit the organization. In this case, Z decides by himself (i.e., noncooperatively) to deviate from the organizational joint strategies. If two engineers, X and Y, find out that by putting their efforts together they can establish a new engineering company which will bring higher welfare levels to both of them, then they will create their own firm $\{X, Y\}$. In this case, X and Y decide jointly (i.e., cooperatively) to deviate from the strategies of the original organization. This joint deviation is characteristic only of the cooperative behavioral principle. (Chapter 2 reviews formal analysis of various types of descriptive cooperative behavior. Specifically, the fourth through sixth paragraphs of Section 2.1 contain the formal definition of a cooperative game, and Remark 2.3.6 presents the view that contrary to the popular conception, the noncooperative "foundation" of cooperative game theory is actually not a foundation of the cooperative behavioral principle. Indeed, the noncooperative behavior is a special case of the cooperative behavior in which only singletons are allowed to form.) The postulate of cooperative behavior becomes more appropriate, if one studies a manufacturer $\{A, B, X, Y, Z, \ldots\}$, in which two executives, A and B, consult with each other in making major corporate decisions. Noncooperative decision-making by A and B (say, the passive decision-making formulated by Cournot (1838) and Nash (1950)) is not appropriate within one organization. The need for the cooperative behavioral principle is more compelling in situations in which several firms are involved. In the above case of Z's quitting the firm $\{A, X, Y, Z, \ldots\}$, Z does so typically because he finds a better job in another firm, say in $\{A', B', \ldots, X', Y', Z', \ldots\}$. What is going on here is that the new firm $\{A', B', \ldots, X', Y', Z', \ldots, Z\}$ is formed (although it may well keep the same name as that of $\{A', B', \ldots, X', Y', Z', \ldots\}$). Forming this new organization is a cooperative behavior (i.e., the employer(s) and the new employee agree on an employment contract), and this coordinated strategy-choice stipulates in part Z's resignation from his old firm $\{A, X, Y, Z, \ldots\}$.

Alchian and Demsetz's (1972) study was the first explicit treatment of the role of incentives of every member in a firm. Laborer X wants to pursue his self-interest, so rather than put all his effort into his firm as promised in the contract, he may devote some of his effort to his personal enjoyment at the sacrifice of the firm's productivity. As long as his shirking behavior is not discovered, he will shirk. More generally, to the extent that his colleagues' observation of his specific labor supply (both quantity and quality) is consistent with the one stipulated in the contract, he will behave in his best interest. Agent X is a decision-maker himself just as his employer is, although the ranges of the decision variables are quite different. Alchian and Demsetz identified this monitoring cost as the transaction cost. A firm is formed to reduce this monitoring cost by appointing a monitor. But the monitor himself may shirk. To avoid this last problem, he must be given an incentive for monitoring such that the more accurately he monitors, the higher reward he receives. He is thus made a residual-claimant. This is Alchian and Demsetz's reasoning for the formation of a specific type of firm, called a classical firm. They also extended implications of this transaction cost (monitoring cost) to other modes of organization, such as profit-sharing firms, socialist firms, big corporations in the capitalistic economy in which the major decision-makers are not stockholders, etc.

Two of the key elements in Alchian and Demsetz's argument are asymmetric information between an employer and an employee and a difference in their interests. The workings of resource allocation mechanisms that would emerge in an organization characterized by these two elements have been studied in the recent literature of the principal-agent theory, albeit under the postulate of noncooperative behavior and in most cases within oversimplified frameworks. See Remark 1.1.1 at the end of this section. Hart (1988) forcefully argued the limits of the principal-agent theory, and provided an account for the appropriateness and power of analysis of the cooperative behavioral principle.

It appears that Alchian and Demsetz were fully aware of the cooperative nature of the firm, when they wrote:

> Team production . . . is production in which 1) several types of resources are used and 2) the product is not a sum of separable outputs of each cooperating resource. An additional factor creates a team organization problem – 3) not all resources used in team production belong to one person (p. 779).

Alchian and Demsetz even talked about a firm having more than one major decision-maker, like a corporation. The purpose of Chapters 3 and 4 of this monograph is to develop an axiomatic theory in order to study the workings of the human-resource allocation mechanism that will emerge in a society characterized by conflicting interests and a cooperative behavioral principle. Recall that there are at least two issues that one has to address to pinpoint an organizational resource allocation mechanism: agents' effective incentives and the cooperative behavioral principle. The axiomatic theory addresses both. In fact, Chapters 3 and 4 study the workings of the conjunction of (1) the cooperative mechanism for the allocation of human resources and (2) the neoclassical market mechanism for the allocation of non-human resources.

The theory developed in Chapters 3 and 4 is descriptive, as it is intended to describe the present-day capitalistic economy and a certain socialistic economy. An organization (firm) is formed as a result of its members' pursuit of self-interest; the members do not care about the society's overall performance. Indeed, its social outcome is in general not Pareto optimal. Chapter 5, on the other hand, develops a normative theory within a simplified framework. In the presence of the increasing returns to scale technology, a new resource allocation mechanism is proposed, so that its social outcome is Pareto optimal.

Williamson (1975, 1985) was the most prominent in identifying various types of transaction costs and their influences on the modes of realized firms. This paragraph reorganizes some of these types and presents them accordingly. Needless to say, the basic concept here is the organization characterized by conflicting interests and coordination of strategies (the second paragraph of this section). The first characteristic (conflicting interests) combined with asymmetric information has the tendency to create the specific behavior emphasized by Williamson as "opportunism." (The point here is that contrary to his treatment, "opportunism" should be explained as a phenomenon the extent of whose realization is endogenously determined in the model.) Williamson (1985, pp. 52–61) introduced three dimensions for transaction cost so that "the factors responsible for differences among transactions be identified and explicated" (p. 52): (1) asset specificity, (2) uncertainty, and (3) frequency. Dimension (1) refers to the job-specific nature of inputs, which does not exist before the contract but shows up continuously after the contract. Examples are site-specificity and specialized labor obtained by on-the-job training. Dimension (2) includes specifically environmental uncertainty and asymmetric information. In the above quotation from Coase (1960, p. 15), there were five contents of transaction costs; the first four are typical examples of dimension (3). In order to see the exact roles that these three dimensions play in Williamson's argument, it is more appropriate to call them three *types* of transaction costs. Another type of transaction cost is: (4) bounded rationality. Radner (1985) contains three precise formulations of the bounded rationality concept, each interpreted differently. The preceding paragraph showed that Alchian and Demsetz emphasized asymmetric information (a specific case of uncertainty) to explain the formation of a classical firm (one mode of organization). Williamson extended the Coasian approach: Asset specificity and frequency in general lead to a long-term contract. A manufacturer's inability to extend quality control to distributors (a specific case of asymmetric information) and hence the possibility of reputation-damage lead to forward integration into distribution. In the US railroad industry of the nineteenth century, the site specificity of operating matters (a specific case of asset specificity), like equipment utilization and maintenance, led to formation of the decentralized line-and-staff mode of organization. In the twentieth century, bounded rationality led to creation of the multidivisional mode of organization (i.e., semiautonomous profit centers organized along product, brand, or geographic lines), and furthermore to creation of conglomerates, and so on. Applicable to all these arguments are exactly the same criticisms as those addressed to Coase (1937, 1988) earlier in this section. It is true that Williamson sometimes looked carefully at the role of effective incentives of agents; the most beautiful example is his explanation of the limits of firm size (Williamson, 1985, Chapter 6). Williamson has carefully identified specificities of various types of transaction costs. Taking them into account while pinpointing and formulating a non-market resource allocation mechanism would surely yield sharper properties of the associated social outcome – but this task is beyond the scope of this monograph.

Remark 1.1.1. The principal-agent theory basically analyzes the following situation: There are the principal and the agents. The strategy of the former is to design a contract (e.g., an employment contract) and make a "take-it-or-leave-it" offer to the latter; the principal is the Stackelberg leader. The agents, if they accept it, then choose their strategies (e.g., supply labor to the principal) as the Stackelberg followers. The return from this activity is distributed at the end among the principal and the agents according to the contract. What makes this theory different from the classical Stackelberg duopoly theory is the explicit treatment of information, asymmetrically held by the principal and by the agents, on some endogenous variables (e.g., quality of labor, and quality of output) and/or on some exogenous data (e.g., agents' productivity). Thus, for example, lack of principal's information about agents' strategy-choice may cause the problem (to the principal) known as moral hazard, and lack of the principal's information about agents' data may cause the problem known as adverse selection. The theory, therefore, emphasizes such results as the non-optimal risk-sharing property of an equilibrium, and design of a contract with which the principal can avoid much of the problem caused by lack of information. In particular, it provides a scenario of how asymmetric information is processed under a specifically designed contract. See, e.g., Sappington (1991) for a survey.

The theory developed in this monograph, on the other hand, concerns design of a contract by more than one individual who will form a coalition (firm). The intended scenario is that these individuals supply their labor to a coalition, managerial or manual, and their contract prescribes how their various labor inputs will be coordinated and how the return of their production activity will be distributed among themselves. Here, each individual serves both as a principal (in the sense that he takes part in drawing up a contract) and as an agent (in the sense that he supplies labor after formation of the firm). It is true that in practice only a few of the individuals (those in managerial positions) have the formal authority to design a contract, yet actually all individuals engage in such a job formally or informally with diverse degrees of authority. Indeed, the implicit bargaining power of the individuals in lower ranks influences the content of the contract, and moreover, re-writing a contract through negotiation between individuals is commonly observed. Difference in the bargaining power of the individuals is the difference in degrees of principality of the individuals.

While the noncooperative approach (including the principal-agent theory) postulates that the individuals within an organization are double-crossing each other, the cooperative approach of this monograph postulates that an organization is formed because each member needs coordination of strategies with the other members.

All the equilibrium concepts proposed in this monograph are *ex ante* notions, so the theory here is essentially static. To investigate how cooperative choice of strategies processes information in *interim* equilibrium, thereby synthesizing the noncooperative theory of information-processing and the static cooperative theory, remains an important, yet little cultivated, research area. □

1.2 Separation of ownership and control of a firm in the capitalistic society

Based upon their celebrated empirical studies, Berle and Means (1932) pointed out two crucial features of the US economy: First, most major industries have come to be dominated by a few huge corporations. Second, most major corporations have moved towards a wider dispersion of stock-ownership. In fact, the first of these phenomena facilitates, and is accelerated by, the second. A natural inference from the first phenomenon is the need for theories of imperfect competition. Of the inferences from the second made by Berle and Means, the following are essential: The majority of stockholders lose control of, and responsibility for, the firm. So, their direct motive for holding stocks, which used to be that of controlling the firm's management in order actively to create yields in their best interest, evolves into that of passive portfolio selection given their subjective probabilities on yields from investing in various firms. Looked at in another way, those who control the firm are no longer all the stockholders. Berle and Means discussed five types of control situations: (1) control through almost complete ownership; (2) majority control; (3) control through a legal device; (4) minority control; and (5) management control. Type (1) is the classical situation in which a single individual or a small group of associates own all, or practically all, the outstanding stock. In this case there is no separation of ownership and control. Alchian and Demsetz (1972) called the firm having this type of control the classical firm, and attempted to explain its *raison d'être* (see Section 1.1). Type (2) is the situation in which a single individual or a small group own the majority of the outstanding stock, thereby holding all the legal powers of control. Type (3) is developed in an attempt to maintain undiminished control of a firm without ownership of the majority of its stock. One device is "pyramiding": Suppose k firms, $F_1, F_2, \ldots, F_k$, are lined up in such a way that firm F_{i-1} holds the majority of F_i's outstanding stock. Then, a single individual who merely owns the majority of F_1's stock extends his complete control to all the k firms. Another device is the use of non-voting stock. Type (4) is the situation in which a single individual or a small group have "working control" of the firm in that although they own less than the majority of stock (e.g., they merely own 14.9 percent of the voting stock), they nevertheless have the ability to attract from scattered owners proxies sufficient when combined

Table 1.1. *Classification of the largest 200 US non-financial corporations according to the types of control situations, 1929*

	By number %	By wealth %
Management control	44	58
Legal device	21	22
Minority control	23	14
Majority control	5	2
Private ownership	6	4
In hands of receiver	1	negligible
Total	100	100

Source: Berle and Means (1932, p. 109).

with their own stock to control the majority of the votes. There is a serious limitation on minority control, hence the emergence of separation of ownership and control, because in case these minority stockholders and the managers are in hostile dispute, the latter can also attract proxies – even more easily than the former. There have been historical cases in which the former won, but the cases also proved the enormity of the financial burden incurred during the proxy fight. Type (5) is the situation in which ownership is so widespread that no individual or small group has even minority control at all. Here, the separation of ownership (stockholding) and control (management) has become virtually complete. There are varieties of managerial work, from highly skilled work empowered with authority such as the executive work to less skilled work such as the routine clerical work to decide on the type of office supplies to purchase, but all these are specific types of labor. In the manager-controlled firm the laborers hire capital, whereas in the classical firm the capitalist hires laborers.

Berle and Means examined the type of control exercised over the 42 railroads, the 52 public utilities, and the 106 industrials which composed the list of 200 largest US non-financial companies at the beginning of 1930. Although certain arbitrary judgments had to be made in their classification (e.g., the dividing line between the minority control and the management control was 20 percent ownership of the total voting stock), their result, reproduced in Table 1.1 here, shows that the management control was the most prevalent at that time. More than thirty years later, Larner (1966) conducted the same investigation following very closely the definitions, procedures, and classifications used in the Berle and Means study (except that the dividing line between the minority control and the management control was lowered to 10 percent ownership of the total voting stock); his result is reproduced in Table 1.2. He concluded, "Berle and Means in 1929

Table 1.2. *Classification of the largest 200 US non-financial corporations according to the types of control situations, 1963*

	By number %	By wealth %
Management control	84.5	85
Legal device	4	3
Minority control	9	11
Majority control	2.5	1
Private ownership	0	0
Total	100%	100%

Source: Larner (1966).

were observing a 'managerial revolution' in process. Now, 30 years later, that observation seems close to complete, at least within the range of the 200 largest nonfinancial corporations" (pp. 786–787). Scherer (1970) contains brief updated empirical discussions of these materials, and Chandler (1962) contains a treatment from a historical perspective.

Several authors have attempted to model the behavior of a manager-controlled firm. All postulated that the firm's behavior is a consequence of the utility-maximization of its sole executive, the manager. Each differs from the others in his definition of the managerial utility function. Baumol (1959), contending that the manager's pecuniary reward and power are positively correlated with firm's revenue rather than with profit, assumed that the manager maximizes the revenue subject to the output-demand function. Marris (1964), contending that the growth rate of the firm and the security from dismissal are the main determinants of the managerial utility, selected several strategies that would be the most crucial for the firm's long-run growth, and illustrated the mechanism that underlies the managerial decision. Williamson (1964) proposed the managerial utility that is a function of the sum of the manager's reward and the staffs' rewards (assuming that the latter represent the manager's power), managerial slack defined as the value of the materials that the manager can personally enjoy at the firm's expense (such as his office furniture), and the value of investment that the manager can make at his discretion. While these three theoretical works were motivated by the thought-provoking empirical observation of Berle and Means, none of them got to the heart of the basic theory of the firm, in particular the thought on the *raison d'être* of the firm (Section 1.1). Indeed, the optimal solution to any of the three managerial utility-maximization problems may be simply unacceptable to potential employees, so that the employment contract may not be drawn up (it fails to take into account the effective incentives of potential employees). Moreover, none of them can explain the behavior of a manager-controlled firm in which there is more than one executive. More fundamentally, none of them can explain why this particular firm (which should be an organization) comes to exist in the economy.

Chapters 3 and 4 of this monograph develop and analyze a new descriptive general equilibrium model of the modern capitalistic economy. The type of control situation is the management control. Organizations of human-resource holders are formed endogenously in equilibrium. These organizations are the firms, and human-resource holders supply labor, managerial or manual, to the firms with which they establish employment contracts. The firms come to exist because no coalition of human-resource holders can do better no matter what coordinated strategies their leaders (entrepreneurs) may propose in an attempt to establish a new organization. Indeed, within a firm realized in equilibrium, the realized coordination of strategies is efficient from its members' point of view. The human-resource holders of an organization hire capital in order to increase their production capacity, and the capitalists, on the other hand, choose the firms in which to invest their money simply as a portfolio selection problem, hence the management control. Chapter 2 makes precise the meanings of the phrases, "no coalition ... can do better," and "efficient from its members' point of view."

1.3 Decision-making in a firm in a socialistic economy

During the 1950s and the 1960s, some socialist countries (Yugoslavia, in particular) came to recognize the efficiency of the decentralized market mechanism, and to introduce it into their own systems. The extent to which decentralization was introduced differed from country to country. Moreover, the extent has been changing, as demonstrated by the series of reforms that have taken place since 1989 in Hungary, Poland, the former East Germany, Czechoslovakia and Bulgaria, and also in the former USSR. As a result, there are many modes of socialist system. Brus (1981) categorized the idealized socialistic economies according to the levels at which decentralized decision-making rules were introduced. His classification is somewhat arbitrary and outdated; nevertheless, it shows the diversity of socialistic modes, which any theorist must seriously take into account in making a formal analysis. According to Brus, there are three levels of decision-making. The "fundamental" level refers to the national and industry levels. The "standard" level refers to the firm (organization) level. The "household" level refers to the level at which commodity-demand for consumption and labor-supply are decided. Table 1.3 reflects the regimes and systems in power as of 1981. Thus, the then-Hungary model is the economy in which centrally planned policies regulate industries, but the decision-

Table. 1.3. *Levels for decentralization as of 1981*

	Fundamentals	Standard	Household
World communism	Centralized	Centralized	Centralized
The Soviet model	Centralized	Centralized	Decentralized
The Hungarian model	Centralized	Decentralized	Decentralized
The Yugoslav model	Decentralized	Decentralized	Decentralized

Source: Brus (1981).

making within a firm (a household, resp.) is left up to the firm (the household, resp.).

The controversy of the *theory of economic calculation* (see, e.g., the collected papers in Hayek (1935)) focused on the infeasibility of central economic planning on the one hand, and the efficiency of the decentralized market mechanism on the other. However, the efficiency of the actual decentralized capitalistic system is questionable. Indeed, Section 1.1 reviewed the theoretical literature that emphasizes the transaction cost of using the market system, and Section 1.2 reviewed the empirical literature that infers the inappropriateness of the profit-maximization hypothesis, and hence the possible inefficiency of the modern capitalistic economy. The above paragraph shows that the idealized world communism and the Soviet model, that are the primary study-objects of the theory of economic calculation as the centrally planned economies, are not the only socialist systems that have actually prevailed in this century. More importantly, the failure of the actual socialist economies with all degrees of decentralization, which has surfaced in the past few years, proves the non-practice of rational economic planning. Thus, the main study-objects of the theory of economic calculation (an idealized capitalistic economy and an idealized planned economy) are not appropriate as the study-objects of any descriptive theory. Chapters 3 and 4 of this monograph develop descriptive models of the capitalistic economy and a socialistic economy (the market-cooperative socialism), which have nothing to do with the theory of economic calculation.

It was the Yugoslav model of market-cooperative socialism that Ward (1958) had in mind when he postulated *per capita* value-added maximization as the objective of a firm, and derived its implications regarding the output-supply curve. Among the subsequent theoretical works are Domar (1966), Jaroslav Vanek (1970) and Meade (1972).

Jan Vanek (1972, Ch. VI) in his Yugoslav case study bitterly opposed the Ward theory, in particular the *per capita* value-added maximization hypothesis. His most serious and relevant criticisms are: (1) Ward's inappropriate modelling of the capital or financial market, and (2) the need for more complex modelling related more or less to the wage differentials. (Jan Vanek actually presented many other criticisms. Some of them are unfounded, and others are applicable not only to the Ward theory but also to the neoclassical theory of the capitalistic economy.) In regard to criticism (1), Jan Vanek rejected Ward's hypothesis of free access to the non-human-resource markets, specifically to the financial market, and emphasized that laborers have to produce the capital resources they need to operate and to expand their firm (p. 146). In regard to (2), Jan Vanek pointed out the facts that a laborer has major avenues to increase his income other than seeking the maximal *per capita* value-added of his firm (e.g., through advancement to a better paid job) (p. 144), and that there is a considerable flexibility of the laborer's remuneration in the short term (p. 148). Indeed, Jan Vanek's careful sketch of the value-added distribution process in practice within a firm (Ch. V) reveals the very difficulty of determining the "right" remuneration according to the actual type, quality and quantity of work, and thus strongly suggests that there arises conflict in interests among the laborers when it comes to dividing the pie. The conflict directly contradicts the simple hypothesis of *per capita* value-added maximization.

An important paper by Prasnikar and Svejnar (1988) provides an up-to-date institutional study of Yugoslav firms. It includes among others the definition of the firm in the Yugoslav system, a sketch of the decision-making process in practice, a description of the output market structure, the financial market condition, characteristics of personal incomes, and foreign trade performance. Of the many conclusions drawn, the following two points are relevant to the discussions of the above two paragraphs: (1) "The Yugoslav system is hence characterized by high rates of capital accumulation together with a surprisingly high degree of misallocation of this resource" (p. 287). (2) "The system of enterprise decision making is a complex one, reflecting the pluralistic management based on a consensus among workers, managers, the Sociopolitical Organizations and Communities" (p. 294). An elaboration of point (1) is in order. Prasnikar and Svejnar first pointed out that bank loans are the most important source of financing for fixed capital investment: See Table 1.4 (the WOAL – work organization of associated labor – may be considered the firm). The problem here is that the banks are partly controlled by large established firms, so the latter hold the "priority status" (for funding). Bogomil Ferfila of the University of Ljubljana provided further up-dated information that, effective from January 1, 1990, the terms WOAL, BOAL (basic organization of associated labor), COAL (composite organization of associated labor), etc. are no longer used in Yugoslavia; these terms were replaced by

Table 1.4. *The structure of investment funds in the 150 interviewed WOALs by source of investment*

		Enterprises with up to 500 employees					Enterprises with more than 500 employees					Total				
		1975	1976	1977	1978	1979	1975	1976	1977	1978	1979	1975	1976	1977	1978	1979
Equity	(1)	26.39	55.23	58.06	49.15	41.89	41.36	32.79	27.44	26.50	34.28	39.78	35.21	30.45	28.94	34.88
Long-term banking loans	(2)	42.22	24.45	27.40	45.16	40.53	31.60	43.54	40.08	43.81	35.75	32.72	41.49	38.84	43.96	36.15
Loans of suppliers	(3)	7.31	2.51	6.29	3.30	12.77	6.54	5.15	5.34	5.41	5.06	6.62	4.87	5.44	5.18	5.75
Pooling of resources	(4)	7.34	0.04	0.00	0.02	1.33	0.53	0.99	0.81	4.33	8.39	1.25	0.88	0.73	3.87	7.82
Loans of foreign supplier	(5)	13.72	10.95	1.68	1.22	1.43	17.20	13.41	22.49	16.61	13.90	16.83	13.15	20.45	14.95	12.90
Short-term banking investment loans	(6)	2.28	0.67	0.57	0.18	1.78	2.69	2.45	2.68	2.10	2.29	2.65	2.25	2.47	1.89	2.25
Other funds	(7)	0.72	6.13	5.97	0.98	0.27	0.01	1.66	1.34	1.23	0.22	0.13	2.14	1.62	1.20	0.23
		100.0	100.0	100.0	100.0	100.0	100.0	100.0	100.0	100.0	100.0	100.0	100.0	100.0	100.0	100.0

Source: Prasnikar and Svejnar (1988, p. 286).

terms familiar to the capitalistic economy, such as proprietorship, partnership with or without liability, and shareholding corporation.

Chapter 3 of this monograph formulates the idealized economy of market-cooperative socialism, characterized by (1) the lack of a financial market; (2) diversity of (and most likely, conflict among) the interests of members of a firm; (3) coordination of the members' activities in a firm; and (4) the perfectly competitive non-financial, non-human resource markets. Properties (2)–(4) are also characteristics of the modern capitalistic economy whose control situation is the management control (the last paragraph of Section 1.2). Firms in the capitalistic economy do have access to the financial markets, specifically the stock market. Chapter 4 analyzes in what sense property (1) causes the Pareto inefficiency of the market-cooperative socialistic economy compared with the manager-controlled capitalistic economy.

1.4 Entrepreneurship

The postulate of the cooperative behavioral principle is a fundamental requirement for analyzing the workings of an organizational resource allocation mechanism. Section 1.4 shows that, based on this postulate, one can find a new way to look at the controversial issue: the definition of, and the roles of, the "entrepreneur". Very roughly speaking, an entrepreneur is a residual claimant who makes effective decisions in his firm. In all the classical economic literature, the firms were decision units given *a priori* to the models, and the entrepreneurial activities were considered to represent the firm activities. Much of the analysis of firm activities, therefore, has been centered around the workings of entrepreneurship.

Two definitions of the "entrepreneur" have been widely discussed in the economic literature: Knight (1921) defined an entrepreneur as a person who plays two roles; one as a risk-bearer (i.e., stockholder), and the other as a member of the board of directors, having the final control of his firm by selecting the men in control. The entrepreneur defined by Schumpeter (1911), on the other hand, is a more specific functionary: the one who introduces new combinations of productive factors into his firm. Both definitions of the "entrepreneur" are based on the assumption of inseparability of ownership and control, and the two definitions differ only in the exact content of risk the entrepreneur is taking. The Knightian entrepreneur takes the risk of stockholding. The Schumpeterian entrepreneur takes the risk of technological uncertainty. In either definition, the entrepreneur's incentive to do his job is the residual he can claim. (Of course the "residual" is defined slightly differently in the two types.)

Stauss (1944) pointed out that the class of entrepreneurs, be it as defined by Knight or by Schumpeter, is impossible to identify, since (1) different people bear different degrees of risk and (2) effective decision-making is done by different functionaries within a firm depending upon particular situations. Stauss then defined a firm as an abstract entity, and claimed that the firm itself should be regarded by definition as the entrepreneur, particularly because of difficulty (2) above. Stauss is correct in raising the difficulties on the concept of entrepreneur, both Knight's and Schumpeter's concept. But his own concept of entrepreneur is useless, because one cannot formulate incentives of the "abstract" entity, and so cannot draw conclusions on entrepreneurial behavior. Thus, one faces a serious dilemma: According to the traditional viewpoint, firm activities cannot be understood without analyzing entrepreneurial behavior. The class of entrepreneurs, however, cannot be identified precisely.

The fallacy of the traditional viewpoint lies in its assumption that a firm has a single objective (i.e., the entrepreneurial utility). This assumption implies the unique existence of an entrepreneur in each firm, which incurred Stauss' criticism.

Given the cooperative behavioral principle, as will be assumed throughout the subsequent Chapters 3–6, every economic agent is an effective decision-maker, where the range of effectiveness varies from agent to agent depending upon individual ability. The ability reflects (1) the type of labor he can supply, which characterizes in particular his administrative drive and skill, technological knowledge and skill, and his physical capacity; and (2) his initial endowment, which determines his financial influence over the others. Each agent is, therefore, an entrepreneur, broadly defined. Formation of a firm (organization) is simply a coordinated strategy-choice as a result of individual pursuit of self-interest. Indeed, a firm consisting of k members has k objectives. Those agents who have a broader range of effectiveness of their decision, in particular those agents who occupy the top portion of a hierarchical structure and supply the managerial labor, show up as the *entrepreneurs, narrowly defined.* They are not necessarily residual claimants, just as the management control (Section 1.2) suggests. In reality, most agents have so limited a range of effectiveness that their decision is simply whether or not to accept another agent's proposed task with the possible intention to shirk. These people are not the entrepreneur narrowly defined (they can never be the entrepreneur in the Knight or Schumpeter sense). There is no "abstract" entity here. The entrepreneurs' decisions are explained not by a single constrained maximization problem (like the managerial-utility maximization problem), but by a multiperson cooperative game.

The new entrepreneur concept (narrowly defined) developed in the preceding paragraph is close in spirit to the entrepreneur concept developed by Coase (1937) and Alchian and Demsetz (1972). Coase pointed out the coordinating ability of his entrepreneur, but did not consider the effective incentives of the other entrepreneurs (broadly defined). Alchian and Demsetz emphasized the importance of conflicting incentives, but paid little attention to agents' ability. Indeed, even a highschool dropout without an engineering mind could become a monitor (entrepreneur in Alchian and Demsetz's sense) of a high-tech engineering company. More importantly, Coase and Alchian and Demsetz confined their attention to the *rationale* for the existence of a firm, and did not ask *which* firms are formed or *which* agents become the entrepreneurs (narrowly defined). The general equilibrium theory of the firm developed in Chapters 3 and 4 of this monograph implicitly answers this last question.

1.5 Related issues

Two issues related to Section 1.1 are discussed in Section 1.5: the internal labor "market", and unemployment.

A series of research studies in labor economics, which originated in the empirical observations of the institutional framework of the US labor market, turned out to be closely related to Coase's (1937) view on the nature of the firm. Kerr (1954) was the first to distinguish the internal labor market and the external labor market (he called the former the institutional market). Typical examples of the internal labor market are the institution within a craft union for labor allocation, and the institution within a firm for labor allocation, both governed to some extent by administrative rules. The external labor market refers to the neoclassical labor market, governed by individualistic competition. (The terminology "market" of the internal labor market is misleading.) Kerr observed that administrative rules in an internal "market" establishes more boundaries between the internal "markets", and make them more specific and harder to cross. He also noted that inside an internal labor "market", the workers have better information on the "market" than the outsiders have. The internal labor "market" within a firm was studied further by Doeringer and Piore (1971) (it was called the "enterprise market" in Doeringer and Piore's study), who identified some institutional concepts essential to its allocation mechanism. They also discussed the pattern of the wage setting process, and pointed out that the observed pattern contradicts the neoclassical theory in that (1) the administrative rule is given more attention and priority than the wages prevailing in the external market, and (2) the fixed costs of recruitment, screening, and training cause permanency of employment even when the wage is not equal to the value of the marginal product of labor. For an extraordinarily comprehensive survey of the literature on segmented labor market theories, the readers may refer to Cain (1976).

The internal resource allocation mechanism is the Coasian non-market resource allocation mechanism instituted in the firm. Since the neoclassical labor market allocation mechanism was rejected for its high transaction cost, the external labor market should have been rejected in this literature as well. Doeringer and Piore's notion of influence of the external labor market on the enterprise "market" is then replaced by the notion of the bargaining power of human-resource holders in their society-wide cooperative game. Doeringer and Piore's observation on the firm's wage setting process is an important predecessor of Williamson's (1985) concept, asset specificity. In order to provide full axiomatic analysis of asset specificity, one needs to rely on the dynamic method, which is beyond the scope of the present monograph.

Keynes (1936) had so many deep insights into the workings – and hence into the non-workings – of the capitalistic economy that it was probably impossible for him to formulate it all in a single consistent general equilibrium model. The Keynesians have attempted to formulate what they interpreted as Keynes' view. The early Keynesians, like Modigliani (1944) and Klein (1947), constructed a macro general equilibrium model, and asserted that rigidity in price, be it in the interest rate or in the wage rate, is the cause of disequilibrium in the labor market, and hence involuntary unemployment. Several authors subsequently pushed this argument one step further, claiming that study of the individual behavior in market disequilibrium (including the commodity market disequilibrium) is *the* subject of Keynes' economics: see Clower (1966); Leijonhufvud (1968); Barro and Grossman (1976) among others. Motivated by this, there arose the formal disequilibrium analysis literature (see, e.g., Benassy (1975)).

If one of the trends in the development of Keynesian thought is to drop more and more market equilibrium conditions, then the model of Chapters 3 and 4 of this monograph represents an extreme case of the trend: The labor market itself is dropped. A cooperative game played by human-resource holders is introduced instead. Unemployment is readily explained in the model: Suppose no group of people want to include agent X in their coalition (firm). The singleton $\{X\}$ is then formed as one of the equilibrium organizations. If, moreover, X has no ability to engage in production activity by himself, then he is considered unemployed. (One can make this argument precise, distinguishing voluntary unemployment and involuntary unemployment within the framework of this model, as in Ichiishi (1985, pp. 127–128)). Unemployed agents are thus the losers of the cooperative game.

2 Descriptive cooperative game theory

Each economic agent, given his own interest, coordinates his strategy-choice with other economic agents in an organization, because by doing so he and his colleagues can better serve their diverse interests, that is, the economic agents play a cooperative game.[1] This chapter focuses on some of the centrally important descriptive solution concepts in the formal cooperative game theory, core and core-like solutions. Basic results on these solution concepts in various setups with diverse degrees of generality are briefly surveyed. Section 2.1 discusses the core of the simplest setup of side-payment game. Among the concepts and results discussed are: Bondareva (1962, 1963) and Shapley's (1967) characterization of a game with a nonempty core (balanced game); an exact game and Schmeidler's (1972) characterization of an exact game; the exact envelope; marginal worth vectors; a convex game and its characterizations. Section 2.2 discusses the core of a generalized setup of non-side-payment game. The balanced side-payment games are extended to the balanced non-side-payment games. The convex side-payment games are extended in two different ways, to the ordinal convex games and to the cardinal convex games. Scarf's (1967a) theorem on the nonemptiness of the core of a balanced non-side-payment game; Vilkov (1977) and Peleg's (1982) theorem on the nonemptiness of the core of an ordinal convex game; a theorem on marginal worth vectors for an ordinal convex game and its non-converse; and a theorem on a λ-transfer value for a cardinal convex game are presented. Section 2.3 first discusses the core-like solutions for a game in normal form: the α-core, the β-core, and a strong equilibrium. Scarf's (1971) theorem for the nonemptiness of the α-core, and a strong equilibrium existence theorem are presented. Then, in order to bridge the gap between this chapter and Chapters 3 and 5 – in particular, in order to propose economically meaningful setups that are

[1] Throughout this monograph, a cooperative game is defined according to a behavioral principle, rather than according to a specific game-theoretical model. See the fourth through sixth paragraphs of Section 2.1.

appropriate for strategic analysis of cooperative behavior – a somewhat more general model is introduced, and the strong equilibrium concept is discussed within the generalized framework; the model is a special case of the model of society that will be introduced in Section 3.4. Section 2.4 presents the decomposition of a normal-form game into a game form and a preference profile, and the decomposition of a non-side-payment game into an effectivity function and a preference profile. The effectivity function approach to the core and its relationship with the non-side-payment game theory – in particular, the stability concept, Peleg's (1982) theorem on stability of a convex effectivity function and its partial converse, an α-stable game form, a β-stable game form, and a strongly consistent game form – are discussed. The Appendix to Chapter 2 contains simple economic examples which illustrate some of the theorems of Sections 2.1–2.4. Many of these examples capture diverse aspects of the main models of Chapters 3–6. All the results presented in this chapter (except Theorems 2.3.1, 2.4.11 and 2.4.12, which are not used in any part of this monograph) are either given a more systematic presentation with a complete proof in Ichiishi (1983), or proved here or in a later chapter. Among other textbooks where the cooperative theory is introduced along with many examples are: Moulin (1981a); Rosenmüller (1981); Owen (1982); Shubik (1982, 1984); Suzuki and Muto (1985); Friedman (1986); and Peleg (1988/89).

2.1 The core of a side-payment game

Let N be a finite set of players, *a priori* given and fixed throughout this chapter. Denote by $\mathcal{N}$ the family of nonempty coalitions $2^N \setminus \{\phi\}$. When the players of coalition S coordinate their strategy-choice in spite of their diverse interests, one says that cooperation among members of S is made, or equivalently that coalition S forms. To model cooperative behavior it is necessary to formulate explicitly what each coalition can achieve by the cooperation of its members. The simplest model of this class would be a *game in characteristic function form with side payments* (or simply a *side-payment game*) defined as a function $v: \mathcal{N} \to \mathbf{R}$. The intended interpretation is that $v(S)$ is the maximal total payoff of coalition S that the members of S can bring about by their cooperation. Here, the concept of strategy is hidden behind the model, and one studies directly the payoff allocation that is implicitly determined by a cooperative strategy-choice of the players. The model of the side-payment game is due to von Neumann and Morgenstern (1947). Their interpretation of the characteristic function v was specific (see von Neumann and Morgenstern (1947, Chapter VI)), however, and will not be adopted in any part of the present monograph. A payoff allocation $\{u_j\}_{j \in S} \in \mathbf{R}^S$ is feasible within coalition S, if $\sum_{j \in S} u_j \leqslant v(S)$. Two restrictions imposed by this formulation should be noticed: First, the feasibility of payoff allocations within S is determined regardless of actions of the players outside S. Second, the maximal "total" payoff value $v(S)$ presupposes the addition of different players' payoff levels, so the payoff can hardly be interpreted as ordinal utility; it is interpreted most naturally as a monetary value. Due to the simplicity and tractability of the model, however, all cooperative solution concepts can be given the most lucid analysis within this setup. Any result thus obtained serves as a crucial stepping stone for analysis of the same concept within more general setups.

An important descriptive cooperative equilibrium concept is now given: The *core* of a side-payment game v is the set $C(v)$ of all $u \in \mathbf{R}^N$ such that (1) $\sum_{j \in N} u_j \leqslant v(N)$ and (2) it is not true that there exists $S \in \mathcal{N}$ for which $\sum_{j \in S} u_j < v(S)$. Condition (1) is the feasibility of the payoff vector u in the grand coalition N. The grand coalition is indeed formed in equilibrium. Condition (2) is the coalitional stability of u. If on the contrary there exists $S \in \mathcal{N}$ for which $\sum_{j \in S} u_j < v(S)$, then coalition S will deviate from the grand coalition to form an independent cooperative unit, realize its maximal total payoff $v(S)$, and divide it among its members so that each member j receives a payoff greater than u_j, that is, S will improve upon u. The coalitional stability means that no coalition can improve upon u. The concept of the core of a side-payment game was discovered by Gillies (1959) and Lloyd S. Shapley during their investigation of the von Neumann-Morgenstern solutions in 1952–1953.

Example 2A.1 of the Appendix to Chapter 2 presents a simple economic model, defines associated side-payment games, and discusses their cores. Notice that different games can be obtained from the same economic model by postulating different institutional setups for players' interaction.

The traditional cutting edge between the cooperative and the noncooperative worlds is that in the former players are allowed to communicate before each play and to make binding agreements about the strategies they will use (see, e.g., Aumann (1967, p. 3)). There are two criteria here: (1) the possibility of entering binding agreements, and (2) the possibility of jointly choosing a coordinated strategy within a coalition. The descriptive cooperative behavior, like the one modelled in the first two paragraphs of this section, has sometimes been criticized as unrealistic, because it assumes a "binding commitment" to cooperation within a coalition (criterion (1) above). Perhaps, the primitive concept of a set of all feasible payoff allocations in a coalition S, $\{\{u_j\}_{j \in S} \in \mathbf{R}^S \mid \sum_{j \in S} u_j \leqslant v(S)\}$, induces this criticism, because one tends to interpret that a payoff allocation $\{u_j\}_{j \in S}$ is in S's feasible set only when the members of S make a binding commitment to cooperation in order to realize $\{u_j\}_{j \in S}$. The above criticism does not apply, and the definition of a cooperative game adopted in the present monograph is different from the traditional one. The feasible set simply describes the constraint on coalition S, just as in the neoclassical economic theory a budget set describes the constraint on a consumer. Whether or not the choice of a strategy bundle will bind the members once it is made is a separate issue from whether or not a strategy bundle satisfies the constraint. In the present monograph a *cooperative game* is defined simply as the way players interact based on the behavioral principle that any set of players can freely communicate with each other and then jointly choose their strategy bundle, that is, it allows players to coordinate their strategies (criterion (2) above). This definition differs from the traditional one in that a chosen joint strategy may not bind the players involved, so that some of them may deviate from the decision afterwards. Should some members defect, then the original coalition will break down. In a descriptive cooperative game theory, therefore, it is essential to address which coalitions are formed and sustained in equilibrium. Notice that the present definition of a cooperative game is made according to a behavioral principle, and not according to a game-theoretical model. Thus, one can define a cooperative game as well as a non-cooperative game within the framework specified by a given model, each leading to its own solution concept; this point will be elaborated in the following two paragraphs.

The core is a central solution concept in a cooperative game. Within the present setup of side-payment game v, the grand coalition N is indeed formed, and the members agree to choose a payoff allocation $u^* \in \mathbf{R}^N$. The binding nature of this agreement is not assumed here, so if players S see that it is to their advantage to defect from N and coordinate their strategies within their capacity (i.e., if there is a payoff allocation $\{u_j\}_{j \in S}$ such that $\sum_{j \in S} u_j \leqslant v(S)$ and $u_j > u_j^*$ for all $j \in S$), then the grand coalition will break down and a new coalition S will be formed. However, if u^* is in the core, no group of people S has *incentives* jointly to defect from N, because they cannot find such an improving allocation $\{u_j\}_{j \in S}$. Coalition N is thus sustained. Under the binding-agreement assumption, there would be no point of looking at the core, because even if a new coalition S sees the opportunity to improve upon u^*, the players S cannot defect from N due to their binding commitment to N.

According to the behavioral principle that no player can coordinate strategy choice with other players, that is, in a *noncooperative game*, a descriptive solution $u^* \in \mathbf{R}^N$ would stipulate that no singleton has an incentive to deviate from it. In the present setup player j has an incentive to deviate if $v(\{j\}) > u_j^*$. A payoff allocation u^* for which $u_j^* \geqslant v(\{j\})$ for all $j \in N$ is called *individually rational*. The cooperative theory and the noncooperative theory provide different predictions, when the coalitional stability condition and the individual rationality condition are different; this occurs when the constraint on coalition S (i.e., $v(S)$) is different from the sum of the constraints on the individuals of S (i.e., $\sum_{j \in S} v(\{j\})$). The spirit of the individual rationality can be extended to more complex game-theoretical models. When it is extended to the game in normal form (Section 2.3) and when the passive behavioral principle is postulated, one obtains the central noncooperative solution concept, the Nash equilibrium (Nash, 1950, 1951). Likewise, the spirit of coalitional stability can be extended to more complex game-theoretical models, including the normal-form game.[2] The present distinction between cooperative and noncooperative games applies to all these models. In both cases, if the theory is to be descriptive, an equilibrium would stipulate that there be no incentives for players to deviate from it.

A *coalition structure* is a partition of N; it describes which coalitions are formed and coexist. In many economic applications, it is desirable to have the modified core concept, where the feasibility condition (1) (via the grand coalition) is relaxed to: (1′) there exists a coalition structure $\mathcal{T}$ such that $\sum_{j \in T} u_j \leqslant v(T)$ for each $T \in \mathcal{T}$. The coalitions $T \in \mathcal{T}$ are then formed in equilibrium. This modification will play an essential role in Chapters 3 and 4. It will not be discussed in the present chapter, however, in order to keep the exposition as simple as possible.

Going back to the formal definition of the core $C(v)$, it is straightforward to see that it is the set of solutions of the linear inequality system,

$$-\sum_{j \in N} x_j \geqslant -v(N),$$
$$\sum_{j \in S} x_j \geqslant v(S), \text{ for all } S \in \mathcal{N}.$$

The core of a side-payment game is therefore a compact, convex polyhedron.

The rest of this section will be devoted to discussions of three important classes of side-payment games. The first class characterizes nonemptiness of the core. A subfamily $\mathcal{B}$ of $\mathcal{N}$ is called *balanced*, if there exists an indexed set $\{\lambda_S \mid S \in \mathcal{B}\}$ of nonnegative real numbers such that $\sum_{S \in \mathcal{B}} \lambda_S \chi_S = \chi_N$, where χ_S is the characteristic vector of S. Note that $\sum_{S \in \mathcal{B}} \lambda_S \chi_S = \chi_N$ iff[3] $\sum_{S \in \mathcal{B}: S \ni j} \lambda_S = 1$ for every $j \in N$. The set $\{\lambda_S \mid S \in \mathcal{B}\}$ is called *associated balancing coefficients*. A side-payment game v is called *balanced* if for every balanced family $\mathcal{B}$ with associated balancing coefficients $\{\lambda_S \mid S \in \mathcal{B}\}$, it follows that $\sum_{S \in \mathcal{B}} \lambda_S v(S) \leqslant v(N)$. Bondareva (1962, 1963) and Shapley (1967) independently established the following basic result:

Theorem 2.1.1 (Bondareva, Shapley). *Let v: $\mathcal{N} \to \mathbf{R}$ be a side-payment game. The core of v is nonempty if and only if v is balanced.*

[2] The correlated equilibrium of Aumann (1974) for a game in normal form with randomized strategies is a noncooperative solution concept. This clarification will be made in detail in Remark 2.3.9 of Section 2.3.

[3] The term "iff" is an abbreviation for "if and only if."

For a proof of Theorem 2.1.1, see, e.g., Ichiishi (1983, pp. 81–82).

Here is one interpretation of the balancedness condition on v: Suppose that each player can put fractions of his total effort into several coalitions. Nobody puts positive effort in coalitions other than those of $\mathscr{B}$. Player j puts fraction λ_S of his total effort into coalition S for which $j \in S$. Since the fractions are summed up to 1, $\sum_{S \in \mathscr{B}: S \ni j} \lambda_S = 1$ for every player j. Each member of coalition S puts fraction λ_S of his total effort, so coalition S produces the total payoff of $\lambda_S v(S)$. The society as a whole then produces the total payoff of $\sum_{S \in \mathscr{B}} \lambda_S v(S)$. The balancedness condition says that the grand coalition is efficient enough to produce its total payoff at no less than this amount.

When game v is constructed from an economic model, like the two games of Example 2A.1, the balancedness condition may be derived from some meaningful conditions on the original economic model. Examples 2A.3 and 2A.4 illustrate this. Example 2A.5 presents an economic model whose associated side-payment game is not balanced.

The next class: A side-payment game v is called *exact* if for every $T \in \mathscr{N}$ there exists a member of the core u such that $\sum_{j \in T} u_j = v(T)$. (Shapley (1971) called this a game with a *complete core*.) An exact game is necessarily balanced. Game v is exact, iff for every T, the optimal value of the linear programming problem,

$$
\begin{aligned}
(P) \qquad & \min && \sum_{j \in T} x_j \\
& \text{subject to} && \sum_{j \in S} x_j \geqslant v(S) \text{ for all } S \in \mathscr{N}, \text{ and} \\
& && -\sum_{j \in N} x_j \geqslant -v(N),
\end{aligned}
$$

exists and is precisely $v(T)$. Here, x satisfies the constraint of problem (P) iff it is in the core of v. Applying the duality theorem of linear programming (see, e.g., Ichiishi, 1983, Exercise 4, p. 115), one can prove the following finite-dimensional version of a result of Schmeidler (1972):

Theorem 2.1.2 (Schmeidler). *A side-payment game v: $\mathscr{N} \to \mathbf{R}$ is exact, if and only if for every $T \in \mathscr{N}$,*

$$
v(T) = \max\left\{ \sum_{S \in \mathscr{N}} \lambda_S v(S) - \kappa v(N) \in \mathbf{R} \;\middle|\; \begin{array}{l} \sum_S \lambda_S \chi_S - \kappa \chi_N = \chi_T \\ \lambda_S,\ \kappa \geqslant 0 \end{array} \right\}.
$$

Notice that the set

$$
D(T) := \left\{ \sum_{S \in \mathscr{N}} \lambda_S v(S) - \kappa v(N) \in \mathbf{R} \;\middle|\; \begin{array}{l} \sum_S \lambda_S \chi_S - \kappa \chi_N = \chi_T \\ \lambda_S,\ \kappa \geqslant 0 \end{array} \right\}
$$

is always nonempty (indeed, $v(T) \in D(T)$, by setting $\lambda_T = 1$, $\lambda_S = 0$ for all $S \neq T$, and $\kappa = 0$). It is bounded from above, iff the core of v is nonempty. To prove this last equivalence, recall that the primary problem of any linear programming problem has an optimal solution iff its dual problem has an optimal solution (Ichiishi, 1983, Exercise 3 (viii), p. 114). As mentioned before, the constraint set of the present primary problem (P) is precisely the core, and it is compact. The image of the objective function of its dual problem is the set $D(T)$. Therefore, the core is nonempty, iff (P) has an optimal solution, and this in turn is the case, iff $D(T)$ is nonempty and bounded from above.

Due to the very definition of exactness, study of the core of an exact game is simpler than study of the core of a balanced game in general. In order to exploit this fact, the *exact envelope* of a balanced game v is defined as the game,

$$\bar{\bar{v}}: \mathscr{N} \to \mathbf{R},\ T \mapsto \max D(T).$$

Then, game $\bar{\bar{v}}$ is exact, and $C(\bar{\bar{v}}) = C(v)$. Indeed, the identity of $C(\bar{\bar{v}})$ and $C(v)$ easily follows from the fact that $\bar{\bar{v}}(T)$ is the optimal value of problem (P). Exactness of $\bar{\bar{v}}$ then follows from this identity. See Schmeidler (1972) for the usefulness of the exact envelope in his study of the core of a side-payment game with infinitely many players.

The third class characterizes increasing returns with respect to the coalition size. Let v: $\mathscr{N} \to \mathbf{R}$ be a side-payment game, and define $v(\phi) := 0$. Game v is called *convex*, if for any $S, T \in \mathscr{N}$

$$v(S) + v(T) \leqslant v(S \cap T) + v(S \cup T).$$

The following discussion justifies this terminology: Let G^N be the family of all side-payment games with a player set N. Fix any $R \in \mathscr{N}$, and define the "difference operator" Δ_R: $G^N \to G^N$ by

$$[\Delta_R v](S) := v(S \cup \mathrm{R}) - v(S \setminus \mathrm{R}).$$

Given $Q, R \in \mathscr{N}$, the "second-order difference operator" Δ_{QR}: $G^N \to G^N$ is defined as $\Delta_{QR} v := \Delta_Q(\Delta_R v)$. Now it is easy to check that game v is convex iff for all $Q, R, S \in \mathscr{N}$ it follows that $[\Delta_{QR} v](S) \geqslant 0$. This last condition is analogous to the standard condition of convexity of a function from $\mathbf{R}$ to $\mathbf{R}$.

A side-payment game v: $\mathscr{N} \to \mathbf{R}$ is said to satisfy *increasing returns with respect to the coalition size* if for any $S, T \subset N$ and any $j \in N$ such that $S \subset T \subset N \setminus \{j\}$, it follows that

$$v(T \cup \{j\}) - v(T) \geqslant v(S \cup \{j\}) - v(S).$$

The term $v(S \cup \{j\}) - v(S)$ is interpreted as the marginal worth of player j to coalition S. The increasing returns condition says that the marginal worth of j is larger as he joins in a bigger coalition.

The marginal worth of each player can be systematically described by the concept of marginal worth vectors. Let $n := \# N$. A linear order on the player set N is identified with a bijection, $\sigma: N \to \{1, 2, \ldots, n\}$. Denote by G_n the family of all linear orders on N. Given $\sigma \in G_n$, the *marginal worth vector* $a^\sigma(v)$ is defined by $a_j^\sigma(v) := v(P_j^\sigma \cup \{j\}) - v(P_j^\sigma)$, where P_j^σ is the set of all players who precede j with respect to σ, i.e., $P_j^\sigma := \{i \in N \mid \sigma(i) < \sigma(j)\}$ (recall the convention, $v(\phi) := 0$). Since $\# G_n = n!$, there are in general $n!$ marginal worth vectors. The implications (i)⇔(ii)⇒(iii) of the following Theorem 2.1.3 is due to Shapley (1971), and the implication (iii)⇒(ii) is due to Ichiishi (1981c).

Theorem 2.1.3. *Let $v: \mathcal{N} \to \mathbf{R}$ be a side-payment game. Then the following three conditions are equivalent*:

(i) *Game v is convex*;
(ii) *Game v satisfies increasing returns with respect to the coalition size*;
(iii) *For each $\sigma \in G_n$, the marginal worth vector $a^\sigma(v)$ is in the core of game v.*

For a proof of Theorem 2.1.3, see, e.g., Ichiishi (1983, pp. 121–122). Here is an intuition for the proof: Given a linear order $\sigma \in G_n$, the associated marginal worth vector $a^\sigma(v)$ is re-defined inductively in the order of σ by

$$a_j^\sigma(v) := \max\left\{x_j \in \mathbf{R} \;\middle|\; \begin{array}{l} \sum_{i:\sigma(i) \leqslant \sigma(j)} x_i \leqslant v(P_j^\sigma \cup \{j\}), \\ x_i = a_i^\sigma(v) \text{ for all } i \in P_j^\sigma \end{array}\right\}.$$

Here, the increasing sequence of coalitions $\{S_k\}_{k=1}^n$, $S_k := S_{k-1} \cup \{\sigma^{-1}(k)\}$, is considered, and in each coalition S_k its "last" member $\sigma^{-1}(k)$ greedily grabs as high payoff as he can given the payoffs already allocated to the other members, S_{k-1}. Of course,

$$\begin{aligned}\textstyle\sum_{j \in N} a_j^\sigma(v) &= a_{\sigma^{-1}(1)}^\sigma(v) + a_{\sigma^{-1}(2)}^\sigma(v) + \ldots + a_{\sigma^{-1}(n)}^\sigma(v) \\ &= v(\{S_1\}) + (v(S_2) - v(S_1)) + \ldots + (v(S_n) - v(S_{n-1})) \\ &= v(N).\end{aligned}$$

The increasing returns with respect to the coalition size says that this *greedy algorithm* works in the sense that the payoff vector determined this way is a solution of the problem,

$$\begin{array}{ll}\min & \sum_{j \in N} x_j, \\ \text{subject to} & \sum_{j \in S} x_j \geqslant v(S), \text{ for all } S \in \mathcal{N},\end{array}$$

i.e., it is a member of the core. See Ichiishi (1981c, pp. 285–286) for the detail.

Examples 2A.6 and 2A.7 present economic models whose associated side-payment games are convex. Further examples of a convex game that is derived from an economy with production are found in Topkis (1987).

Consider an arbitrary increasing finite sequence of coalitions, $\phi \neq S_1 \subsetneqq S_2 \subsetneqq \ldots \subsetneqq S_m$. One may choose $\sigma \in G_n$, so that the first $\# S_1$

members according to σ are precisely the players of S_1, the next $\#(S_2\backslash S_1)$ members are precisely the players of $S_2\backslash S_1$, and so on. Formally, choose σ so that for each $k=1, \ldots, m-1$,

$$\sigma(i)<\sigma(j) \text{ for all } i\in S_k \text{ and } j\in S_{k+1}\backslash S_k.$$

Then, for each k, $v(S_k)=\sum_{j\in S_k} a_j^\sigma(v)$. Notice that if $m=n$, the payoff vector u for which $v(S_k)=\sum_{j\in S_k} u_j$ is uniquely determined (for $\{j\}=S_{k+1}\backslash S_k$, $u_j=v(S_{k+1})-v(S_k)$). In view of condition (iii) of Theorem 2.1.3, therefore, one can easily establish:

Corollary 2.1.4. *Let v: $\mathcal{N}\to\mathbf{R}$ be a side-payment game. Game v is convex if and only if for any increasing finite sequence of coalitions $\phi\neq S_1\subsetneqq S_2\subsetneqq \ldots \subsetneqq S_m$, there exists $u\in C(v)$ such that $\sum_{j\in S_k} u_j=v(S_k)$ for all $k=1, \ldots, m$.*

In particular, a convex game is exact.

Several remarks related to the marginal worth vectors are in order: (1) The Shapley value of game v (see, e.g., Shapley (1953) or Ichiishi (1983, Ch. 6)) is $\sum_{\sigma\in G_n} a^\sigma(v)/(n!)$. By Theorem 2.1.3, the Shapley value of a convex game is in the core. Rabie (1981) constructed an example of an exact game whose Shapley value is outside the core. (2) Shapley (1971) established that for a convex game, the extreme points of its core are precisely the marginal worth vectors. (3) Robert J. Weber (1988) established that for any side-payment game v, its core $C(v)$ is contained in the convex hull of the set of marginal worth vectors co $\{a^\sigma(v) \mid \sigma\in G_n\}$.

2.2 The core of a non-side-payment game

Let N be given as the finite set of players, and hence let $\mathcal{N}$ $(:=2^N\backslash\{\phi\})$ be given as the family of nonempty coalitions of players. Two of the restrictions imposed by the modelling of a side-payment game were emphasized earlier (the first paragraph of Section 2.1): Actions of the outsiders $N\backslash S$ impose no constraints on the feasibility of payoff allocations within coalition S, and the payoff can hardly be interpreted as utility. In order to remove the second restriction, a more general model is now constructed; the model is due to Aumann and Peleg (1960). For each S, space $\mathbf{R}^S$ is identified with the subspace $\{u\in\mathbf{R}^N \mid \forall j\notin S: u_j=0\}$ of the utility allocation space $\mathbf{R}^N$. A *game in characteristic function form without side payments* (or simply a *non-side-payment game*) is a correspondence (set-valued map) $\tilde{V}$: $\mathcal{N}\to\mathbf{R}^N$ such that $\tilde{V}(S)\subset\mathbf{R}^S$ for every $S\in\mathcal{N}$. The intended interpretation is that $u\in\tilde{V}(S)$ iff the utility allocation $\{u_j\}_{j\in S}$ is feasible within coalition S through the cooperation of its members. An equivalent definition: A *non-side-payment game* is a correspondence V: $\mathcal{N}\to\mathbf{R}^N$ such that $[u, v\in\mathbf{R}^N, \forall i\in S: u_i=v_i]$ implies $[u\in V(S)$ iff $v\in V(S)]$ for every $S\in\mathcal{N}$.

Clearly, $V(S)$ is the cylinder based on $\tilde{V}(S)$, i.e., it is the set of $u \in \mathbf{R}^N$ whose natural projection to $\mathbf{R}^S$ is in $\tilde{V}(S)$. Many conditions on a non-side-payment game can be concisely expressed in terms of the second definition rather than in terms of the first definition above. The second definition of a non-side-payment game will be adopted throughout this text.

The *core* of a non-side-payment game V is the set $C(V)$ of all $u \in \mathbf{R}^N$ such that (1) $u \in V(N)$ and (2) it is not true that there exist $S \in \mathcal{N}$ and $u' \in V(S)$ such that $u_j < u'_j$ for every $j \in S$. Condition (1) is the feasibility of the utility allocation u in the grand coalition N. The grand coalition is indeed formed in equilibrium. Condition (2) is the coalitional stability of u in that no coalition can improve upon u. The geometry of the core of a non-side-payment game may sometimes become hard to capture. Even if each $V(S)$ is a convex set (an assumption too stringent in this ordinal context), the core $C(V)$ could be a disconnected set. Aumann (1961) developed the core concept systematically for a non-side-payment game.

A non-side-payment game V is called *balanced* if for every balanced subfamily $\mathcal{B}$ of $\mathcal{N}$, it follows that $\bigcap_{S \in \mathcal{B}} V(S) \subset V(N)$. A fundamental result due to Scarf (1967a) is:

Theorem 2.2.1 (Scarf). *Let $V\colon \mathcal{N} \to \mathbf{R}^N$ be a non-side-payment game, and define $b \in \mathbf{R}^N$ by $b_j := \sup \{u_j \in \mathbf{R} \mid u \in V(\{j\})\}$ for each $j \in N$. The core of V is nonempty if*

(i) *$V(S) - \mathbf{R}^N_+ = V(S)$ for every $S \in \mathcal{N}$;*
(ii) *there exists $M \in \mathbf{R}$ such that for every $S \in \mathcal{N}$, $[u \in V(S),\ u \geqslant b]$ implies $[u_i < M$ for every $i \in S]$;*[4]
(iii) *$V(S)$ is closed in $\mathbf{R}^N$ for every $S \in \mathcal{N}$; and*
(iv) *V is balanced.*

For a proof of Theorem 2.2.1, see, e.g., Ichiishi (1983, p. 84). The theorem will be derived from a more general theorem in Section 3.4. Its relevance to the fixed-point literature will be discussed in Section 3.6, where still other proofs will be given.

One can interpret the balancedness condition on V in the same way as before (the paragraph following the statement of Theorem 2.1.1). Of course, alternative and more appropriate interpretations may be given, depending upon specific contexts. Indeed, Examples 2A.8 and 2A.14 construct non-side-payment games from the model of pure exchange $\mathscr{E}_{pe}$, and derive the balancedness of the games from well-known assumptions on economy $\mathscr{E}_{pe}$. Example 2A.9 constructs a balanced non-side-payment game from an economic model with production.

[4] For any two vectors $x, y \in \mathbf{R}^N$, $x \leqslant y$ means $x_j \leqslant y_j$ for all $j \in N$; $x < y$ means $x \leqslant y$ and $x \neq y$; and $x \ll y$ means $x_j < y_j$ for all $j \in N$.

A side-payment game can be considered a special case of a non-side-payment game. Indeed, given a side-payment game v, the associated non-side-payment game V is defined by

$$V(S) := \{u \in \mathbf{R}^N \mid \sum_{j \in S} u_j \leqslant v(S)\}.$$

In this case it is straightforward to check that the core $C(v)$ of v (defined in the second paragraph of Section 2.1) and the core $C(V)$ of V (defined in the second paragraph of this section) are identical, that assumptions (i)–(iii) of Theorem 2.2.1 are automatically satisfied, and that the balancedness condition on v (defined in the paragraph preceding the statement of Theorem 2.1.1) and the balancedness condition on V (defined in the paragraph preceding the statement of Theorem 2.2.1) are equivalent.

The convexity condition on a side-payment game has been extended to a non-side-payment game in two ways: ordinal convexity and cardinal convexity. The former will be discussed first. A non-side-payment game V: $\mathcal{N} \to \mathbf{R}^N$ is called *ordinal convex*, if for any $S, T \in \mathcal{N}$

$$V(S) \cap V(T) \subset V(S \cap T) \cup V(S \cup T),$$

where $V(\phi) := \phi$. Vilkov (1977) established the nonemptiness of the core of an ordinal convex game under certain regularity conditions, and Peleg (1982) strengthened the theorem as:

Theorem 2.2.2 (Vilkov, as strengthened by Peleg). *Let V: $\mathcal{N} \to \mathbf{R}^N$ be a non-side-payment game, and define $b \in \mathbf{R}^N$ by $b_j := \sup \{u_j \in \mathbf{R} \mid u \in V(\{j\})\}$ for each $j \in N$. The core of V is nonempty if*

(i) *$V(S) - \mathbf{R}^N_+ = V(S)$ for every $S \in \mathcal{N}$;*
(ii) *there exists $M \in \mathbf{R}$ such that for every $S \in \mathcal{N}$, $[u \in V(S),\ u \geqslant b]$ implies $[u_i < M$ for every $i \in S]$;*
(iii) *$V(S)$ is closed in $\mathbf{R}^N$ for every $S \in \mathcal{N}$; and*
(iv) *V is ordinal convex.*

(Peleg (1982) assumed, instead of (ii), that (ii′) *there exist*[5] $c \in \bigcap_{S \in \mathcal{N}} \mathring{V}(S)$ *and $M \in \mathbf{R}$ such that for every $S \in \mathcal{N}$, $[u \in V(S), u \geqslant c]$ implies $[u_i < M$ for every $i \in S]$*. Replacing assumption (ii′) by the weaker assumption (ii) as in the above theorem is straightforward.)

Examples 2A.10 and 2A.14, and also Example 4.2.4 of Chapter 4, present economic models whose associated non-side-payment games are ordinal convex.

Let $n := \# N$. Denote by G_n the family of all linear orders on N, each identified with a bijection from N to $\{1, 2, \ldots, n\}$. Given $\sigma \in G_n$, the *marginal*

[5] For a set X in a topological space E, $\mathring{X}$ is the interior of X in E, and $\bar{X}$ is the closure of X in E. If E is a topological vector space, icr X is the relative interior of X.

worth vector $a^\sigma(V)$ is inductively defined as follows: Let P_j^σ be the set of all players who precede j with respect to σ, i.e., $P_j^\sigma := \{i \in N \mid \sigma(i) < \sigma(j)\}$. Assume that $a_i^\sigma(V)$ has been defined for each $i \in P_j^\sigma$. Then $a_j^\sigma(V)$ is defined by:

$$a_j^\sigma(V) := \max\left\{ u_j \in \mathbf{R} \;\middle|\; \begin{array}{l} u \in V(P_j^\sigma \cup \{j\}) \\ u_i = a_i^\sigma(V) \text{ for all } i \in P_j^\sigma \end{array} \right\}.$$

Theorem 2.2.2 is a consequence of the following theorem:

Theorem 2.2.3. *Let* $V\colon \mathcal{N} \to \mathbf{R}^N$ *be a non-side-payment game. Assume that all the conditions (i)–(iv) of Theorem 2.2.2 are satisfied. Then for each* $\sigma \in G_n$, *the marginal worth vector* $a^\sigma(V)$ *is in the core of game* V.

Theorem 2.2.3 will be proved in Section 4.3; the proof is based on two lemmas of Peleg (1986). Unlike Theorem 2.1.3 the converse of Theorem 2.2.3 is false, as demonstrated by the following example:

Example 2.2.4. A non-ordinal-convex game V whose marginal worth vectors are all in the core $C(V)$: $N = \{1, 2, 3\}$, $V(\{j\}) = \{u \in \mathbf{R}^3 \mid u_j \leqslant 0\}$,

$$\begin{aligned} V(\{i, j\}) &= \{u \in \mathbf{R}^3 \mid u_i \leqslant 1, u_j \leqslant 1\} \text{ for } i \neq j, \text{ and} \\ V(N) &= \{u \in \mathbf{R}^3 \mid u_1 \leqslant 0, u_2 \leqslant 1, u_3 \leqslant 1\} \\ &\quad \cup \{u \in \mathbf{R}^3 \mid u_1 \leqslant 1, u_2 \leqslant 0, u_3 \leqslant 1\} \\ &\quad \cup \{u \in \mathbf{R}^3 \mid u_1 \leqslant 1, u_2 \leqslant 1, u_3 \leqslant 0\}. \end{aligned}$$

This game satisfies conditions (i)–(iii). In Table 2.1, $\sigma \in G_n$ is represented by the column vector whose jth component is $\sigma^{-1}(j)$, $j = 1, 2, 3$.

Then, $a^\sigma(V) \in C(V)$ for all $\sigma \in G_n$. This game is not ordinal convex, however, because

$$\begin{pmatrix} 1 \\ 1 \\ 1 \end{pmatrix} \in V(\{1, 2\}) \cap V(\{2, 3\}), \text{ and}$$

$$\begin{pmatrix} 1 \\ 1 \\ 1 \end{pmatrix} \notin V(\{2\}) \cup V(\{1, 2, 3\}). \ \square$$

The second extension of convexity is formulated in terms of the base $\tilde{V}(S)$ of a cylinder $V(S)$. Recall:

$$\tilde{V}(S) := \{u \in V(S) \mid u_j = 0 \text{ for each } j \in N \setminus S\}.$$

A non-side-payment game $V\colon \mathcal{N} \to \mathbf{R}^N$ is called *cardinal convex*, if for any S, $T \in \mathcal{N}$

$$\tilde{V}(S) + \tilde{V}(T) \subset \tilde{V}(S \cap T) + \tilde{V}(S \cup T),$$

where $\tilde{V}(\phi) := \{\mathbf{0}\}$.

The concept of the Shapley value of a side-payment game has been

Table 2.1. *Computation of $a^{\sigma}(V)$*

σ / $a^{\sigma}(V)$	1 2 3	1 3 2	2 1 3	2 3 1	3 1 2	3 2 1
$a_1^{\sigma}(V)$	0	0	1	1	1	1
$a_2^{\sigma}(V)$	1	1	0	0	1	1
$a_3^{\sigma}(V)$	1	1	1	1	0	0

extended to a non-side-payment game in several ways. The following concept is one of the extensions, and is due to Shapley (1969). Let V: $\mathcal{N} \to \mathbf{R}^N$ be a non-side-payment game. Set $\Delta^N := \{x \in \mathbf{R}^N \mid x \geqslant \mathbf{0}, \sum_{j \in N} x_j = 1\}$, and for each $\lambda \in \Delta^N$ define a side-payment game v_λ: $\mathcal{N} \to \mathbf{R}$ by

$$v_\lambda(S) := \sup \{\sum_{j \in S} \lambda_j u_j \mid u \in V(S)\}.$$

Here, vector λ is interpreted as the exchange rates of utilities. Then $u^* \in \mathbf{R}^N$ is called a *λ-transfer value* of V, if (1) $u^* \in V(N)$ and (2) there exists $\lambda^* \in \Delta^N$ such that $\{\lambda_j^* u_j^*\}_{j \in N}$ is the Shapley value of side-payment game v_{λ^*}. Recall that the Shapley value of a convex game is in the core (the last paragraph of Section 2.1). The following theorem (or its variant) is due independently to Kern (1985) and to Ichiishi (1983, Ch. 6, Exercise 2):

Theorem 2.2.5. *Let V: $\mathcal{N} \to \mathbf{R}^N$ be a non-side-payment game. There exists a λ-transfer value in the core $C(V)$, if*

(i) *there exists a convex, compact set K such that $V(N) = K - \mathbf{R}_+^N$; and*
(ii) *V is cardinal convex.*

When a non-side-payment game V is actually a side-payment game v, i.e., $V(S) = \{u \in \mathbf{R}^N \mid \sum_{j \in S} u_j \leqslant v(S)\}$, convexity of v, ordinal convexity of V, and cardinal convexity of V are equivalent. For a general non-side-payment game V, ordinal convexity and cardinal convexity are different, as pointed out by Sharkey (1981).

Example 2.2.6. An ordinal convex game V which is not cardinal convex:

$N = \{1, 2, 3\}$, $V(\{j\}) = \{u \in \mathbf{R}^3 \mid u_j \leqslant 0\}$, $V(\{i, j\}) = \{u \in \mathbf{R}^3 \mid u_i \leqslant 1, u_j \leqslant 1\}$ for $i \neq j$, and $V(\{1, 2, 3\}) = \{u \in \mathbf{R}^3 \mid u_j \leqslant 1, j = 1, 2, 3\}$. □

Example 2.2.7. A cardinal convex game V which is not ordinal convex:

$N = \{1, 2, 3, 4\}$, $V(\{2, 3\}) = \{u \in \mathbf{R}^4 \mid u_2 \leqslant 1, u_3 \leqslant 3\}$, $V(\{1, 2, 3\}) = \{u \in \mathbf{R}^4 \mid u_1 \leqslant 1, u_2 \leqslant 2, u_3 \leqslant 2\}$, $V(\{2, 3, 4\}) = \{u \in \mathbf{R}^4 \mid u_2 \leqslant 2, u_3 \leqslant 2, u_4 \leqslant 1\}$,

$$V(\{1,2,3,4\}) = \{u \in \mathbf{R}^4 \mid u_1 \leqslant 1, u_2 \leqslant 2, u_3 \leqslant 2, u_4 \leqslant 0\}, \\ \cup \{u \in \mathbf{R}^4 \mid u_1 \leqslant 0, u_2 \leqslant 2, u_3 \leqslant 2, u_4 \leqslant 1\} \\ \cup \{u \in \mathbf{R}^4 \mid u_1 \leqslant 1, u_2 \leqslant 3, u_3 \leqslant 1, u_4 \leqslant 1\},$$

and $V(S) = \{u \in \mathbf{R}^4 \mid u_j \leqslant 0 \text{ for each } j \in S\}$ for all other S. □

2.3 Core-like solutions for a game in normal form and for a more general model

Let N be given as the finite set of players, and hence let $\mathcal{N}(:=2^N \setminus \{\phi\})$ be given as the family of nonempty coalitions of players. The modelling of the non-side-payment game still imposes the restriction that the set of feasible utility allocations within coalition S is given exogenously, independent of actions of the outsiders $N \setminus S$. This section will discuss how such restriction can be removed.

For player j denote by X^j the set of all strategies available to him. Define $X^S := \prod_{j \in S} X^j$ for each $S \in \mathcal{N}$, and set for simplicity $X := X^N$. It is postulated that j's preference relation is represented by a utility function $u^j: X \to \mathbf{R}$. A *game in normal form* is a list of specified data, $G := \{X^j, u^j\}_{j \in N}$.

The central noncooperative solution for G is the *Nash equilibrium*, defined as the strategy bundle x^* such that

$$\neg \exists j \in N: \exists x^j \in X^j: u^j(x^j, x^{*N \setminus \{j\}}) > u^j(x^*).$$

The phrase "$\exists j \in N$" is the key to understanding the Nash equilibrium as a noncooperative solution, because it is used in the context whether or not player j, acting alone, will improve upon a given strategy bundle. On the other hand, all the descriptive cooperative solution concepts involve instead the phrase "$\exists S \in \mathcal{N}$."

Different types of cooperative behavior can be modelled within game G, each reflecting specific perception by the members of a coalition about their capabilities *vis-à-vis* outsiders' strategy-choice, or about their own internal stability. These are summarized by certain non-side-payment games derived from G. The first three types of cooperative behavior and the associated solution concepts for G (the α-core, the β-core, and the strong equilibrium) presented in this section are due to Aumann (1959).

The *α-characteristic function* of game G is the non-side-payment game V_α: $\mathcal{N} \to \mathbf{R}^N$ defined by

$$V_\alpha(S) := \bigcup_{x^S \in X^S} \bigcap_{y^{N \setminus S} \in X^{N \setminus S}} \{u \in \mathbf{R}^N \mid \forall j \in S: u_j \leqslant u^j(x^S, y^{N \setminus S})\}.$$

According to the non-side-payment game V_α, the members of coalition S perceive utility allocation $\{u_j\}_{j \in S}$ to be feasible if they find one of their strategy bundles such that as long as they hang on to it, every member j in S can enjoy his utility level no less than u_j regardless of the strategy-choice of the outsiders. Coalition S is formed (and enforces its utility allocation $\{u_j\}_{j\in S}$), therefore, based upon its members' *prudent* or *pessimistic* perception about their capability to react to outsiders' strategy-choice. The *α-core* of a normal-form game G is the core of the associated α-characteristic function, and is denoted by $C_\alpha(G)$. The following theorem is due to Scarf (1971):

Theorem 2.3.1 (Scarf). *Let G be a game in normal form. Its α-core is nonempty if for every* $j\in N$,

(i) X^j *is a nonempty, convex, compact subset of a Euclidean space; and*
(ii) u^j *is continuous and quasi-concave in* X.

Examples 2A.11 and 2A.12 present economic models whose associated games in normal form satisfy the assumption of quasi-concavity of u^j in X.

The *β-characteristic function* of game G is the non-side-payment game V_β: $\mathcal{N}\to\mathbf{R}^N$ defined by

$$V_\beta(S):=\bigcap_{y^{N\setminus S}\in X^{N\setminus S}}\ \bigcup_{x^S\in X^S}\{u\in\mathbf{R}^N\mid\forall j\in S: u_j\leqslant u^j(x^S, y^{N\setminus S})\}.$$

According to the non-side-payment game V_β, the members of coalition S perceive utility allocation $\{u_j\}_{j\in S}$ to be feasible if for any strategy-choice of the outsiders, they can counteract it so as to make member j's utility level to be no less than u_j for all $j\in S$. Coalition S is formed, therefore, based upon its members' *optimistic* perception about their reaction capability. The *β-core* of a normal-form game G is the core of the associated β-characteristic function, and is denoted by $C_\beta(G)$.

Remark 2.3.2. For a two-person game in normal form, a stronger theorem than Theorem 2.3.1 can be established. Let $N=\{1, 2\}$. *The α-core of a two-person game in normal form,* $\{X^j, u^j\}_{j=1}^2$, *is nonempty, if* X^j *is a nonempty compact subset of a Euclidean space and* u^j *is continuous in* X. This is the case, because the only nonempty non-grand coalitions are the two singletons. Indeed, let

$$c_\alpha^1:=\max_{x^1}\min_{x^2} u^1(x^1, x^2),\ c_\alpha^2:=\max_{x^2}\min_{x^1} u^2(x^1, x^2).$$

Then, $x^*\in X$ is an α-core strategy, iff

$$\forall j\in\{1, 2\}: u^j(x^*)\geqslant c_\alpha^j, \text{ and}$$

$$\neg\exists x\in X: \forall j\in\{1, 2\}: u^j(x)>u^j(x^*).$$

The set $IR_\alpha:=\{x\in X\mid\forall j\in\{1, 2\}: u^j(x)\geqslant c_\alpha^j\}$ is always nonempty, because for $\hat{x}^j$ defined by $\min_{x^{N\setminus\{j\}}} u^j(\hat{x}^j, x^{N\setminus\{j\}})=c_\alpha^j$, it follows that $(\hat{x}^1, \hat{x}^2)\in IR_\alpha$. Under the topological assumptions one may choose a point $x^*\in IR_\alpha$ for which

$$\neg\exists x\in X: \forall j\in\{1, 2\}: u^j(x)>u^j(x^*).$$

Also for the two-person case, the assumptions of Theorem 2.3.1 guarantee the nonemptiness of the β-core. In fact, a stronger theorem is true: *The β-core of a two-person game in normal form, $\{X^j, u^j\}_{j=1}^2$, is nonempty, if X^j is a nonempty, convex, compact subset of a Euclidean space, u^j is continuous in X, and $u^j(\cdot, x^{N\setminus\{j\}})$ is quasi-concave in X^j.* Indeed, let

$$c_\beta^1 := \min_{x^2} \max_{x^1} u^1(x^1, x^2), \; c_\beta^2 := \min_{x^1} \max_{x^2} u^2(x^1, x^2).$$

Then, x^* is a β-core strategy, iff

$$x^* \in IR_\beta := \{x \in X \mid \forall j \in \{1, 2\}: u^j(x) \geqslant c_\beta^j\}, \text{ and}$$

$$\neg \exists x \in X: \forall j \in \{1, 2\}: u^j(x) > u^j(x^*).$$

But under the present assumptions there exists a Nash equilibrium $\bar{x}$ (see, e.g., Ichiishi (1983, Theorem 4.1.1, p. 57)), and it is easy to see that $\bar{x} \in IR_\beta$. Again under the topological assumptions, one may choose a point $x^* \in IR_\beta$ for which

$$\neg \exists x \in X: \forall j \in \{1, 2\}: u^j(x) > u^j(x^*).$$

The β-core nonemptiness theorem for the two-person case is no longer true, if the quasi-concavity assumption on $u^j(\cdot, x^{N\setminus\{j\}})$ is dropped.

Example:

$$X^1 = X^2 = [0, 4] \subset \mathbf{R},$$

$$u^1(x) = \begin{cases} 2x_1 + x_2, & \text{if } 2x_1 + x_2 \leqslant 1, \\ 2 - (2x_1 + x_2), & \text{if } 1 \leqslant 2x_1 + x_2 \leqslant 6, \\ 2x_1 + x_2 - 10, & \text{if } 6 \leqslant 2x_1 + x_2 \leqslant 11, \\ 12 - (2x_1 + x_2), & \text{if } 11 \leqslant 2x_1 + x_2, \end{cases}$$

$$u^2(x) = \begin{cases} -x_1 + 2x_2, & \text{if } -x_1 + 2x_2 \leqslant -3, \\ -6 - (-x_1 + 2x_2), & \text{if } -3 \leqslant -x_1 + 2x_2 \leqslant 2, \\ -x_1 + 2x_2 - 10, & \text{if } 2 \leqslant -x_1 + 2x_2 \leqslant 7, \\ 4 - (-x_1 + 2x_2), & \text{if } 7 \leqslant -x_1 + 2x_2. \end{cases}$$

In this example, $IR_\beta = \phi$. □

Given game G, construct non-side-payment games V_x, parameterized by the strategy bundles $x \in X$, by

$$V_x(S) := \bigcup_{\xi^S \in X^S} \{u \in \mathbf{R}^N \mid \forall j \in S: u_j \leqslant u^j(\xi^S, x^{N\setminus S})\}.$$

Here, a coalition is formed based on the *passive* cooperative behavior of its members in that they take the outsiders' strategy-choice as given. One can consider the core of game V_x, but a strategy bundle which gives rise to a core utility allocation may not be the same as the given parameter x. A *strong* *equilibrium* of game G is a strategy bundle $x^* \in X$ such that $\{u^j(x^*)\}_{j \in N}$ is in the core of V_{x^*}, or equivalently such that

$$\neg \exists S \in \mathcal{N}: \exists \xi^S \in X^S: \forall j \in S: u^j(\xi^S, x^{*N \setminus S}) > u^j(x^*).$$

A strong equilibrium is a Pareto optimal Nash equilibrium. Denote by $SE(G)$ the set of all strong equilibrium utility allocations of G. The following Claim 2.3.3 is straightforward. A strong equilibrium existence theorem (Theorem 2.3.4) was noted in Ichiishi (1982a).

Claim 2.3.3. *Let G be a game in normal form. Then,* $SE(G) \subset C_\beta(G) \subset C_\alpha(G)$.

Theorem 2.3.4. *Let G be a game in normal form. A strong equilibrium of G exists if*

(i) X^j *is a nonempty, convex, compact subset of a Euclidean space for every* $j \in N$;
(ii) u^j *is continuous and quasi-concave in X for every* $j \in N$; *and*
(iii) *the non-side-payment game* V_x *is balanced for every* $x \in X$.

Theorem 2.3.4 will be derived from a more general theorem (Theorem 3.4.15) in Section 3.4. Dubey (1986) clarified that if a strong equilibrium exists, then in general it has to be on the boundary of X (see Remark 2.3.5 for a detailed presentation). Here is an intuitive account for this: Let G be a game in normal form such that for each player j, the strategy space X^j is a compact convex subset of $\mathbf{R}^{m_j}$ with a nonempty interior, and the utility function u^j is differentiable. Let $x^* \in X$ be a strong equilibrium of G, and assume that $x^{*T} \in \mathring{X}^T$ for some $T \subset N$. For each subcoalition S of T, S cannot improve upon x^{*S} given $x^{*N \setminus S}$, so the standard Lagrangean technique applied to the problem,

$$\begin{aligned}&\text{Max} \qquad u^j(x^S, x^{*N \setminus S})\\ &\text{subject to } u^i(x^S, x^{*N \setminus S}) = u^i(x^*) \text{ for all } i \in S \setminus \{j\},\\ &\text{given } j \in S \text{ and } x^*,\end{aligned}$$

yields the first order conditions,

$$\frac{\partial u^j}{\partial x_h^k} = \sum_{i \in S \setminus \{j\}} \lambda_i \frac{\partial u^i}{\partial x_h^k}, \text{ for all } k \in S \text{ and } h = 1, \ldots, m_k,$$

where the λ_i are the Lagrangean multipliers. There are $\sum_{k \in S} m_k - \#S + 1$ equations for each $S \subset T$, and there are $2^{\#T} - 1$ nonempty subcoalitions S of T. On the other hand, there are only $\sum_{k \in T} m_k$ variables that T has to determine. This overdetermination problem arises out of the assumption that x^{*T} is in the interior of X^T.

No general theorem for nonemptiness of the β-core has been established yet, apart from the combination of Claim 2.3.3 and Theorem 2.3.4. For certain games G the associated α- and β-characteristic functions are proved identical, so that $C_\alpha(G) = C_\beta(G)$; see, e.g., Mertens (1980) for the repeated games, and Moulin (1983) and Kolpin (1988) for a class of extensive games.

Chakrabarti (1985, 1988) refined the core-like solution concepts for a normal-form game by formulating explicitly the "credibility" of threat to coalition S by the outsiders $N \backslash S$, and reconsidered several fundamental theorems on core-like solutions using his own refined core-like solutions. Yano (1990) initiated the differential geometry approach by proposing the local α- and β-core concepts.

Bernheim, Peleg and Whinston (1987) proposed the *coalition-proof Nash equilibrium* concept as the solution for the situation in which the members of a coalition take into account internal stability when choosing their strategies. Peleg (1987) established an existence theorem for a subgame-perfect coalition-proof Nash equilibrium by characterizing it as a subgame-perfect Nash equilibrium, for the case in which each player has a linear order on the outcome space as his preference relation.

Remark 2.3.5. On Dubey's (1980, 1986) generic non-existence theorems about a strong equilibrium: Let X_0 be a subset of a set X. There are many circumstances in which one may interpret that X_0 is "big" in X. This is the case, for example, if (1) X is a probability space and $X \backslash X_0$ is a null set. Another circumstance which allows for this interpretation is that (2) X is a Baire space and $X \backslash X_0$ is a set of the first category. Notice that the criteria (1) and (2) are different, in spite of the logical similarity; see, e.g., Oxtoby (1971). A property (P) is said to hold *almost everywhere* in a probability space X, if there exists a subset X_0 such that $X \backslash X_0$ is a null set and every member of X_0 satisfies (P). A property (P) is said to hold *generically* in a Baire space X, if there exists a subset X_0 such that $X \backslash X_0$ is a set of the first category and every member of X_0 satisfies (P). Let X^j be a strategy space for player $j \in N$, and assume that it is a simplex in a Euclidean space. Set $n := \# N$. Choose any neighborhood V^j of X^j, and set $V := \prod_{j \in N} V^j$. Let U be the vector space of all C^2 functions from V to $\mathbf{R}$, endowed with the C^2-norm. Then a point $(u^j)_{j \in N} \in U^N$ gives rise to a game in normal form $\{X^j, u^j\}_{j \in N}$, so the Baire space U^N is considered the space of games. Dubey (1986) established that *the following is a generic property in* U^N: *If an n-tuple* $\{x^{*j}\}_{j \in N}$ *is a strong equilibrium, then at least* $n-1$ *of the strategies are vertices of the strategy spaces*. Thus, if vertices can *a priori* be ruled out of the Nash equilibria, then in general a strong equilibrium does not exist. Theorem 2.3.4 is, therefore, best understood in the context which allows for vertices to become a strong equilibrium strategy. Indeed, one can easily see that the class of games in U^N which possess a strong equilibrium is of the second category.

In another paper, Dubey (1980) constructed a normal-form game from a model of pure exchange, so in this context the space $\mathscr{E}_{pe}$ of all games that are derived from pure exchange economies is the normed space of economies. Dubey (1980) looked at the subset of $\mathscr{E}_{pe}$ that are derived from the pure exchange economies in which a consumer does not have a corner equilibrium. In this subset of $\mathscr{E}_{pe}$, vertices are excluded from the Nash equilibria, so he has shown a meaningful generic non-existence theorem on strong equilibria.

Given the same pure exchange economy, $\mathscr{E}_{pe}$, however, one can construct another type of normal-form game, and prove that its strong equilibria coincide with the competitive equilibria, which do exist; see Schmeidler (1980). Dubey (1982) also has other types of normal-form game, for which strong equilibria do exist. Therefore, the (non-) existence of a strong equilibrium depends upon the specificity of a given normal-form game. As pointed out by Dubey (1982, Remark 4, p. 125), the common feature about the games that are constructed from $\mathscr{E}_{pe}$ and have a strong equilibrium (like those of Schmeidler (1980) and Dubey (1982)) is that the utility functions (as functions of a strategy bundle, and not as functions of a commodity bundle) are discontinuous. Thus, discontinuity of utility functions (in the strategy-bundle space X) is one way to open up the possibility of the existence of a strong equilibrium in the interior of X. Of course, Theorem 2.3.4 cannot encompass this situation.

Another way to ensure the existence of a strong equilibrium as an interior point is to introduce an additional structure into the game in normal form: To be specific, one postulates that the *feasible* joint-strategy space F^N of N is larger than the product $\prod_{j \in N} F^j$ of the *feasible* individual strategy spaces $\{F^j\}_{j \in N}$. An introduction to this approach is given at the end of the present section. It turns out that Theorem 2.3.4 can be meaningfully extended to this situation, as will be seen in Chapters 3 and 5. □

Remark 2.3.6. Let G be a game in normal form. The "noncooperative foundation of cooperative theory" is the study which establishes (1) that for an economically meaningful specific case of G, the utility allocations associated with a cooperative solution are identical to the Nash equilibrium utility allocations, or (2) that given another normal-form game G^* that is constructed from G, the utility allocations associated with a cooperative solution of G are identical to the Nash equilibrium utility allocations of G^*. With equivalence theorems of nature (1) or (2), there arose the popular conception that the cooperative theory is a subset of the noncooperative theory, or that the cooperative theory assumes a kind of "black box" whose contents can be revealed only by the noncooperative theory. This perception is false. In order to clarify how wrong the perception is, one of the propositions of the nature of (2) above is now briefly reviewed. The *repeated game* G^* associated with G is defined as a repetition of G over infinitely many periods, where each player chooses his strategy of period t conditioned on realized strategy bundles of the periods up to $t-1$. In contrast to this repeated game G^*, the original game G is sometimes called a *one-shot game*; see, e.g., Mertens (1987) for a survey. One topic is to explain certain outcomes of a one-shot game G from a specified behavior of the players in the repeated game G^* (and hence from a specified solution concept for G^*). Let F be the set of "feasible" utility allocations in the one-shot game, grossly defined, e.g., $F := \text{co } \{\{u^j(x)\}_{j \in N} \mid x \in X\}$ (the precise definition may be different depending upon specific work in this area). A utility allocation $\bar{u} \in \mathbf{R}^N$ is called *β-individually rational*, if

$$\neg \exists j \in N: \forall x^{N\setminus\{j\}} \in X^{N\setminus\{j\}}: \exists x^j \in X^j: u^j(x^j, x^{N\setminus\{j\}}) > \bar{u}_j.$$

The *folk theorem* (whose authorship is not known) says that *the set of feasible, β-individually rational utility allocations of G is precisely the set of Nash equilibrium utility allocations of* G^*. Specifically a cooperative outcome in G can be explained from a noncooperative behavior in G^*. For an application of the folk theorem to altruism, see, e.g., Hammond (1975) and Kurz (1977). Nevertheless, the folk theorem does not provide a justification for the popular perception quoted above. First, while a cooperative *outcome* (in terms of the utility allocation) in G can be derived from a noncooperative solution in G^*, cooperative *behavior* itself in G, that is, the very possibility of joint choice of strategies, has not been explained. Given the current state of the art in game theory, a behavioral principle is best chosen as an axiom of the theory, rather than as a phenomenon to be explained. Second, it is not the noncooperative behavior in G^* alone that has been used to explain an outcome of G. Indeed, just as the noncooperative behavior in G^* is assumed in the folk theorem, several types of cooperative behavior may also be assumed in G^* as alternative behavioral principles, with which one can establish different equivalence theorems to explain yet other cooperative outcomes in G. This second point is elaborated as follows:

The coalitional analogue of the β-individual rationality can be formulated as

$$\neg \exists S \in \mathcal{N}: \forall x^{N\setminus S} \in X^{N\setminus S}: \exists x^S \in X^S: \forall j \in S: u^j(x^S, x^{N\setminus S}) > \bar{u}_j,$$

that is,

$$\neg S \in \mathcal{N}: \bar{u} \in \mathring{V}_\beta(S).$$

The Aumann proposition is a coalitional analogue of the folk theorem, and says that *the β-core of a one-shot game is precisely the set of strong equilibrium utility allocations of the associated repeated game* (Aumann (1959)). See also Yanovskaya (1971/72), Rubinstein (1980) and Ichiishi

(1987c). Chakrabarti (1990) introduced a certain cost of changing one-shot strategies over periods in the repeated game, and established that *the α-core of a one-shot game is the set of strong equilibrium utility allocations of the associated repeated game with this inertia.*

Thus, if one takes the passive cooperative behavior in the repeated game as a primitive axiom, then (1) a feasible, individually rational outcome in the one-shot game can be explained in the case where formation of any coalition of more than one player is extremely costly in the repeated game (the folk theorem); (2) the β-core can be explained in the case where changing one-shot strategies over periods can be made costlessly (the Aumann proposition); and (3) the α-core can be explained in the case where the repeated game has inertia (Chakrabarti's theorem). The choice of a behavioral principle in G^* as an axiom is actually subject to a specific economic context to which the associated equivalence theorem is applied. □

The model of a game in normal form is already close to the economic models that will be developed in Chapters 3–6 of this monograph. Some of these economic models require richer structures than the normal-form game, and these additional structures play a fundamental role in the study of cooperative solution concepts. To illustrate this point, recall that in a normal-form game G the joint strategy space of coalition S is given as $X^S := \prod_{j \in S} X^j$. It is sometimes necessary, however, to allow for the situation in which S's joint strategy space is different from X^S. Consider, for example, the pure exchange economy $\mathscr{E}_{pe} := \{X^i, u^i, \omega^i\}_{i \in N}$ of a consumer set N, a consumption set $X^i (\subset \mathbf{R}^l)$, a utility function $u^i: X^i \to \mathbf{R}$, and an initial endowment vector $\omega^i (\in \mathbf{R}^l)$ for every $i \in N$ (Example 2A.8 in the Appendix to Chapter 2 – see also Definition 3.3.1). A natural game-theoretical model within which to discuss cooperative behavior is now constructed from $\mathscr{E}_{pe}$: The player set is the same as the consumer set N. For each player i, his utility function is $u^i: X^i \to \mathbf{R}$, and his *feasible* strategy space is $F^i := \{x^i \in X^i \mid x^i \leqslant \omega^i\}$. The game in normal form $\{F^i, u^i\}_{i \in N}$ is not interesting here, because coalition S can do more than $\prod_{i \in S} F^i$. The *feasible* strategy space of coalition S is given by $F^S := \{(x^i)_{i \in S} \in \prod_{i \in S} X^i \mid \sum_{i \in S} x^i \leqslant \sum_{i \in S} \omega^i\}$. A *strong equilibrium* of this model $(\{X^i, u^i\}_{i \in N}, \{F^S\}_{S \in \mathscr{N}})$ is defined as a strategy bundle $x^* \in F^N$ for which it is not true that there exist $S \in \mathscr{N}$ and $x^S \in F^S$ such that $u^i(x^i) > u^i(x^{*i})$ for all $i \in S$. It is precisely a core strategy, whose existence is guaranteed in Example 2A.8. By looking at this strong equilibrium in the Edgeworth box diagram, one can easily verify that it is in general in the relative interior of the face $\{x \in F^N \mid \sum_{i \in N} x^i = \sum_{i \in N} \omega^i\}$ (compare with Remark 2.3.5). Notice also that in general $x^{*i} \notin F^i$ for every i. The models developed in Chapters 3 and 5 are essentially this model $(\{X^i, u^i\}_{i \in N}, \{F^S\}_{S \in \mathscr{N}})$, further generalized to such an extent that for each coalition S, its feasible strategy space F^S varies, reflecting different strategy-choice by the outsiders $N \backslash S$ (so it is more appropriately denoted by $F^S(x^{N\backslash S})$, or more generally by $F^S(x^N)$), and for each $i \in S$, his utility function u^i depends not only on x^i but also on $\{x^j\}_{j \in N\backslash\{i\}}$ and S itself (so it is more appropriately denoted by $u^i_S(x^{N\backslash S}, x^S)$). Moreover, realization of a coalition structure in equilibrium, rather than formation of the grand coalition, is allowed for. For now, a special case of the model of Section 3.4 is introduced, in order to discuss the strong equilibrium concept in several economic setups in the Appendix to Chapter 2, which are simple yet have a richer structure than the normal-form game (Examples 2A.8, 2A.9, 2A.13, 2A.14). A *society* is a list of data $(\{X^i, u^i\}_{i \in N}, \{F^S\}_{S \in \mathcal{N}})$ of a player set N, a strategy set X^i and a utility function u^i: $X \to \mathbf{R}$ for every $i \in N$, and a feasible-strategy correspondence F^S: $X \to X^S$ for every $S \in \mathcal{N}$ (see Definition 3.4.9 for a more general model). A *strong equilibrium* of the society is a strategy bundle $x^* \in X$ such that

$$x^* \in F^N(x^*), \text{ and}$$
$$\neg \exists S \in \mathcal{N}: \exists \xi^S \in F^S(x^*): \forall j \in S: u^j(\xi^S, x^{*N\backslash S}) > u^j(x^*).$$

The following existence theorem is a straightforward consequence of Theorem 3.4.15:

Theorem 2.3.7. *Let* $(\{X^i, u^i\}_{i \in N}, \{F^S\}_{S \in \mathcal{N}})$ *be a society. There exists a strong equilibrium if:*

(i) *for any* j, X^j *is a nonempty, compact and convex subset of a Euclidean space;*
(ii) *for any* j, u^j *is continuous and quasi-concave in* X;
(iii) *for any* S, *the feasible-strategy correspondence* F^S *is both upper and lower semicontinuous, and is nonempty-, closed-, and convex-valued; and*
(iv) *for any* $\bar{x}$, *the non-side-payment game* $V_{\bar{x}}$ *defined by* $V_{\bar{x}}(S) := \{u \in \mathbf{R}^N \mid \exists x^S \in F^S(\bar{x}): \forall j \in S: u_j \leq u^j(x^S, \bar{x}^{N\backslash S})\}$ *is balanced.*

Many economic models, like a production economy with externalities or with public goods, can be formulated as a society $\mathcal{S} = (\{X^j, u^j\}_{j \in N}, \{F^S\}_{S \in \mathcal{N}})$. In these examples, among the intrinsic facts are the inequality $F^S(x) \neq \prod_{j \in S} F^j(x)$ and the dependence of u^j on X (rather than merely on X^j). One may, however, re-formulate the same economic model as another society $\hat{\mathcal{S}} = (\{\hat{X}^j, \hat{u}^j\}_{j \in N}, \{\hat{F}^S\}_{S \in \mathcal{N}})$, such that there is a one-to-one correspondence between the strong equilibria of $\mathcal{S}$ and the strong equilibria of $\hat{\mathcal{S}}$, and such that $\hat{u}^j$ depends only on $\hat{X}^j$ (see, e.g., Example 2A.13). This remark justifies the following Corollary 2.3.8.

Corollary 2.3.8. *Let* $\mathcal{S}$ *be a society. Assume that each utility function* u^j *depends only on* X^j. *Then there exists a strong equilibrium, if assumptions (i)–(iii) of Theorem 2.3.7 are satisfied, and if:*

(iv′) *for any* $\bar{x}$ *and any balanced family* $\mathscr{B}$ *with the associated balancing coefficients* $\{\lambda_S\}_{S\in\mathscr{B}}$, *it follows that* $\sum_{S\in\mathscr{B}} \lambda_S \tilde{F}^S(\bar{x}) \subset F^N(\bar{x})$, *where* $\tilde{F}^S(\bar{x}) := \{x \mid x^S \in F^S(\bar{x}),\ x^{N\setminus S} = \mathbf{0}\}$.

Proof of Corollary 2.3.8. One needs to show that assumption (iv) of Theorem 2.3.7 is satisfied. Choose any $\bar{x}$, any balanced family $\mathscr{B}$ with the associated balancing coefficients $\{\lambda_S\}_{S\in\mathscr{B}}$, and any $u \in \bigcap_{S\in\mathscr{B}} V_{\bar{x}}(S)$. For each $S \in \mathscr{B}$, there exists $(x^{(S),j})_{j\in S} \in F^S(\bar{x})$ such that $u_j \leqslant u^j(x^{(S),j})$ for all $j \in S$. Define $x^j := \sum_{S\in\mathscr{B}:S\ni j} \lambda_S x^{(S),j}$ for all $j \in N$. By quasi-concavity of u^j, $u^j(x^j) \geqslant u_j$, and by (iv′), $x \in F^N(\bar{x})$. So, $u \in V_{\bar{x}}(N)$. □

Remark 2.3.9. Let $G := \{X^j, u^j\}_{j\in N}$ be a game in normal form, where u^j is explicitly interpreted as a von Neumann-Morgenstern utility function. Two types of probabilistic choice of strategies can be defined here. To distinguish the given notion of strategy from these two types, a strategy $x^j \in X^j$ is called a *pure strategy*. The first type presupposes a probability space $(\Omega, \mathscr{A}, p)$ on uncertain states ω's in Ω. The information on Ω held by player j is summarized by a sub-σ-algebra $\mathscr{A}^j$ of $\mathscr{A}$. A *randomized strategy* of player j is a measurable function f^j: $(\Omega, \mathscr{A}^j) \to X^j$; one may view space $L_1(\Omega, \mathscr{A}^j, p; X^j)$ (the space of integrable functions from $(\Omega, \mathscr{A}^j, p)$ to X^j) as j's randomized-strategy space. To define the second type, denote by $\mathscr{M}(X^S)$ the space of all probabilities on X^S. A *correlated strategy* of coalition S is a probability $\mu^S \in \mathscr{M}(X^S)$. When S is a singleton $\{j\}$, correlated strategy μ^j reduces to the traditional concept of *mixed strategy*.

The distribution of a randomized strategy bundle $f^S := (f^j)_{j\in S}$ – that is, the probability $p \circ (f^S)^{-1}$ on X^S – is a correlated strategy. Conditions under which any correlated strategy can be derived as the distribution of some randomized-strategy bundle are known (see, e.g., Ichiishi, 1988a). The product measure of a mixed-strategy bundle $(\mu^j)_{j\in S}$ is a correlated strategy $\bigotimes_{j\in S} \mu^j \in \mathscr{M}(X^S)$, but in general a correlated strategy cannot be expressed as the product of mixed strategies.

When a randomized-strategy bundle $f \in \prod_{j\in N} L_1(\Omega, \mathscr{A}^j, p; X^j)$ is chosen, the *expected utility* of player j is given by

$$Eu^j(f) := \int_\Omega u^j(f(\omega))\, p(d\omega).$$

A Nash equilibrium f^* of the normal-form game $G_r := \{L_1(\Omega, \mathscr{A}^j, p; X^j), Eu^j\}_{j\in N}$ is called a *correlated equilibrium*, a concept due to Aumann (1974). This is a noncooperative solution, because the players do not coordinate strategies when playing the game G_r. It is true that f^* gives rise to a correlated strategy, $p \circ (f^*)^{-1}$, but the behavioral principle according to which randomized strategies are chosen is a different issue from the properties of the resulting distribution that would govern space X.

Relationships among some cooperative solutions in randomized or correlated strategies were investigated in Ichiishi (1988a). □

2.4 The effectivity function approach to the core

Let $\{X^j, u^j\}_{j \in N}$ be a game in normal form, as defined in Section 2.3. Set $\mathcal{N} := 2^N \setminus \{\phi\}$, $X^S := \prod_{j \in S} X^j$ for every $S \in \mathcal{N}$, and $X := X^N$. In many economic contexts, it is essential to distinguish the concept of strategy bundle (a point in X) and the concept of outcome. Choice of a strategy bundle results in realization of an outcome, and it is on the space of outcomes that individual preference relations are defined. One is thus led to define a *game in strategic form* as a list of specified data, $(\{X^j\}_{j \in N}, Z, g, \{h^j\}_{j \in N})$, where Z is an outcome set, g: $X \to Z$ is an outcome function which is *postulated to be surjective*, and h^j: $Z \to \mathbf{R}$ is a utility function of player j. A strategy bundle x gives rise to outcome $g(x)$ of the game. Notice that $\{X^j, h^j \circ g\}_{j \in Z}$ is the reduced normal-form game. The triple $(\{X^j\}_{j \in N}, Z, g)$ is called a *game form*. A strategic-form game has an advantage over a normal-form game in that in the former there is a separate treatment of a game form $(\{X^j\}_{j \in N}, Z, g)$ and a preference profile $\{h^j\}_{j \in N}$. In some important instances a game form has a very specific inherent property, from which one may be able to deduce a strong conclusion without imposing any assumption on a preference profile. Indeed, a game form $(\{X^j\}_{j \in N}, Z, g)$ is called *Nash consistent*, if for every preference profile $\{h^j\}_{j \in N}$ on Z the associated game in normal form $\{X^j, h^j \circ g\}_{j \in N}$ possesses a Nash equilibrium (in pure strategies). See the work of Zermelo (1913), von Neumann, Kuhn (1953) and Dalkey (1953) on characterization of the Nash consistent extensive game forms.

Throughout this section, the player set N and the outcome set Z are assumed finite.

An effectivity function is to a non-side-payment game, what a game form is to a game in normal form. Robert W. Rosenthal (1972) proposed an approach to the core through his new game-theoretical model, a game in effectivity form. A special case of its crucial ingredient, which Rosenthal called effectiveness functions, is what Moulin and Peleg (1982) called an effectivity function. Moulin and Peleg (1982) came up with the effectivity function concept through their works in social choice theory, and initiated its axiomatic study. The present section reviews some basic results on the effectivity function theory. Motivations for the effectivity function concept and relevant concepts, and relationships with the game-theoretical models of Sections 2.2 and 2.3 are emphasized. This section unfairly spares little space for the social-choice-theoretical motivations. Indeed, readers may refer to Moulin (1983) and Peleg (1984a) for comprehensive presentations of these motivations. Formally, a correspondence E: $2^N \to 2^Z$ is called an *effectivity function*, if (1) $\phi \notin E(S)$ for every $S \in 2^N$; (2) $B \notin E(\phi)$ for every $B \in 2^Z$; (3) $Z \in E(S)$ for every $S \in \mathcal{N} := 2^N \setminus \{\phi\}$; and (4) $B \in E(N)$ for every $B \in 2^Z \setminus \{\phi\}$. As in a non-side-payment game, the concept of strategy is hidden behind the model. The intended interpretation is that $B \in E(S)$ if coordination of strategy-choice by the members of coalition S can force the outcome to fall into set B. Which point of B is actually realized depends on the behavior of the outsiders $N \backslash S$. Different coordination by S may result in $B' \in E(S)$, $B' \neq B$, hence the multi-valuedness of the mapping E. Condition (1) says that no coalition can bring about the situation in which no outcome is realized. Condition (2) says that the empty coalition has no power. Condition (3) says that any nonempty coalition can impose no constraint on realization of an outcome. Condition (4) says that the grand coalition can enforce realization of any outcome; it corresponds to the postulate on a game form that the outcome function be surjective. A more general concept: a correspondence E is called a *semi-well-behaved function*, if it satisfies conditions (1) and (2).

Just as a pair of a game form and a preference profile gives rise to the associated game in normal form, a pair of an effectivity function $E: 2^N \to 2^Z$ and a preference profile $h: Z \to \mathbf{R}^N$ gives rise to the associated non-side-payment game. Indeed, define $\underline{h}^j(B) := \min \{h^j(z) \mid z \in B\}$. Then the required non-side-payment game is given by:

$$V(S) := \{u \in \mathbf{R}^N \mid \exists B \in E(S): \forall j \in S: u_j \leqslant \underline{h}^j(B)\}.$$

Let $E: 2^N \to 2^Z$ be an effectivity function and let $h: Z \to \mathbf{R}^N$ be a preference profile. A *core outcome of E with respect to h* is a member $z^* \in Z$ such that

$$\neg \exists S \in \mathcal{N}: \exists B \in E(S): \forall j \in S: \underline{h}^j(B) > h^j(z^*).$$

It characterizes coalitional stability. Feasibility of z^* in the grand coalition is guaranteed by condition (4) of the definition of an effectivity function, i.e., N can enforce realization of any outcome, in particular realization of z^*. Denote by $C(E, h)$ the set of all core outcomes of E with respect to h. As in Section 2.2 one can define the core $C(V)$ of the non-side-payment game V, where V is associated with (E, h) (defined in the preceding paragraph). The inclusion $\{z \in Z \mid h(z) \in C(V)\} \subset C(E, h)$ of the following Claim 2.4.1 is due to Peleg (1984a).

Claim 2.4.1 (Peleg). *Let $E: 2^N \to 2^Z$ be an effectivity function and let $h: Z \to \mathbf{R}^N$ be a preference profile. Let V be the non-side-payment game associated with (E, h). Then*:

$$C(E, h) = \{z \in Z \mid h(z) \in C(V)\}.$$

Proof. Choose any $z \in Z$ such that $h(z) \notin C(V)$. Then there exist $S \in \mathcal{N}$ and $u \in V(S)$ such that $u_j > h^j(z)$ for each $j \in S$. By the definition of V, there exists $B \in E(S)$ such that $\underline{h}^j(B) \geqslant u_j$, hence $\underline{h}^j(B) > h^j(z)$, for every $j \in S$. Therefore, $z \notin C(E, h)$.

To show the other inclusion, choose any $z \in Z$ such that $z \notin C(E, h)$. Then there exist $S \in \mathcal{N}$ and $B \in E(S)$ such that $\underline{h}^j(B) > h^j(z)$ for every $j \in S$. Choose $u \in \mathbf{R}^N$ such that $u_j = \underline{h}^j(B)$ for each $j \in S$. Then $u \in V(S)$, and $u_j > h^j(z)$ for every $j \in S$. Therefore, $h(z) \notin C(V)$. □

An effectivity function E: $2^N \to 2^Z$ is called *stable*, if $C(E, h) \neq \phi$ for every preference profile h defined on Z. Several conditions for stability of E have been established in the past, of which the convexity condition (defined below) has appeared the most useful.

An effectivity function E is called *superadditive* if for every $S_i \in \mathcal{N}$ and every $B_i \in E(S_i)$, $i = 1, 2$, for which $S_1 \cap S_2 = \phi$, it follows that $B_1 \cap B_2 \in E(S_1 \cup S_2)$. It is called *subadditive* if for every $S_i \in \mathcal{N}$ and every $B_i \in E(S_i)$, $i = 1, 2$, for which $B_1 \cap B_2 = \phi$, it follows that $B_1 \cup B_2 \in E(S_1 \cap S_2)$. It is called *convex* if for every $S_i \in \mathcal{N}$ and $B_i \in E(S_i)$, $i = 1, 2$, it follows that $B_1 \cap B_2 \in E(S_1 \cup S_2)$ or $B_1 \cup B_2 \in E(S_1 \cap S_2)$. Clearly, a convex effectivity function is both superadditive and subadditive. The following Claim 2.4.2 and a fundamental result in the effectivity function theory (Theorem 2.4.3) are due to Peleg (1982).

Claim 2.4.2 (Peleg). *Let E: $2^N \to 2^Z$ be a convex effectivity function. Then for any preference profile h: $Z \to \mathbf{R}^N$, the non-side-payment game V associated with (E, h) is ordinal convex.*

Proof. Choose any $S, T \in \mathcal{N}$ and any $u \in V(S) \cap V(T)$. Then,

$$\exists B \in E(S): \forall j \in S: \underline{h}^j(B) \geqslant u_j; \text{ and}$$
$$\exists C \in E(T): \forall j \in T: \underline{h}^j(C) \geqslant u_j.$$

Therefore,

$$B \cap C \neq \phi \Rightarrow \underline{h}^j(B \cap C) \geqslant u_j \text{ for every } j \in S \cup T. \qquad (1)$$
$$S \cap T \neq \phi \Rightarrow \underline{h}^j(B \cup C) \geqslant u_j \text{ for every } j \in S \cap T. \qquad (2)$$

By convexity of E, either $B \cap C \in E(S \cup T)$, in which case $u \in V(S \cup T)$ in view of (1), or else $B \cup C \in E(S \cap T)$, in which case $u \in V(S \cap T)$ in view of (2). □

Theorem 2.4.3 (Peleg). *A convex effectivity function is stable.*

Proof. Let E: $2^N \to 2^Z$ be a convex effectivity function. Choose any preference profile h: $Z \to \mathbf{R}^N$. By Claim 2.4.2, the non-side-payment game V associated with (E, h) is ordinal convex. By Theorem 2.2.2, $C(V) \neq \phi$. By Claim 2.4.1, $C(E, h) \neq \phi$. Since h was arbitrarily chosen, E is stable. □

Theorem 2.4.3 was thus proved by applying the non-side-payment game theory. At the end of the present section, however, an alternative proof will be provided; the proof does not make use of the non-side-payment game theory. Demange (1987) contains still another proof.

Example 2A.15 presents a specific class of convex effectivity functions, called the additive effectivity functions, which play a central role in social choice theory. Moulin and Peleg (1982) established the stability of an additive effectivity function, prior to the development of the study of a convex effectivity function. Examples 2A.16 and 2A.17 present models in social choice theory which give rise to additive effectivity functions. Example 2A.18 presents a convex non-additive effectivity function.

A partial converse of Theorem 2.4.3 (Theorem 2.4.5 below) is also due to Peleg (1982). It is based on the work of Abdou (1982). An effectivity function E is called *maximal* if for every $S \in \mathcal{N}$ and every $B \in 2^Z \setminus \{\phi\}$ such that $B \notin E(S)$, it follows that $Z \setminus B \in E(N \setminus S)$.

Lemma 2.4.4 (Abdou). *Every stable maximal effectivity function is superadditive and subadditive.*

Proof. Let E: $2^N \to 2^Z$ be a stable maximal effectivity function. Suppose E were not superadditive. Then there would exist $S_i \in \mathcal{N}$ and $B_i \in E(S_i)$, $i=1$, 2, such that $S_1 \cap S_2 = \phi$ and $B_1 \cap B_2 \notin E(S_1 \cup S_2)$. Consider the preference profile h: $Z \to \mathbf{R}^N$ defined by:

$$\forall j \in S_i \colon h^j(z) := \begin{cases} 1 \text{ if } z \in B_i \\ 0 \text{ if } z \in Z \setminus B_i \end{cases}$$

$$\forall j \in N \setminus (S_1 \cup S_2) \colon h^j(z) := \begin{cases} 1 \text{ if } z \in Z \setminus (B_1 \cap B_2) \\ 0 \text{ if } z \in B_1 \cap B_2) \end{cases}$$

It will be shown that $C(E, h) = \phi$, thereby contradicting the stability assumption of E.

Suppose $B_1 \cap B_2 = \phi$. If $z \in B_2$, then for all $j \in S_1$, $\underline{h}^j(B_1) = 1 > 0 = h^j(z)$, so S_1 can improve upon z. If $z \in Z \setminus B_2$, then for all $j \in S_2$, $\underline{h}^j(B_2) > h^j(z)$, so S_2 can improve upon z. Therefore, $C(E, h) = \phi$ if $B_1 \cap B_2 = \phi$.

Suppose $B_1 \cap B_2 \neq \phi$. Then by maximality of E, $Z \setminus (B_1 \cap B_2) \in E(N \setminus (S_1 \cup S_2))$. If $z \in B_1 \cap B_2$, then for all $j \in N \setminus (S_1 \cup S_2)$, $\underline{h}^j(Z \setminus (B_1 \cap B_2)) > h^j(z)$, so $N \setminus (S_1 \cup S_2)$ can improve upon z. If $z \in B_1 \setminus B_2$, then for all $j \in S_2$, $\underline{h}^j(B_2) > h^j(z)$, so S_2 can improve upon z. If $z \in Z \setminus B_1$, then for all $j \in S_1$, $\underline{h}^j(B_1) > h^j(z)$, so S_1 can improve upon z. Therefore, $C(E, h) = \phi$ if $B_1 \cap B_2 \neq \phi$.

Suppose E were not subadditive. Then there would exist $S_i \in \mathcal{N}$ and $B_i \in E(S_i)$, $i=1$, 2, such that $B_1 \cap B_2 = \phi$ and $B_1 \cup B_2 \notin E(S_1 \cap S_2)$. Consider the preference profile h: $Z \to \mathbf{R}^N$ defined by:

$$\forall j \in N \setminus S_2 \colon h^j(z) := \begin{cases} 2 \text{ if } z \in Z \setminus (B_1 \cup B_2) \\ 1 \text{ if } z \in B_1 \\ 0 \text{ if } z \in B_2 \end{cases}$$

$$\forall j \in S_2 \setminus S_1 \colon h^j(z) := \begin{cases} 2 \text{ if } z \in B_2 \\ 1 \text{ if } z \in Z \setminus (B_1 \cup B_2) \\ 0 \text{ if } z \in B_1 \end{cases}$$

$$\forall j \in S_2 \cap S_1 \colon h^j(z) := \begin{cases} 2 \text{ if } z \in B_1 \\ 1 \text{ if } z \in B_2 \\ 0 \text{ if } z \in Z \setminus (B_1 \cup B_2) \end{cases}$$

It will be shown that $C(E, h) = \phi$.

Suppose $S_1 \cap S_2 = \phi$. Then S_1 will improve upon any $z \in B_2$, and S_2 will improve upon any $z \in Z \setminus B_2$. Therefore, $C(E, h) = \phi$ in this case.

Suppose $S_1 \cap S_2 \neq \phi$. Then by maximality of E, $Z \setminus (B_1 \cup B_2) \in E(N \setminus (S_1 \cap S_2))$. So, S_2 will improve upon any $z \in Z \setminus (B_1 \cup B_2)$, S_1 will improve upon any $z \in B_2$, and $N \setminus (S_1 \cap S_2)$ will improve upon any $z \in B_1$. Therefore, $C(E, h) = \phi$ in this case as well. □

Theorem 2.4.5 (Peleg). *Every stable maximal effectivity function is convex.*

Proof. Let E: $2^N \to 2^Z$ be any maximal, superadditive and subadditive effectivity function. In view of Lemma 2.4.4, it suffices to show that this effectivity function E is convex. Choose any $S_i \in \mathcal{N}$ and $B_i \in E(S_i)$, $i = 1, 2$, and assume that $B_1 \cap B_2 \notin E(S_1 \cup S_2)$. One needs to show that $B_1 \cup B_2 \in E(S_1 \cap S_2)$. By maximality of E, $Z \setminus (B_1 \cap B_2) \in E(N \setminus (S_1 \cup S_2))$. By superadditivity of E, $B_1 \setminus B_2 = B_1 \cap [Z \setminus (B_1 \cap B_2)] \in E(S_1 \cup [N \setminus (S_1 \cup S_2)]) = E(N \setminus (S_2 \setminus S_1))$. By subadditivity of E, $B_1 \cup B_2 = B_2 \cup (B_1 \setminus B_2) \in E(S_2 \cap [N \setminus (S_2 \setminus S_1)]) = E(S_2 \cap S_1)$. □

Just as several non-side-payment games are derived from a game in normal form, several effectivity functions can be derived from a game form, $\Gamma := (\{X^j\}_{j \in N}, Z, g)$.

The *α-effectivity function* of game form Γ is the correspondence E_α: $2^N \to 2^Z$ defined by:

$$B \in E_\alpha(S) \text{ iff } \exists x^S \in X^S \colon \forall y^{N \setminus S} \in X^{N \setminus S} \colon g(x^S, y^{N \setminus S}) \in B.$$

Since g is surjective, E_α is an effectivity function. It summarizes all the cooperative possibilities, in terms of subsets of Z, based upon the *prudent* or *pessimistic* perception by the members of S about their capability to react to outsiders' strategy-choice. Let h: $Z \to \mathbf{R}^N$ be a preference profile. A core outcome of E_α with respect to h is called an *α-core outcome* of game form Γ *with respect to h*. Set $C_\alpha(\Gamma, h) := C(E_\alpha, h)$. A game form Γ is called *α-stable* if $C_\alpha(\Gamma, h) \neq \phi$ for every preference profile h: $Z \to \mathbf{R}^N$.

The *β-effectivity function* of a game form Γ is the correspondence E_β: $2^N \to 2^Z$ defined by:

$$B \in E_\beta(S) \text{ iff } \forall\, y^{N \setminus S} \in X^{N \setminus S}: \exists\, x^S \in X^S: g(x^S, y^{N \setminus S}) \in B.$$

The set $C_\beta(\Gamma, h)$ of *β-core outcomes* of game form Γ *with respect to* preference profile h on Z is the set $C(E_\beta, h)$. A game form Γ is called *β-stable* if $C_\beta(\Gamma, h) \neq \phi$ for every preference profile h: $Z \to \mathbf{R}^N$. The same interpretation as before (i.e., the *optimistic* perception) can be made here.

Let $\Gamma := (\{X^j\}_{j \in N}, Z, g)$ be a game form, and let h: $Z \to \mathbf{R}^N$ be a preference profile. Define $V_{G,\alpha}$ ($V_{G,\beta}$, resp.) as the α-characteristic function (β-characteristic function, resp.) derived from the reduced normal-form game $\{X^j, h^j \circ g\}_{j \in N}$ as defined in Section 2.3, and define $V_{E,\alpha}$ ($V_{E,\beta}$, resp.) as the non-side-payment game associated with (E_α, h) (associated with (E_β, h), resp.) as defined in this section. Then, one can easily check:

$$V_{G,\alpha} = V_{E,\alpha}, \text{ and } V_{G,\beta} = V_{E,\beta}.$$

This fact is summarized in Figure 2.1.

Combining this fact and Claim 2.4.1, one establishes:

Claim 2.4.6. *Let* $(\Gamma, h) := (\{X^j\}_{j \in N}, Z, g, \{h^j\}_{j \in N})$ *be a game in strategic form, and let* $G := \{X^j, h^j \circ g\}_{j \in N}$ *be the associated game in normal form. Then*:

$$C_\alpha(\Gamma, h) = \{z \in Z \mid h(z) \in C_\alpha(G)\},$$
$$C_\beta(\Gamma, h) = \{z \in Z \mid h(z) \in C_\beta(G)\}.$$

Given a game in strategic form (Γ, h), construct effectivity functions E_x, parameterized by the strategy bundles $x \in X$, by:

$$B \in E_x(S) \text{ iff } \exists\, \xi^S \in X^S: g(\xi^S, x^{N \setminus S}) \in B.$$

A *strong equilibrium outcome* of game from Γ *with respect to* preference profile h is an outcome $z^* \in Z$ such that there exists $x^* \in X$ for which $z^* = g(x^*) \in C(E_{x^*}, h)$, or equivalently, such that there exists a strong equilibrium x^* of the reduced normal-form game $\{X^j, h^j \circ g\}_{j \in N}$ for which $z^* = g(x^*)$. The set of all strong equilibrium outcomes of Γ with respect to h is denoted by $SE(\Gamma, h)$. A game form Γ is called *strongly consistent* if $SE(\Gamma, h) \neq \phi$ for every preference profile h: $Z \to \mathbf{R}^N$.

Claim 2.4.7. *Let* (Γ, h) *be a game in strategic form. Then,* $SE(\Gamma, h) \subset C_\beta(\Gamma, h) \subset C_\alpha(\Gamma, h)$.

No general theorems have been established to characterize the α-stability, β-stability, strong consistency of a given game form. There are, however, some basic results on these properties. A game form is called *tight*, if its associated α-effectivity function and β-effectivity function are identical. The α-effectivity function and the β-effectivity of a tight game

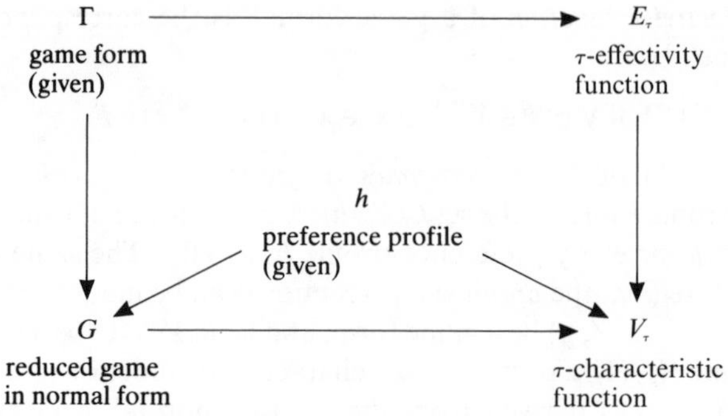

2.1 τ-characteristic function and τ-effectivity function, $\tau = \alpha, \beta$

form Γ is called *the* effectivity function of Γ. The following Lemma 2.4.8 is due to Moulin (1983) and Peleg (1984a):

Lemma 2.4.8 (Moulin, Peleg). *Let $\Gamma := (\{X^j\}_{j \in N}, Z, g)$ be a game form, and let E_α and E_β be its associated α-effectivity function and β-effectivity function, respectively. Then, the following two conditions (i) and (ii) are equivalent:*

(i) *The game form Γ is tight;*
(ii) *The associated α-effectivity function E_α is maximal.*
Moreover, any one of the two conditions (i) and (ii) implies:
(iii) *The associated β-effectivity function E_β is maximal.*

Proof. (i)⇒(ii). Suppose Γ is tight. Choose any $S \in \mathcal{N}$ and $B \in 2^Z \backslash \{\phi\}$ such that $B \notin E_\alpha(S)$, i.e., such that

$$\neg \exists x^S \in X^S: \forall y^{N \backslash S} \in X^{N \backslash S}: g(x^S, y^{N \backslash S}) \in B.$$

This means that $Z \backslash B \in E_\beta(N \backslash S)$. By tightness of Γ, $Z \backslash B \in E_\alpha(N \backslash S)$. Therefore, E_α is maximal.

(ii)⇒(i). It suffices to show that maximality of E_α implies $E_\beta(S) \subset E_\alpha(S)$. Choose any $B \notin E_\alpha(S)$. If $S = \phi$ or $B = \phi$, then $B \notin E_\beta(S)$, so assume $S \neq \phi$ and $B \neq \phi$. By maximality of E_α, $Z \backslash B \in E_\alpha(N \backslash S)$, i.e.,

$$\neg \neg \exists y^{N \backslash S} \in X^{N \backslash S}: \forall x^S \in X^S: g(x^S, y^{N \backslash S}) \notin B.$$

This means $B \notin E_\beta(S)$.

(ii)⇒(iii). Maximality of E_β follows from maximality of E_α, in view of the inclusion, $E_\alpha(S) \subset E_\beta(S)$. □

Moulin and Peleg (1982) established that every strongly consistent game form is tight. Kolpin (1986) sharpened the result as:

Lemma 2.4.9 (Kolpin). *Every β-stable game form is tight.*

Proof. Let $\Gamma := (\{X^j\}_{j\in N}, Z, g)$ be a game form. In view of Lemma 2.4.8, it suffices to show that non-maximality of E_α implies β-instability of Γ. Assume, therefore, that there exist $S \in \mathcal{N}$ and $B \in 2^Z \backslash \{\phi\}$ such that

$$B \notin E_\alpha(S) \text{ and } Z\backslash B \notin E_\alpha(N\backslash S).$$

Necessarily, $S \neq N$ (so $N\backslash S \neq \phi$) and $B \neq Z$ (so $Z\backslash B \neq \phi$). The above two conditions mean:

$$Z\backslash B \in E_\beta(N\backslash S), \quad (1)$$
$$B \in E_\beta(S). \quad (2)$$

Consider the preference profile h: $Z \rightarrow \mathbf{R}^N$ defined by:

$$\forall j \in S: h^j(z) := \begin{cases} 1 \text{ if } z \in B, \\ 0 \text{ if } z \in Z\backslash B, \end{cases}$$
$$\forall j \in N\backslash S: h^j(z) := \begin{cases} 1 \text{ if } z \in Z\backslash B, \\ 0 \text{ if } z \in B. \end{cases}$$

It will be shown that $C_\beta(\Gamma, h) = \phi$, yielding the required β-instability. If $z \in Z\backslash B$, then coalition S can β-improve upon z, in view of (2). If $z \in B$, then coalition $N\backslash S$ can β-improve upon z, in view of (1). No outcome is, therefore, a member of $C_\beta(\Gamma, h)$. □

Corollary 2.4.10. *Let Γ be a game form. Then, the following three conditions (i)–(iii) are equivalent*:

(i) *The game form Γ is β-stable*;
(ii) *The game form Γ is tight, and the effectivity function associated with Γ is convex*;
(iii) *The β-effectivity function associated with Γ is convex.*

A kind of the converse of tightness of a strongly consistent game form (Theorem 2.4.11 below) is deeper and is due to Moulin and Peleg (1982):

Theorem 2.4.11 (Moulin and Peleg). *Let E: $2^N \rightarrow 2^Z$ be a stable maximal effectivity function. Then there exists a strongly consistent game form Γ with the player set N and the outcome set Z such that*

(i) *the effectivity function associated with Γ is precisely the given function E; and*
(ii) *$SE(\Gamma, h) = C(E, h)$ for any preference profile h: $Z \rightarrow \mathbf{R}^N$.*

A Nash consistent game form Γ is called *acceptable* if for every preference profile h, every Nash equilibrium of the game (Γ, h) is Pareto optimal. A game form Γ is called *non-dictatorial* if it is not true that there exists $j \in N$ (dictator) such that $E_\alpha(\{j\}) = 2^Z \backslash \{\phi\}$. The following result is due to Dutta (1984) (see also a positive result of Dutta (1984, Theorem 4.4)):

Theorem 2.4.12 (Dutta). *There is no non-dictatorial game form with $\# N \geqslant 3$ and $\# Z \geqslant 3$, which is both acceptable and strongly consistent.*

Remark 2.4.13. Several effectivity functions were associated with a given game form in the preceding several paragraphs. One can construct effectivity functions also from other game-theoretical or social-choice-theoretical models. Indeed, a pair of a simple game and an outcome set is a special case of the effectivity functions. Given a social choice correspondence, one can associate with it several simple games and hence several effectivity functions. Actually, one can directly associate with a social choice correspondence several effectivity functions which describe the power distribution more adequately. These effectivity functions are, however, outside the scope of this section; see, e.g., Peleg (1984a). □

The rest of this section will be devoted to a combinatorial proof of Theorem 2.4.3. Recall that given a finite player set N and a finite outcome set Z, a correspondence E: $2^N \to 2^Z$ is called a semi-well-behaved function if $\phi \notin E(S)$ and $B \notin E(\phi)$ for any $S \in 2^N$ and any $B \in 2^Z$.

Let E: $2^N \to 2^Z$ be a semi-well-behaved function and let h: $Z \to \mathbf{R}^N$ be a preference profile. A *core outcome of E with respect to h* is a member $z^* \in Z$ such that

$$\neg \exists S \in \mathcal{N}: \exists B \in E(S): \forall j \in S: \underline{h}^j(B) > h^j(z^*).$$

(Feasibility of z^* is not necessarily guaranteed.) The set of all core outcomes of E with respect to h is denoted by $C(E, h)$. E is called *stable*, if $C(E, h) \neq \phi$ for every preference profile h defined on Z. It is called *convex*, if for every $S_i \in \mathcal{N}$ and $B_i \in E(S_i)$, $i = 1, 2$, it follows that $B_1 \cap B_2 \in E(S_1 \cup S_2)$ or $B_1 \cup B_2 \in E(S_1 \cap S_2)$. The following generalization of Theorem 2.4.3 and its proof is due to Ichiishi (1989):

Theorem 2.4.14. *A convex semi-well-behaved function is stable.*

Proof. Let E: $2^N \to 2^Z$ be a convex semi-well-behaved function. The theorem is proved by induction on $(\# N + \# Z)$. If $\# N = 1$ or $\# Z = 1$ then the assertion is trivial, so assume $\#\mathrm{N} \geqslant 2$ and $\# Z \geqslant 2$. The inductive hypothesis says that any convex semi-well-behaved function E': $2^{N'} \to 2^{Z'}$ for which $\# N' + \# Z' < \# N + \# Z$ is stable. Choose any preference profile on Z, $h = \{h^j\}_{j \in N}$. One has to show that $C(E, h) \neq \phi$.

Step 1. There are two mutually exclusive and exhaustive cases: $(K) \exists z \in Z$: $\exists k \in N$: $\exists B \in E(\{k\})$: $\underline{h}^k(B) > h^k(z)$; and $(P) \forall z \in Z$: $\forall k \in N$: $\forall B \in E(\{k\})$: $\underline{h}^k(B) \leqslant h^k(z)$. [Case (K) reflects the work of Keiding (1985), and Case (P) reflects the work of Peleg (1986).]

Step 2. Suppose Case (K) is valid. Definitions of C_k, z_k, and B_k: Define

$$C_k := \{z \in Z \mid \exists B \in E(\{k\}): \underline{h}^k(B) > h^k(z)\} \neq \phi.$$

Choose a maximal element z_k of C_k with respect of h^k. Then

$$\left.\begin{aligned} C_k &= \{z \in Z \mid h^k(z_k) \geqslant h^k(z)\}, \\ Z\backslash C_k &= \{z \in Z \mid h^k(z) > h^k(z_k)\}. \end{aligned}\right\} \tag{1}$$

Choose $B_k \in E(\{k\})$ so that $\underline{h}^k(B_k) > h^k(z_k)$. Then $B_k \subset Z\backslash C_k$.

Step 3. In Case (K), for every $S \in \mathcal{N}$ such that $S \not\ni k$ and for every $B \in E(S)$ it follows that $B\backslash C_k \neq \phi$. Indeed, since E is convex and $S \cap \{k\} = \phi$, it follows that $B \cap B_k \in E(S \cup \{k\})$, in particular $B \cap B_k \neq \phi$ hence $B\backslash C_k \neq \phi$.

Step 4. In Case (K), define a correspondence E_K: $2^N \to 2^{Z\backslash C_k}$ by

$$E_K(S) := \begin{cases} \{B\backslash C_k \mid B \in E(S)\}, \text{ if } \phi \neq S \not\ni k; \\ \{B \mid B \subset Z\backslash C_k, B \in E(S)\}, \text{ if } S \ni k; \\ \phi, \text{ if } S = \phi. \end{cases}$$

Then E_K is a convex semi-well-behaved function. (Remark that for a convex effectivity function E the associated convex semi-well-behaved function E_K is an effectivity function.) Indeed, in view of Step 3, E_K is a semi-well-behaved function. Let $B_i \in E_K(S_i)$, $i = 1, 2$. One has to show $B_1 \cap B_2 \in E_K(S_1 \cup S_2)$ or $B_1 \cup B_2 \in E_K(S_1 \cap S_2)$. There are four mutually exclusive and exhaustive cases: (a) $k \in S_i$, $i = 1, 2$; (b) $k \in S_1$ and $k \notin S_2$; (c) $k \notin S_1$ and $k \in S_2$; and (d) $k \notin S_i$, $i = 1, 2$. Define $B_i' \in E(S_i)$ by $B_i = B_i'$ $(\subset Z\backslash C_k)$ if $S_i \ni k$; and by $B_i = B_i'\backslash C_k$ if $S_i \not\ni k$, $i = 1, 2$. Then

$$B_1' \cap B_2' \in E(S_1 \cup S_2) \text{ or } B_1' \cup B_2' \in E(S_1 \cap S_2). \tag{2}$$

For Case (a), $S_1 \cup S_2 \ni k$ and $S_1 \cap S_2 \ni k$. Also in this case, $B_i = B_i' \subset Z\backslash C_k$, $i = 1, 2$, so $B_1 \cap B_2 = B_1' \cap B_2' \subset Z\backslash C_k$ and $B_1 \cup B_2 = B_1' \cup B_2' \subset Z\backslash C_k$. Consequently, (2) implies the required result.

For Case (b), $S_1 \cup S_2 \ni k$ and $S_1 \cap S_2 \not\ni k$. Also in this case, $B_1 = B_1' \subset Z\backslash C_k$ and $B_2 = B_2'\backslash C_k$, so $B_1 \cap B_2 = B_1' \cap B_2' \subset Z\backslash C_k$ and $B_1 \cup B_2 = (B_1' \cup B_2')\backslash C_k$. Consequently (2) implies the required result.

A symmetric argument establishes the required result for Case (c).

For Case (d), $S_1 \cup S_2 \not\ni k$ and $S_1 \cap S_2 \not\ni k$. Also in this case, $B_i = B_i'\backslash C_k$, $i = 1, 2$, so $B_1 \cap B_2 = (B_1' \cap B_2')\backslash C_k$ and $B_1 \cup B_2 = (B_1' \cup B_2')\backslash C_k$. Consequently (2) implies the required result.

Step 5. Now, suppose $C(E, h) = \phi$ in Case (K). Then $\forall z \in Z$: $\exists S_z \in \mathcal{N}$: $\exists B_z \in E(S_z)$:

$$\forall j \in S_z: \underline{h}^j(B_z) > h^j(z). \tag{3}$$

Define $B_z' := B_z\backslash C_k$ if $S_z \not\ni k$; $B_z' := B_z$ if $S_z \ni k$. If $S_z \not\ni k$, $B_z' \in E_K(S_z)$. If $z \in Z\backslash C_k$ and $S_z \ni k$ then for any $y \in B_z$, $h^k(y) > h^k(z) > h^k(z_k)$ so $y \in Z\backslash C_k$ in view of (1). Consequently $B_z' \in E_K(S_z)$ for all $z \in Z\backslash C_k$. Then by (3),

$$\begin{aligned} &\forall z \in Z\backslash C_k: \exists S_z \in \mathcal{N}: \exists B_z' \in E_K(S_z): \\ &\qquad \forall j \in S_z: \underline{h}^j(B_z') > h^j(z), \end{aligned}$$

which contradicts the inductive hypothesis and Step 4 that E_K is stable. Thus $C(E, h) \neq \phi$ in Case (K).

Step 6. Suppose Case (P) is valid. Definitions of k, $\bar{z}$, and N': Choose any $k \in N$, and let $\bar{z} \in Z$ be a minimal element of Z with respect to h^k.

$$\forall z \in Z\colon h^k(z) \geqslant h^k(\bar{z}). \tag{4}$$

Then,

$$\forall B \in E(\{k\})\colon \underline{h}^k(B) \leqslant h^k(\bar{z}). \tag{5}$$

Set $N' := N \backslash \{k\}$, and $\mathcal{N}' := 2^{N'} \backslash \{\phi\}$.

Step 7. In Case (P), define a correspondence E_P: $2^{N'} \to 2^Z$ by

$$E_P(S) := \begin{cases} E(S) \cup \{B \mid B \in E(S \cup \{k\}),\ \underline{h}^k(B) > h^k(\bar{z})\}, \text{ if } S \neq \phi; \\ \phi, \text{ if } S = \phi. \end{cases}$$

Then E_P is a convex semi-well-behaved function. (Remark that for a convex effectivity function E the associated convex semi-well-behaved function E_P may not be an effectivity function.) Indeed, let $B_i \in E_P(S_i)$, $i = 1, 2$. One has to show $B_1 \cap B_2 \in E_P(S_1 \cup S_2)$ or $B_1 \cup B_2 \in E_P(S_1 \cap S_2)$. By symmetry, one has only to consider the following three cases: (a) $B_i \in E(S_i)$, $i = 1, 2$; (b) $B_1 \in E(S_1)$, $B_2 \in E(S_2 \cup \{k\})$, and $\underline{h}^k(B_2) > h^k(\bar{z})$; and (c) $B_i \in E(S_i \cup \{k\})$, $\underline{h}^k(B_i) > h^k(\bar{z})$, $i = 1, 2$.

For Case (a), $B_1 \cap B_2 \in E(S_1 \cup S_2)$ or $B_1 \cup B_2 \in E(S_1 \cap S_2)$, so $B_1 \cap B_2 \in E_P(S_1 \cup S_2)$ or $B_1 \cup B_2 \in E_P(S_1 \cap S_2)$.

For Case (b), $B_1 \cap B_2 \in E(S_1 \cup S_2 \cup \{k\})$ or $B_1 \cup B_2 \in E(S_1 \cap [S_2 \cup \{k\}]) = E(S_1 \cap S_2)$. But $\underline{h}^k(B_1 \cap B_2) > h^k(\bar{z})$ in this case, so $B_1 \cap B_2 \in E_P(S_1 \cup S_2)$ or $B_1 \cup B_2 \in E_P(S_1 \cap S_2)$.

For Case (c), $B_1 \cap B_2 \in E(S_1 \cup S_2 \cup \{k\})$ or $B_1 \cup B_2 \in E([S_1 \cap S_2] \cup \{k\})$. But $\underline{h}^k(B_1 \cap B_2) > h^k(\bar{z})$ and $\underline{h}^k(B_1 \cup B_2) > h^k(\bar{z})$ in this case. Moreover, the present Case (P) implies:

$$[S \subset N',\ B \in E(S \cup \{k\}),\ \underline{h}^k(B) > h^k(\bar{z})] \Rightarrow S \neq \phi.$$

So in view of $\underline{h}^k(B_1 \cup B_2) > h^k(\bar{z})$, if $B_1 \cup B_2 \in E([S_1 \cap S_2] \cup \{k\})$ then $S_1 \cap S_2 \neq \phi$. Thus, $B_1 \cap B_2 \in E_P(S_1 \cup S_2)$ or $B_1 \cup B_2 \in E_P(S_1 \cap S_2)$.

Step 8. By the inductive hypothesis and Step 7, there exists $z^* \in C(E_P, \{h^j\}_{j \in N'})$ in Case (P). It suffices to show that $z^* \in C(E, h)$ in this case. Indeed, by (4) and (5),

$$\forall B \in E(\{k\})\colon \underline{h}^k(B) \leqslant h^k(z^*). \tag{6}$$

If $S \in \mathcal{N}'$, then (recalling again that $h^k(z^*) \geqslant h^k(\bar{z})$)

$$\forall B \in E(S \cup \{k\})\colon \neg\, \forall j \in S \cup \{k\}\colon \underline{h}^j(B) > h^j(z^*) \tag{7}$$

$$\forall B \in E(S)\colon \neg\, \forall j \in S\colon \underline{h}^j(B) > h^j(z^*). \tag{8}$$

Results (6)–(8) establish the required result. □

Appendix to Chapter 2: Examples

Example 2A.1. Consider a production economy with l primary goods, one final good, and a finite set N of economic agents. Each agent j is endowed with an initial endowment vector $\omega^j (\in \mathbf{R}^l_+)$ of primary goods. His utility function depends only on consumption of the final good, so a utility level is identified with consumption of the final good. All coalitions S $(\subset N)$ are potential production units and can use the identical production function g: $\mathbf{R}^l_+ \to \mathbf{R}_+$, which is assumed to be strictly increasing and to satisfy $g(\mathbf{0})=0$. This is a special case of the coalition production economy introduced in Section 3.5 (Definition 3.5.1) and Section 5.1 (Definition 5.1.1).

Consider the scenario that a coalition can use its members' primary goods for production, and then distribute the output only to its members. The associated side-payment game is the function v: $\mathcal{N} \to \mathbf{R}$ defined by $v(S) := g(\sum_{j \in S} \omega^j)$. The core of game v is the set of final-good allocations y^* $(\in \mathbf{R}^N_+)$, such that (1) it is made feasible by the grand coalition (the agents supply their initial endowments to the grand coalition, engage in production, and distribute the output among themselves, so $\sum_{j \in N} y^*_j \leqslant g(\sum_{j \in N} \omega^j)$), and (2) it is coalitionally stable (it is not true that the members of some coalition S find it more advantageous to defect from N and use their resources $\{\omega^j\}_{j \in S}$ for their own production activity, because by doing so they could find a final-good allocation $\{y_j\}_{j \in S}$ such that $\sum_{j \in S} y_j \leqslant g(\sum_{j \in S} \omega^j)$ and $y_j > y^*_j$ for all $j \in S$).

Consider the following alternative scenario: There is a market for each commodity, and the final good is chosen as a numéraire. Each agent is a price-taker. Let p be a primary-good price vector. Agents now have two options: to contribute primary goods to their coalition for production, or to exchange primary goods for the final good in the market. The associated side-payment game is then defined by

$$v_p(S) := \max \{p \cdot x + g(\textstyle\sum_{j \in S} \omega^j - x) \mid \mathbf{0} \leqslant x \leqslant \sum_{j \in S} \omega^j\},$$

where $p \cdot x$ denotes the Euclidean inner product, $\sum_{h=1}^{l} p_h x_h$. Game v_p reflects a broader class of strategies available to each coalition than game v. Therefore,

$$v_p(S) \geqslant v(S), \text{ for all } S \in \mathcal{N}.$$

If $v_p(N) = v(N)$, then $C(v_p) \subset C(v)$.

A production function g is called *supportable*, if for any $\bar{x} \in \mathbf{R}^l_+$ there exists $\bar{p} \in \mathbf{R}^l_+$ such that

(i) $\bar{p} \cdot \bar{x} = g(\bar{x})$, and
(ii) $(\forall x\colon \mathbf{0} \leqslant x \leqslant \bar{x})\colon \bar{p} \cdot x \geqslant g(x)$.

The supportability concept was studied by Sharkey and Telser (1978) in the context of the multiproduct cost function of a natural monopoly. See also Baumol, Bailey and Willig (1977) and Sharkey (1982a). Remark 2A.2 below characterizes the supportability condition on g in terms of the function g. In the rest of this example, assume that production function g is supportable.

Let $\bar{p}$ be the primary-good price vector that satisfies the supportability condition (i) and (ii) for $\bar{x} := \sum_{j \in N} \omega^j$. Then by (ii), for each S and any x for which $\mathbf{0} \leqslant x \leqslant \sum_{j \in S} \omega^j$

$$\sum_{j \in S} \bar{p} \cdot \omega^j = \bar{p} \cdot x + \bar{p} \cdot (\sum_{j \in S} \omega^j - x) \geqslant \bar{p} \cdot x + g(\sum_{j \in S} \omega^j - x), \tag{1}$$

so, by taking the maximum of the right-hand side of (1) with respect to such x, one obtains

$$\sum_{j \in S} \bar{p} \cdot \omega^j \geqslant v_{\bar{p}}(S).$$

On the other hand, $v_{\bar{p}}(S)$ is no less than the value of the right-hand side of (1) for $x = \sum_{j \in S} \omega^j$, so

$$\sum_{j \in S} \bar{p} \cdot \omega^j \leqslant v_{\bar{p}}(S).$$

Therefore, one concludes

$$\sum_{j \in S} \bar{p} \cdot \omega^j = v_{\bar{p}}(S).$$

In particular, game $v_{\bar{p}}$ is *additive*, i.e., $v_{\bar{p}}(S) = \sum_{j \in S} v_{\bar{p}}(\{j\})$. It is straightforward to check the general facts that the core $C(w)$ of an additive game w defined by $w(S) = \sum_{j \in S} w_j$ is nonempty, and that $C(w)$ consists only of the single element $\{w_j\}_{j \in N}$. Thus, the final-good-value allocation $\{\bar{p} \cdot \omega^j\}_{j \in N}$ is the unique element of the core of game $v_{\bar{p}}$. It is also in the core of v, since the supportability condition (i) guarantees that $v_{\bar{p}}(N) = g(\sum_{j \in N} \omega^j) = v(N)$ and consequently $C(v_{\bar{p}}) \subset C(v)$. □

Remark 2A.2. For any set X, denote by $\oplus_X \mathbf{R}$ the set of all functions from X to $\mathbf{R}$, $x \mapsto \lambda_x$, with a finite support (i.e., $\lambda_x = 0$ for all but finitely many x). Choose any $\bar{x} \in \mathbf{R}^l_+$, and define $I := \{x \in \mathbf{R}^l \mid \mathbf{0} \leqslant x \leqslant \bar{x}\}$. As pointed out by Sharkey and Telser (1978), the supportability condition at $\bar{x}$ on a strictly increasing production function g: $\mathbf{R}^l_+ \to \mathbf{R}_+$ is characterized by the condition: *For any* $\lambda \in \oplus_I \mathbf{R}_+$ *for which* $\sum_{x \in I} \lambda_x x \leqslant \bar{x}$, *it follows that* $\sum_{x \in I} \lambda_x g(x) \leqslant g(\bar{x})$. To prove this equivalence by using the method of Kannai (1969, pp. 229–230), assume first that $\bar{x} \gg \mathbf{0}$. A special case of Fan

(1956, Theorem 13, pp. 126–127) says: *For any indexed family* $\{x_\mu\}_{\mu\in I_0}$ *of points in* $\mathbf{R}^l$ *and any family* $\{\alpha_\mu\}_{\mu\in I_0}$ *of real numbers indexed by the same set* I_0, (1) *there exists* $p^0\in\mathbf{R}^l$ *such that* $p^0\cdot x_\mu \geqslant \alpha_\mu$ *for all* $\mu\in I_0$, *iff*

$$\sigma := \sup\{\textstyle\sum_{\mu\in I_0}\lambda_\mu\alpha_\mu \mid \lambda\in\oplus_{I_0}\mathbf{R}_+,\ \|\sum_{\mu\in I_0}\lambda_\mu x_\mu\|_\infty = 1\} < \infty,$$

and (2) *if* $\sigma<\infty$, *then*

$$\sigma = \min\{\|p\|_1 \mid p\in\mathbf{R}^l,\ p\cdot x_\mu \geqslant \alpha_\mu \text{ for all } \mu\in I_0\}.$$

Here, $\|x\|_\infty := \max_{1\leqslant h\leqslant l}|x_h|$, and $\|p\|_1 := \sum_{h=1}^{l}|p_h|$. Now, let $\mathbf{1}$ be the vector in $\mathbf{R}^l$ each of whose components is 1, and let $I_0 := \{x\in\mathbf{R}^l \mid \mathbf{0}\leqslant x\leqslant\mathbf{1}\}$. Identify the vector x_μ with the index $\mu\in I_0$, and let $\alpha_x := g(x_1\bar{x}_1, \ldots, x_l\bar{x}_l)$ for all $x\in I_0$. Then, by Fan's theorem (1) above, there exists $p^0\in\mathbf{R}^l$ satisfying

$$p^0\cdot x \geqslant g(x_1\bar{x}_1, \ldots, x_l\bar{x}_l) \text{ for all } x\in I_0,$$

iff

$$\sigma := \sup\{\textstyle\sum_{x\in I_0}\lambda_x g(x_1\bar{x}_1, \ldots, x_l\bar{x}_l) \mid \lambda\in\oplus_{I_0}\mathbf{R}_+,\ \sum_{x\in I_0}\lambda_x x\leqslant\mathbf{1}\} < \infty.$$

Any of such p^0 has to be strictly positive, so that $\|p^0\|_1 = p^0\cdot\mathbf{1}$. To see this, choose any h: $1\leqslant h\leqslant l$. Let e^h be the hth unit vector in $\mathbf{R}^l$, defined by $e^h_h := 1$, and $e^h_i := 0$ for all $i\neq h$. Then, $e^h\in I_0$, so $p^0_h = p^0\cdot e^h \geqslant g(\bar{x}_h e^h) > 0$. Define $\bar{p} \gg \mathbf{0}$ by $\bar{p}_h := p^0_h/\bar{x}_h$. Then, $\bar{p}$ satisfies the supportability conditions (i) and (ii) (in Example 2A.1), iff $p^0\cdot\mathbf{1} = g(\bar{x})$. Also by Fan's theorem (2) above, if $\sigma<\infty$, then

$$\sigma = \min\{p\cdot\mathbf{1} \mid p\in\mathbf{R}^l,\ p\cdot x\geqslant g(x_1\bar{x}_1, \ldots, x_l\bar{x}_l), \text{ for all } x\in I_0\}.$$

Thus, g is supportable at $\bar{x}$, iff for any $\lambda\in\oplus_{I_0}\mathbf{R}_+$ for which $\sum_{x\in I_0}\lambda_x x\leqslant\mathbf{1}$, it follows that $\sum_{x\in I_0}\lambda_x g(x_1\bar{x}_1, \ldots, x_l\bar{x}_l)\leqslant g(\bar{x})$. This last condition is equivalent to: For any $\lambda\in\oplus_I\mathbf{R}_+$ for which $\sum_{x\in I}\lambda_x x\leqslant\bar{x}$, it follows that $\sum_{x\in I}\lambda_x g(x)\leqslant g(\bar{x})$. For the case $\bar{x}_h=0$ for some h, assume without loss of generality that $\bar{x}_1, \bar{x}_2, \ldots, \bar{x}_k>0$ and $\bar{x}_{k+1}=\ldots=\bar{x}_l=0$, apply the same argument as above in the subspace $\mathbf{R}^k$, obtain the required $\bar{p}\in\mathbf{R}^k_+$, and redefine $\bar{p}\in\mathbf{R}^l_+$ by setting $\bar{p}_h := 0$ for all $h\geqslant k+1$. □

Example 2A.3. This is the same model as in Example 2A.1. The core of game v is nonempty, if the production function g satisfies constant returns to scale,

$$g(rx) = rg(x) \text{ for all } r\geqslant 0,$$

and superadditivity,

$$g(x)+g(x')\leqslant g(x+x').$$

To show this fact, let $\mathscr{B}$ be a balanced family with the associated coefficients $\{\lambda_S\}_{S\in\mathscr{B}}$. Then,

$$\sum_{S\in\mathscr{B}} \lambda_S v(S) = \sum_{S\in\mathscr{B}} \lambda_S g(\sum_{j\in S} \omega^j) \leqslant g(\sum_{S\in\mathscr{B}} \lambda_S \sum_{j\in S} \omega^j)$$
$$= g(\sum_{j\in N} \sum_{S\in\mathscr{B}:S\ni j} \lambda_S \omega^j) = g(\sum_{j\in N} \omega^j) = v(N),$$

so game v is balanced. By Theorem 2.1.1, $C(v) \neq \phi$. □

Example 2A.4. This is also the same model as in Example 2A.1. It was shown in Example 2A.1 that if production function g is supportable, then $C(v) \neq \phi$. This fact can also be demonstrated by using Theorem 2.1.1. Indeed, let $\mathscr{B}$ be a balanced family with the associated coefficients $\{\lambda_S \mid S \in \mathscr{B}\}$. Choose $\bar{p}$ as in Example 2A.1. Then,

$$\sum_{S\in\mathscr{B}} \lambda_S v(S) = \sum_{S\in\mathscr{B}} \lambda_S g(\sum_{j\in S} \omega^j) \leqslant \sum_{S\in\mathscr{B}} \lambda_S \bar{p}\cdot \sum_{j\in S} \omega^j$$
$$= \sum_{j\in N} (\sum_{S\in\mathscr{B}:S\ni j} \lambda_S) \bar{p}\cdot\omega^j = \sum_{j\in N} \bar{p}\cdot\omega^j = g(\sum_{j\in N} \omega^j) = v(N).$$

Game v is, therefore, balanced. Unlike Example 2A.3, this example allows for increasing returns to scale. Indeed, Section 5.3 clarifies that the supportability condition on g is equivalent to Scarf's (1986) condition of distributiveness on the underlying production set (Remark 5.3.2). □

Example 2A.5. A model taken from Shapley and Shubik (1967, pp. 100–101) (see also Shubik (1984, pp. 494–495)), but presented here in a different economic context: In the present-day Yugoslav economy, many firms have inherited or accumulated assets in the past. These assets are conceived as *social property*, but are in effect owned by nobody. Consider a firm endowed with a social property, in which the human-resource holders $N := \{1, 2, \ldots, n\}$ work, using the technology represented by the production function,

$$g: \mathbf{R}_+ \to \mathbf{R}_+,$$

which associates to each labor-input level the maximal output level produced from it. Function g reflects the given available social property. There are no initial endowments of assets held by the individuals. The output price is set equal to 1. Assume that the utility function of a human-resource holder does not depend upon his labor-supply but only upon consumption of output, and that each human-resource holder supplies 1 unit of labor to the firm regardless of wage levels. Then, the total value-added made by the firm is given as

$$y_{\max} := \max\{g(j) \mid 1 \leqslant j \leqslant n\},$$

which is assumed positive. The problem is how to distribute $y_{\max}$ to the n members as their wages. Consider the extreme case in which the majority exercises absolute control – control of the assets (social property), control of decision on work order, and control of decision on wage distribution – so that once it has decided, the minority is in no position to obstruct. No individuals of the minority have incentives to abstain from the ordered work and leave the firm, since they cannot find better deals in other firms; in the other firms assets are controlled by their majority groups. The majority can acquire the whole value-added, so

$$v(S)=\begin{cases} y_{\max}, & \text{if } \#S>n/2,\\ 0, & \text{otherwise.}\end{cases}$$

For any $n \geqslant 3$, the core of this game is empty. To see this, let $S_j := N\backslash\{j\}$. Then, the family $\{S_j\}_{j\in N}$ is balanced (indeed, the associated balancing coefficients are $\lambda_{S_j}=1/(n-1), j\in N$). Since $n\geqslant 3$, $\#S_j>n/2$. Game v is now shown to be non-balanced, as

$$\sum_{j\in N}\lambda_{S_j}v(S_j)=\frac{n}{n-1}y_{\max}>v(N).$$

Shapley and Shubik (1967) wrote, "The absence of a core implies that there is no distribution of the output that is free from social pressure: some coalition will always be able to obstruct any proposal" (p. 101). This model, albeit oversimplified, illustrates one of the major difficulties inherent in the present-day economy of market-cooperative socialism. See Remark 3.2.6 for other difficulties that arise in the presence of social properties.

In Section 3.2, a general equilibrium model of market-cooperative socialism is proposed (Definition 3.2.3), in which every asset is privately owned as an initial endowment, so there is no social property. The economy can be interpreted as the initial stage of the idealized market-cooperative socialism. Here, a new firm is created when its founders provide assets, and according to the practice in Yugoslavia, these founders in return collect dividends in the name of *past labor*. Another interpretation of this economy is a possible future of the market-cooperative socialism upon completion of the privatization process. □

Example 2A.6. The same model as in Example 2A.1: Suppose that production function g satisfies:

$$(\forall x, x'\in \mathbf{R}^l_+ : x'\geqslant x): (\forall z\in\mathbf{R}^l_+): g(x'+z)-g(x')\geqslant g(x+z)-g(x).$$

This is a version of increasing returns to scale. In this case,

$$v(T\cup\{j\})-v(T)\geqslant v(S\cup\{j\})-v(S), \text{ if } S\subset T\subset N\backslash\{j\},$$

so by Theorem 2.1.3, game v is convex. □

Example 2A.7. An example taken from Champsaur (1975): Consider a production economy with one primary good, one final good, and a finite set N of economic agents. All coalitions $S\,(\subset N)$ are potential production units and can use the identical production function g: $\mathbf{R}_+ \to \mathbf{R}_+$, which is assumed to be strictly increasing. Unlike Examples 2A.1–2A.5, the final good here is a public good. The primary good is a private good, as before. The utility function of each agent, u^j: $\mathbf{R}^2_+ \to \mathbf{R}$, depends both on consumption of the primary good and on consumption of the final good, and is assumed to be non-decreasing. For each $u \in \mathbf{R}^N$ and each $S \in \mathcal{N}$, let $c(S, u)$ be the minimal amount of the primary good that coalition S needs in order to realize utility allocation $\{u_j\}_{j\in S}$ for its members:

$$c(S, u) := \min \{\textstyle\sum_{j\in S} x^j + g^{-1}(z) \mid \forall j \in S\colon u_j \leqslant u^j(x^j, z)\}.$$

Then, for each $u \in \mathbf{R}^N$, the function $-c(\cdot, u)$ is convex. In order to show this fact, choose any S_1, $S_2 \in \mathcal{N}$. For each $i = 1, 2$, there exists $(\{x^{(i),j}\}_{j\in S_i}, z^{(i)}) \in \mathbf{R}^{\#S_i}_+ \times \mathbf{R}_+$ such that

$$u_j \leqslant u^j(x^{(i),j}, z^{(i)}), \text{ for every } j \in S_i, \text{ and}$$
$$\sum_{j\in S_i} x^{(i),j} + g^{-1}(z^{(i)}) = c(S_i, u).$$

Without loss of generality, let $z^{(1)} \leqslant z^{(2)}$, so that $g^{-1}(z^{(1)}) \leqslant g^{-1}(z^{(2)})$. Then,

$$\begin{aligned}
&c(S_1, u) + c(S_2, u)\\
&= \sum_{j\in S_1} x^{(1),j} + g^{-1}(z^{(1)}) + \sum_{j\in S_2} x^{(2),j} + g^{-1}(z^{(2)})\\
&= \Bigl(\sum_{j\in S_1\cap S_2} x^{(1),j} + g^{-1}(z^{(1)})\Bigr) +\\
&\quad + \Bigl(\sum_{j\in S_1\setminus S_2} x^{(1),j} + \sum_{j\in S_2} x^{(2),j} + g^{-1}(z^{(2)})\Bigr)\\
&\geqslant c(S_1 \cap S_2, u) + c(S_1 \cup S_2, u).
\end{aligned}$$

This result will be used in Example 2A.10. □

Example 2A.8. An example taken from Scarf (1967a, pp. 54–55): A *pure exchange economy* introduced in Section 3.3 (Definition 3.3.1) is a list of specified data $\mathscr{E}_{pe} := \{X^i, u^i, \omega^i\}_{i\in N}$ of a finite set of consumers N, consumer i's consumption set X^i (a subset of the commodity space $\mathbf{R}^l$), his utility function u^i: $X^i \to \mathbf{R}$, and his initial endowment ω^i (a point in the commodity space $\mathbf{R}^l$). In the absence of markets for the l commodities, consumers get together and exchange their initial endowments among themselves for a better allocation of commodities. The associated non-side-payment game is the correspondence V: $\mathcal{N} \to \mathbf{R}^N$ defined by

$$V(S):=\left\{u\in\mathbf{R}^N \,\middle|\, \exists\,(x^i)_{i\in S}\in\prod_{i\in S}X^i\colon \begin{array}{l}\sum_{i\in S}x^i\leqslant\sum_{i\in S}\omega^i,\\ \forall\, i\in S\colon u_i\leqslant u^i(x^i)\end{array}\right\}.$$

If each consumption set X^i is convex and each utility function u^i is quasi-concave, then the associated non-side-payment game V is balanced. Indeed, let $\mathscr{B}$ be a balanced family with the associated balancing coefficients $\{\lambda_S \mid S\in\mathscr{B}\}$, and choose any $u\in\bigcap_{S\in\mathscr{B}}V(S)$. One needs to show that $u\in V(N)$. For each $S\in\mathscr{B}$, there exists $(x^{i,S})_{i\in S}\in\prod_{i\in S}X^i$ such that $\sum_{i\in S}x^{i,S}\leqslant\sum_{i\in S}\omega^i$ and $u_i\leqslant u^i(x^{i,S})$ for every $i\in S$. Define $\bar{x}^i:=\sum_{S\in\mathscr{B}:S\ni i}\lambda_S x^{i,S}$ for every $i\in N$. By convexity of X^i, $\bar{x}^i\in X^i$; and by quasi-concavity of u^i, $u_i\leqslant u^i(\bar{x}^i)$. Moreover,

$$\begin{aligned}\sum_{i\in N}\bar{x}^i &= \sum_{i\in N}\sum_{S\in\mathscr{B}:S\ni i}\lambda_S x^{i,S}=\sum_{S\in\mathscr{B}}\lambda_S\sum_{i\in S}x^{i,S}\\ &\leqslant\sum_{S\in\mathscr{B}}\lambda_S\sum_{i\in S}\omega^i=\sum_{i\in N}\sum_{S\in\mathscr{B}:S\ni i}\lambda_S\omega^i=\sum_{i\in N}\omega^i.\end{aligned}$$

Therefore, $u\in V(N)$. A mild regularity condition on the economy $\mathscr{E}_{pe}$ guarantees the validity of assumptions (i)–(iii) of Theorem 2.2.1. So, the core of V is nonempty.

One can also construct a model of society $(\{X^i, u^i\}_{i\in N}, \{F^S\}_{S\in\mathscr{N}})$ as done in the paragraph between Remark 2.3.6 and Theorem 2.3.7. Specifically, $F^S:=\{(x^i)_{i\in S}\in\prod_{i\in S}X^i \mid \sum_{i\in S}x^i\leqslant\sum_{i\in S}\omega^i\}$. To show that condition (iv′) of Corollary 2.3.8 is satisfied, choose any balanced family $\mathscr{B}$ with the associated balancing coefficients $\{\lambda_S\}_{S\in\mathscr{B}}$, and any $\{x^{i,S}\}_{i\in S}\in F^S$. Define $\tilde{x}^S\in\tilde{F}^S$ by: $(\tilde{x}^S)^i=x^{i,S}$, if $i\in S$; and $(\tilde{x}^S)^i=\mathbf{0}$, otherwise. Then, $\sum_{S\in\mathscr{B}}\lambda_S\tilde{x}^S=(\bar{x}^i)_{i\in N}\in F^N$, by the argument of the preceding paragraph. □

Example 2A.9. A special case of the work by Böhm (1974): A *coalition production economy* is a list of specified data, $\mathscr{E}_{cp}:=(\{X^j, u^j, \omega^j\}_{j\in N}, \{Y(S)\}_{S\in\mathscr{N}})$ of a finite set of economic agents N, a consumption set X^j (a subset of the commodity space $\mathbf{R}^l$), a utility function $u^j\colon X^j\to\mathbf{R}$ and an initial endowment vector $\omega^j\,(\in\mathbf{R}^l)$ for each agent j, and a production set $Y(S)\,(\subset\mathbf{R}^l)$ for each coalition S (Definition 3.5.1). If no market mechanism is to be introduced to this economy, cooperative behavior of agents in $\mathscr{E}_{cp}$ can be modelled by the associated non-side-payment game V defined by

$$V(S):=\left\{u\in\mathbf{R}^N \,\middle|\, \begin{array}{l}\exists\{x^j\}_{j\in S}\in\prod_{j\in S}X^j\colon \exists\, y\in Y(S)\colon\\ \sum_{j\in S}x^j\leqslant\sum_{j\in S}\omega^j+y,\text{ and}\\ \forall\, j\in S\colon u_j\leqslant u^j(x^j)\end{array}\right\}.$$

Game V is balanced, if each X^j is convex, each u^j is quasi-concave, and the technology is balanced, i.e., for any balanced family $\mathscr{B}$ with the associated balancing coefficients $\{\lambda_S\}_{S\in\mathscr{B}}$, it follows that $\sum_{S\in\mathscr{B}}\lambda_S Y(S)\subset Y(N)$. Indeed, given any balanced family $\mathscr{B}$ with the associated balancing coefficients $\{\lambda_S\}_{S\in\mathscr{B}}$, choose any $u\in\bigcap_{S\in\mathscr{B}} V(S)$. One needs to show that $u\in V(N)$. For each $S\in\mathscr{B}$, there exist $(x^{i,S})_{i\in S}\in\prod_{i\in S} X^i$ and $y^S\in Y(S)$ such that $\sum_{i\in S} x^{i,S} \leqslant \sum_{i\in S}\omega^i + y^S$ and $u_i\leqslant u^i(x^{i,S})$ for every $i\in S$. Define $\bar{x}^i := \sum_{S\in\mathscr{B}:S\ni i}\lambda_S x^{i,S}$ for every $i\in N$. By convexity of X^i, $\bar{x}^i\in X^i$; and by quasi-concavity of u^i, $u_i\leqslant u^i(\bar{x}^i)$. By the balancedness assumption on technology, $\bar{y} := \sum_{S\in\mathscr{B}}\lambda_S y^S \in Y(N)$. Moreover,

$$\sum_{i\in N}\bar{x}^i = \sum_{i\in N}\sum_{S\in\mathscr{B}:S\ni i}\lambda_S x^{i,S} = \sum_{S\in\mathscr{B}}\lambda_S\sum_{i\in S}x^{i,S} \leqslant \sum_{S\in\mathscr{B}}\lambda_S\Big(\sum_{i\in S}\omega^i + y^S\Big) = \sum_{i\in N}\omega^i + \bar{y}.$$

Therefore, $u\in V(N)$.

One can also construct a model of society $(\{X^i, u^i\}_{i\in N}, \{F^S\}_{S\in\mathscr{B}})$ from this coalition production economy $\mathscr{E}_{cp}$. Define

$$F^S := \{(x^i)_{i\in S}\in\prod_{i\in S}X^i \mid \exists\, y\in Y(S): \sum_{i\in S}x^i\leqslant\sum_{i\in S}\omega^i + y\}.$$

It is easy to show that the balancedness assumption on technology and the convexity assumption on each X^i guarantee condition (iv′) of Corollary 2.3.8. □

Example 2A.10. The model of Example 2A.7 with an additional structure, taken from Champsaur (1975): Let $\omega^j\in\mathbf{R}_+$ be agent j's initial endowment of the primary good. No positive amount of the final good (public good) is given to the economy as an initial endowment. The associated non-side-payment game V is defined as

$$V(S) := \left\{u\in\mathbf{R}^N \,\middle|\, \begin{array}{l}\exists\,(x^j)_{j\in S}\subset\mathbf{R}_+: \sum_{j\in S}x^j\leqslant\sum_{j\in S}\omega^j,\\ \forall\, i\in S: u_i\leqslant u^i(x^i, g(\sum_{j\in S}\omega^j - \sum_{j\in S}x^j))\end{array}\right\}.$$

Game V is ordinal convex. To prove this, notice first that $u\in V(S)$ iff $c(S, u)\leqslant\sum_{j\in S}\omega^j$. Choose any $u\in V(S)\cap V(T)$, and assume that $u\notin V(S\cap T)$. Then,

$$c(S, u)\leqslant\sum_{j\in S}\omega^j,\ c(T, u)\leqslant\sum_{j\in T}\omega^j,\ c(S\cap T, u) > \sum_{j\in S\cap T}\omega^j.$$

By the discussion in Example 2A.7, $-c(\cdot, u)$ is convex, so

$$\begin{aligned}\sum_{j\in S\cup T}\omega^j &= \sum_{j\in S}\omega^j + \sum_{j\in T}\omega^j - \sum_{j\in S\cap T}\omega^j\\ &\geqslant c(S, u) + c(T, u) - c(S\cap T, u)\\ &\geqslant c(S\cup T, u).\end{aligned}$$

Therefore, $u\in V(S\cup T)$. □

Example 2A.11. The result of this example was obtained independently by Jingang Zhao and by the present author. Consider an industry in which n

individuals produce the same type of output. Each individual owns, runs and works by himself for his own firm (e.g., a contractor), and is interested in maximizing his value-added. Let $N:=\{1, 2, \ldots, n\}$ be the set of the individuals. When individual j produces y^j units of output, $j \in N$, the value-added of individual i is $\pi^i(y^1, y^2, \ldots, y^n)$. Assume that there is a function f^i: $\mathbf{R}^2_+ \to \mathbf{R}_+$ such that

$$\pi^i(y^1, y^2, \ldots, y^n) = f^i(y^i, \sum_{j \neq i} y^j).$$

This assumption is justified, if the industry faces the inverse demand function, p: $\mathbf{R}_+ \to \mathbf{R}_+$, and individual i has his non-human cost function, C^i: $\mathbf{R}_+ \to \mathbf{R}_+$, so that i's value-added function is given as

$$\pi^i(y^1, y^2, \ldots, y^n) = p(y^i + \sum_{j \neq i} y^j) \cdot y^i - C^i(y^i). \tag{1}$$

Then, it is easy to establish that *function π^i is quasi-concave in $(y^1, y^2, \ldots, y^n)$, iff function f^i is quasi-concave in the two arguments.* Under the additional assumption that f^i be differentiable, the quasi-concavity assumption on f^i is satisfied if

$$\det \begin{pmatrix} 0 & f^i_1 & f^i_2 \\ f^i_1 & f^i_{11} & f^i_{12} \\ f^i_2 & f^i_{21} & f^i_{22} \end{pmatrix} > 0. \tag{2}$$

If function π^i is given by (1), and if $d^2p/dy^2 = d^2C^i/d(y^i)^2 = 0$, direct computation establishes that condition (2) is satisfied, iff $p > dC^i/dy^i$. It is well-known that the Cournot equilibrium (the Nash equilibrium in the present oligopoly context) is not Pareto optimal with respect to the producer-set N. Needless to say, an α-core strategy is Pareto optimal. □

Example 2A.12. Essentially the same model as in Examples 2A.7 and 2A.10, but given a different economic interpretation here: There are l primary goods which are private goods, one final good which is a public good, and a finite set N of economic agents. All coalitions $S (\subset N)$ are potential production units and can use the identical production function g: $\mathbf{R}^l_+ \to \mathbf{R}_+$, which is assumed to be concave. The utility function of each agent, u^j: $\mathbf{R}^{l+1}_+ \to \mathbf{R}$, depends both on consumption of the private goods and on benefit of the public good, and is assumed to be non-decreasing and quasi-concave. Each agent possesses an initial endowment vector of the primary goods, $\omega^j \in \mathbf{R}^l_+$. The strategy space of agent j is defined as

$$X^j := \{x^j \in \mathbf{R}^l \mid \mathbf{0} \leqslant x^j \leqslant \omega^j\}.$$

Define $X^S := \prod_{j \in S} X^j$ for each $S \subset N$, and set $X := X^N$. Suppose a strategy bundle $x:=(x^j)_{j\in N}\in X$ is chosen. If coalition S is formed, the members in S produce the public good in the amount of $g(\sum_{i\in S}\omega^i-\sum_{i\in S}x^i)$, but they also enjoy the additional amount of public good produced by the complementary coalition $N\backslash S$, $g(\sum_{i\in N\backslash S}\omega^i-\sum_{i\in N\backslash S}x^i)$. So, each member j's utility level is

$$u_S^j(x):=u^j(x^j, g(\sum_{i\in S}\omega^i-\sum_{i\in S}x^i)+g(\sum_{i\in N\backslash S}\omega^i-\sum_{i\in N\backslash S}x^i)).$$

Under the present assumptions on g and u^j, it is easy to show that function u_S^j is quasi-concave in X. By Theorem 2.3.1, the normal-form game $\{X^j, u_N^j\}_{j\in N}$ has a nonempty α-core. If the production function g satisfies constant returns to scale,

$$g(rx)=rg(x) \text{ for all } r\geqslant 0,$$

then together with the concavity assumption, it satisfies the superadditivity,

$$g(x)+g(x')\leqslant g(x+x').$$

In this case, it is easy to show that

$$u_S^j(x)\leqslant u_N^j(x) \text{ for all } S.$$

Then, the α-core is nonempty even in the situation in which any blocking coalition S has to use $\{u_S^j\}_{j\in S}$ instead of $\{u_N^j\}_{j\in S}$, because each coalition would have a smaller blocking power.

The behavioral principle of the members of coalition S that underlies the α-core says that each member expects the worst to himself of the possible strategy choice of $N\backslash S$. No member of S, therefore, enjoys a *free ride* on the prevailing production by $N\backslash S$ of the public good. The passive behavioral principle, which underlies the strong equilibrium concept, says that each member does enjoy such a free ride. Of course, one cannot expect the existence of a strong equilibrium in the present model, that is, there is no strategy bundle which is free from coalitional free ride. □

Example 2A.13. The same model as in Example 2A.12. In order to make a free ride into a *costly ride*, a governmental authority is introduced: Suppose that coalition S is going to defect from the grand coalition N when the latter is choosing strategy bundle $\bar{x}$. Since the members of S would freely enjoy the amount $g(\sum_{j\in N\backslash S}(\omega^j-\bar{x}^j))$ of the public good produced by $N\backslash S$, the authority forces S to transfer to $N\backslash S$ a fraction of the input bundle, $\alpha\cdot\sum_{j\in N\backslash S}(\omega^j-\bar{x}^j)$, where the tax rate $\alpha\in[0, 1]$ is *a priori* set. The feasible-strategy space of coalition S is then given as

$$F^S(\bar{x}):=\{x^S\in X^S \mid \sum_{j\in S}x^j\leqslant\sum_{j\in S}\omega^j-\alpha\cdot\sum\nolimits_{j\in N\backslash S}(\omega^j-\bar{x}^j)\}.$$

(To avoid the possibility $F^S(\bar{x})=\phi$ while keeping the present analysis as simple as possible, the set X^j is enlarged to include negative components, and the functions u^j are extended to $\mathbf{R}^{l+1}$.) Assume as in Example 2A.12 that each utility function u^j is non-decreasing and quasi-concave and that the production function g satisfies concavity and constant returns to scale. As in Example 2A.12, one may show that the analogously defined functions u^j_S are quasi-concave in X. The associated society is given as $\mathscr{S}:=(\{X^j\}_{j\in N}, \{F^S\}_{S\in\mathscr{N}}, \{u^j_S\}_{j\in S\in\mathscr{N}})$. The non-side-payment games $V_{\bar{x}}$, parameterized by $\bar{x}\in X$ is defined by

$$V_{\bar{x}}(S):=\left\{u\in\mathbf{R}^N \;\middle|\; \begin{array}{l}\exists\, x^S\in X^S\!: \sum_{i\in S} x^i\leqslant\sum_{i\in S}\omega^i-\alpha\cdot\sum_{i\in N\setminus S}(\omega^i-\bar{x}^i),\\ \forall j\in S\!: u_j\leqslant u^j(x^j, g(\sum_{i\in N\setminus S}(\omega^i-\bar{x}^i))+\\ \qquad g(\sum_{i\in S}\omega^i-\alpha\cdot\sum_{i\in N\setminus S}(\omega^i-\bar{x}^i)-\sum_{i\in S}x^i))\end{array}\right\}.$$

Any condition under which game $V_{\bar{x}}$ is balanced would be a condition for the existence of strong equilibrium, in view of Theorem 2.3.7.

It appears that Corollary 2.3.8 is easier to use for the present example. To use this corollary, the concept of strategy has to be reformulated: A strategy of agent j is a vector $z^j:=(x^j, y^j)$ of his consumption of the primary goods $x^j\in\mathbf{R}^l$ and the final good y^j. Here, his consumption of the final good means his involvement in collective consumption of the public good. Let Z^j be the strategy space. Given strategy bundle $\bar{z}$, the feasible-strategy set of coalition S is:

$$G^S(\bar{z}):=\left\{z^S \;\middle|\; \begin{array}{l}x^S\in X^S\!: \sum_{i\in S} x^i\leqslant\sum_{i\in S}\omega^i-\alpha\cdot\sum_{i\in N\setminus S}(\omega^i-\bar{x}^i),\\ \forall j\in S\!: y^j\leqslant g(\sum_{i\in N\setminus S}(\omega^i-\bar{x}^i))+\\ \qquad g(\sum_{i\in S}\omega^i-\alpha\cdot\sum_{i\in N\setminus S}(\omega^i-\bar{x}^i)-\sum_{i\in S}x^i)\end{array}\right\}.$$

The associated society is now given as $\hat{\mathscr{S}}:=(\{Z^j, u^j\}_{j\in N}, \{G^S\}_{S\in\mathscr{N}})$. Clearly, the strong equilibria of $\mathscr{S}$ correspond precisely to the strong equilibria of $\hat{\mathscr{S}}$. It will be shown in the following that $\alpha=1$, that is, if a deviating coalition is asked to pick up the entire cost of production of the public good, then assumption (iv′) of Corollary 2.3.8 is satisfied. Choose any balanced family $\mathscr{B}$ with the associated coefficients $\{\lambda_S\}_{S\in\mathscr{B}}$, and any $z\in\sum_{S\in\mathscr{B}}\lambda_S\tilde{G}^S(\bar{z})$. For each $S\in\mathscr{B}$, there exists $(z^{(S),j})_{j\in S}\in G^S(\bar{z})$ such that for every $j\in N$,

$$z^j=\sum_{S\in\mathscr{B}:S\ni j}\lambda_S z^{(S),j}.$$

Notice first

$$\sum_{j\in N}x^j=\sum_{j\in N}\sum_{S\in\mathscr{B}:S\ni j}\lambda_S x^{(S),j},$$

so if the grand coalition adopts the primary-good consumption bundle x, then it can use the input bundle

$$\sum_{j\in N}\omega^j-\sum_{j\in N}\sum_{S\in\mathscr{B}:S\ni j}\lambda_S x^{(S),j}$$
$$=\sum_{S\in\mathscr{B}}\lambda_S\Big(\sum_{i\in S}(\omega^i-x^{(S),i})\Big) \tag{1}$$

for production of the public good. On the other hand, for each $j\in S\in\mathscr{B}$,

$$y^{(S),j}\leqslant g\Big(\sum_{i\in N\setminus S}(\omega^i-\bar{x}^i)\Big)+g\Big(\sum_{i\in S}\omega^i-\sum_{i\in N\setminus S}(\omega^i-\bar{x}^i)-\sum_{i\in S}x^{(S),i}\Big)$$
$$\leqslant g\Big(\sum_{i\in S}\omega^i-\sum_{i\in S}x^{(S),i}\Big),$$

so

$$y^j=\sum_{S\in\mathscr{B}:S\ni j}\lambda_S y^{(S),j}$$
$$\leqslant\sum_{S\in\mathscr{B}:S\ni j}\lambda_S g\Big(\sum_{i\in S}\omega^i-\sum_{i\in S}x^{(S),i}\Big)$$
$$\leqslant g\Big(\sum_{S\in\mathscr{B}:S\ni j}\lambda_S\sum_{i\in S}(\omega^i-x^{(S),i})\Big),$$

which can be produced from the input bundle (1). Thus $z\in G^N$. □

Example 2A.14. An institution which allows the players to take advantage of the market mechanism when making cooperative choice of strategies. This idea underlies all the main models of Chapters 3–5. The results on this example were obtained jointly by Richard P. McLean and the present author. Let $\mathscr{E}_{pe}:=\{X^i, u^i, \omega^i\}_{i\in N}$ be a pure exchange economy (Example 2A.8, Definition 3.3.1), and let $N:=\{1,\ldots,n\}$. A society is now constructed from $\mathscr{E}_{pe}$. The players are the consumers and the newly added hypothetical player (called *market participant* or player 0). A consumer's strategy space is his consumption set, and the market participant's strategy space is the price simplex $\Delta^{l-1}:=\{p\in\mathbf{R}^l_+ \mid \sum_{h=1}^l p_h=1\}$. The feasible-strategy correspondences are defined as follows: Given a pair of price vector and commodity allocation $(\bar{p},\bar{x})$,

$$F^{\{0\}}(\bar{p},\bar{x}):=\Delta^{l-1};$$

and for S for which $0\notin S$,

$$F^S(\bar{p},\bar{x}):=\{x^S\in X^S \mid \bar{p}\cdot\sum_{i\in S}x^i\leqslant\bar{p}\cdot\sum_{i\in S}\omega^i\};$$
$$F^{\{0\}\cup S}(\bar{p},\bar{x}):=F^{\{0\}}(\bar{p},\bar{x})\times F^S(\bar{p},\bar{x}).$$

For player $i\in N$, his utility function as a consumer, u^i, is also the utility function in this society. For the market participant,

$$u^0(\bar{p},\bar{x},p):=p\cdot\sum_{i\in N}(\bar{x}^i-\omega^i).$$

In the society defined above, the non-side-payment game relative to $(\bar{p}, \bar{x})$ is given by:

$$V_{\bar{p},\bar{x}}(\{0\}) := \{u \in \mathbf{R}^{1+n} \mid \exists p \in \Delta^{l-1}: u_0 \leqslant p \cdot \sum_{i \in N} (\bar{x}^i - \omega^i)\};$$

and for S for which $0 \notin S$,

$$V_{\bar{p},\bar{x}}(S) := \left\{ u \in \mathbf{R}^{1+n} \,\middle|\, \begin{array}{l} \exists (x^i)_{i \in S} \in \prod_{i \in S} X^i: \sum_{i \in S} \bar{p} \cdot x^i \leqslant \sum_{i \in S} \bar{p} \cdot \omega^i, \\ \forall i \in S: u_i \leqslant u^i(x^i) \end{array} \right\},$$

$$V_{\bar{p},\bar{x}}(\{0\} \cup S) := V_{\bar{p},\bar{x}}(\{0\}) \cap V_{\bar{p},\bar{x}}(S).$$

As in Arrow and Debreu (1954), it is easy to show that *for any pair* (p^*, x^*), *if* $x^* \in F^N(p^*, x^*)$ *and if* p^* *maximizes* $p \cdot \sum_{i \in N}(x^{*i} - \omega^i)$ *in* Δ^{l-1}, *then* x^* *is attainable in N, that is,* $\sum_{i \in N} x^{*i} \leqslant \sum_{i \in N} \omega^i$. Indeed, for each $h \in \{1, \ldots, l\}$, let $e^h \in \Delta^{l-1}$ be the hth unit vector defined by: $e^h_k := 1$ if $k = h$; and $e^h_k := 0$ if $k \neq h$. Then,

$$\begin{aligned} \textstyle\sum_{i \in N}(x^{*i}_h - \omega^i_h) &= e^h \cdot \textstyle\sum_{i \in N}(x^{*i} - \omega^i) \\ &\leqslant p^* \cdot \textstyle\sum_{i \in N}(x^{*i} - \omega^i) \\ &\leqslant 0. \end{aligned}$$

Moreover, it is also easy to show under the monotonicity assumption on u^i, that *if* (p^*, x^*) *is a strong equilibrium of the society, then* $p^* \cdot x^{*i} = p^* \cdot \omega^i$ *for every* $i \in N$. Indeed, if there exists $i \in N$ for whom $p^* \cdot x^{*i} > p^* \cdot \omega^i$, then by the definition of F^N there exists $j \in N$ for whom $p^* \cdot x^{*j} < p^* \cdot \omega^j$, so player j would be able to improve upon (p^*, x^*) – a contradiction of the choice of (p^*, x^*) as a strong equilibrium. Thus, (p^*, x^*) *is a strong equilibrium of the society, iff it is a competitive equilibrium (Definition 3.3.2) of* $\{X^i, u^i, \omega^i\}_{i \in N}$.

Now, as in Example 2A.8, one can show that *the non-side-payment game* $V_{\bar{p},\bar{x}}$ *relative to* $(\bar{p}, \bar{x})$ *is balanced.* Under the standard assumption of the minimal subsistence level ($p \cdot \omega^i > \min p \cdot X^i$ for every i), the correspondences F^S are both upper and lower semicontinuous. Therefore, a strong equilibrium exists by Theorem 2.3.7.

The non-side-payment game $V_{\bar{p},\bar{x}}$ *is also ordinal convex*. To prove this fact, it suffices to show that the ordinal convexity condition is satisfied for S_1 and S_2 for which $0 \notin S_1 \cup S_2$. Choose such S_k, $k = 1, 2$, and choose any $u \in V_{\bar{p},\bar{x}}(S_1) \cap V_{\bar{p},\bar{x}}(S_2)$. There exists an allocation $(x^{(k)i})_{i \in S_k}$ attainable relative to $\bar{p}$ in S_k which gives rise to u, $k = 1, 2$. If $u \notin V_{\bar{p},\bar{x}}(S_1 \cap S_2)$, then

$$\textstyle\sum_{i \in S_1 \cap S_2} \bar{p} \cdot x^{(2)i} > \sum_{i \in S_1 \cap S_2} \bar{p} \cdot \omega^i,$$

so that

$$\textstyle\sum_{i \in S_2 \setminus S_1} \bar{p} \cdot x^{(2)i} < \sum_{i \in S_2 \setminus S_1} \bar{p} \cdot \omega^i.$$

Define $(y^i)_{i \in S_1 \cup S_2}$ by

$$y^i := \begin{cases} x^{(1)i} \text{ if } i \in S_1, \\ x^{(2)i} \text{ if } i \in S_2 \backslash S_1. \end{cases}$$

Then $(y^i)_{i \in S_1 \cup S_2}$ is attainable relative to $\bar{p}$ and gives rise to u, so

$$u \in V_{\bar{p},\bar{x}}(S_1 \cup S_2).$$

Thus, $V_{\bar{p},\bar{x}}(S_1) \cap V_{\bar{p},\bar{x}}(S_2) \subset V_{\bar{p},\bar{x}}(S_1 \cap S_2) \cup V_{\bar{p},\bar{x}}(S_1 \cup S_2)$, as was to be proved. □

Example 2A.15. An example taken from Moulin and Peleg (1982): This example is still somewhat abstract, yet many important concrete cases fall into this category as Examples 2A.16 and 2A.17 below suggest. Let N and Z be a finite player set and a finite outcome set, respectively. An effectivity function (correspondence) E: $2^N \to 2^Z$ is called *additive*, if there exists $(\zeta, \nu) \in \mathbf{R}^Z \times \mathbf{R}^N$ satisfying $\zeta \gg \mathbf{0}$, $\sum_{z \in Z} \zeta_z = 1$, $\nu \gg \mathbf{0}$ and $\sum_{j \in N} \nu_j = 1$ (that is, there exist strictly positive weights on Z and on N), such that

$$B \in E(S) \text{ iff } \sum_{z \in B} \zeta_z + \sum_{j \in S} \nu_j > 1.$$

An additive effectivity function is convex. Indeed, suppose that $B \in E(S)$, $C \in E(T)$, and $B \cap C \notin E(S \cup T)$. Then, $\sum_{z \in B} \zeta_z + \sum_{j \in S} \nu_j > 1$, $\sum_{z \in C} \zeta_z + \sum_{j \in T} \nu_j > 1$, and $\sum_{z \in B \cap C} \zeta_z + \sum_{j \in S \cup T} \nu_j \leqslant 1$, so $\sum_{z \in B \cup C} \zeta_z + \sum_{j \in S \cap T} \nu_j > 1$, which establishes that $B \cup C \in E(S \cap T)$. □

Example 2A.16. An example taken from Moulin (1981b): Let N be a finite set of voters, and let Z be a finite set of outcomes. Set $n := \# N$, and $p := \# Z$. A *neutral and anonymous veto function* (called simply a *veto function* in this example) is a function $v: \{1, 2, \ldots, n\} \to \{1, 2, \ldots, p-1\}$ such that $v(n) = p-1$. The intended interpretation is that a coalition of s voters can veto any set of at most $v(s)$ outcomes, and that the grand coalition can realize any outcome by vetoing the other $p-1$ outcomes. It is neutral, because for two sets of outcomes B and C having the same number of outcomes, a coalition S can veto B iff it can veto C. It is anonymous, because for two coalitions S and T having the same number of voters, S can veto an outcome set B iff T can veto B. Coalition S is effective on outcome set B, iff it can veto $Z \backslash B$, so the associated effectivity function E is defined by:

$$B \in E(S) \text{ iff } p - \# B \leqslant v(\# S).$$

Here, $E(\phi) := \phi$. The *proportional veto function* is the veto function $\bar{v}$ defined by: $\bar{v}(s)$ is the unique integer satisfying

$$p \cdot \frac{s}{n} - 1 \leqslant \bar{v}(s) < p \cdot \frac{s}{n}.$$

The associated effectivity function $\bar{E}$ is then given by:

$$B \in \bar{E}(S) \text{ iff } \frac{\# B}{p} + \frac{\# S}{n} > 1.$$

Clearly, function $\bar{E}$ is additive, hence is stable (Example 2A.15). A stronger theorem is due to Moulin (1981b): *A veto function v is stable, that is, its associated effectivity function is stable, iff* $v(t) \leqslant \bar{v}(t)$ *for all t.* (Moulin assumed superadditivity of v, but it is actually not needed, as the following proof shows.) The sufficiency is straightforward, in view of the fact that for two effectivity functions E and $\bar{E}$, if $E(S) \subset \bar{E}(S)$ for all S, and if $\bar{E}$ is stable, then E is also stable.

In order to prove the necessity, suppose on the contrary that there exists $s \in \{1, 2, \ldots, n\}$ for which $v(s) > \bar{v}(s)$. Necessarily, $1 \leqslant s \leqslant n-1$. Since $\bar{v}(s)$ is the greatest integer satisfying $\bar{v}(s) < p \cdot \frac{s}{n}$, and since $v(s)$ is an integer greater than $\bar{v}(s)$, it follows that $p \cdot \frac{s}{n} \leqslant v(s)$. Define the integer c by $p - c = v(s)$. Then, a coalition of size s is effective on an outcome set of size c, and

$$\frac{p}{p-c} s \leqslant n. \tag{1}$$

Clearly, $1 \leqslant c \leqslant p-1$. Define $p = Ac + B$, where A and B are nonnegative integers such that $B < c$.

It suffices to show that there exists a preference profile with respect to which any outcome z is vetoed by some coalition S of size s because S can find an outcome set C of size c (so that S is effective on C) and every member of S prefers each outcome of C to z. It will appear that a particular preference profile h of the Condorcet type is the required one. So, introduce linear orders on N and on Z; without loss of generality, set $N = \{1, 2, \ldots, n\}$ and $Z = \{1, 2, \ldots, p\}$. For each positive integer j, define $h^j\colon Z \to Z$ by

$$h^j(i) := i - (j-1)c \bmod p.$$

See Table 2A.1 for the case $p = 7, c = 2, n = 8, s = 5$. Notice that the numbers in the table represent the utility levels; so, the higher the number, the higher is the ranking. Choose any $i \in Z$. Let $j_1 < j_2 < \ldots < j_s$ be the first s integers j for which $h^j(i) \leqslant p - c$. One needs to show only that $j_s \leqslant n$, because then coalition $\{j_1, j_2, \ldots, j_s\}$ would be effective on $C := \{(i+1 \bmod p), (i+2 \bmod p), \ldots, (i+c \bmod p)\}$, and improve upon i. Also, one needs to show this only for $i = p$.

Assume $B = 0$. Then, necessarily, $A > 1$. By setting $t := n - s$, condition (1) becomes in this case

$$\frac{s}{A-1} \leqslant t. \tag{1'}$$

Consider the first k sets of players,

Table 2A.1. $h^j(i)$ for $p=7$, $c=2$, $n=8$, $s=5$

j	A			A				n ‖		
$i \in Z$	1	2	3	4	5	6	7	8	9	10
1	1	6	4	2	7	5	3	1	6	4
2	2	7	5	3	1	6	4	2	7	5
3	3	1	6	4	2	7	5	3	1	6
4	4	2	7	5	3	1	6	4	2	7
5	5	3	1	6	4	2	7	5	3	1
6	6	4	2	7	5	3	1	6	4	2
7	7	5	3	1	6	4	2	7	5	3

$$\{1, \ldots, A\}, \{A+1, \ldots, 2A\}, \ldots, \{(k-2)A+1, \ldots, (k-1)A\}, \{k-1)A+1, \ldots, j_s\},$$

such that $(k-1)A+1 \leqslant j_s \leqslant kA$. Since each of the first $(k-1)$ sets contains precisely $(A-1)$ players whose utility levels are no greater than $p-c$, and since the last set contains at most one player whose utility level is greater than $p-c$,

$$j_s - s = (k-1) \text{ or } k,$$

so it suffices to show that $k \leqslant t$. But by the same reasoning,

$$(k-1)(A-1) < s \leqslant k(A-1).$$

This is equivalent to

$$\frac{s}{A-1} \leqslant k < \frac{s}{A-1} + 1.$$

Therefore, by (1′), $k \leqslant t$.

Assume $B > 0$. For any real number x, denote by $[x]$ the smallest integer that is greater than or equal to x. In view of (1), it suffices to establish

$$\forall s\colon j_s \leqslant \left[\frac{p}{p-c}s\right],$$

that is,

$$\forall s\colon j_s \leqslant s + \left[\frac{c}{p-c}s\right]. \tag{2}$$

Inequalities (2) will be proved by induction on s for the case $A>1$; proof of (2) for the case $A=1$ is left as an exercise.

For $s=1$, one has $j_s \leqslant 2$, so (2) is trivial. Assume that (2) is true for all $s'=1, \ldots, s-1$.

To prove (2) for s, notice that there are two mutually exclusive and exhaustive cases: (I) $c<h^{j_{s-1}}(p)$; and (II) $0<h^{j_{s-1}}(p) \leqslant c$.

Case (I). In this case, $j_s=j_{s-1}+1$, and by the inductive hypothesis made on $(s-1)$,

$$j_{s-1} \leqslant (s-1)+\left\lceil \frac{c}{p-c}(s-1) \right\rceil \leqslant s-1+\left\lceil \frac{c}{p-c}s \right\rceil.$$

The required inequality follows now.

Case (II). In this case, $j_s=j_{s-1}+2$. There are two subcases: (II.1) $0<h^{j_{s-1}}(p) \leqslant B$; and (II.2) $B<h^{j_{s-1}}(p) \leqslant c$.

If (II.1) is the case exactly A consecutive members,

$$j_{s-1}-(A-1), j_{s-1}-(A-2), \ldots, j_{s-1},$$

have utilities no greater than $p-c$. Set $r:=s-A$. Then, $j_r=j_{s-1}-(A-1)$, so $j_s=j_r+A+1$. One needs to show

$$j_r+A+1 \leqslant r+A+\left\lceil \frac{c}{p-c}(r+A) \right\rceil.$$

By the inductive hypothesis made on r,

$$j_r \leqslant r+\left\lceil \frac{c}{p-c}r \right\rceil.$$

Therefore, it suffices to show

$$r+\left\lceil \frac{c}{p-c}r \right\rceil < r+\frac{c}{p-c}(r+A),$$

that is,

$$\frac{c}{p-c}A > \left\lceil \frac{c}{p-c}r \right\rceil - \frac{c}{p-c}r.$$

But the left-hand side of the last inequality is greater than 1, while the right-hand side is less than 1.

Assume that (II.2) is the case. Define $c=\alpha B+\beta$, $1 \leqslant \alpha$, $0 \leqslant \beta < B$. Consider the α sets of players,

$$\begin{aligned}
&\{j_{s-1}-\alpha A-(A-1), j_{s-1}-\alpha A-(A-1)+1, \quad \ldots, \quad j_{s-1}-\alpha A\},\\
&\{j_{s-1}-(\alpha-1)A-(A-1), \quad \ldots, \quad j_{s-1}-(\alpha-1)A\},\\
&\ldots,\\
&\{j_{s-1}-(A-1), \quad j_{s-1}-(A-1)+1, \quad \ldots, \quad j_{s-1}\}.
\end{aligned}$$

Set $m := j_{s-1} - \alpha A$. Then, by applying the identity, $Ac + u \equiv -B + u \pmod{p}$, repeatedly, one obtains two further subcases: (II.2.1) $B - \alpha B \bmod p < h^m(p) \leqslant p$; and (II.2.2) $0 < h^m(p) \leqslant \beta$.

If (II.2.1) is the case, all the A members of the second set have utilities no greater than $p - c$. Set $j_r := j_{s-1} - (\alpha - 1)A - (A - 1)$ for this subsubcase. Then, (1) all the A members of set $\{j_r, j_r + 1, \ldots, j_r + (A-1)\}$ have utility levels no greater than $p - c$; (2) the last $(A - 1)$ members of set $\{j_r + aA, j_r + aA + 1, \ldots, j_r + aA + (A - 1)\}$ are precisely the members whose utility levels are no greater than $p - c$, $a = 1, 2, \ldots, \alpha - 1$; and (3) $j_r + (\alpha - 1)A + (A - 1) = j_{s-1}$. Such r exists by the present assumption $i = p$. Therefore,

$$j_s = j_r + 1 + \alpha A, \text{ and}$$
$$s = r + 1 + \alpha(A - 1).$$

By the inductive hypothesis,

$$j_r \leqslant r + \left\lceil \frac{c}{p-c} r \right\rceil.$$

To prove (2), one needs to show

$$j_r + 1 + \alpha A \leqslant r + 1 + \alpha(A-1) + \left\lceil \frac{c}{p-c}(r + 1 + \alpha(A-1)) \right\rceil.$$

This would be true if

$$1 - \alpha + \frac{c}{p-c}(1 + \alpha(A-1)) > \left\lceil \frac{c}{p-c} r \right\rceil - \frac{c}{p-c} r.$$

But

$$\text{the left-hand side} = 1 + \frac{c - \alpha B}{(A-1)c + B} \geqslant 1 > \text{the right-hand side}.$$

Assume (II.2.2) is the case. Necessarily, $\beta \geqslant 1$. Notice that for each positive integer k, $(k-1)\beta \bmod p < h^{j_{s-1} - k\alpha A - k + 1}(p) \leqslant k\beta \bmod p$. Choose the smallest integer $\bar{k}$ for which $p - c < (\bar{k} - 1)\beta$. Necessarily, $\bar{k}\beta \leqslant p$. Set $j_r := j_{s-1} - \bar{k}\alpha A - \bar{k} + 2$. Then, from j_r to j_{s-1}, there must be $\bar{k}$ distinct sets of consecutive A members whose utility levels are no greater than $p - c$. So,

$$j_s = j_{s-1} + 2 = j_r + \bar{k}\alpha A + \bar{k},$$
$$s = r + \bar{k}\alpha(A-1) + \bar{k}.$$

To prove (2), one needs to show

$$j_r + \bar{k}\alpha A + \bar{k} \leqslant r + \bar{k}\alpha(A-1) + \bar{k} + \left\lceil \frac{c}{p-c}[r + \bar{k}\alpha(A-1) + \bar{k}] \right\rceil,$$

which would be true (by the inductive hypothesis on r) if

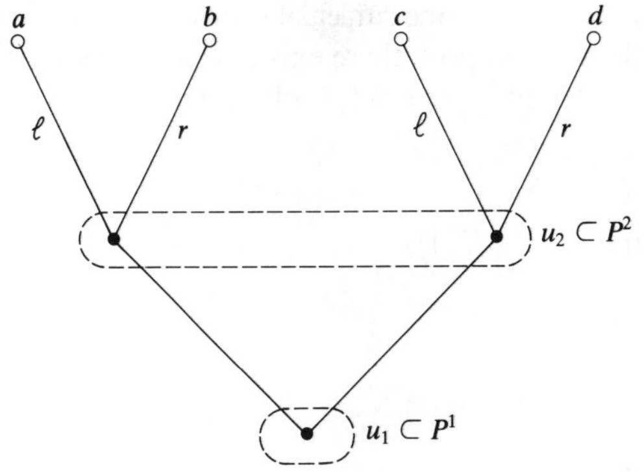

2A.1 Non-additive, convex effectivity function

$$1-\bar{k}\alpha+\frac{c}{p-c}\{\bar{k}\alpha(A-1)+\bar{k}\}>\left[\frac{c}{p-c}r\right]-\frac{c}{p-c}r.$$

But

$$\text{the left-hand side}=1+\frac{1}{(A-1)c+B}\bar{k}(c-\alpha B)$$
$$>1\geqslant\text{the right-hand side. } \square$$

Example 2A.17. An example taken from Peleg (1978): Let N be a finite set of voters, and let Z be a finite set of outcomes. Set $n:=\#N$, and $p:=\#Z$. Assume $n\geqslant p-1$. Choose any function β: $Z\to\{1, \ldots, n\}$ satisfying $\sum_{z\in Z}\beta(z)=n+1$. The intended interpretation is that in order to veto an outcome set $C(\subset Z)$ one needs a coalition of size $\sum_{z\in C}\beta(z)$. The associated effectivity function E is defined by:

$$B\in E(S) \text{ iff } \#S\geqslant\sum_{z\in Z\setminus B}\beta(z).$$

It is easy to show that function E is additive (Example 2A.15). Peleg's (1978) proof of the stability of E is based on his *feasible elimination procedure*; the procedures characterize $C(E, h)$ (Moulin and Peleg (1982, Theorem 4.13) and Peleg (1984a, Theorem 5.4.2, p. 101)). □

Example 2A.18. A convex non-additive effectivity function: There are two players, $N=\{1, 2\}$, and four outcomes $Z=\{a, b, c, d\}$. Define

$$E(\{1\}):=\{B\in 2^Z\setminus\{\phi\}\mid B\supset\{a, b\} \text{ or } B\supset\{c, d\}\},$$
$$E(\{2\}):=\{B\in 2^Z\setminus\{\phi\}\mid B\supset\{a, c\} \text{ or } B\supset\{b, d\}\}, \text{ and}$$
$$E(N):=2^Z\setminus\{\phi\}.$$

This effectivity function arises as the α-effectivity function out of the extensive game given in Figure 2A.1. By the general theorem of Chapter 6

(Theorem 6.3.3), E is convex; but one can easily verify this fact directly. To show that E is not additive, suppose there exists $(\zeta, \nu) \in \mathbf{R}^Z \times \mathbf{R}^N$ satisfying $\zeta \gg \mathbf{0}$, $\sum_{z \in Z} \zeta_z = 1$, $\nu \gg \mathbf{0}$, and $\sum_{j \in N} \nu_j = 1$, such that

$$B \in E(S) \text{ iff } \sum_{z \in B} \zeta_z + \sum_{j \in S} \nu_j > 1.$$

Since $\{a, b\} \in E(\{1\})$ and $\{a, c\} \notin E(\{1\})$,

$$\zeta_a + \zeta_b \quad + \nu_1 > 1 \tag{1}$$
$$\zeta_a \quad + \zeta_c + \nu_1 \leqslant 1. \tag{2}$$

Since $\{a, b\} \notin E(\{2\})$ and $\{a, c\} \notin E(\{2\})$,

$$\zeta_a + \zeta_b \quad + \nu_2 \leqslant 1 \tag{3}$$
$$\zeta_a \quad + \zeta_c + \nu_2 > 1 \tag{4}$$

By (1) and (3), $\nu_1 > \nu_2$. On the other hand, by (2) and (4), $\nu_1 < \nu_2$ – a contradiction. □

3 General equilibrium analysis of the nature of the firm

In this chapter a new general equilibrium model of an economy and an equilibrium concept are proposed. The model embodies both the economic forces identified by specialists in the theory of the firm (Chapter 1) and the neoclassical market mechanism. Every effort has been made to make the model simple, while retaining all the essential economic ingredients; it is an improved version of the models of Ichiishi (1982b, 1990b). The foci of this chapter are the economic interpretations of the formal model and the existence of equilibria. Section 3.1 presents the basic model of an economy and the equilibrium concept. The model features the allocation of non-human resources through the neoclassical markets, and the allocation of human resources through a cooperative game played by human-resource holders. This cooperative game is an explicit interpretation and formulation of the Coasian non-market human-resource allocation mechanism discussed in Section 1.1. The equilibrium concept is a hybrid of the market equilibrium concept and the strong equilibrium concept. Section 3.2 introduces ownership structures into the basic model, and formulates its two special cases, the capitalistic economy and a socialistic economy. The difference between the two special cases lies in the fact that a firm in the former can obtain non-human investments from outsiders by issuing its stock, but there is no such channel for re-allocation of initial resources in the latter. The two reflect Berle and Means' (1932) observation of the separation of ownership and control in the modern capitalistic firms (Section 1.2), and the decentralized market-cooperative socialism (Section 1.3), respectively. Section 3.3 presents three traditional models and equilibrium concepts: the pure exchange economy and its competitive equilibrium, the private ownership economy (the Arrow-Debreu model) and its competitive equilibrium, and the non-side-payment game and its core. It is shown how the basic model and equilibrium concept of Section 3.1 can be specialized to each of the three. Section 3.4 establishes two equilibrium existence theorems for the basic model of Section 3.1. This is done by applying the social coalitional equilibrium existence theorem of Ichiishi

(1981b); the statement of this theorem and a sketch of its proof is also given. Also proved as applications of the social coalitional equilibrium existence theorem are Scarf's (1967a) theorem for nonemptiness of the core of a non-side-payment game, strong equilibrium existence theorems for a game in normal form and for a society, and Arrow and Debreu's (1954) competitive equilibrium existence theorem for the private ownership economy. From the formal point of view, the basic model of Section 3.1 may be considered an extension of the model of coalition production economy. Section 3.5 briefly surveys the works on core allocations of the coalition production economy and Böhm's concept of market equilibrium with a stable firm structure. The proof of the social coalitional equilibrium existence theorem is heavily based on a certain technique to prove Scarf's theorem for nonemptiness of the core. This technique involves (1) Shapley's (1973) theorem on closed coverings of a simplex, a generalization of Knaster, Kuratowski and Mazurkiewicz's (1929) theorem (the latter theorem, called the K-K-M theorem, is equivalent to Brouwer's (1912) fixed-point theorem), and (2) Fan's (1969, 1972) coincidence theorem, one of the highest achievements in the recent fixed-point theory. There are other generalizations of the K-K-M theorem, many of which are also related to the Scarf theorem. Section 3.6 provides a unified treatment of these generalizations. The capitalistic version specified in Section 3.2 assumes that stocks of all possible firms are traded in the neoclassical market. The Appendix to Chapter 3 sketches the formulation of a variant of this capitalistic version, in which stocks are issued and purchased not through the neoclassical market, but rather as a part of the cooperative game played by the n economic agents.

3.1 General equilibrium model

A general equilibrium model of production, which features the neoclassical market mechanism and cooperative behavior of the economic agents in firms (organizations), is constructed in this section. It is the basic model that will be specialized in Section 3.2 into the model of the capitalistic economy, and also into the model of a socialistic economy.

There are l marketed commodities. These are commodities that are traded in perfectly competitive spot markets. A price vector is normalized so that the sum of all prices is equal to 1 (instead of choosing a numéraire); the *price domain* is then the unit simplex,

$$\Delta^{l-1} := \{p \in \mathbf{R}^l_+ \mid \sum_{h=1}^{l} p_h = 1\}.$$

Besides the l marketed commodities, there are other commodities whose allocation is determined by a non-market (but economic) mechanism. In light of the insight of Coase (1937, 1988), human resources are typical examples of these *non-marketed commodities* (see the discussion of Section 1.1). Throughout this text a human-resource holder will be called a *laborer* for short. The term "labor", therefore, includes not only manual labor but also highly skilled labor such as engineering and managerial labor. In both Sections 1.2 and 1.3, it was argued that a firm is managed by the laborers who work for it. The following facts then emerge: People can communicate with each other while working in a firm or when establishing a new firm, and each agent is aware of this possibility. These facts prompt economic theorists to introduce a new behavioral principle as a part of the appropriate modelling: Each laborer in a firm, given his own interest, coordinates his strategy-choice with the other laborers of the firm, because by doing so he and his colleagues can better serve their diverse interests, that is, the laborers play a cooperative game. Indeed, this cooperative behavioral principle is modelled in this section. It is through this cooperative game that non-marketed commodities are allocated. In many economies any set of laborers can come together to form a coalition (cooperative unit, i.e., firm) if everyone of the set wants to. This is certainly the case in the free society of capitalism. This is also true in the market-cooperative socialistic economy, as evidenced in the Yugoslav case study (see, e.g., Jan Vanek (1972)). It is necessary, therefore, to model a mechanism for determination of firm membership in equilibrium. The approach adopted here does provide such a mechanism; the laborers play a nation-wide cooperative game in which each decides whom and whom not to cooperate with.

There are *n economic agents*; denote by N the set of all economic agents. Each agent plays at least two roles in the economy: that of a consumer, and that of a member of the firm he works for. A subset S of N, called a *coalition*, is identified with a potential firm; denote by $\mathscr{N}$ the family of all nonempty coalitions $2^N \setminus \{\phi\}$. When firm S is actually formed, agent j works for S as a full-time laborer (human-resource holder) if and only if $j \in S$. A *coalition structure* is a partition of N; it describes realization and coexistence of firms. Some coalition structures may be forbidden by law as inadmissible. Let $\mathscr{T}$ be the nonempty family of *admissible coalition structures* of N, *a priori* given. The model here will explain which coalition structure in $\mathscr{T}$ is realized in equilibrium.

Example 3.1.1. If $N = \{1, 2, 3\}$, then $\mathscr{T}$ consists of some members of $\{\{1\}, \{2\}, \{3\}\}$, $\{\{1\}, \{2, 3\}\}$, $\{\{2\}, \{3, 1\}\}$, $\{\{3\}, \{1, 2\}\}$, and $\{\{1, 2, 3\}\}$. □

Formally the model under construction is static, but it is best interpreted as a model of temporary equilibrium.[1] There are two periods, today and

[1] For the temporary equilibrium analysis, see, e.g., Grandmont (1974, 1977, 1983). The earlier literature includes the original treatment by Hicks (1939, Parts III and IV) and its formal study by Morishima (1947, 1948).

future. All the endogenous variables are determined today; these variables include today's transactions and subjective probabilities (held today) on future transactions. Joint products are allowed in production. A firm uses commodities, marketed or non-marketed, as inputs today, and produces marketed commodities today and in the future.

For each agent j, his *strategy space* X^j is a subset of $\mathbf{R}^l \times \mathbf{R}^l \times E^j$, where E^j is a real Hausdorff locally convex topological vector space. A generic element x^j of X^j is denoted by $(x^j_{\mathrm{I}}, x^j_{\mathrm{II}}, x^j_{\mathrm{III}})$, with $x^j_{\mathrm{I}} \in \mathbf{R}^l$, $x^j_{\mathrm{II}} \in \mathbf{R}^l$, $x^j_{\mathrm{III}} \in E^j$. Agent j in his capacity as a consumer demands a marketed-commodity bundle x^j_{I} for his consumption today. He chooses the other part $(x^j_{\mathrm{II}}, x^j_{\mathrm{III}})$ of his strategy in his capacity as a member of the firm he works for. The subvector x^j_{II} is a marketed-commodity bundle signifying the quantity of inputs and outputs that are used or produced in his firm today. The subvector x^j_{III} represents the part of his strategy that is not directly related to today's spot markets; it includes specifically the types and quantity of labor he supplies to his firm and the wage he receives. Wage rates are not prices but a part of strategies to be determined in the cooperative game. The subvector also includes other non-marketed commodities, if any. The other components of x^j_{III} is j's subjective probability on his future consumption of marketed commodities. The usual sign convention for demand and supply is adopted, i.e., consumer j's demand for (supply of, resp.) a commodity is measured by a positive number (negative number, resp.), and firm S's supply of (demand for, resp.) a commodity is measured by a positive number (negative number, resp.).

Example 3.1.2. Suppose that the only non-marketed commodities are k types of labor, and that there are m commodities in the future. Denote by $\mathrm{ca}(\mathbf{R}^m)$ the space of all countably additive measures on the Borel σ-algebra of subsets of $\mathbf{R}^m$, endowed with the weak* topology. Then,

$$E^j = \mathbf{R}^k \times \mathbf{R} \times \mathrm{ca}(\mathbf{R}^m),$$

and the space of probabilities on future consumption is the subset of $\mathrm{ca}(\mathbf{R}^m)$,

$$\mathcal{M}(\mathbf{R}^m) := \{\mu \in \mathrm{ca}(\mathbf{R}^m) \mid \mu \geqslant \mathbf{0},\ \mu(\mathbf{R}^m) = 1\},$$

so that

$$X^j \subset \mathbf{R}^l \times \mathbf{R}^l \times \mathbf{R}^k \times \mathbf{R} \times \mathcal{M}(\mathbf{R}^m).$$

The intended interpretation of $(L^j, w^j, \mu^j) \in E^j$ is that L^j signifies j's labor supply, w^j signifies his wage, and μ^j signifies the probability on his future consumption. A generic element of X^j is then written as $(x^j_{\mathrm{I}}, x^j_{\mathrm{II}}, L^j, w^j, \mu^j)$ with

$$x^j_{\mathrm{I}},\ x^j_{\mathrm{II}} \in \mathbf{R}^l,\ L^j \in \mathbf{R}^k,\ w^j \in \mathbf{R},\ \mu^j \in \mathcal{M}(\mathbf{R}^m).$$

By the sign convention, $x_{\mathrm{I}}^j \geqslant \mathbf{0}$, $x_{\mathrm{II}h}^j \geqslant 0$ if commodity h is an output, $x_{\mathrm{II}h}^j \leqslant 0$ if commodity h is an input, $L^j \leqslant \mathbf{0}$, and the support of μ^j is contained in $\mathbf{R}_+^m$. □

Each economic agent j has a marketed-commodity bundle ω^j ($\in \mathbf{R}^l$) as his *initial endowment*.

Define $X^S := \prod_{j \in S} X^j$ for each $S \in \mathcal{N}$, and set for simplicity $X := X^N$. Suppose $(\bar{x}, \bar{p}, \bar{\mathcal{T}}) \in X \times \Delta^{l-1} \times \mathcal{T}$ is given at the outset. Firm S is formed, once the members of S agree to cooperate; they agree to choosing the input-output vector, $x_{\mathrm{II}}^{(S)}$ $(= x_{\mathrm{II}}^j$, for all $j \in S)$, and the other firm-related part of strategies, $\{x_{\mathrm{III}}^j\}_{j \in S}$. Let w^j denote j's wage (a component of x_{III}^j). Not all strategies $\{x^S \in X^S \mid x_{\mathrm{II}}^i = x_{\mathrm{II}}^j (=: x_{\mathrm{II}}^{(S)})$ for all $i, j \in S\}$ are feasible to firm S. The cost of marketed inputs plus the wage payment cannot exceed the revenue from marketed outputs today, so

$$\sum_{j \in S} w^j \leqslant \bar{p} \cdot x_{\mathrm{II}}^{(S)}.$$

Once agent j agrees to his wage w^j in his firm S, his income level today is determined as $w^j + \bar{p} \cdot \omega^j$. He demands a marketed-commodity bundle x_{I}^j in the l markets subject to his budget constraint,

$$\bar{p} \cdot x_{\mathrm{I}}^j \leqslant w^j + \bar{p} \cdot \omega^j,$$

by himself (i.e., noncooperatively) as a consumer.

Agent j forms his subjective probability on his future consumption. This subjective probability is considered feasible when it is reasonably formed as follows: Firm S's future-wage policy (which takes into account its future outputs and hence its future revenue, given today's inputs) and the "externalities" $\bar{x}^{N \setminus S}$ $(:= \{\bar{x}^j\}_{j \in N \setminus S})$ determine the subjective probability on j's future income level. Here, the precise nature of the "externalities" will be made explicit for the special case of capitalistic version in Section 3.2. Each possible pair of future income level and future commodity price vector determines the set of possible future commodity bundles (the budget set in the future). Since only a subjective probability on the future incomes and future prices is given, one obtains the set of possible probabilities on future consumption.

The constraints specified in the preceding three paragraphs are summarized by the *feasible-strategy set* $F^S(\bar{x}, \bar{p}, \bar{\mathcal{T}})$ $(\subset X^S)$. This set depends not only on $\bar{p}$ but also on $\bar{x}^{N \setminus S}$, because of the "externalities" that influence the reasonableness of the subjective probabilities on future consumption. To re-state some of these constraints, each $x^S \in F^S(\bar{x}, \bar{p}, \bar{\mathcal{T}})$ has to satisfy

$$x_{\mathrm{II}}^i = x_{\mathrm{II}}^j =: x_{\mathrm{II}}^{(S)}, \text{ for all } i, j \in S,$$

and (by summing up all the budget constraints)

$$\bar{p} \cdot \sum_{j \in S} x_{\mathrm{I}}^j \leqslant \bar{p} \cdot x_{\mathrm{II}}^{(S)} + \bar{p} \cdot \sum_{j \in S} \omega^j.$$

The following condition is weaker than the family of budget constraints obtained by varying coalitions S in a coalition structure, and is called *Walras' law*: For every $(\bar{x}, \bar{p}, \bar{\mathcal{T}}) \in X \times \Delta^{l-1} \times \mathcal{T}$, for every admissible coalition structure $\mathcal{T} \in \mathcal{T}$, and for every strategy bundle x for which $x^T \in F^T(\bar{x}, \bar{p}, \bar{\mathcal{T}})$ for all $T \in \mathcal{T}$, it follows that

$$\bar{p} \cdot \sum_{j \in N} x_{\mathrm{I}}^j \leqslant \bar{p} \cdot \sum_{T \in \mathcal{T}} x_{\mathrm{II}}^{(T)} + \bar{p} \cdot \sum_{j \in N} \omega^j.$$

Denote by $\mathrm{gr}F^S$ the graph of the correspondence F^S: $X \times \Delta^{l-1} \times \mathcal{T} \rightarrow X^S$;

$$\mathrm{gr}F^S := \{(\bar{x}, \bar{p}, \bar{\mathcal{T}}, x^S) \in X \times \Delta^{l-1} \times \mathcal{T} \times X^S \mid x^S \in F^S(\bar{x}, \bar{p}, \bar{\mathcal{T}})\}.$$

For each member j of S, his utility function u_S^j: $\mathrm{gr}F^S \rightarrow \mathbf{R}$ is given. Here, the dependence of the utility function on S reflects the possible fact that the members in S enjoy the environment (i.e., non-strategic elements) specific to S.

Example 3.1.3. Consider the strategy sets $\{X^j\}_{j \in N}$ of Example 3.1.2. Each x_{III}^j is denoted by (L^j, w^j, μ^j). The utility of j is determined by the list $(x_{\mathrm{I}}^j, L^j, \mu^j)$, that is, there exists a function u^j: $\mathbf{R}^l \times \mathbf{R}^k \times \mathcal{M}(\mathbf{R}^m) \rightarrow \mathbf{R}$ such that

$$u_S^j(\bar{x}, \bar{p}, \bar{\mathcal{T}}, x^S) = u^j(x_{\mathrm{I}}^j, L^j, \mu^j). \ \square$$

Definition 3.1.4. An *economy* is a list of specified data, $\mathcal{E} := (\{X^j, \omega^j\}_{j \in N}, \{F^S(\cdot)\}_{S \in \mathcal{N}}, \{u_S^j(\cdot)\}_{j \in S \in \mathcal{N}}, \mathcal{T})$, of the strategy spaces, the initial endowment vectors, the feasible-strategy correspondences, the utility functions and the admissible coalition structures, such that $[x^S \in F^S(\bar{x}, \bar{p}, \bar{\mathcal{T}})]$ implies $[x_{\mathrm{II}}^i = x_{\mathrm{II}}^j =: x_{\mathrm{II}}^{(S)}$, for all $i, j \in S]$, and such that Walras' law holds true.

In economy $\mathcal{E}$ the two resource allocation mechanisms work in the following way: Given $(\bar{x}, \bar{p}, \bar{\mathcal{T}})$, the agents play a nation-wide cooperative game; this changes the strategical part $(\bar{x}, \bar{\mathcal{T}})$ of $(\bar{x}, \bar{p}, \bar{\mathcal{T}})$ in disequilibrium. At the same time, given $(\bar{x}, \bar{p}, \bar{\mathcal{T}})$, the market mechanism works in the spot commodity markets; this changes the price vector $\bar{p}$ of $(\bar{x}, \bar{p}, \bar{\mathcal{T}})$ in disequilibrium. An equilibrium $(x^*, p^*, \mathcal{T}^*)$ is achieved (formulated as the feasibility condition (i) of the following Definition 3.1.5), in which no coalition as a price-taker can bring about by its own effort a higher utility level to each of its members, and specifically no coalition has an incentive to change the strategies (formulated as the coalitional stability condition (ii)), and all the l commodity markets are cleared (formulated as the market clearance condition (iii)).

Definition 3.1.5. An *equilibrium* of economy $\mathcal{E}$ is a triple $(x^*, p^*, \mathcal{T}^*)$ of members of X, Δ^{l-1}, $\mathcal{T}$, respectively, such that:

(i) $x^{*T} \in F^T(x^*, p^*, \mathcal{T}^*)$ for every $T \in \mathcal{T}^*$;
(ii) it is not true that there exist $S \in \mathcal{N}$ and $x^S \in F^S(x^*, p^*, \mathcal{T}^*)$ such that $u^j_S(x^*, p^*, \mathcal{T}^*, x^S) > u^j_{T(j)}(x^*, p^*, \mathcal{T}^*, x^{*T(j)})$ for every $j \in S$, where $T(j)$ is the unique member of $\mathcal{T}^*$ such that $T(j) \ni j$; and
(iii) $\sum_{j \in N} x^{*j}_{\mathrm{I}} \leqslant \sum_{T \in \mathcal{T}^*} x^{*(T)}_{\mathrm{II}} + \sum_{j \in N} \omega^j$.

The equilibrium concept is thus a hybrid of the strong equilibrium (see Section 2.3) and the competitive market equilibrium. In particular, for each agent j, the types and quantity of labor he supplies and the wage he receives (components of x^{*j}_{III}) are determined as a result of the cooperative game. The non-human investment made in a realized coalition, $x^{*(T)}_{\mathrm{II}}$, $T \in \mathcal{T}^*$, may well be firm-specific in that it is good for the firm T (as T has no incentive to revise this investment) but not for other firms, realized or potential.

One might wish to weaken the equilibrium condition (ii) so that the only possible blocking coalitions are those *admissible* S for which there exists an admissible coalition structure $\mathcal{T}$ such that $S \in \mathcal{T}$. Formally this does not change the model; for a non-admissible coalition T, one simply defines $F^T(\bar{x}, \bar{p}, \bar{\mathcal{T}})$ so that the utility level $u^j_T(\bar{x}, \bar{p}, \bar{\mathcal{T}}, x^T)$ is sufficiently small (like $-\infty$) for each $x^T \in F^T(\bar{x}, \bar{p}, \bar{\mathcal{T}})$ and each $j \in T$. One might also wish that the admissible coalitions be small. This does not change the model either, since $\mathcal{T}$ is arbitrarily given.

Example 3.1.6. A deterministic economy with l marketed commodities and k types of non-marketed labor today, a finite set N of economic agents, and no trade in the future: Each agent j has his consumption set $C^j \subset \mathbf{R}^l \times (-\mathbf{R}^k_+)$, whose generic element is denoted by (x^j_{I}, L^j). The intended interpretation is that j consumes marketed commodity bundle x^j_{I} and supplies non-marketed labor bundle $-L^j$ today. His preference relation defined on C^j is represented by a utility function u^j: $C^j \rightarrow \mathbf{R}$. He has an initial endowment of marketed commodities $\omega^j \in \mathbf{R}^l$. Each coalition as a potential firm $S \in \mathcal{N} := 2^N \setminus \{\phi\}$ has its production set $Y(S) \subset \mathbf{R}^l \times (-\mathbf{R}^k_+)$, whose generic element is denoted by $(x^{(S)}_{\mathrm{II}}, L^{(S)})$. The intended interpretation is that firm S chooses an input-output vector $(x^{(S)}_{\mathrm{II}}, L^{(S)})$ today. The set $Y(S)$ is the set of all technologically feasible input-output vectors. A family of admissible coalition structures $\mathcal{T}$ is given *a priori*. The associated economy $\mathscr{E} := (\{X^j, \omega^j\}_{j \in N}, \{F^S(\cdot)\}_{S \in \mathcal{N}}, \{u^j_S(\cdot)\}_{j \in S \in \mathcal{N}}, \mathcal{T})$ is constructed as follows: For each j, X^j is defined as a subset of $\mathbf{R}^l \times \mathbf{R}^l \times E^j$, where E^j is the labor-wage space, $\mathbf{R}^k \times \mathbf{R}$. A generic element of X^j is denoted by $x^j := (x^j_{\mathrm{I}}, x^j_{\mathrm{II}}, L^j, w^j)$. The initial endowment vectors $\{\omega^j\}_{j \in N}$ and the admissible coalition structures $\mathcal{T}$ are already given here, and the utility functions $\{u^j_S(\cdot)\}_{j \in S \in \mathcal{N}}$ are defined by $u^j_S(\bar{x}, \bar{p}, x^S) := u^j(x^j_{\mathrm{I}}, L^j)$. The feasible-strategy correspondences F^S: $X \times \Delta^{l-1} \rightarrow X^S$ are defined by: $x^S \in F^S(\bar{x}, \bar{p})$, iff

$$\forall j \in S: (x_{\rm I}^j, L^j) \in C^j \text{ and } \bar{p}\cdot x_{\rm I}^j \leqslant w^j + \bar{p}\cdot\omega^j;$$
$$\forall j, j' \in S: x_{\rm II}^j = x_{\rm II}^{j'} \,(=: x_{\rm II}^{(S)});$$
$$\sum_{j\in S} w^j \leqslant \bar{p}\cdot x_{\rm II}^{(S)}; \text{ and}$$
$$(x_{\rm II}^{(S)}, \sum_{j\in S} L^j) \in Y(S).$$

The economy and equilibrium concept of the present section were first proposed in this specific context by Ichiishi (1975). This deterministic context cannot describe any capitalistic economy, however, because in the latter investment in capital (i.e., stockholding) is made with the speculative motive, which presupposes uncertainty about the future. □

Example 3.1.7. An economy with l marketed commodities and k types of non-marketed labor today, m commodities in the future, and a finite set N of economic agents: Each agent j has his consumption set $C^j \subset \mathbf{R}^l \times (-\mathbf{R}_+^k) \times \mathscr{M}(\mathbf{R}^m)$, whose generic element is denoted by $(x_{\rm I}^j, L^j, \mu^j)$. The intended interpretation is that j consumes marketed commodity bundle $x_{\rm I}^j$ and supplies non-marketed labor bundle $-L^j$ today, and that he has a subjective probability μ^j on future consumption of commodities. His preference relation defined on C^j is represented by a utility function u^j: $C^j \to \mathbf{R}$; see Examples 3.1.2 and 3.1.3. He also has an initial endowment of marketed commodities $\omega^j \in \mathbf{R}^l$. Each coalition as a potential firm $S \in \mathscr{N} := 2^N \setminus \{\phi\}$ has its production set $Y(S) \subset \mathbf{R}^l \times (-\mathbf{R}_+^k) \times [\mathscr{M}(\mathbf{R}^k)]^S$, whose generic element is denoted by $(x_{\rm II}^{(S)}, L^{(S)}, \{\nu^j\}_{j\in S})$. The intended interpretation is that firm S chooses an input-output vector $(x_{\rm II}^{(S)}, L^{(S)})$ today, and this activity also yields an output vector in the future, the subjective probability of which is given by ν^j, $j \in S$. When today's input-output vector is technologically feasible and each subjective probability on future outputs is reasonable, $(x_{\rm II}^{(S)}, L^{(S)}, \{\nu^j\}_{j\in S}) \in Y(S)$. A family of admissible coalition structures $\mathscr{T}$ is given *a priori*. The associated economy $\mathscr{E} := (\{X^j, \omega^j\}_{j\in N}, \{F^S(\cdot)\}_{S\in\mathscr{N}}, \{u_S^j(\cdot)\}_{j\in S\in\mathscr{N}}, \mathscr{T})$ is constructed as follows: For each j, X^j is defined as a subset of $\mathbf{R}^l \times \mathbf{R}^l \times E^j$, where $E^j := \mathbf{R}^k \times \mathbf{R} \times \mathscr{M}(\mathbf{R}^m)$ (Example 3.1.2), such that the projection of X^j to the appropriate subspace $\mathbf{R}^l \times (-\mathbf{R}_+^k) \times \mathscr{M}(\mathbf{R}^m)$ contains C^j, and the projection of X^j to another appropriate subspace $\mathbf{R}^l \times (-\mathbf{R}_+^k)$ contains the corresponding projection of $Y(S)$ for all S for which $S \ni j$. The initial endowment vectors $\{\omega^j\}_{j\in N}$ and the admissible coalition structures $\mathscr{T}$ are already given here, and the utility functions $\{u_S^j(\cdot)\}_{j\in S\in\mathscr{N}}$ are defined as in Example 3.1.3. The feasible-strategy correspondences F^S: $X \times \Delta^{l-1} \to X^S$ is defined by: $x^S \in F^S(\bar{x}, \bar{p})$, iff

$$\forall j \in S: (x_{\rm I}^j, L^j, \mu^j) \in C^j \text{ and } \bar{p}\cdot x_{\rm I}^j \leqslant w^j + \bar{p}\cdot\omega^j;$$
$$\forall j, j' \in S: x_{\rm II}^j = x_{\rm II}^{j'} \,(=: x_{\rm II}^{(S)});$$
$$\sum_{j\in S} w^j \leqslant \bar{p}\cdot x_{\rm II}^{(S)}; \text{ and}$$

$$\exists \{\nu^j\}_{j\in S}\in[\mathscr{M}(\mathbf{R}^m)]^S\colon (x_{\mathrm{II}}^{(S)}, \sum_{j\in S} L^j, \{\nu^j\}_{j\in S})\in Y(S), \text{ and}$$
$$\{\mu^j\}_{j\in S} \text{ and } \{\nu^j\}_{j\in S} \text{ are compatible.}$$

Here, $\{\mu^j\}_{j\in S}$ and $\{\nu^j\}_{j\in S}$ are *compatible*, if each agent j expects that his future consumption is described by probability μ^j, based on his firm's future-production probability ν^j, firm's future-wage policy and the "externalities, $\bar{x}^{N\setminus S}$" (the precise nature of "externalities" for the capitalistic version requires the discussion of Section 3.2). □

Remark 3.1.8. It should be emphasized that the cooperative *behavior* is not restricted to narrowly defined "cooperative" decision-making *rules* such as the unanimity or majority decision rule and decision rules in workers' profit-sharing cooperatives. While the cooperative behavior is consistent with these "cooperative" decision rules on the one hand, it is certainly consistent on the other hand with the top-down decision-making rule given a hierarchical structure of a firm. Suppose that the executives of Firm A (i.e., those at the top of the firm's hierarchy) decide on the wage structure of the firm, and that some workers at the bottom of the hierarchy do not like their wage levels. Those workers may quit and find jobs in other firms, or may even establish their own firm. In this case, new coalitions of laborers are formed, and the decision on wage structure in Firm A turns out to be coalitionally unstable. If the workers' grievance reaches their executives, say with a strike or with a threat of mass resignation, an alternative decision on wages in Firm A may be made. In this case, no new coalitions of laborers are formed, but the original decision turns out to be infeasible or coalitionally unstable. If those workers cannot improve their working conditions in Firm A with their own power, nor can find better jobs or establish a new firm, they have no choice but to accept their wages in Firm A. In this case, no new coalitions of laborers are formed, and the decision is enforced in Firm A (the aggrieved workers coordinate their strategies favorably with the executives' decision, having no effective objections), so it is coalitionally stable. □

The descriptive cooperative game outlined in this section can be one explicit interpretation of the Coasian human-resource allocation mechanism that replaces the neoclassical labor market. Indeed, this is the interpretation adopted here. While planning on coordination of strategies, the laborers in a firm (managers and workers) can process information and come up with a labor allocation which might be Pareto superior to the one that would be made through a labor market with incomplete information. Notice that information processing is not modelled here, but its consequence is summarized by the feasible-strategy set $F^S(x, p, \mathscr{T})$.

In reality a laborer bargains individually or collectively for his wage with each potential coalition, knowing the current strategies (in particular, the prevailing wages) chosen in the existing coalitions, and conversely each coalition bargains with a possible joiner for his wage having similar knowledge about the others' strategies. This cooperative decision-making process can be costly, yet it has been put into practice, providing the information needed for production activities. The perfect information on the labor market postulated in the neoclassical paradigm has never been experienced in reality.

Remark 3.1.9. The information needed for the cooperative behavior can be kept minimal, contrary to the common misconception. To illustrate this point, consider Firm S that adopts the top-down decision-making rule (Remark 3.1.8), and its member j at the bottom of the hierarchy. Assume $E^j = \mathbf{R}^k \times \mathbf{R} \times \mathrm{ca}(\mathbf{R}^m)$, and $u^j_S(\bar{x}, \bar{p}, \bar{\mathcal{T}}, x^S) = u^j(x^j_{\mathrm{I}}, L^j, \mu^j)$ (Example 3.1.3). Then he does not care about his firm's marketed input-output vector $x^{(S)}_{\mathrm{II}}$ nor about his colleagues' strategies $\{x^i\}_{i \in S \setminus \{j\}}$, let alone his colleagues' preference relations $\{u^i\}_{i \in S \setminus \{j\}}$. Suppose the executives of S decide to enforce $(\hat{x}^{(S)}_{\mathrm{II}}, \{(\hat{L}^i, \hat{w}^i, \hat{\mu}^i)\}_{i \in S})$, but they tell agent j only j's work condition $(\hat{L}^j, \hat{w}^j, \hat{\mu}^j)$. As long as j and any other agents have no power to improve upon this decision by forming a new coalition, j has to accept it. (Here, agent j takes into account a variety of forms as his new potential coalition – e.g., the other agents may constitute an existing firm whose executives are trying to hire j, or j may play an entrepreneurial role in establishing a new firm, etc.) His acceptance means that he stays in S and chooses x^j so that $L^j = \hat{L}^j$, $w^j = \hat{w}^j$, $\mu^j = \hat{\mu}^j$ without knowing his colleagues' work conditions. The dummy part of j's strategy, x^j_{II}, is automatically set equal to $\hat{x}^{(S)}_{\mathrm{II}}$ even without j's knowing $\hat{x}^{(S)}_{\mathrm{II}}$ upon his acceptance of the executives's decision. To use the terminology of the extensive game, agent j has the information set which consists of the vertices, each specifying $(x^{(S)}_{\mathrm{II}}, \{L^i, w^i, \mu^i\}_{i \in S})$ such that $(L^j, w^j, \mu^j) = (\hat{L}^j, \hat{w}^j, \hat{\mu}^j)$, and his choice at this information set is either acceptance or blocking. If he chooses acceptance, the edge that specifies $(\hat{x}^{(S)}_{\mathrm{II}}, \{(\hat{L}^i, \hat{w}^i, \hat{\mu}^i)\}_{i \in S})$ will be realized. He can choose blocking either singly or jointly with other agents (acting singly is a special case of acting jointly). This illustration also shows that the cooperative behavioral principle encompasses the noncooperative behavioral principle.

The point of this remark is that what an economic agent needs to know to be able to act is minimal. An economic analyst as the third person would need to know virtually all the exogenous data (economy) in order to compute the endogenously determined value (equilibrium), but this is not an agent's concern. The same point is well-known in regard to the neoclassical paradigm: Each consumer can be myopic in that he needs to know only the prevailing price vector. He is not concerned with whether the observed price vector is in equilibrium or not; indeed, he does not even need to know the total demand or the total supply of a commodity. The competitive equilibrium is well-defined. It is considered a robust social outcome of the market mechanism in the neoclassical paradigm, because the dynamic theory of disequilibrium process (like the *tâtonnement* process) establishes that the sequence of strategy bundles chosen by the myopic behavior converges to the competitive allocation. Likewise, the equilibrium (Definition 3.1.5) of the present model (Definition 3.1.4) is well-defined. To confirm the view that this equilibrium is indeed the social outcome of the mechanisms embodied in the model, an economic theorist needs to develop a theory of disequilibrium process of coalition formation – this task is, however, beyond the scope of this monograph. □

3.2 Capitalistic version versus socialistic version

In the basic economic model constructed in the preceding section (Definition 3.1.4), while management of a firm was formulated as its laborers' strategy-choice in the cooperative game, ownership of a firm was not defined yet. The purpose of this section is to introduce into the model two concepts of ownership. The two specialized models obtained this way describe the present-day capitalistic economy (e.g., the US economy) and a certain socialistic economy (i.e., the Yugoslav model of market-cooperative socialism), respectively. The capitalistic model will be specified first.

The notation for the basic model of Section 3.1 is also adopted throughout this section. In the capitalistic economy there are m marketed physical commodities and services; denote by M the index set for these m commodities. Besides the market for each commodity in M, there are stock markets. Since there are $2^n - 1 (= \# \mathcal{N})$ potential firms, each having the potential to issue its own stock, there are $2^n - 1$ types of stocks. All stocks are traded in the perfectly competitive spot markets. The economy has, therefore, $l = m + (2^n - 1)$ markets, indexed by $h \in M \cup \mathcal{N}$. Commodity $h \in M$ is a marketed physical commodity or service, and commodity $h \in \mathcal{N}$ is the stock of firm h.

Suppose $(\bar{x}, \bar{p}, \bar{\mathcal{T}}) \in X \times \Delta^{l-1} \times \mathcal{T}$ prevails at the outset, and firm S is going to form and choose its strategy $x^S \in F^S(\bar{x}, \bar{p}, \bar{\mathcal{T}})$. The firm's only output today is its own stock. Indeed, in order to run the firm S, funds are raised first through the stock market, and these funds in the total value of $\bar{p}_S x^{(S)}_{\mathrm{II},S}$, listed as liabilities in the balance sheet, are used to pay wages and buy marketed inputs today. Of the input bundle, the physical commodities and services $(\{x^{(S)}_{\mathrm{II},h}\}_{h \in M})$ and labor (a part of $\{x^j_{\mathrm{III}}\}_{j \in S}$) are used to produce future outputs (random variable). The other component of the input bundle is firm's portfolio, $\{x^{(S)}_{\mathrm{II},T}\}_{T \in \mathcal{N} \setminus \{S\}}$, listed as assets in the balance sheet; they will yield returns in the future (random variable). It is also postulated that no firm owns any commodity as its initial endowment. Thus, $x^{(S)}_{\mathrm{II},S} \geqslant 0$, and

$x^{(S)}_{\mathrm{II},h} \leqslant 0$ for all $h \in M \cup \mathscr{N} \backslash \{S\}$. The firm's budget constraint may be rewritten in more detail as:

$$\sum_{h\in M} \bar{p}_h(-x^{(S)}_{\mathrm{II},h}) + \sum_{T\in \mathscr{N}\backslash\{S\}} \bar{p}_T(-x^{(S)}_{\mathrm{II},T}) + \sum_{j\in S} w^j \leqslant \bar{p}_S x^{(S)}_{\mathrm{II},S},$$

where the first term (the second term, the third term, resp.) in the left-hand side is the cost of marketed commodities and services (the market value of portfolio, the wage payment, resp.).

The owners of firm S are defined as the holders of stock S. In the future, the market value of the outputs and the dividend on (the firm's) portfolio constitute the firm's revenue, and all the revenue will be distributed in part to the laborers as future wages (random variable) and in part to the firm's owners as dividend (random variable). Stocks are, therefore, held with the speculative motive (see Keynes (1936, p. 170)). From the viewpoint of agent j in S, his own portfolio $\{x^j_{\mathrm{I},T}\}_{T\in\mathscr{N}}$ will bring in a dividend in the future. This dividend is determined by the stockholding structures as described by ($\bar{x}$, x^S), as well as by the performance of the firms. His future income level (random variable) thus depends upon $\bar{x}^{N\backslash S}$, and this dependence was called in Section 3.1 the "externalities" to the feasible subjective probabilities on his future consumption.

The type of firm-control situation modelled here is the *management control*, i.e., control of a firm by its managers (certain laborers). Indeed, the model describes the present-day capitalistic economy, where "ownership of wealth without appreciable control and control of wealth without appreciable ownership" (Berle and Means (1932, p. 66)) are observed. Stockowners without appreciable control can no longer order their firm to maximize its profit. There is no real-valued objective function of a firm either, since a firm is subject to conflict among those laborers with varying degrees of power. Thus, the present model bypasses any concept of *individual* firm equilibrium, and uses directly a *general* equilibrium concept of the n person game.

Definition 3.2.1. A *capitalistic economy* $\mathscr{E}_c$ is an economy $\mathscr{E}$ (Definition 3.1.4), such that the l marketed commodities are m marketed physical commodities and services and $(2^n - 1)$ marketed stocks (commodity $h \in M$ is a physical commodity or service, and commodity $S \in \mathscr{N}$ is the stock of firm S), and $[x^S \in F^S(\bar{x}, \bar{p}, \bar{\mathscr{T}})]$ further implies $[x^{(S)}_{\mathrm{II},S} \geqslant 0$, and $x^{(S)}_{\mathrm{II},h} \leqslant 0$ for all $h \in M \cup \mathscr{N} \backslash \{S\}]$.

The same equilibrium concept as in the preceding section (Definition 3.1.5) is adopted for the capitalistic economy. Let $(x^*, p^*, \mathscr{T}^*)$ be an equilibrium of a capitalistic economy $\mathscr{E}_c$, and choose any $j \in N$ and $T \in \mathscr{T}^*$. Then agent j's *relative share* in firm T is defined as

$$\theta^*_{jT} := x^{*j}_{\mathrm{I},T} / x^{*(T)}_{\mathrm{II},T},$$

where (assuming that the stock market clearance condition is satisfied with equality)

$$x^{*(T)}_{\mathrm{II},T} = \sum_{i\in N} x^{*i}_{\mathrm{I},T} + \sum_{S\in\mathcal{T}^*\setminus\{T\}} (-x^{*(S)}_{\mathrm{II},T}).$$

It was pointed out in Section 1.4 that both the Schumpeterian entrepreneur and the Knightian entrepreneur are defined based on the assumption of inseparability of ownership and control, and that the two definitions differ only in the exact content of the risk undertaken. The former takes the risk of technological uncertainty and the latter takes the risk of stockholding. For either definition, the entrepreneur's incentive to do his job is the residual he can claim (of course, the "residual" is defined slightly differently in the two types). In all the traditional economics literature, the firms were decision units given *a priori* to the models, and the entrepreneurial activities were considered to represent the firm activities. Much of the analysis of the firm activities, therefore, has been centered around the workings of the entrepreneurship. In the present model of the capitalistic economy, however, a firm is endogenously formed, there is no Schumpeterian entrepreneur (the technological knowledge is *a priori* given), and there is no Knightian entrepreneur either (stockholders are no longer effective decision-makers of their firm). The laborers, in particular, those laborers who supply managerial labor, play the role of entrepreneur here with varying degrees of responsibility. The propelling force of the firm is the maximization of the utility of every laborer (therefore, a firm consisting of r laborers has r conflicting objective functions), each of whom is so competitive as to seek the advantages that will be derived from coordinating his strategy with other members. The entrepreneurship defined this way makes sense only given the separation of ownership and control.

Remark 3.2.2. The take-overs issue may be understood as follows. Firm A can buy up Firm B basically in three ways: A purchases B's stock, by (1) using the existing asset of A, or (2) issuing new junk bond, or (3) issuing new equity. In all three cases, the purchased B's stock becomes a part of A's asset. The stockholders of A (new owners of B) cannot, however, manage this part of A's asset. The managers of A extend their control to B due to this asset, and possibly dismiss some managers of B. Denote by S the set of laborers who have been working for A; by T the set of laborers who have been working for B; and by T_0 the set of those dismissed managers of B. Before the take-overs there were two coalitions, S identified with Firm A, and T identified with Firm B. After the take-overs the new coalition of laborers $S \cup (T\setminus T_0)$ is formed, and is called Firm A. Coalition T_0 could not prevent formation of this new firm. □

The rest of this section will specify a socialistic model. Section 1.3 presented Brus' (1981) categorization of the socialistic economies. The category of the market-cooperative socialism, in which all the three levels are decentralized (the fundamental national level, the firm level, and the household level), will be studied here. There is no stock, nor stockholders who would own a firm. The assets in a firm of this economy are legally conceived as *social property*, but are in effect owned by nobody. Jan Vanek (1972, Ch. 4) reports:

In the case of existing enterprises, this meant that such means or funds which were actually at their disposal were entrusted for management to the work collectivity at various times. As regards new enterprises, the assets are supplied by the founder, normally as a repayable grant under contract. They are formally taken over by the newly elected workers' council when the enterprise is ready to start productive operation (p. 90).

The "initial stage" of the idealized market-cooperative socialism is, therefore, the economy in which no firms have accumulated their assets as social properties, and in which laborers come together to manage their new firms, some as founders bringing their own non-human resources, and trade non-human inputs and outputs through the neoclassical markets. This is the economy that is being modelled here as the socialistic economy. Another interpretation of the economy modelled here is the possible future of the market-cooperative socialism upon completion of the privatization process. The point is that social properties are excluded from the present model. As in the capitalistic economy (Definition 3.2.1), it is postulated that it takes a firm one period to produce outputs. Funds for operating firm S today are, therefore, collected from its members in the form of negative wages. The socialistic economy so defined may be considered a special case of the capitalistic economy in which firms have no access to the capital markets. In a nutshell, while stock in the capitalistic economy serves as a channel for the redistribution of funds, there is no such mechanism in this socialistic economy. A welfare implication of this difference will be established in Section 4.2. The following two formal definitions are made in such a way as to facilitate comparison of the capitalistic economy and the socialistic economy.

Definition 3.2.3. A *socialistic economy* $\mathscr{E}_s$ is an economy $\mathscr{E}$ (Definition 3.1.4), such that the l marketed commodities are m marketed physical commodities and services (indexed by $h \in M$) and $(2^n - 1)$ marketed "commodities" (indexed by $S \in \mathcal{N}$), $\omega_S^j = 0$ for all $j \in N$ and all $S \in \mathcal{N}$, and $[x^S \in F^S(\bar{x}, \bar{p}, \bar{\mathscr{T}})]$ further implies $[x_{\mathrm{II},h}^{(S)} \leqslant 0$ for all $h \in M$, and $x_{\mathrm{II},T}^{(S)} = 0$ for all $T \in \mathcal{N}]$.

Definition 3.2.4. A socialistic economy $(\{\tilde{X}^j, \tilde{\omega}^j\}_{j \in N}, \{\tilde{F}^S(\cdot)\}_{S \in \mathcal{N}},$

$\{\tilde{u}^j_S(\cdot)\}_{j\in S\in\mathcal{N}}, \tilde{\mathcal{T}})$ is *associated with* a capitalistic economy $(\{X^j, \omega^j\}_{j\in N}, \{F^S(\cdot)\}_{S\in\mathcal{N}}, \{u^j_S(\cdot)\}_{j\in S\in\mathcal{N}}, \mathcal{T})$, if for all j and S,

$$\tilde{X}^j = X^j,\ \tilde{\omega}^j = \omega^j,\ \tilde{\mathcal{T}} = \mathcal{T},$$
$$\tilde{F}^S(\bar{x}, \bar{p}, \bar{\mathcal{T}}) = \{x^S \in F^S(\bar{x}, \bar{p}, \bar{\mathcal{T}}) \mid x^{(S)}_{\mathrm{II},T} = 0 \text{ for all } T \in \mathcal{N}\},$$
$$\tilde{u}^j_S = \text{the restriction of } u^j_S \text{ to } \mathrm{gr}\tilde{F}^S.$$

The same equilibrium concept as in the preceding section (Definition 3.1.5) is adopted for the socialistic economy. Here, the price domain Δ^{l-1} is replaced by its subface Δ^{m-1}.

Example 3.2.5. The simplest example of a socialistic economy might be the case obtained by further specializing Example 3.1.3, $(\{X^j, \omega^j, u^j\}_{j\in N}, \{G^S(\cdot)\}_{S\in\mathcal{N}}, \mathcal{T})$, in which (1) $m=1$ (so that one may set $M=\{c\}, p_c\equiv 1$); (2) labor supply does not enter the utility function (so that each laborer always supplies his maximal labor time to his firm); (3) there is no uncertainty in the future (so that the future consumption is completely determined as today's strategy, i.e., $[\mu^j \in \mathcal{M}(\mathbf{R})]$ is replaced by $[x^j_{\mathrm{III},c} \in \mathbf{R}]$); and (4) the technology of firm S is described by a production function, $g^S\colon \mathbf{R}_+ \to \mathbf{R}_+$. Observe $w^j = x^j_{\mathrm{I},c} - \omega^j_c$. Then, $G^S(\cdot)$ is the constant correspondence, $(\bar{x}, \bar{p}, \bar{\mathcal{T}}) \mapsto G^S$, given by

$$G^S = \left\{ x^S \in X^S \,\middle|\, \begin{array}{l} \sum_{j\in S} x^j_{\mathrm{I},c} + (-x^{(S)}_{\mathrm{II},c}) \leq \sum_{j\in S} \omega^j_c \\ \sum_{j\in S} x^j_{\mathrm{III},c} \leq g^S(-x^{(S)}_{\mathrm{II},c}) \end{array} \right\},$$

and the utility function $u^j(x^j_{\mathrm{I}}, L^j, \mu^j)$ may be re-defined as $u^j(x^j_{\mathrm{I},c}, x^j_{\mathrm{III},c})$. □

Remark 3.2.6. As is made explicit in Definition 3.2.3, the model does not allow for the presence of an initial endowment of assets that are not owned by individuals. Specifically, it does not allow for the presence of an initial endowment of social properties entrusted for management to the work collectivity. In the presence of social properties as an initial endowment, several economic issues would arise: (1) It amounts to an ownership dilution for existing assets, so removes all incentives to proper monitoring of managers. (2) Laborers, in particular those laborers close to retirement age, try to appropriate the returns of the social properties by paying themselves high wages, instead of investing in their firms. These issues are more appropriately studied in a multi-stage setup (rather than the two-period temporary equilibrium setup). Full analysis of an economy with social properties is yet to be given as a future research agenda. See also Example 2A.5 in the Appendix to Chapter 2. Ferfila (1991) contains historical and institutional accounts for the difficulties and failure of the collective management of social properties. □

Remark 3.2.7. The Mondragon cooperatives (see, e.g., Thomas and Logan (1982) for an account of its historical and institutional aspects) are examples of the firms in the capitalistic economy. The economic agents in these cooperatives *can* raise funds by issuing stock under the Spanish law, but they *choose* not to. That is, non-issuance of stock is their equilibrium strategy. □

3.3 Special cases

The purpose of this section is to clarify the conceptual contributions of the materials of Sections 3.1–3.2 to the existing general equilibrium literature. This will be done by presenting three economic or game-theoretical models along with solution concepts, and by showing that they are special cases of the basic model and equilibrium concept formulated in Section 3.1 (Definitions 3.1.4 and 3.1.5). The three models and solution concepts are: the pure exchange economy and the competitive equilibrium; the private ownership economy and the competitive equilibrium; and the non-side-payment game and the core.

The first model is the pure exchange economy. There are l commodities and n_c consumers. All l commodities are marketed, and the price domain is the unit simplex Δ^{l-1}. Denote by N_c the set of all consumers. Consumer i is characterized by the triple (X^i, u^i, ω^i) of his consumption set X^i, his utility function u^i, and his initial endowment vector ω^i. The *consumption set* X^i, a subset of $\mathbf{R}^l$, represents all the commodity bundles with which consumer i can physically survive, i.e., X^i signifies the "physical needs" of i. The *utility function* u^i: $X^i \to \mathbf{R}$ represents consumer i's preference relation on the commodity bundles. The *initial endowment vector* ω^i is a point of $\mathbf{R}^l$ and is interpreted as the commodity bundle consumer i holds initially.

Definition 3.3.1. A *pure exchange economy* is a list of specified data, $\mathscr{E}_{pe} := \{X^i, u^i, \omega^i\}_{i \in N_c}$, of the consumption sets, the utility functions and the initial endowment vectors.

In the pure exchange economy $\mathscr{E}_{pe}$ the market mechanism works in the following way: Each consumer is a price-taker. Given any $\bar{p} \in \Delta^{l-1}$, consumer i chooses a maximal element $x^{*i}(\bar{p}, \bar{p}\cdot\omega^i)$ of his budget set $\{x^i \in X^i \mid \bar{p}\cdot x^i \leqslant \bar{p}\cdot\omega^i\}$ with respect to u^i. The total excess demand is, therefore, $E(\bar{p}) := \sum_{i \in N_c}(x^{*i}(\bar{p}, \bar{p}\cdot\omega^i) - \omega^i)$. The price of commodity h then rises (falls, resp.) if $E_h(\bar{p}) > 0$ (<0, resp.). A competitive equilibrium price vector p^* is eventually established, at which $E(p^*) \leqslant \mathbf{0}$.

Definition 3.3.2. A *competitive equilibrium* of pure exchange economy $\mathscr{E}_{pe}$ is an (n_c+1)-triple $(\{x^{*i}\}_{i \in N_c}, p^*)$ of members of X^i's, Δ^{l-1}, respectively, such that

(i) $x^{*i} \in X^i$, $p^*\cdot x^{*i} \leqslant p^*\cdot\omega^i$ for every $i \in N_c$;

(ii) it is not true that there exist $i \in N_c$ and $x^i \in X^i$ satisfying $p^* \cdot x^i \leqslant p^* \cdot \omega^i$ such that $u^i(x^i) > u^i(x^{*i})$; and

(iii) $\sum_{i \in N_c} x^{*i} \leqslant \sum_{i \in N_c} \omega^i$.

To show that a pure exchange economy and its competitive equilibrium are a special case of the model/equilibrium of Section 3.1, let a pure exchange economy $\mathscr{E}_{pe} := \{X^i, u^i, \omega^i\}_{i \in N_c}$ be arbitrarily given, and construct the associated economy $\mathscr{E}$ as follows:

$N := N_c$,
strategy space of $j := X^j$,
initial endowment vector of $j := \omega^j$,
$F^{\{j\}}(\bar{x}, \bar{p}, \bar{\mathscr{T}}) := \{x^j \in X^j \mid \bar{p} \cdot x^j \leqslant \bar{p} \cdot \omega^j\}$,
$u^j_{\{j\}}(\bar{x}, \bar{p}, \bar{\mathscr{T}}, x^j) := u^j(x^j)$,
$F^S(\bar{x}, \bar{p}, \bar{\mathscr{T}}) :=$ arbitrary for all S for which $\# S \geqslant 2$,
$u^j_S(\bar{x}, \bar{p}, \bar{\mathscr{T}}, x^S) := -\infty$ for all S for which $\{j\} \subsetneqq S$,
$\mathscr{T} := \{$the finest coalition structure$\}$.

Here, the *finest coalition structure* is the partition of N into the singletons, $\{\{j\} \mid j \in N\}$. Agent j's strategy space is a subset of $\mathbf{R}^l$, rather than a subset of $\mathbf{R}^l \times \mathbf{R}^l \times E^j$. This does not cause any problem, however, since X^j is identified with $X^j \times \{\mathbf{0}\} \times \{\mathbf{0}\}$ $(\subset \mathbf{R}^l \times \mathbf{R}^l \times E^j)$. Then, it is straightforward to verify that (x^*, p^*, the finest coalition structure) is an equilibrium of $\mathscr{E}$, iff (x^*, p^*) is a competitive equilibrium of $\mathscr{E}_{pe}$.

The second model is the Arrow-Debreu model of the private ownership economy (Arrow and Debreu, 1954). There are l commodities, n_c consumers and n_f firms. All l commodities are marketed. Denote by N_c and N_f the set of all consumers and the set of all firms, respectively. Consumer i is characterized by his consumption set X^i $(\subset \mathbf{R}^l)$, his utility function u^i: $X^i \to \mathbf{R}$, and his initial endowment vector ω^i $(\in \mathbf{R}^l)$, as in the pure exchange economy. Firm j is characterized by its production set Y^j. The *production set* Y^j, a subset of $\mathbf{R}^l$, represents the technology of firm j, i.e., an input-output vector y^j is technologically feasible in firm j iff $y^j \in Y^j$. The usual sign convention for demand and supply is adopted, i.e., consumer i's demand for (supply of, resp.) a commodity is measured by a positive number (negative number, resp.), and firm j's supply of (demand for, resp.) a commodity is measured by a positive number (negative number, resp.). In particular, given a price vector $\bar{p}$, the profit made by an input-output vector y^j is the inner product $\bar{p} \cdot y^j$. The next and final ingredient characterizes the Arrow-Debreu model as the private ownership economy: The *relative shares*, $\{\theta_{ij}\}_{i \in N_c, j \in N_f}$, nonnegative real numbers indexed by $(i, j) \in N_c \times N_f$ such that $\sum_{i \in N_c} \theta_{ij} = 1$ for every $j \in N_f$, describe the stockholding structure;

consumer i in his capacity as a shareholder has the relative share θ_{ij} in firm j, so he receives $100 \times \theta_{ij}$ percent of j's profit as dividend.

The concept of relative shares presupposes the existence of stocks. The constancy of the relative shares as exogenous data, however, means that stocks are not traded.

Definition 3.3.3. A *private ownership economy* is a list of specified data, $\mathscr{E}_{po}:=(\{X^i, u^i, \omega^i\}_{i\in N_c}, \{Y^j\}_{j\in N_f}, \{\theta_{ij}\}_{i\in N_c, j\in N_f})$, of the consumption sets, the utility functions, the initial endowment vectors, the production sets and the relative shares.

In the private ownership economy $\mathscr{E}_{po}$ the owners (stockholders) control a firm. Suppose a price vector $\bar{p}\in\Delta^{l-1}$ prevails. If firm j chooses its input-output vector $y^j\in Y^j$ (hence realizes its profit $\bar{p}\cdot y^j$), then consumer i automatically receives the dividend $\theta_{ij}\bar{p}\cdot y^j$, which will constitute a part of i's income. Since i wants to receive as high a dividend as possible, and since θ_{ij} is a given constant, he orders firm j to make the maximal profit. Consumer i', another owner of the same firm j, receives the dividend of $\theta_{i'j}\bar{p}\cdot y^j$. Since $\theta_{i'j}$ is a given constant, he also orders firm j to make the maximal profit. Thus, all the owners unanimously order firm j to make the maximal profit. Let $y^{*j}(\bar{p})\in Y^j$ be a profit-maximizing input-output vector of firm j. Then, consumer i's income level is $I^i(\bar{p}):=\bar{p}\cdot\omega^i+\sum_{j\in N_f}\theta_{ij}\bar{p}\cdot y^{*j}(\bar{p})$. He chooses a maximal element $x^{*i}(\bar{p}, I^i(\bar{p}))$ of his budget set $\{x^i\in X^i \mid \bar{p}\cdot x^i\leqslant I^i(\bar{p})\}$ with respect to u^i. The total excess demand is, therefore,

$$E(\bar{p}):=\sum_{i\in N_c}(x^{*i}(\bar{p}, I^i(\bar{p}))-\omega^i)-\sum_{j\in N_f}y^{*j}(\bar{p}).$$

A competitive equilibrium price vector p^* is eventually established, at which $E(p^*)\leqslant\mathbf{0}$.

Definition 3.3.4. A *competitive equilibrium* of private ownership economy $\mathscr{E}_{po}$ is an (n_c+n_f+1)-triple $(\{x^{*i}\}_{i\in N_c}, \{y^{*j}\}_{j\in N_f}, p^*)$ of members of X^i's, Y^j's, Δ^{l-1}, respectively, such that

(i$_c$) $x^{*i}\in X^i$, $p^*\cdot x^{*i}\leqslant p^*\cdot\omega^i+\sum_{j\in N_f}\theta_{ij}p^*\cdot y^{*j}$ for every $i\in N_c$;

(i$_f$) $y^{*j}\in Y^j$ for every $j\in N_f$;

(ii$_c$) it is not true that there exist $i\in N_c$ and $x^i\in X^i$ satisfying $p^*\cdot x^i\leqslant p^*\cdot\omega^i+\sum_{j\in N_f}\theta_{ij}p^*\cdot y^{*j}$ such that $u^i(x^i)>u^i(x^{i*})$;

(ii$_f$) it is not true that there exist $j\in N_f$ and $y^j\in Y^j$ such that $p^*\cdot y^j>p^*\cdot y^{*j}$; and

(iii) $\sum_{i\in N_c}x^{*i}\leqslant\sum_{i\in N_c}\omega^i+\sum_{j\in N_f}y^{*j}$.

The private ownership economy fails to incorporate several basic issues of the theory of the firm. First, all the l commodities, including labor, are traded in the perfectly competitive markets. The market mechanism is the only resource allocation mechanism. What is missing here is a non-market human-resource allocation mechanism, which Coase (1937) emphasized as the nature of the firm. Indeed, the "firm" in the private ownership economy is not an organization of human-resource holders. Second, there is no separation of ownership (stockholding) and control (management). The private ownership economy is a specific model of the owner-managed market economy, which Berle and Means (1932) empirically refuted as not applicable to the present-day capitalistic economy. The third point, of which Arrow and Debreu (1954) were fully aware, is that the model does not encompass any of the socialistic economies.

To show that a private ownership economy and its competitive equilibrium are a special case of the model/equilibrium of Section 3.1, let a private ownership economy $\mathscr{E}_{po} := (\{X^i, u^i, \omega^i\}_{i\in N_c}, \{Y^j\}_{j\in N_f}, \{\theta_{ij}\}_{i\in N_c, j\in N_f})$ be arbitrarily given, and construct the associated economy $\mathscr{E}$ as follows:

$$N := N_c \cup N_f,$$
$$\text{strategy space of } k := \begin{cases} X^k \times \{\mathbf{0}\}, \text{ if } k \in N_c \\ \{\mathbf{0}\} \times Y^k, \text{ if } k \in N_f, \end{cases}$$
$$\text{initial endowment vector of } k := \begin{cases} \omega^k, \text{ if } k \in N_c \\ \{\mathbf{0}\}, \text{ if } k \in N_f, \end{cases}$$
$$F^{\{k\}}(\bar{x}, \bar{p}, \bar{\mathscr{T}}) := \begin{cases} \{(x^k, \mathbf{0}) \mid x^k \in X^k, \bar{p}\cdot x^k \leqslant I^k(\bar{p})\}, \text{ if } k \in N_c, \\ \{\mathbf{0}\} \times Y^k, \text{ if } k \in N_f, \end{cases}$$
$$u^k_{\{k\}}(\bar{x}, \bar{p}, \bar{\mathscr{T}}, x^k) := \begin{cases} u^k(x^k_{\mathrm{I}}), \text{ if } k \in N_c, \\ \bar{p}\cdot x^k_{\mathrm{II}}, \text{ if } k \in N_f, \end{cases}$$
$$F^S(\bar{x}, \bar{p}, \bar{\mathscr{T}}) := \text{arbitrary set in } (\mathbf{R}^l \times \mathbf{R}^l)^S \text{ for all } S \text{ for which } \#S \geqslant 2,$$
$$u^k_S(\bar{x}, \bar{p}, \bar{\mathscr{T}}, x^S) := -\infty \text{ for all } S \text{ for which } \{k\} \subsetneq S,$$
$$\mathscr{T} := \{\text{the finest coalition structure}\}.$$

Then, it is straightforward to verify that (x^*, p^*, the finest coalition structure) is an equilibrium of $\mathscr{E}$, iff (x^*, p^*) is a competitive equilibrium of $\mathscr{E}_{po}$.

The third model and its solution concept are the non-side-payment game and the core. Although they were given a systematic presentation in Section 2.2, the definitions will be reproduced here for completeness. Let N be given as the finite set of players, and hence let $\mathscr{N}$ $(:= 2^N \backslash \{\phi\})$ be given as the family of nonempty coalitions of players.

Definition 3.3.5. A *non-side-payment game* is a correspondence $V: \mathscr{N} \to \mathbf{R}^N$ such that $[u, v \in \mathbf{R}^N, \forall i \in S: u_i = v_i]$ implies $[u \in V(S)$ iff $v \in V(S)]$ for every $S \in \mathscr{N}$.

Definition 3.3.6. A utility allocation u^* is in the *core* of non-side-payment game V, if

(i) $u^* \in V(N)$; and
(ii) it is not true that there exist $S \in \mathcal{N}$ and $u \in V(S)$ such that for every $i \in S$, $u_i > u_i^*$.

To show that a non-side-payment game and a utility allocation in its core are a special case of the model/equilibrium of Section 3.1, let a non-side-payment game V be arbitrarily given, and construct the associated economy $\mathscr{E}$ as follows: Choose $X^j (\subset \mathbf{R})$ so that it contains all the attainable and individually rational utility levels of player j; i.e., if

$$u \in \bigcup_{S \in \mathcal{N}: S \ni j} V(S), \text{ and } u_j \geqslant \sup \{u_j' \in \mathbf{R} \mid u' \in \mathrm{V}(\{j\})\},$$

then $u_j \in X^j$. The set X^j is considered a subset of the space $E^j := \mathbf{R}$ in $\mathscr{E}$.

the player set: $= N$,
strategy space of j: $= X^j$, identified with $\{\mathbf{0}\} \times \{\mathbf{0}\} \times X^j$,
initial endowment vector of j: $= \mathbf{0}$,
$F^S(\bar{x}, \bar{p}, \bar{\mathscr{T}}) := \{x^S \in X^S \mid \exists\, r^{N \setminus S} \in \mathbf{R}^{N \setminus S} : (x^S, r^{N \setminus S}) \in V(S)\}$,
$u_S^j(\bar{x}, \bar{p}, \bar{\mathscr{T}}, x^S) := x^j$,
$\mathscr{T} := \{$the coarsest coalition structure$\}$.

Here, the *coarsest coalition structure* is the partition of N which consists only of the grand coalition N. Then, it is straightforward to verify that (x^*, p^*, the coarsest coalition structure) is an equilibrium of $\mathscr{E}$, iff x^* is a utility allocation in the core of V.

3.4 Equilibrium existence theorems

Two existence theorems for equilibria (Definition 3.1.5) of the economy (Definition 3.1.4) are presented here. The first theorem states conditions for the equilibrium existence in terms of the given data, $(\{X^j\}_{j \in N}, \{F^S\}_{S \in \mathcal{N}}, \{u_S^j\}_{j \in S \in \mathcal{N}}, \mathscr{T})$. The second theorem, which includes the first, states conditions in terms of the derivative concepts of parameterized non-side-payment games. The second theorem will be proved by applying a social coalitional equilibrium existence theorem. Also proved here as applications of the social coalitional equilibrium existence theorem are Scarf's (1967a) theorem for nonemptiness of the core of a non-side-payment game (Theorem 2.2.1), the strong equilibrium existence theorems for a normal-form game (Theorem 2.3.4) and for a society (Theorem 2.3.7), and Arrow and Debreu's (1954) competitive equilibrium existence theorem for a private ownership economy (see Definitions 3.3.3 and 3.3.4).

To prove the existence of equilibria (Definition 3.1.5), a weaker concept of equilibrium with transfer will first be introduced. Under mild assumptions an equilibrium with transfer is proved to be the required equilibrium

(Proposition 3.4.3). The main results (Theorems 3.4.4 and 3.4.6) actually establish the existence of an equilibrium with transfer.

An equilibrium with transfer is based on the extension of the feasible-strategy set concept $F^S(\bar{x}, \bar{p}, \bar{\mathscr{T}})$ to the *feasible-strategy set with transfer* $F_t^S(\bar{x}, \bar{p}, \bar{\mathscr{T}})$ given transfer of nominal value $t \in \mathbf{R}$ to coalition S. The intended interpretation is that $x^S \in F_t^S(\bar{x}, \bar{p}, \bar{\mathscr{T}})$ if strategy bundle x^S is feasible in S when the nominal value of S's initial endowment is $\sum_{j\in S} \bar{p}\cdot\omega^j + t$ instead of $\sum_{j\in S} \bar{p}\cdot\omega^j$. Therefore, such a feasible strategy bundle has to satisfy

$$x_{\mathrm{II}}^i = x_{\mathrm{II}}^j =: x_{\mathrm{II}}^{(S)}, \text{ for all } i, j \in S, \text{ and}$$
$$\bar{p}\cdot\sum_{j\in S} x_{\mathrm{I}}^j \leqslant \bar{p}\cdot x_{\mathrm{II}}^{(S)} + \bar{p}\cdot\sum_{j\in S}\omega^j + t.$$

The value t could be positive, zero, or negative. For a negative number t, $F_t^S(\bar{x}, \bar{p}, \bar{\mathscr{T}})$ could be the empty set. Conditions (i) and (ii) of the following Postulate 3.4.1 say that there is no secret deal, that is, no coalition can expect a larger future return by freely giving away today's asset.

Postulate 3.4.1.
(i) $F_0^S(\bar{x}, \bar{p}, \bar{\mathscr{T}}) = F^S(\bar{x}, \bar{p}, \bar{\mathscr{T}})$;
(ii) $F_s^S(\bar{x}, \bar{p}, \bar{\mathscr{T}}) \subset F_t^S(\bar{x}, \bar{p}, \bar{\mathscr{T}}) \subset X^S$, if $s < t$; and
(iii) For each $\{t_T\}_{T\in\mathscr{T}} \subset \mathbf{R}$ for which $\sum_T t_T = 0$, Walras' law holds true, that is, for every admissible coalition structure $\mathscr{T}$ and every strategy bundle x for which $x^T \in F_{t_T}^T(\bar{x}, \bar{p}, \bar{\mathscr{T}})$ for all $T \in \mathscr{T}$, it follows that $\bar{p}\cdot\sum_{j\in N} x_{\mathrm{I}}^j \leqslant \bar{p}\cdot\sum_{T\in\mathscr{T}} x_{\mathrm{II}}^{(T)} + \bar{p}\cdot\sum_{j\in N}\omega^j$.

Definition 3.4.2. Let $\mathscr{E}$ be an economy for which each utility function u_S^j: $\mathrm{gr}F^S \to \mathbf{R}$ is extended to $X \times X^S$. An *equilibrium with transfer* of $\mathscr{E}$ is a quadruple $(x^*, p^*, \mathscr{T}^*, \{t_T^*\}_{T\in\mathscr{T}^*})$ of members of X, Δ^{l-1} $\mathscr{T}$, $\prod_{\mathscr{T}^*}\mathbf{R}$, respectively, such that

(i′) $\sum_{T\in\mathscr{T}^*} t_T^* = 0$, $x^{*T} \in F_{t_T^*}^T(x^*, p^*, \mathscr{T}^*)$ for every $T \in \mathscr{T}^*$;

(ii) it is not true that there exist $S \in \mathscr{N}$ and $x^S \in F^S(x^*, p^*, \mathscr{T}^*)$ such that $u_S^j(x^*, p^*, \mathscr{T}^*, x^S) > u_{T(j)}^j(x^*, p^*, \mathscr{T}^*, x^{*T(j)})$ for every $j \in S$, where $T(j)$ is the unique member of $\mathscr{T}^*$ such that $T(j) \ni j$; and

(iii) $\sum_{j\in N} x_{\mathrm{I}}^{*j} \leqslant \sum_{T\in\mathscr{T}^*} x_{\mathrm{II}}^{*(T)} + \sum_{j\in N}\omega^j$.

Compared with the equilibrium concept (Definition 3.1.5), (1) the feasibility condition (i) is relaxed here to (i′) which assumes transfer among the realized coalitions, (2) but blocking coalitions cannot count on any transfer from outsiders, so the same stability condition (ii) is retained. Notice that transfer of commodities (hence transfer of their nominal values) is being made here, and not interpersonal transfer of utility levels. The present framework is different from the side-payment games introduced in Section 2.1; the latter is sometimes called the game with transferable utilities.

Proposition 3.4.3. *Let $\mathscr{E}$ be an economy (Definition 3.1.4) which allows no secret deal (Postulate 3.4.1). Assume that each utility function u_S^j: $\mathrm{gr}F^S \to \mathbf{R}$ is extended to $X \times X^S$, and that the following two conditions are satisfied:*

(i) *If $x^S \in F_t^S(\bar{x}, \bar{p}, \bar{\mathscr{T}})$ and $t<0$, then there exists $x'^S \in F^S(\bar{x}, \bar{p}, \bar{\mathscr{T}})$ such that $x_{\mathrm{I}}^j < x_{\mathrm{I}}'^j$, $x_{\mathrm{II}}^j = x_{\mathrm{II}}'^j$ and $x_{\mathrm{III}}^j = x_{\mathrm{III}}'^j$ for all $j \in S$; and*

(ii) *If $x_{\mathrm{I}}^j < x_{\mathrm{I}}'^j$, $x_{\mathrm{II}}^j = x_{\mathrm{II}}'^j$ and $x_{\mathrm{III}}^j = x_{\mathrm{III}}'^j$ for all $j \in S$, then $u_S^j(\bar{x}, \bar{p}, \bar{\mathscr{T}}, x^S) < u_S^j(\bar{x}, \bar{p}, \bar{\mathscr{T}}, x'^S)$.*

Then an equilibrium with transfer of $\mathscr{E}$ is an equilibrium of $\mathscr{E}$.

Condition (i) says that if a coalition has money to give away, then that money can be used by the members of the coalition to purchase marketed commodities for their personal consumption. Condition (ii) is a weak form of monotonicity of the preference relations.

Proof. Let $(x^*, p^*, \mathscr{T}^*, \{t_T^*\}_{T \in \mathscr{T}^*})$ be an equilibrium with transfer of the economy $\mathscr{E}$. One needs to show that $t_T^* = 0$ for all $T \in \mathscr{T}^*$. Suppose not. Then by the equilibrium (with transfer) condition (i′), there exists T for which $t_T^* < 0$. By the present assumptions (i) and (ii), there exists $x'^T \in F^T(x^*, p^*, \mathscr{T}^*)$ for which $u_T^j(x^*, p^*, \mathscr{T}^*, x'^T) > u_T^j(x^*, p^*, \mathscr{T}^*, x^{*T})$ for all $j \in T$, which contradicts the equilibrium (with transfer) condition (ii). □

In the subsequent paragraphs through the end of the proof of the main theorems (Theorems 3.4.4 and 3.4.6), except in Claim 3.4.7, the feasibility of a strategy bundle in economy $\mathscr{E}$ is understood as the feasibility that assumes transfer among realized coalitions (conditions (i′) of Definition 3.4.2).

Let $\mathscr{E}$ be an economy (Definition 3.1.4). In most of the meaningful cases the utility function, $(\bar{x}, \bar{p}, \bar{\mathscr{T}}, x^S) \mapsto u_S^j(\bar{x}, \bar{p}, \bar{\mathscr{T}}, x^S)$, does not depend on $\{x_{\mathrm{II}}^j\}_{j \in S}$ (e.g., Example 3.1.3). To focus on these cases, define

$$X_{\mathrm{II}}^j := \{x_{\mathrm{II}}^j \in \mathbf{R}^l \mid \exists\, (x_{\mathrm{I}}^j, x_{\mathrm{III}}^j) : (x_{\mathrm{I}}^j, x_{\mathrm{II}}^j, x_{\mathrm{III}}^j) \in X^j\},$$
$$X_{-\mathrm{II}}^j := \{(x_{\mathrm{I}}^j, x_{\mathrm{III}}^j) \in \mathbf{R}^l \times E^j \mid \exists\, x_{\mathrm{II}}^j : (x_{\mathrm{I}}^j, x_{\mathrm{II}}^j, x_{\mathrm{III}}^j) \in X^j\}.$$

A generic element of $X_{-\mathrm{II}}^j$ is denoted by $x_{-\mathrm{II}}^j$. Recall that a subfamily $\mathscr{B}$ of $\mathscr{N}$ is called *balanced*, if there exist nonnegative real numbers $\{\lambda_S\}_{S \in \mathscr{B}}$ such that $\sum_{S \in \mathscr{B} : S \ni j} \lambda_S = 1$ for every $j \in N$ (Section 2.1).

Theorem 3.4.4. *Let $\mathscr{E}$ be an economy (Definition 3.1.4) which satisfies Postulate 3.4.1. There exists an equilibrium with transfer of $\mathscr{E}$ if*

(i) *for any j, $X^j = X_{\mathrm{II}}^j \times X_{-\mathrm{II}}^j$, it is a nonempty, compact and convex subset of $\mathbf{R}^l \times \mathbf{R}^l \times E^j$, and $\mathbf{0} \in X_{\mathrm{II}}^j$;*

(ii) *for any S, the correspondence F^S is both upper semicontinuous and lower* *semicontinuous in* $X \times \Delta^{l-1} \times \mathscr{T}$, *and for each* $(\bar{x}, \bar{p}, \bar{\mathscr{T}})$, $F^S(\bar{x}, \bar{p}, \bar{\mathscr{T}})$ *is nonempty and closed;*

(ii$_h$) *the correspondence*

$$(\bar{x}, \bar{p}) \mapsto \cup \left\{ \prod_{T \in \mathscr{T}} F^T_{t_T}(\bar{x}, \bar{p}, \mathscr{T}) \,\middle|\, \begin{matrix} \mathscr{T} \in \mathscr{T}: \\ \{t_T\}_{T \in \mathscr{T}} \subset \mathbf{R}, \sum_T t_T = 0 \end{matrix} \right\}$$

is closed-valued and both upper semicontinuous and lower semicontinuous in $X \times \Delta^{l-1}$, *and for each* $S \in \mathscr{N}$, $F^S_t(\bar{x}, \bar{p}, \mathscr{T})$ *depends actually only upon* $(\{\bar{x}^j_{-\mathrm{II}}\}_{j \in N}, \sum_{T \in \mathscr{T}} \bar{x}^{(T)}_{\mathrm{II}}, \bar{p}, \mathscr{T})$ *if* $\bar{x}^i_{\mathrm{II}} = \bar{x}^j_{\mathrm{II}}$ *for all* $i, j \in T \in \mathscr{T}$;

(iii) *for every balanced family* $\mathscr{B}$ *with the associated balancing coefficients* $\{\lambda_S\}_{S \in \mathscr{B}}$, *if*

$$\{x^{S,j}\}_{j \in S} \in F^S(\bar{x}, \bar{p}, \mathscr{T}^S) \text{ and } \mathscr{T}^S \in \mathscr{T}, \textit{for all } S \in \mathscr{B},$$

then there exist $\mathscr{T} \in \mathscr{T}$, $\{t_T\}_{T \in \mathscr{T}} \subset \mathbf{R}$ *for which* $\sum_{T \in \mathscr{T}} t_T = 0$, *and* $\{x^j\}_{j \in T} \in F^T_{t_T}(\bar{x}, \bar{p}, \mathscr{T})$ *for each* $T \in \mathscr{T}$ *such that*

$$\sum_{S \in \mathscr{B}: S \ni j} \lambda_S(x^{S,j}_{\mathrm{I}}, x^{S,j}_{\mathrm{III}}) = (x^j_{\mathrm{I}}, x^j_{\mathrm{III}}) \textit{ for all } j \in N,$$

and

$$\sum_{S \in \mathscr{B}} \lambda_S x^{(S)}_{\mathrm{II}} = \sum_{T \in \mathscr{T}} x^{(T)}_{\mathrm{II}},$$

where $x^{(S)}_{\mathrm{II}} := x^{S,j}_{\mathrm{II}}$ *for all* $j \in S$ *and* $x^{(T)}_{\mathrm{II}} := x^j_{\mathrm{II}}$ *for all* $j \in T$; *and*

(iv) *for any* j, *there exists a continuous function* u^j: $X_{-\mathrm{II}} \times \Delta^{l-1} \times X^j_{-\mathrm{II}} \to \mathbf{R}$ *such that*

$$u^j_S(\bar{x}, \bar{p}, \bar{\mathscr{T}}, x^S) = u^j(\bar{x}_{-\mathrm{II}}, \bar{p}, x^j_{-\mathrm{II}}) \textit{ for all } (\bar{x}, \bar{p}, \bar{\mathscr{T}}, x^S),$$

and for each $(\bar{x}, \bar{p})$, $u^j(\bar{x}_{-\mathrm{II}}, \bar{p}, \cdot)$ *is quasi-concave in* $X^j_{-\mathrm{II}}$.

Of course, a finite set is endowed with the discrete topology here. Actually, the feasible-strategy correspondences, F^S: $X \times \Delta^{l-1} \times \mathscr{T} \to X^S$, make sense only on the restricted domain,

$$D := \{(x, p, \mathscr{T}) \in X \times \Delta^{l-1} \times \mathscr{T} \mid \forall\, T \in \mathscr{T}: \forall\, i, j \in T: x^i_{\mathrm{II}} = x^j_{\mathrm{II}}\}.$$

Conditions (ii) and (ii$_h$) of Theorem 3.4.4 say that the correspondences F^S_t can be both upper and lower semicontinuously extended from D to $X \times \Delta^{l-1} \times \mathscr{T}$. Notice that an equilibrium with or without transfer (Definitions 3.1.5 or 3.4.2) is necessarily a member of D. The last condition in (ii$_h$) says that the "externalities" are brought about by the *total* marketed input-output vector $\sum_{T \in \mathscr{T}} \bar{x}^{(T)}_{\mathrm{II}}$, rather than by the *individual* marketed input-output vectors $\{\bar{x}^{(T)}_{\mathrm{II}}\}_{T \in \mathscr{T}}$. The *balanced feasibility constraint* condition (iii) says that the set of feasible strategies

$$\cup \left\{ \prod_{T \in \mathscr{T}} F^T_{t_T}(\bar{x}, \bar{p}, \mathscr{T}) \,\middle|\, \begin{matrix} \mathscr{T} \in \mathscr{T}, \\ \{t_T\}_{T \in \mathscr{T}} \subset \mathbf{R}, \sum_T t_T = 0 \end{matrix} \right\}$$

is efficient enough to realize the maximal technological capability of $\mathscr{E}$. This extends Böhm's balanced technology assumption (Example 2A.9 of the Appendix to Chapter 2), as shown in the following Example 3.4.5.

Example 3.4.5. The same example as Example 3.1.6: To model the situation in which the labor-supply to coalition S comes only from those agents within S, labor is classified not only according to the types but also according to the agents. Thus, agent j can supply k_j types of labor, $\sum_{j\in N} k_j = k$, j's consumption set C^j is a subset of $\mathbf{R}^l \times (-\mathbf{R}^{k_j}_+)$, and coalition S's production set $Y(S)$ is a subset of $\mathbf{R}^l \times (-\mathbf{R}^{\sum_{j\in S} k_j}_+)$, where $\mathbf{R}^{k_j}$ is identified with the appropriate subspace of $\mathbf{R}^k$. Then, one of the conditions for $x^S \in F^S(\bar{x}, \bar{p})$, that is, $(x^{(S)}_{\mathrm{II}}, \sum_{j\in S} L^j) \in Y(S)$, implies not only that coalition S uses as much labor bundle as $\sum_{j\in S} L^j$, but also that the labor-supply to coalition S comes only from those agents in S. Assume the standard conditions on the data $(\{C^j, u^j, \omega^j\}_{j\in N}, \{Y(S)\}_{S\in\mathscr{N}})$ that each C^j is nonempty, convex and compact; each u^j is continuous, monotone and quasi-concave; $(\omega^j, \mathbf{0})$ is in the interior of $C^j + \mathbf{R}^{l+k_j}_+$; each $Y(S)$ is nonempty, convex and closed; $Y(S) \cap \mathbf{R}^{l+k_j}_+ = \{\mathbf{0}\}$; free disposal in production is allowed; and only a bounded set of outputs is technologically feasible from a bounded set of inputs. The feasible-strategy set with transfer $F^S_t(\bar{x}, \bar{p}, \bar{\mathscr{T}})$, defined by: $x^S \in F^S_t(\bar{x}, \bar{p}, \bar{\mathscr{T}})$ iff

$$\begin{aligned}
&\forall j \in S\colon (x^j_{\mathrm{I}}, L^j) \in C^j \text{ and } \bar{p}\cdot x^j_{\mathrm{I}} \leqslant w^j + \bar{p}\cdot\omega^j;\\
&\forall j, j' \in S\colon x^j_{\mathrm{II}} = x^{j'}_{\mathrm{II}} \; (=: x^{(S)}_{\mathrm{II}});\\
&\sum_{j\in S} w^j \leqslant \bar{p}\cdot x^{(S)}_{\mathrm{II}} + t; \text{ and}\\
&(x^{(S)}_{\mathrm{II}}, \sum_{j\in S} L^j) \in Y(S),
\end{aligned}$$

satisfies Postulate 3.4.1. Notice the equivalence,

$$x \in \bigcup \left\{ \prod_{T\in\mathscr{T}} F^T_{t_T}(\bar{x}, \bar{p}, \mathscr{T}) \,\middle|\, \begin{array}{l} \mathscr{T} \in \mathscr{T}\colon \\ \{t_T\}_{T\in\mathscr{T}} \subset \mathbf{R},\ \sum_T t_T = 0 \end{array} \right\},$$

iff

$$\begin{aligned}
&(x^j_{\mathrm{I}}, L^j) \in C^j \text{ for all } j \in N,\\
&\text{for some } \mathscr{T} \in \mathscr{T},\ (x^{(T)}_{\mathrm{II}}, \sum_{j\in T} L^j) \in Y(T) \text{ for all } T \in \mathscr{T},\\
&\bar{p}\cdot \sum_{j\in N} x^j_{\mathrm{I}} \leqslant \bar{p}\cdot \sum_{T\in\mathscr{T}} x^{(T)}_{\mathrm{II}} + \bar{p}\cdot \sum_{j\in N} \omega^j_{\mathrm{I}},
\end{aligned}$$

where $x^j_{\mathrm{II}} = x^{(T)}_{\mathrm{II}}$ for all $j \in T$. If, further, the technology satisfies Böhm's balancedness condition (Example 2A.9 of the Appendix to Chapter 2), i.e., if $\sum_{S\in\mathscr{B}} \lambda_S Y(S) \subset \bigcup_{\mathscr{T}\in\mathscr{T}} \sum_{T\in\mathscr{T}} Y(T)$ for every balanced subfamily $\mathscr{B}$ of $\mathscr{N}$ with the associated $\{\lambda_S\}_{S\in\mathscr{B}}$, then assumption (iii) of Theorem 3.4.4 is satisfied. Needless to say, the continuity and quasi-concavity conditions on

u^j are precisely assumption (iv) of Theorem 3.4.4. Assumptions (i) and (ii) of Proposition 3.4.3 are trivially satisfied. □

In order to state the second existence theorem, define for each $(\bar{x}, \bar{p}, \bar{\mathcal{T}}) \in X \times \Delta^{l-1} \times \mathcal{T}$ the non-side-payment games,

$$V_{\bar{x},\bar{p},\mathcal{T}}(S) := \left\{ u \in \mathbf{R}^N \,\middle|\, \begin{array}{l} \exists x^S \in F^S(\bar{x}, \bar{p}, \bar{\mathcal{T}}): \\ \forall j \in S: u_j \leqslant u_S^j(\bar{x}, \bar{p}, \bar{\mathcal{T}}, x^S) \end{array} \right\},$$

$$V_{\bar{x},\bar{p}}(S) := \bigcup_{\mathcal{T} \in \mathcal{T}} V_{\bar{x},\bar{p},\mathcal{T}}(S)$$

and also the set of feasible utility allocations

$$H_{\bar{x},\bar{p}} := \left\{ u \in \mathbf{R}^N \,\middle|\, \begin{array}{l} \exists \mathcal{T} \in \mathcal{T}: \exists \{t_T\}_{T \in \mathcal{T}} \subset \mathbf{R}: \sum_T t_T = 0: \\ \forall T \in \mathcal{T}: \exists x^T \in F_{t_T}^T(\bar{x}, \bar{p}\, \mathcal{T}): \\ \forall j \in T: u_j \leqslant u_T^j(\bar{x}, \bar{p}, \mathcal{T}, x^T) \end{array} \right\}.$$

Recall that a non-side-payment game V is called *balanced* if $\bigcap_{S \in \mathcal{B}} V(S) \subset V(N)$ for every balanced family $\mathcal{B}$ (Section 2.2). A weak version of the balancedness condition appears as condition (iv) in the following second existence theorem, which allows for realization of an admissible coalition structure (rather than realization of the coarsest coalition structure) in equilibrium with transfer.

Theorem 3.4.6. *Let $\mathcal{E}$ be an economy (Definition 3.1.4) which satisfies Postulate 3.4.1. Assume that each utility function u_S^j: $\mathrm{gr}F^S \to \mathbf{R}$ is extended to $X \times X^S$. There exists an equilibrium with transfer of $\mathcal{E}$ if*

(i) *for any j, $X^j = X_{\mathrm{II}}^j \times X_{-\mathrm{II}}^j$, it is a nonempty, compact and convex subset of $\mathbf{R}^l \times \mathbf{R}^l \times E^j$;*

(ii) *for any S, the correspondence F^S is both upper semicontinuous and lower semicontinuous in $X \times \Delta^{l-1} \times \mathcal{T}$, and for each $(\bar{x}, \bar{p}, \bar{\mathcal{T}})$, $F^S(\bar{x}, \bar{p}, \bar{\mathcal{T}})$ is nonempty and closed;*

(ii_h) *the correspondence $(x, p) \mapsto H_{x,p}$ is closed-valued and both upper semicontinuous and lower semicontinuous in $X \times \Delta^{l-1}$, and for each $S \in \mathcal{N}$, $F_t^S(\bar{x}, \bar{p}, \mathcal{T})$ depends actually only upon $(\{\bar{x}_{-\mathrm{II}}^j\}_{j \in N}, \sum_{T \in \mathcal{T}} \bar{x}_{\mathrm{II}}^{(T)}, \bar{p}, \mathcal{T})$ if $\bar{x}_{\mathrm{II}}^i = \bar{x}_{\mathrm{II}}^j$ for all $i, j \in T \in \mathcal{T}$;*

(iii) *u_S^j depends only on $(\bar{x}_{-\mathrm{II}}, \bar{p}, \bar{\mathcal{T}}, \bar{x}_{-\mathrm{II}}^S)$, and is continuous in $X \times \Delta^{l-1} \times \mathcal{T} \times X_{-\mathrm{II}}^S$ for every $S \in \mathcal{N}$ and every $j \in S$;*

(iv) *for any $(\bar{x}, \bar{p}) \in X \times \Delta^{l-1}$,*

$$\bigcap_{S \in \mathcal{B}} V_{\bar{x},\bar{p}}(S) \subset H_{\bar{x},\bar{p}}$$

for every balanced subfamily $\mathcal{B}$ of $\mathcal{N}$; and

(v) *given any $(\bar{x}, \bar{p}) \in X \times \Delta^{l-1}$ and any $\bar{u} \in H_{\bar{x},\bar{p}} \setminus \bigcup_{S \in \mathcal{N}} \mathring{V}_{\bar{x},\bar{p}}(S)$, the set of feasible essential strategy bundles that give rise to $\bar{u}$,*

$$\bigcup_{T\in\mathcal{T}}\left\{(\{x^j_{-\mathrm{II}}\}_{j\in N}, \sum_{T\in\mathcal{T}} x^{(T)}_{\mathrm{II}}) \;\middle|\; \begin{array}{l}\exists\{t_T\}_{T\in\mathcal{T}}\subset\mathbf{R}\colon \sum_T t_T=0\colon\\ \forall T\in\mathcal{T}\colon x^T\in F^T_{t_T}(\bar{x},\bar{p}\,\mathcal{T})\colon\\ \forall j\in T\colon u_j\leqslant u^j_T(\bar{x},\bar{p},\mathcal{T},X^T)\end{array}\right\},$$

is convex.

The set of utility allocations $H_{\bar{x},\bar{p}}\setminus \bigcup_{S\in\mathcal{N}} \mathring{V}_{\bar{x},\bar{p}}(S)$ is of course the core of the non-side-payment game with admissible coalition structures and possible transfers. Condition (v) of Theorem 3.4.6 says that given any utility allocation $\bar{u}$ in the core, the set of feasible modified strategy bundles that give rise to $\bar{u}$ is convex. For capitalistic economy $\mathcal{E}_c$, this condition implies that there exists a unique coalition structure $\mathcal{T}^*$ which makes these strategy bundles feasible. Indeed, choose any two strategy bundles x and y, each giving rise to $\bar{u}$, and suppose they are made feasible by coalition structures $\mathcal{T}$ and $\mathcal{U}$, respectively. If $\mathcal{T}\neq\mathcal{U}$, there exist $T\in\mathcal{T}$ and $U\in\mathcal{U}$ such that $T\neq U$ and $T\cap U\neq\phi$. Assuming that $x^{(T)}_{\mathrm{II},T}>0$ and $y^{(U)}_{\mathrm{II},U}>0$, a strict convex combination z of x and y has the property, $z^j_{\mathrm{II},T}>0$ and $z^j_{\mathrm{II},U}>0$ for each $j\in T\cap U$, which is impossible. Theorem 3.4.6 is stated in its present form rather than in terms of this unique coalition structure $\mathcal{T}^*$, however, because the theorem as stated can be used to establish an equilibrium existence theorem for an alternative model of capitalistic economy in the Appendix to Chapter 3; in the alternative model, two strategy bundles made feasible by distinct coalition structures may give rise to a utility allocation $\bar{u}$ in the core.

Condition (v) of Theorem 3.4.6 may be understood as an extension of the convexity assumption on the feasible strategy sets and the quasi-concavity assumption on the utility functions, as the following Claim 3.4.7 suggests:

Claim 3.4.7. *Let $\mathcal{E}$ be an economy (Definition 3.1.4), and choose any $(\bar{x}, \bar{p})\in X\times\Delta^{l-1}$. Assume that $\mathcal{T}$ is a singleton $\{\mathcal{T}\}$ and that for each $T\in\mathcal{T}$ and each $j\in T$, $F^T(\bar{x},\bar{p},\mathcal{T})$ is compact and $u^j_T(\bar{x},\bar{p},\mathcal{T},\cdot)$ is continuous. Then, the following two conditions are equivalent:*

(i) *Given any $\bar{u}\in\mathbf{R}^N$, the set of feasible strategy bundles without transfer that give rise to $\bar{u}$,*

$$\left\{x\in X \;\middle|\; \begin{array}{l}\forall T\in\mathcal{T}\colon \exists x^T\in F^T(\bar{x},\bar{p},\mathcal{T})\colon\\ \qquad\qquad \forall j\in T\colon u^j_T(\bar{x},\bar{p},\mathcal{T},x^T)\geqslant\bar{u}_j\end{array}\right\}$$

is convex;

(ii) *For each $T\in\mathcal{T}$ and each $j\in T$, the feasible strategy set $F^T(\bar{x},\bar{p},\mathcal{T})$ is convex, and $u^j_T(\bar{x},\bar{p},\mathcal{T},\cdot)$ is quasi-concave in $F^T(\bar{x},\bar{p},\mathcal{T})$.*

Proof. (i)⇒(ii). Choose $\underline{u}\in\mathbf{R}^N$ so that $\underline{u}_j\leqslant\min\{u^j_T(\bar{x},\bar{p},\mathcal{T},x^T)\mid x^T\in F^T(\bar{x},\bar{p},\mathcal{T})\}$ for every j. Then, the set of feasible strategy bundles that give rise to $\underline{u}$ is precisely $\prod_{T\in\mathcal{T}} F^T(\bar{x},\bar{p},\mathcal{T})$, so each $F^T(\bar{x},\bar{p},\mathcal{T})$ is convex. To show the convexity of the upper contour set $P^j(u_j):=\{x^T\in F^T(\bar{x},\bar{p},\mathcal{T})\mid u_j\leqslant u^j_T(\bar{x},\bar{p},\mathcal{T},x^T)\}$ for each $u_j\in\mathbf{R}$, it suffices to observe that the set of feasible strategy bundles that give rise to $(u_j,\underline{u}^{T\setminus\{j\}})$ is

$$P^j(u_j)\times\prod_{T\in\mathcal{T}:T\not\ni j}F^T(\bar{x},\bar{p},\mathcal{T}).$$

(ii)⇒(i). The set of feasible strategy bundles that give rise to $\bar{u}$ is $\prod_{T\in\mathcal{T}}(\bigcap_{j\in T}P^j(\bar{u}_j))$, which is a convex subset of X. □

Theorem 3.4.4 is included in Theorem 3.4.6. In order to prove this fact, it suffices to show that conditions (i), (iii) and (iv) of Theorem 3.4.4 together imply both conditions (iv) and (v) of Theorem 3.4.6.

Proof that conditions (i), (iii) and (iv) of Theorem 3.4.4 together imply both conditions (iv) and (v) of Theorem 3.4.6.

Balancedness. Choose any balanced family $\mathcal{B}$ with associated balancing coefficients $\{\lambda_S\}_{S\in\mathcal{B}}$, and any $u\in\bigcap_{S\in\mathcal{B}}V_{\bar{x},\bar{p}}(S)$. Then, for each $S\in\mathcal{B}$ there exist $\mathcal{T}^S\in\mathcal{T}$ and $\{x^{S,j}\}_{j\in S}\in F^S(\bar{x},\bar{p},\mathcal{T}^S)$ such that $u_j\leqslant u^j(\bar{x}_{-\mathrm{II}},\bar{p},x^{S,j}_{-\mathrm{II}})$ for every $j\in S$. By the balanced feasibility constraint condition (iii) of Theorem 3.4.4, there exist $\mathcal{T}\in\mathcal{T}$, $\{t_T\}_{T\in\mathcal{T}}\subset\mathbf{R}$ for which $\sum_T t_T=0$, and $x^T\in F^T_{t_T}(\bar{x},\bar{p},\mathcal{T})$ for every $T\in\mathcal{T}$, such that

$$\sum_{S\in\mathcal{B}:S\ni j}\lambda_S x^{S,j}_{-\mathrm{II}}=x^j_{-\mathrm{II}},\ \text{for every}\ j\in N.$$

By the quasi-concavity of $u^j(\bar{x}_{-\mathrm{II}},\bar{p},\cdot)$,

$$u_j\leqslant u^j(\bar{x}_{-\mathrm{II}},\bar{p},x^j_{-\mathrm{II}}),\ \text{for every}\ j\in N.$$

Therefore,

$$u\in H_{\bar{x},\bar{p}}.$$

Convexity. Choose any $\bar{u}\in H_{\bar{x},\bar{p}}\setminus\bigcap_{S\in\mathcal{N}}\mathring{V}_{\bar{x},\bar{p}}(S)$. Let x, y be two feasible strategy bundles that give rise to $\bar{u}$, i.e.,

$$\begin{aligned}
&\exists\,\mathcal{T}\in\mathcal{T}:\exists\{t_T\}_{T\in\mathcal{T}}\subset\mathbf{R}:\textstyle\sum_T t_T=0,\\
&\exists\,\mathcal{U}\in\mathcal{T}:\exists\{t_U\}_{U\in\mathcal{U}}\subset\mathbf{R}:\textstyle\sum_U t_U=0,\\
&\forall\,T\in\mathcal{T}: x^T\in F^T_{t_T}(\bar{x},\bar{p},\mathcal{T}),\\
&\forall\,U\in\mathcal{U}: y^U\in F^U_{t_U}(\bar{x},\bar{p},\mathcal{U}),\ \text{and}\\
&\forall\,j\in N: \bar{u}_j\leqslant u^j(\bar{x}_{-\mathrm{II}},\bar{p},x^j_{-\mathrm{II}}),\ \text{and}\ \bar{u}_j\leqslant u^j(\bar{x}_{-\mathrm{II}},\bar{p},y^j_{-\mathrm{II}}).
\end{aligned}$$

Choose also any $\alpha\in[0,1]$. The family[2] $\mathcal{T}+\mathcal{U}$ is balanced; indeed, $\{\lambda_S\}_{S\in\mathcal{T}+\mathcal{U}}$ defined by

[2] For two sets A and B, $A\cup B$ denotes the *union* of A and B defined as the set of those x for which $x\in A$ or $x\in B$, and $A+B$ denotes the *sum* of A and B identified with the set of those (i,x) for which $(1,x)\in\{1\}\times A$ or $(2,x)\in\{2\}\times B$. When both A and B are subsets of a vector space, $A+B$ may also denote the *vector sum* of A and B defined as the set of those $x+y$ for which $x\in A$ and $y\in B$; no confusion arises.

$$\lambda_S := \begin{cases} \alpha & \text{if } S \in \mathcal{T} \\ 1-\alpha & \text{if } S \in \mathcal{U} \end{cases}$$

are associated balancing coefficients. By the balancedness feasibility constraint condition (iii) of Theorem 3.4.4, there exists $\mathcal{T}^* \in \mathcal{T}$, $\{t_T^*\}_{T \in \mathcal{T}^*} \subset \mathbf{R}$ for which $\sum_{T \in \mathcal{T}^*} t_T^* = 0$, and $z^T \in F^T_{t_T^*}(\bar{x}, \bar{p}, \mathcal{T}^*)$ for each $T \in \mathcal{T}^*$ such that

$$\alpha x^j_{-\mathrm{II}} + (1-\alpha) y^j_{-\mathrm{II}} = z^j_{-\mathrm{II}} \text{ for all } j \in N$$

and

$$\alpha \sum_{T \in \mathcal{T}} x^{(T)}_{\mathrm{II}} + (1-\alpha) \sum_{U \in \mathcal{U}} y^{(U)}_{\mathrm{II}} = \sum_{T \in \mathcal{T}^*} z^{(T)}_{\mathrm{II}}.$$

By the quasi-concavity assumption (iv) of Theorem 3.4.4,

$$\forall j \in N: \bar{u}_j \leqslant u^j(\bar{x}_{-\mathrm{II}}, \bar{p}, z^j_{-\mathrm{II}}). \ \square$$

Example 3.4.8. The same example as Example 3.1.7: Assumption (iii) of Theorem 3.4.4 or assumptions (iv) and (v) of Theorem 3.4.6 have been imposed, in order to pin down in terms of $F^S(\bar{x}, \bar{p}, \mathcal{T})$ or in terms of $V_{\bar{x},\bar{p}}(S)$ and $H_{\bar{x},\bar{p}}$ the general class of subjective probabilities needed for the existence of an equilibrium (with transfer). □

Theorem 3.4.6 for the economy will be proved by applying an existence theorem for the seemingly simpler, abstract model of society. The latter model is now presented: Let N be given as a finite set of *players*, and hence let $\mathcal{N}(:=2^N \backslash \{\phi\})$ be given as the set of nonempty *coalitions* of players. For player j denote by X^j his *strategy space*, and define $X^S := \prod_{j \in S} X^j$ for every $S \in \mathcal{N}$. Put $X := X^N$ for notational convenience. The *feasible-strategy correspondence* of coalition S is a correspondence $F^S\colon X \to X^S$. The subset $F^S(x)$ of X^S is interpreted as the set of all feasible strategy bundles for S as a cooperative unit when $x\,(\in X)$ has been chosen. For each member j of S, his *utility function* $u^j_S\colon \mathrm{gr}F^S \to \mathbf{R}$ is given. Here the dependence of the utility function on S reflects the possible fact that members of S enjoy the environment (i.e., non-strategic elements) specific to S. Thus the players outside coalition S influence the members of S (1) indirectly by restricting the feasible strategies of the members of S to $F^S(x)$ and (2) directly by affecting the utility level u^j_S for all $j \in S$. Let $\mathcal{T}$ be the family of *admissible coalition structures*.

Definition 3.4.9. A *society* is a list of specified data, $\mathcal{S} := (\{X^j\}_{j \in N}, \{F^S\}_{S \in \mathcal{N}}, \{u^j_S\}_{j \in S \in \mathcal{N}}, \mathcal{T}\}$, of the strategy spaces, the feasible-strategy correspondences, the utility functions and the admissible coalition structures.

The following equilibrium concept for a society characterizes the feasibility (condition (i) of Definition 3.4.10) and the coalitional stability (condition (ii)).

Definition 3.4.10. A *social coalitional equilibrium* of society $\mathscr{S}$ is a pair $(x^*, \mathscr{T}^*)$ of members of X and $\mathscr{T}$, respectively, such that:
(i) $x^{*T} \in F^T(x^*)$ for every $T \in \mathscr{T}^*$; and
(ii) it is not true that there exist $S \in \mathscr{N}$ and $x^S \in F^S(x^*)$ such that $u_S^j(x^*, x^S) > u_{T(j)}^j(x^*, x^{*T(j)})$ for every $j \in S$, where $T(j)$ is the unique member of $\mathscr{T}^*$ such that $T(j) \ni j$.

Theorem 3.4.11. *Let $\mathscr{S}$ be a society. There exists a social coalitional equilibrium of $\mathscr{S}$ if*
(i) *for any j, X^j is a nonempty, compact and convex subset of a real Hausdorff locally convex topological vector space;*
(ii) *for any S, the correspondence F^S is both upper semicontinuous and lower semicontinuous in X, and for each $\bar{x}$, $F^S(\bar{x})$ is nonempty and closed;*
(iii) *u_S^j is continuous in $\mathrm{gr}F^S$ for every $S \in \mathscr{N}$ and every $j \in S$;*
(iv) *for any $\bar{x} \in X$,*

$$\bigcap_{S \in \mathscr{B}} V_{\bar{x}}(S) \subset \bigcup_{\mathscr{T} \in \mathscr{T}} \bigcap_{T \in \mathscr{T}} V_{\bar{x}}(T)$$

for every balanced subfamily $\mathscr{B}$ of $\mathscr{N}$ where

$$V_{\bar{x}}(S) := \{u \in \mathbf{R}^N \mid \exists x^S \in F^S(\bar{x}): \forall j \in S: u_j \leq u_S^j(\bar{x}, x^S)\};$$

and
(v) *given any $\bar{x} \in X$ and any $\bar{u} \in \bigcup_{\mathscr{T} \in \mathscr{T}} \bigcap_{T \in \mathscr{T}} V_{\bar{x}}(T) \setminus \bigcup_{S \in \mathscr{N}} \mathring{V}_{\bar{x}}(S)$, the set of feasible strategy bundles that give rise to $\bar{u}$,*

$$\bigcap_{\mathscr{T} \in \mathscr{T}} \left\{ x \in X \;\middle|\; \begin{array}{l} \forall T \in \mathscr{T}: x^T \in F^T(\bar{x}), \text{ and} \\ \bar{u}_j \leq u_T^j(\bar{x}, x^T) \text{ for each } j \in T \end{array} \right\},$$

is convex.

A complete proof of Theorem 3.4.11 can be found in Ichiishi (1981b), and the proof for the finite dimensional setup was reproduced in Ichiishi (1983, pp. 96–98) (see Remark 3.4.13 below, however). Here, the proof of Theorem 3.4.11 will be outlined after the statement of another theorem (Theorem 3.4.12) which is basic to it.

A correspondence F from a topological space X to a topological vector space E is called *upper demicontinuous* (*u.d.c.*, for short) *in* X, if for each $x \in X$ and each open half-space H in E such that $F(x) \subset H$, there exists a neighborhood $N(x)$ of x in X such that $F(x') \subset H$ for all $x' \in N(x)$. Two of the advantages of this concept are: (1) it is weaker than the upper semicontinuity concept, and (2) given a compact-valued, u.d.c. correspondence F, the correspondence $\overline{\mathrm{co}}F$: $X \to E$ defined by $(\overline{\mathrm{co}}F)(x) := \overline{\mathrm{co}}(F(x))$, the closed convex hull of $F(x)$, is also u.d.c. [Unless E is finite dimensional, it is not known whether compact-valuedness and upper semicontinuity of F imply upper semicontinuity of $\overline{\text{co}}\text{F}$.] The following coincidence theorem is due to Fan (1972):

Theorem 3.4.12 (Fan). *Let X be a nonempty compact convex subset of a real Hausdorff locally convex topological vector space E, and let F, G be two u.d.c. correspondences defined on X. Let E* be the topological dual of E. If for each $x \in X$, $F(x)$ and $G(x)$ are nonempty closed convex sets in E and at least one of them is compact, and if*
(*) *for any $x \in X$ and any $p \in E^*$ such that $p(x) = \min\{p(y) \mid y \in X\}$, there exist $u \in F(x)$ and $v \in G(x)$ such that $p(u) \geqslant p(v)$,*
then there exists $x^* \in X$ such that $F(x^*) \cap G(x^*) \neq \phi$.

Outline of the Proof of Theorem 3.4.11. *Step 1.* Define for each $x \in X$, $H_x := \bigcup_{\mathcal{T} \in \mathscr{T}} \bigcap_{T \in \mathcal{T}} V_x(T)$. The correspondences from X to $\mathbf{R}^N$, $x \mapsto V_x(S)$ and $x \mapsto H_x$, are both upper semicontinuous (u.s.c.) and lower semicontinuous in X. Let $m(x) \in \mathbf{R}^N$ be the individually rational point defined by $m_j(x) := \max\{u_j \in \mathbf{R} \mid u \in V_x(\{j\})\}$. There exists a real number $M > 0$ such that for every $x \in X$, every $S \in \mathscr{N}$, and every $v \in V_x(S)$, $v_j - m_j(x) < M$ for all $j \in S$. Denote by D^S the simplex in the negative cone defined as $\text{co}\{-Mn\chi_{\{j\}} \mid j \in S\}$, where $n := \# N$ and χ_T is the characteristic vector of $T \subset N$, and choose its center $\chi'_S := -Mn\chi_S/(\# S)$. Define functions, τ: $X \times D^N \to \mathbf{R}$, and f: $X \times D^N \to \mathbf{R}^N$ by,

$$\tau(x, y) := \max\{r \in \mathbf{R} \mid y + m(x) + r\chi_N \in \bigcup_{S \in \mathscr{N}} V_x(S)\},$$
$$f(x, y) := y + m(x) + \tau(x, y)\chi_N.$$

Both functions τ and f are continuous.

Step 2. For each $x \in X$, define a closed covering of D^N, $\{C_S(x)\}_{S \in \mathscr{N}}$, by $C_S(x) := \{y \in D^N \mid f(x, y) \in V_x(S)\}$. For each $S \in \mathscr{N}$, the correspondence, $x \mapsto C_S(x)$, is u.s.c. By the choice of the number M, one can show that [S, $T \in \mathscr{N}$, $D^T \cap C_S(x) \neq \phi$] implies [$S \subset T$].

Step 3. Let d be the Euclidean distance, and let ρ be the distance between a point and a set in $\mathbf{R}^N$ defined by $\rho(u, A) := \inf\{d(u, a) \mid a \in A\}$. Define a correspondence F: $X \times D^N \to X \times D^N$ by

$$\begin{aligned} F(\bar{x}, \bar{y}) := \overline{\text{co}} \bigcup_{\mathcal{T} \in \mathscr{T}} \{x \in X \mid \forall T \in \mathcal{T}: x^T \in F^T(\bar{x}), \text{ and} \\ \rho(u^{\mathcal{T}}(\bar{x}, x), \{f(\bar{x}, \bar{y})\} + \mathbf{R}^N_+) \leqslant \rho(f(\bar{x}, \bar{y}), H_{\bar{x}})\} \\ \times \{\chi'_N\}, \end{aligned}$$

where the jth component of $u^{\mathcal{T}}(\bar{x}, x)$ is $u^j_{T(j)}(\bar{x}, x^{T(j)})$ with $j \in T(j) \in \mathcal{T}$. Define another correspondence G: $X \times D^N \to X \times D^N$ by

$$G(\bar{x}, \bar{y}) := \{\bar{x}\} \times \text{co}\{\chi'_S \mid C_S(\bar{x}) \ni \bar{y}\}.$$

Both correspondences F and G are u.d.c. in $X \times D^N$ and are nonempty- and convex-valued. By Step 2, one can show that all the assumptions of Fan's coincidence theorem (Theorem 3.4.12) are satisfied. There exist, therefore (x^*, y^*) and $(\bar{x}, \bar{y}) \in X \times D^N$ such that

$$(\bar{x}, \bar{y}) \in F(x^*, y^*) \cap G(x^*, y^*).$$

Step 4. The previous step has shown the existence of (x^*, y^*), $(\bar{x}, \bar{y}) \in X \times D^N$ such that

$$\bar{x} \in \overline{\text{co}} \bigcup_{\mathcal{T} \in \mathscr{T}} \{x \in X \mid \forall\, T \in \mathcal{T}: x^T \in F^T(x^*), \text{ and } \rho(u^{\mathcal{T}}(x^*, x), \{f(x^*, y^*)\} + \mathbf{R}^N_+) \leqslant \rho(f(x^*, y^*), H_{x^*})\}; \quad (1)$$

$$\bar{y} = \chi'_N; \quad (2)$$

$$\bar{x} = x^*; \text{ and} \quad (3)$$

$$\bar{y} \in \text{co}\{\chi'_S \mid C_S(x^*) \ni y^*\}. \quad (4)$$

By (2) and (4), the collection $\mathscr{B}^* := \{S \in \mathscr{N} \mid C_S(x^*) \ni y^*\}$ is balanced. By assumption (iv), therefore, $f(x^*, y^*) \in H_{x^*}$. Indeed,

$$f(x^*, y^*) \in H_{x^*} \setminus \bigcup_{S \in \mathscr{N}} \mathring{V}_{x^*}(S). \quad (5)$$

Then, $\rho(f(x^*, y^*), H_{x^*}) = 0$, and the above results (1) and (3) become

$$x^* \in \overline{\text{co}} \bigcup_{\mathcal{T} \in \mathscr{T}} \{x \in X \mid \forall\, T \in \mathcal{T}: x^T \in F^T(x^*), \text{and} f(x^*, y^*) \leqslant u^{\mathcal{T}}(x^*, x^T)\}.$$

By assumption (v), this last set is identical to

$$\bigcup_{\mathcal{T} \in \mathscr{T}} \{x \in X \mid \forall\, T \in \mathcal{T}: x^T \in F^T(x^*), \text{ and } f(x^*, y^*) \leqslant u^{\mathcal{T}}(x^*, x^T)\},$$

so there exists $\mathcal{T}^* \in \mathscr{T}$ such that

$$x^{*T} \in F^T(x^*) \text{ for every } T \in \mathcal{T}^*; \text{ and} \quad (6)$$

$$f(x^*, y^*) \leqslant u^{\mathcal{T}^*}(x^*, x^{*T}). \quad (7)$$

The pair $(x^*, \mathcal{T}^*)$ is the required social coalitional equilibrium of society $\mathscr{S}$, in view of (5), (6), and (7). □

Remark 3.4.13. In the original proof of Theorem 3.4.11, the correspondence $F: X \times D^N \to X \times D^N$ of Step 3 was defined as

$$F(\bar{x}, \bar{y}) := \overline{\text{co}} \bigcup_{\mathcal{T} \in \mathscr{T}} \{x \in X \mid \forall\, T \in \mathcal{T}: x^T \in F^T(\bar{x}), \text{ and } d(f(\bar{x}, \bar{y}), u^{\mathcal{T}}(\bar{x}, x)) \leqslant \rho(f(\bar{x}, \bar{y}), H_{\bar{x}})\} \times \{\chi'_N\},$$

(Ichiishi (1981b, p. 373), and Ichiishi (1983, p. 97)). A problem then arises: $F(\bar{x}, \bar{y})$ may become the empty set. Kim C. Border pointed out this error, and proposed the appropriate correspondence F as in the above outline of the proof. □

Remark 3.4.14. For a somewhat *generalized society* $\mathscr{S}:=(\{X^j\}_{j\in N}, \{F^S\}_{S\in\mathscr{N}}, G, \{u_S^j\}_{j\in S\in\mathscr{N}}, \mathscr{T})$ in which F^S is defined on $X\times\mathscr{T}$ rather than merely on X, and in which society's attainability of (strategy bundle, coalition structure) pairs is given by an arbitrarily given correspondence G: $X\to X\times\mathscr{T}$ rather than by the correspondence $x\mapsto\cup_{\mathscr{T}\in\mathscr{T}}(\prod_{T\in\mathscr{T}}F^T(x), \mathscr{T})$, a *social coalitional equilibrium* of $\mathscr{S}$ is defined as a pair $(x^*, \mathscr{T}^*)$ of members of X and $\mathscr{T}$ respectively, such that (1) $(x^*, \mathscr{T}^*)\in G(x^*)$, and (2) it is not true that there exist $S\in\mathscr{N}$ and $x^S\in F^S(x^*, \mathscr{T}^*)$ such that $u_S^j(x^*, \mathscr{T}^*, x^S)>u_{T(j)}^j(x^*, \mathscr{T}^*, x^{*T(j)})$ for every $j\in S$. By applying the same proof, one can establish the following social coalitional equilibrium existence theorem for this generalized society: Define

$$V_{\bar{x},\mathscr{T}}(S):=\left\{u\in\mathbf{R}^N \;\middle|\; \begin{array}{l}\exists x^S\in F^S(\bar{x}, \bar{\mathscr{T}}):\\ \forall j\in S\colon u_j\leqslant u_S^j(\bar{x}, \bar{\mathscr{T}}, x^S)\end{array}\right\},$$

$$V_{\bar{x},}(S):=\bigcup_{\mathscr{T}\in\mathscr{T}}V_{\bar{x},\mathscr{T}}(S), \text{ and}$$

$$H_{\bar{x}}^G:=\left\{u\in\mathbf{R}^N \;\middle|\; \begin{array}{l}\exists(x, \mathscr{T})\in G(\bar{x}):\\ \forall T\in\mathscr{T}\colon\forall j\in T\colon u_j\leqslant u_T^j(\bar{x}, x^T)\end{array}\right\}.$$

Then, a social coalitional equilibrium exists under the same assumptions of Theorem 3.4.11, except that conditions (ii), (iii), (iv), and (v) be replaced by

(ii′) *for any S, the correspondence F^S is both upper semicontinuous and lower semicontinuous in $X\times\mathscr{T}$, the correspondence G is both upper semicontinuous and lower semicontinuous in X, and for each $(\bar{x}, \bar{\mathscr{T}})$, $F^S(\bar{x}, \bar{\mathscr{T}})$ and $G(\bar{x})$ are nonempty and closed;*

(iii′) *u_S^j is continuous in $X\times X^S$ for every $S\in\mathscr{N}$ and every $j\in S$;*

(iv′) *for any $\bar{x}\in X$, there is $H_{\bar{x}}\subset H_{\bar{x}}^G$ such that*

$$\bigcup_{S\in\mathscr{B}}V_{\bar{x}}(S)\subset H_{\bar{x}}$$

for every balanced subfamily $\mathscr{B}$ of $\mathscr{N}$; and

(v′) *given any $\bar{x}\in X$ and any*

$$\bar{u}\in H_{\bar{x}}\setminus\bigcup_{S\in\mathscr{N}}\overset{\circ}{\overbrace{\bigcup_{\mathscr{T}\in\mathscr{T}}V_{\bar{x},\mathscr{T}}(T)}},$$

the set of feasible strategy bundles that give rise to $\bar{u}$,

$$\bigcup_{\mathscr{T}\in\mathscr{T}}\left\{x\in X \;\middle|\; \begin{array}{l}(x, \mathscr{T})\in G(\bar{x}),\\ \bar{u}_j\leqslant u_T^j(\bar{x}, x^T)\text{ for all } j\in T\in\mathscr{T}\end{array}\right\},$$

is convex. □

Proof of Theorem 3.4.6. *Step 1.* Based on economy $\mathscr{E}$ given in the theorem, an auxiliary economy $\ddot{\mathscr{E}}$ is constructed: Since $\mathbf{0}\in X_{\mathrm{II}}^j$, the linear subspace of $\mathbf{R}^l$ spanned by X_{II}^j, span X_{II}^j, and the affine hull of X_{II}^j, aff X_{II}^j, coincide. Choose a compact, convex subset $\ddot{X}_{\mathrm{II}}^j$ of span X_{II}^j so that for every $S\in\mathscr{N}$ and every $x^S \in X^S$ for which $x^i_{\text{II}} = x^j_{\text{II}}$ $(=: x^{(S)}_{\text{II}})$ for all $i, j \in S$ there exists $\ddot{x}^S_{\text{II}} \in \ddot{X}^S_{\text{II}}$ such that $x^{(S)}_{\text{II}} = \sum_{j \in S} \ddot{x}^j_{\text{II}}$. The jth agent's strategy space in $\ddot{\mathscr{E}}$ is given as $\ddot{X}^j := \ddot{X}^j_{\text{II}} \times X^j_{-\text{II}}$. Define as usual, $\ddot{X}^S := \prod_{j \in S} \ddot{X}^j$, $\ddot{X} := \ddot{X}^N$. The intended interpretation of strategy $\ddot{x}^j \in \ddot{X}^j$ is that $\ddot{x}^j_{\text{II}}$ is the *portion* of the marketed input-output vector that j proposes to any firm he belongs to, so when firm T is formed, the marketed input-output vector $\sum_{j \in T} \ddot{x}^j_{\text{II}}$ is actually proposed by its members. For each $\ddot{x}^S \in \ddot{X}^S$, therefore, define $x(\ddot{x}^S, S)^j \in X^j$ by:

$$x(\ddot{x}^S, S)^j_{\text{II}} := \sum_{i \in S} \ddot{x}^i_{\text{II}}, \text{ and } x(\ddot{x}^S, S)^j_{-\text{II}} := \ddot{x}^j_{-\text{II}}.$$

For $\ddot{x} \in \ddot{X}$ and $\mathscr{T} \in \mathscr{T}$, $x(\ddot{x}, \mathscr{T})^j$ is defined as $x(\ddot{x}^{T(j)}, T(j))^j$ where $T(j)$ is the unique member of $\mathscr{T}$ that contains j. Set $x(\ddot{x}, \mathscr{T}) := \{x(\ddot{x}, \mathscr{T})^j\}_{j \in N}$.

By compactness and convexity of X^j_{II}, there exists a continuous function f^j: aff $X^j_{\text{II}} \to X^j_{\text{II}}$ such that f^j restricted to X^j_{II} is the identity. (Indeed, choose a relative interior point θ of X^j_{II}, and define a function t: aff $X^j_{\text{II}} \to [0, 1]$ by

$$t(y) := \max \{\alpha \in [0, 1] \mid \alpha y + (1 - \alpha)\theta \in X^j_{\text{II}}\}.$$

Then, the required function can be defined by $f^j(y) := t(y)y + (1 - t(y))\theta$.) Extend the feasible-strategy correspondence F^S (without changing its range, that is, keeping $F^S(X \times \Delta^{l-1} \times \mathscr{T})$ as the range) upper and lower semicontinuously to $[\prod_{j \in N} ((\text{span } X^j_{\text{II}}) \times X^j_{-\text{II}})] \times \Delta^{l-1} \times \mathscr{T}$ by

$$F^S(x, p, \mathscr{T}) := F^S(\{f^j(x^j_{\text{II}}), x^j_{-\text{II}}\}_{j \in N}, p, \mathscr{T}).$$

The feasible-strategy correspondences $\ddot{F}^S$: $\ddot{X} \times \Delta^{l-1} \times \mathscr{T} \to \ddot{X}^S$ of the auxiliary economy $\ddot{\mathscr{E}}$ are constructed from the extended feasible-strategy correspondences F^S of $\mathscr{E}$ as follows: $\ddot{x}^S \in \ddot{F}^S(\bar{\ddot{x}}, \bar{p}, \bar{\mathscr{T}})$, iff $\ddot{x}^S \in \ddot{X}^S$ and $\{x(\ddot{x}^S, S)^j\}_{j \in S} \in F^S(x(\bar{\ddot{x}}, \bar{\mathscr{T}}), \bar{p}, \bar{\mathscr{T}})$. The feasible-strategy-with-transfer correspondence $\ddot{F}^S_t$ are analogously defined. The auxiliary economy's set of feasible strategy bundles with transfer $G(\bar{\ddot{x}}, \bar{p})$ is the set of those $(\ddot{x}, \mathscr{T})$ for which

$$\begin{aligned}
&\exists \{t_T\}_{T \in \mathscr{T}} \subset \mathbf{R}\colon \sum_{T \in \mathscr{T}} t_T = 0\colon \\
&\forall T \in \mathscr{T}\colon \exists x^T \in F^T_{t_T}(x(\bar{\ddot{x}}, \mathscr{T}), \bar{p}, \mathscr{T})\colon \\
&\qquad \sum_{j \in N} \ddot{x}^j_{\text{II}} = \sum_{T \in \mathscr{T}} x^{(T)}_{\text{II}}, \text{ and } \forall j \in N\colon \ddot{x}^j_{-\text{II}} = x^j_{-\text{II}}.
\end{aligned}$$

The utility functions $\ddot{u}^j_S$: $\ddot{X} \times \Delta^{l-1} \times \mathscr{T} \times \ddot{X}^S_{-\text{II}} \to \mathbf{R}$ of the auxiliary economy $\ddot{\mathscr{E}}$ are defined by:

$$u^j_S(\bar{\ddot{x}}, \bar{p}, \bar{\mathscr{T}}, \ddot{x}^S_{-\text{II}}) := u^j_S(x(\bar{\ddot{x}}, \bar{\mathscr{T}}), \bar{p}, \bar{\mathscr{T}}, \ddot{x}^S_{-\text{II}}).$$

It is easy to check that for every $(\bar{\ddot{x}}, \bar{p}, \bar{\mathscr{T}})$,

$$\begin{aligned}
\ddot{V}_{\bar{\ddot{x}}, \bar{p}, \bar{\mathscr{T}}}(S) &:= \left\{ u \in \mathbf{R}^N \;\middle|\; \begin{array}{l} \exists \ddot{x}^S \in \ddot{F}^S(\bar{\ddot{x}}, \bar{p}, \bar{\mathscr{T}})\colon \\ \forall j \in S\colon u_j \leqslant \ddot{u}^j_S(\bar{\ddot{x}}, \bar{p}, \bar{\mathscr{T}}, \ddot{x}^S_{-\text{II}}) \end{array} \right\} \\
&= V_{x(\bar{\ddot{x}}, \bar{\mathscr{T}}), \bar{p}, \bar{\mathscr{T}}}(S), \text{ and}
\end{aligned}$$

$$\ddot{H}_{\bar{\bar{x}},\bar{p}} := \left\{ u \in \mathbf{R}^N \,\middle|\, \begin{array}{l} \exists (\ddot{x}, \mathscr{T}) \in G(\bar{\bar{x}}, \bar{p}): \\ \forall j \in T: u_j \leqslant \ddot{u}^j_T(\bar{\bar{x}}, \bar{p}, \mathscr{T}, \ddot{x}^T_{-\mathrm{II}}) \end{array} \right\} \supset H_{\bar{x},\bar{p}},$$

where $\bar{x}$ in the right-hand side is given by $\bar{x}_{-\mathrm{II}} := \bar{\bar{x}}_{-\mathrm{II}}$ and $\sum_{T \in \mathscr{T}} \bar{x}^{(T)}_{\mathrm{II}} := \sum_{j \in N} \bar{\bar{x}}_{\mathrm{II}}$ (choice of an admissible $\mathscr{T}$ does not affect $H_{\bar{x},\bar{p}}$ due to assumptions (ii_h) and (iii)). The *auxiliary economy* is defined as $\ddot{\mathscr{E}} := (\{\ddot{X}^j, \omega^j\}_{j \in N}, \{\ddot{F}^S_t(\cdot)\}_{S \in \mathscr{N}}, \ddot{H}_., \{\ddot{u}^j_S(\cdot)\}_{j \in S \in \mathscr{N}}, \mathscr{T})$. The advantage of using this concept is that the total excess demand given by strategy bundle $\ddot{x} \in \ddot{X}$ is $\sum_{j \in N}(\ddot{x}^j_{\mathrm{I}} - \omega^j - \ddot{x}^j_{\mathrm{II}})$, which is independent of a coalition structure.

Step 2. Introduce a fictitious "market participant" as the zeroth agent, and define $N_0 := \{0\} \cup N$, $\mathscr{N}_0 := \{S \mid \phi \neq S \subset N_0\}$. A model of generalized society $\ddot{\mathscr{S}}_0$ with player set N_0 (Remark 3.4.14) is now constructed from the auxiliary economy $\ddot{\mathscr{E}}$. The strategy space of player 0 is the price domain Δ^{l-1}. For each $j \in N$ and each $S \in \mathscr{N}$, the strategy space $\ddot{X}^j$, the feasible-strategy correspondence $\ddot{F}^S$, $\ddot{G}$ and the utility function $\ddot{u}^j_S$ of $\ddot{\mathscr{E}}$ are used as the corresponding concepts for $\ddot{\mathscr{S}}_0$. Define for each $S \subset N$,

$$\begin{aligned} &\ddot{F}^{\{0\} \cup S}(\bar{\bar{x}}, \bar{p}, \bar{\mathscr{T}}) := \Delta^{l-1} \times \ddot{F}^S(\bar{\bar{x}}, \bar{p}, \bar{\mathscr{T}}), \\ &\ddot{u}^j_{\{0\} \cup S}(\bar{\bar{x}}, \bar{p}, \bar{\mathscr{T}}, \ddot{x}^S, p) \\ &\quad := \begin{cases} p \cdot \sum_{j \in N}(\bar{\bar{x}}^j_{\mathrm{I}} - \omega^j - \bar{\bar{x}}^j_{\mathrm{II}}) \text{ if } j = 0, \\ \ddot{u}^j_S(\bar{\bar{x}}, \bar{p}, \bar{\mathscr{T}}, \ddot{x}^S) \text{ if } j \in S. \end{cases} \end{aligned}$$

The admissible coalition structures of $\ddot{\mathscr{S}}_0$ are $\{\{\{0\}\} \cup \mathscr{T} \mid \mathscr{T} \in \mathscr{T}\}$. It is easy to show that if the n-agent economy $\mathscr{E}$ satisfies conditions (i)–(v) of Theorem 3.4.6, then the $(n+1)$-player society $\ddot{\mathscr{S}}_0$ satisfies conditions (i), (ii′), (iii′), (iv′) and (v′) of Theorem 3.4.11 (modified in Remark 3.4.14). There exists, therefore, a social coalitional equilibrium $(\ddot{x}^*, p^*, \{\{0\}\} \cup \mathscr{T}^*)$ of $\ddot{\mathscr{S}}_0$.

Step 3. Define x^* by

$$x^{*T} \in F^T_{t^*_T}(x(\ddot{x}^*, \mathscr{T}^*), p^*, \mathscr{T}^*), \; T \in \mathscr{T}^*,$$

$$\sum_{T \in \mathscr{T}^*} x^{*(T)}_{\mathrm{II}} = \sum_{j \in N} \ddot{x}^{*j}_{\mathrm{II}}, \text{ and } \forall j \in N: x^{*j}_{-\mathrm{II}} = \ddot{x}^{*j}_{-\mathrm{II}}.$$

In view of assumption (ii_h) that $F^T_{t^*_T}(x^*, \bar{p}, \mathscr{T}^*)$ depends only upon $(\{x^{*j}_{-\mathrm{II}}\}_{j \in N}, \sum_{T \in \mathscr{T}^*} x^{*(T)}_{\mathrm{II}}, p^*, \mathscr{T}^*)$, whose second argument is equal to $\sum_{j \in N} \ddot{x}^{*j}_{\mathrm{II}}$, the feasibility condition (i′) of the equilibrium with transfer (Definition 3.4.2), $\forall T \in \mathscr{T}^*: x^{*T} \in F^T_{t^*_T}(x^*, \bar{p}, \mathscr{T}^*)$, is satisfied by $(x^*, p^*, \mathscr{T}^*)$. Similarly, in view of assumptions (ii_h) and (iii), the coalitional stability condition (ii) of the equilibrium with transfer is satisfied. To show the market clearance condition (iii), choose any market commodity h. Notice that

$$e^h := (0, \ldots, \overset{h}{\overbrace{1}}, \ldots, 0) \in \Delta^{l-1}.$$

Now, the total excess demand for commodity h is nonpositive, since

$$\begin{aligned}
&\sum_{j\in N} x^{*j}_{\mathrm{I},h} - \sum_{T\in\mathscr{T}^*} x^{*(T)}_{\mathrm{II},h} - \sum_{j\in N}\omega^j_h \\
&= \sum_{j\in N}(\ddot{x}^{*j}_{\mathrm{I},h} - \ddot{x}^{*j}_{\mathrm{II},h} - \omega^j_h) \\
&= e^h \cdot \sum_{j\in N}(\ddot{x}^{*j}_{\mathrm{I}} - \ddot{x}^{*j}_{\mathrm{II}} - \omega^j) \\
&\leqslant p^* \cdot \sum_{j\in N}(\ddot{x}^{*j}_{\mathrm{I}} - \ddot{x}^{*j}_{\mathrm{II}} - \omega^j) \\
&= p^* \cdot \Big(\sum_{j\in N} x^{*j}_{\mathrm{I}} - \sum_{T\in\mathscr{T}^*} x^{*(T)}_{\mathrm{II}} - \sum_{j\in N}\omega^j\Big) \leqslant 0.
\end{aligned}$$

Here, the last inequality is due to Walras' law. □

The rest of this section will be devoted to applications of the social coalitional equilibrium existence theorem (Theorem 3.4.11) to the existence problems for other economic or game-theoretical models. Before moving on to this issue, notice that Theorem 3.4.11 includes the Nash equilibrium existence theorem (Nash, 1950, 1951). Indeed, the former reduces to the latter when $F^S(x) = X^S$, $u^j_S(x, \xi^S) = -\infty$ if $\# S \geqslant 2$, and $\mathscr{T}$ consists only of the finest partition.

The first application is on the core of a non-side-payment game (Definitions 3.3.5 and 3.3.6). It was shown in the paragraph following Definition 3.3.6 how the economy (Definition 3.1.4) and its equilibrium (Definition 3.1.5) can be specialized to a non-side-payment game and a utility allocation in its core. The direct application of Theorem 3.4.6 or Theorem 3.4.11 does not yield Scarf's theorem for nonemptiness of the core (Theorem 2.2.1), however, as Figure 3.1 illustrates: The example of this figure is a two-person balanced game, such that $V(\{j\}) = \{u \in \mathbf{R}^2 \mid u_j \leqslant 0\}$. The core is the part $\widehat{ABCDE}$ of the boundary of $V(\{1, 2\})$. Here, the segment $\overline{BC}$ is vertical, and the segment $\overline{CD}$ is horizontal. Then, for the member C of the core, the set of all feasible strategies that give rise to C is the set $\overline{BC} \cup \overline{CD}$, which is not convex; the convexity condition (condition (v) of Theorem 3.4.6, condition (v) of Theorem 3.4.11) is thus violated. A little elaboration will, however, yield Scarf's theorem.

Proof of Theorem 2.2.1. *Step 1.* Let V be a non-side-payment game which satisfies all the conditions (i)–(iv) of Theorem 2.2.1. Recall that vector $b \in \mathbf{R}^N$ is defined by

$$b_j := \max\{u_j \in \mathbf{R} \mid u \in V(\{j\})\}.$$

Let $V_+(S) := \{u \in V(S) \mid u \geqslant b\}$, and define another non-side-payment game W by

$$W(S) := V_+(S) - \mathbf{R}^N_+.$$

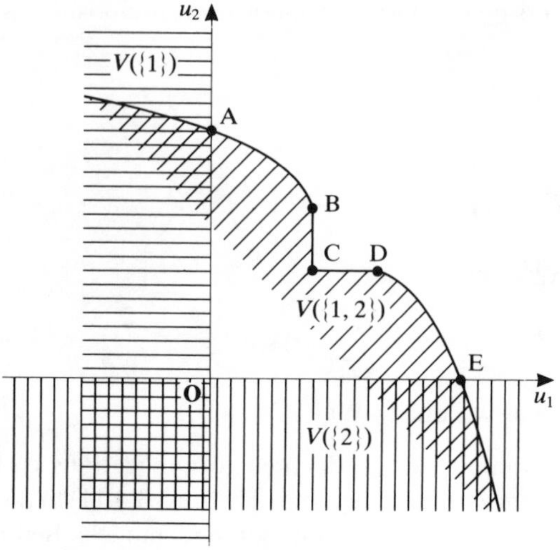

3.1 Balanced non-side-payment game which does not satisfy the convexity condition

Then, W satisfies all the conditions (i)–(iv) of Theorem 2.2.1, and $C(W) = C(V)$. Choose any $c \ll b$; without loss of generality, $c = \mathbf{0}$. The advantage of using game W instead of game V is that there exists $M' > 0$ such that for any $u \in W(S)$, $u_j < M'$ for all $j \in S$. However, one still cannot avoid the difficulty of Figure 3.1 even with this game W. Define

$$U := \{u \in \bigcup_{S \in \mathcal{N}} W(S) \mid \forall j \in N: u_j \leqslant M'\}.$$

A bijection from the unit simplex $\Delta^N := \{x \in \mathbf{R}^N_+ \mid \sum_{j \in N} x_j = 1\}$ to the boundary of $U \cap \mathbf{R}^N_+$ in $\mathbf{R}^N_+$ is now constructed. Define t: $\Delta^N \rightarrow \mathbf{R}_+$ by

$$t(x) := \max \{t \in \mathbf{R}_+ \mid tx \in U\}.$$

The required bijection f is then defined by $f(x) := t(x)x$. It is continuous, in view of the choice of c. Define for each $S \in \mathcal{N}$,

$$C_S := \{x \in \Delta^N \mid f(x) \in W(S)\}.$$

The family $\{C_S\}_{S \in \mathcal{N}}$ covers Δ^N. Define yet another non-side-payment game W' by

$$W'(S) := C_S + \mathbf{R}^{N \setminus S} - \mathbf{R}^N_+,$$

where $\mathbf{R}^{N \setminus S}$ is identified with the subspace $\{x \in \mathbf{R}^N \mid x_j = 0 \text{ for all } j \in S\}$. The game W' satisfies all the assumptions (i)–(iv) of Theorem 2.2.1, and $[x \in C(W') \text{ iff } f(x) \in C(W)]$. Thus, one needs to prove $C(W') \neq \phi$.

Step 2. A model of society $\mathscr{S}$ will be constructed from game W'. For each player j, his strategy space X^j is the compact interval $[0, M']$. For each coalition S, its feasible-strategy correspondence is the constant correspondence, $F^S(\bar{x}) := \{x^S \in X^S \mid \exists x^{N\setminus S}: (x^S, x^{N\setminus S}) \in W'(S)\}$. The utility functions are the projections, $u_S^j(\bar{x}, x^S) := x^j$. The only admissible coalition structure is the coarsest coalition structure $\{N\}$. Then, $\mathscr{S}$ satisfies all the conditions (i)–(v) of Theorem 3.4.11 (indeed, the convexity condition (v) is a consequence of the fact, $C(W') \subset \Delta^N$). A social coalitional equilibrium of $\mathscr{S}$ is a utility allocation in the core of W'. □

The next existence problem is about the strong equilibrium introduced in Section 2.3. The two existence theorems (Theorems 2.3.4 and 2.3.7) are consequences of the following theorem:

Theorem 3.4.15. *Let $\mathscr{T}$ be a coalition structure and let $\mathscr{S} := (\{X^j, u^j\}_{j \in N}, \{F^S\}_{S \in \mathscr{N}}, \{\mathscr{T}\})$ be a society (defined in Section 2.3). There exists a strong equilibrium x^*, whose feasibility is defined by $x^{*T} \in F^T(x^*)$ for every $T \in \mathscr{T}$, if*

(i) *for every $j \in N$, X^j is a nonempty, convex, compact subset of a real Hausdorff locally convex topological vector space;*

(ii) *for every $j \in N$, u^j is continuous in X, and for each $\bar{x} \in X$, $u^j(\bar{x}^{N\setminus T}, \cdot)$ is quasi-concave in $F^T(\bar{x})$, where T is the unique member of $\mathscr{T}$ such that $T \ni j$;*

(iii) *for every $S \in \mathscr{N}$, the feasible-strategy correspondence F^S is both upper semicontinuous and lower semicontinuous in X, and for each $\bar{x}$, $F^S(\bar{x})$ is nonempty, closed, and convex; and*

(iv) *for every $\bar{x} \in X$, the non-side-payment game $V_{\bar{x}}$ defined by $V_{\bar{x}}(S) := \{u \in \mathbf{R}^N \mid \exists x^S \in F^S(\bar{x}): \forall j \in S: u_j \leqslant u^j(x^S, \bar{x}^{N\setminus S})\}$ is balanced with respect to $\mathscr{T}$, i.e.,*

$$\bigcap_{S \in \mathscr{B}} V_{\bar{x}}(S) \subset \bigcap_{T \in \mathscr{T}} V_{\bar{x}}(T)$$

for every balanced subfamily $\mathscr{B}$ of $\mathscr{N}$.

Proof. By the same argument as in the proof of Claim 3.4.7, convexity of $F^T(\bar{x})$ and quasi-concavity of $u^j(\bar{x}^{N\setminus T}, \cdot)$ in $F^T(\bar{x})$ imply condition (v) of Theorem 3.4.11 on the society $(\{X^j\}_{j \in N}, \{F^S\}_{S \in \mathscr{N}}, \{u^j_S\}_{j \in S \in \mathscr{N}}, \{\mathscr{T}\})$ defined by $u^j_S(\bar{x}, x^S) := u^j(\bar{x}^{N\setminus S}, x^S)$. Therefore, by Theorem 3.4.11, there exists a social coalitional equilibrium, which is a strong equilibrium. □

Zhao (1992) proposed a *hybrid solution* concept for a game in normal form $\{X^j, u^j\}_{j \in N}$ and a coalition structure $\mathscr{T}$: It is a strategy bundle $x^* \in X$ such that for each $T \in \mathscr{T}$, x^{*T} is an α-core strategy of the subgame $\{X^j, u^j(x^{*N\setminus T}, \cdot)\}_{j \in T}$. Zhao established that *a hybrid solution exists under the assumptions (i) and (ii) of Theorem 3.4.15 in which $F^T(\bar{x}) = X^T$.*

The final existence problem in this section is about a competitive equilibrium of a private ownership economy (Definitions 3.3.3 and 3.3.4). It was shown in the second paragraph after the statement of Definition 3.3.4 how the economy (Definition 3.1.4) and its equilibrium (Definition 3.1.5) can be specialized to a private ownership economy and its competitive equilibrium. The direct application of Theorem 3.4.6 yields the following existence theorem of Arrow and Debreu (1954). See also the independent works of McKenzie (1954), Gale (1955), and Nikaido (1956). The application of Theorem 3.4.11 as in the above proof of Theorem 3.4.6 (Steps 2 and 3) also establishes the same theorem.

Theorem 3.4.16. *Let $\mathscr{E}_{po}$ be a private ownership economy (Definition 3.3.3). There exists a competitive equilibrium of $\mathscr{E}_{po}$ if*

(i_c) *for every consumer $i \in N_c$, his consumption set X^i is a nonempty, compact and convex subset of $\mathbf{R}^l$;*

(i_f) *for every producer $j \in N_f$, his production set Y^j is a nonempty, compact and convex subset of $\mathbf{R}^l$;*

(ii_c) *for every consumer $i \in N_c$, his budget-set correspondence F^i: $\Delta^{l-1} \rightarrow X^i$,*

$$F^i(\bar{p}) := \{x^i \in X^i \mid \bar{p} \cdot x^i \leqslant \bar{p} \cdot \omega^i + \sum_{j \in N_f} \theta_{ij} \max \bar{p} \cdot Y^j\},$$

is both upper semicontinuous and lower semicontinuous in Δ^{l-1}, and for each $\bar{p}$, $F^i(\bar{p}) \neq \phi$;

(iii_c) *for every consumer $i \in N_c$, his utility function u^i is continuous and quasi-concave in X^i.*

Remark 3.4.17. Arrow and Debreu (1954, pp. 276–278) also (1) supplied conditions on $\mathscr{E}_{po}$ under which the upper and lower semicontinuities of the budget-set correspondences are satisfied, and (2) relaxed the boundedness assumption on X^is and Y^js. The same technique can relax the boundedness assumption of Theorem 3.4.6 on the strategy spaces of economy $\mathscr{E}$. □

3.5 Coalition production economy literature

Formulation of the economic models of Sections 3.1 and 3.2 was motivated by the need to study the workings of the economic forces that specialists in the theory of the firm had identified since the 1920s. From the formal point of view, the models may be considered extensions of the model of coalition production economy, originally studied by Debreu and Scarf (1963) and Hildenbrand (1968), both in the context of the core convergence/equivalence theorems. The purpose of this section is to review the literature on the coalition production economy.

In the coalition production economy, there are l commodities and n economic agents. Labor is considered one of the l commodities. Denote by N the set of economic agents. Each agent j plays two roles here. The first role is that of consumer/laborer, characterized by his consumer characteristics (X^j, u^j, ω^j) of consumption set $X^j (\subset \mathbf{R}^l)$, utility function u^j: $X^j \to \mathbf{R}$, and initial endowment ω^j $(\in \mathbf{R}^l)$ (see the paragraph preceding the statement of Definition 3.3.1). The second role is that of owner of production units. It is postulated that each coalition S as the set of owners of its own firm can manage production activities constrained by its technology (production set) $Y(S) \subset \mathbf{R}^l$. Set as before, $\mathcal{N} := 2^N \backslash \{\phi\}$. The usual sign convention for demand and supply is adopted.

Definition 3.5.1. A *coalition production economy* is a list of specified data, $\mathscr{E}_{cp} := (\{X^j, u^j, \omega^j\}_{j \in N}, \{Y(S)\}_{S \in \mathcal{N}})$.

If no market mechanism is to be introduced to coalition production economy $\mathscr{E}_{cp}$, cooperative behavior of its agents can be modelled by the associated non-side-payment game V defined by

$$V(S) := \left\{ u \in \mathbf{R}^N \;\middle|\; \begin{array}{l} \exists \{x^j\}_{j \in S} \in \prod_{j \in S} X^j : \exists y \in Y(S): \\ \sum_{j \in S} x^j \leqslant \sum_{j \in S} \omega^j + y, \text{ and} \\ \forall j \in S: u_j \leqslant u^j(x^j) \end{array} \right\}.$$

Assuming that the grand coalition is realized in equilibrium, a core allocation is defined as a commodity allocation which gives rise to a core utility allocation of game V.

Definition 3.5.2. A *core allocation* of coalition production economy $\mathscr{E}_{cp}$ is an $(n+1)$-tuple $(\{x^{*j}\}_{j \in N}, y^*)$ of members of X^j's and $Y(N)$, respectively, such that

(i) $\sum_{j \in N} x^{*j} \leqslant \sum_{j \in N} \omega^j + y^*$; and

(ii) it is not true that there exist $S \in \mathcal{N}$, $\{x^j\}_{j \in S} \in \prod_{j \in S} X^j$ and $y \in Y(S)$ satisfying $\sum_{j \in S} x^j \leqslant \sum_{j \in S} \omega^j + y$, such that $u^j(x^j) > u^j(x^{*j})$ for every $j \in S$.

It was mentioned at the outset of this section that the model of the coalition production economy had been proposed in order to extend the limit theorems and the equivalence theorems on the core allocations to economies with production. This problem is an issue in descriptive economics, as it intends to understand properties of a descriptive solution concept, competitive equilibrium. Indeed, Werner Hildenbrand wrote:

> In this paper we wish to investigate a generalization of Aumann's result – the identity of the core and the set of competitive allocations in a pure exchange economy – namely the study of an economy where production is possible (Hildenbrand, 1968, p. 444).

> In the analysis of the core of an economy it is not sufficient to know for every coalition E the shares of profit of the different production units. What are needed are the production possibilities available to every coalition, since in the core analysis

the allocation process does not involve prices and hence profit is not defined. For this reason we introduced production in Hildenbrand (1968) by specifying for every coalition $E \in \mathscr{C}$ a production set $\mathbf{Y}_E$. As in Hildenbrand (1968, p. 444), we assume that the function $\mathbf{Y}$ of $\mathscr{C}$ into subsets of $\mathbf{R}^l$ is countably additive (Hildenbrand, 1970, p. 611).

Here, the countable additivity assumption on the production-set correspondence $\mathbf{Y}$: $S \mapsto Y(S)$ is crucial: Together with some regularity assumptions, it guarantees that given each price vector p, the maximal profit function v_p which associates to each coalition S the maximal profit that S can make,

$$v_p(S) := \sup \{p \cdot y \mid y \in Y(S)\},$$

is countably additive, so has the Radon-Nikodym derivative $\pi_p(\cdot)$. It was only with the value $\pi_p(j)$ that Hildenbrand (1968, Definition 2, p. 446) could define (1) the budget constraint of consumer j given price vector p, and hence (2) a competitive equilibrium of economy $\mathscr{E}_{cp}$. This assumption says, however, that forming a coalition does not increase or decrease the efficiency of production. The advantage of coalition formation if any, therefore, comes only from the possibility of redistribution of initial endowments among the members of the coalition.

The formal framework of coalition production economy has a great potential to exploit in developing an axiomatic descriptive theory of the firm, since a coalition can naturally be identified with a firm as an organization. To provide a powerful explanation of formation of firms, one needs to allow for the situation in which a coalition has a more efficient production set than the sum of the production sets held by the individuals of the coalition, that is, the production-set correspondence is non-additive. The rest of this section reviews some works which can handle this situation.

Böhm (1974) supplied conditions on $\mathscr{E}_{cp}$ under which the associated game V is balanced, thereby establishing a core allocation existence theorem in the light of Scarf's theorem (Theorem 2.2.1). Notice that in the stability condition (ii) for a core allocation (Definition 3.5.2), a more primitive concept of preference relation (a binary relation on X^j) may be used instead of the utility concept. Border (1984) proposed a generalized model of society with non-ordered preference relations as an extension of the society (Definition 3.4.9), defined the core concept in his new setup, provided conditions for nonemptiness of the core, and applied the result to establish a core allocation existence theorem for a coalition production economy with non-ordered preference relations. Florenzano (1989) considered a coalition production economy with an infinite dimensional commodity space and non-ordered preference relations, and provided a core allocation existence theorem, strengthening Border's result on a coalition production economy (a certain continuity assumption on the preference relations was weakened). In all three works, the convexity assumption on the production set $Y(N)$ (the assumption of non-increasing returns to scale) was essential.

Another line of work on the core allocations of a coalition production economy, pioneered by Scarf (1986) whose first draft had been circulated as a working paper since 1963, is to explore the implications of the non-convexity condition on $Y(N)$, in particular implications of increasing returns to scale. This issue will be fully discussed in Chapter 5. Since a core allocation in this setup is usually Pareto optimal, one obtains a result in normative economics: How to design an economic mechanism to achieve a Pareto optimum in the presence of increasing returns to scale?

Böhm (1973) considered the following private ownership economy based on a coalition production economy. It is a descriptive economic model, quite different in spirit from the private ownership economy of Arrow and Debreu (Definition 3.3.3). Let the unit simplex Δ^{l-1} be the price domain. A *firm structure* is a subset of $\mathcal{N}$, it is not necessarily a partition of N. Let $\mathcal{T}$ be an *a priori* given family of admissible firm structures. Given any price vector $p \in \Delta^{l-1}$, the owners of firm S unanimously want the firm to realize its maximal profit,

$$v_p(S) := \max\{p \cdot y \mid y \in Y(S)\},$$

but conflicts arise among them as to how to divide their profit. If d_j is the sum of dividends that agent j receives from the various firms he owns, then bundle $\{d_j\}_{j \in N}$ is coalitionally stable if for every $S \in \mathcal{N}$, $\sum_{j \in S} d_j \geqslant v_p(S)$. A stable profit distribution is a member of the core of side-payment game v_p, made feasible by some firm structure. Thus, a *market equilibrium with a stable firm structure* is defined as a quintuple $(\{x^{*j}\}_{j \in N}, \{d_j^*\}_{j \in N}, \mathcal{T}^*, \{y^{*T}\}_{T \in \mathcal{T}^*}, p^*)$ of members of $\prod_{j \in N} X^j$, $\mathbf{R}^N$, $\mathcal{T}$, $\prod_{T \in \mathcal{T}^*} Y(T)$, Δ^{l-1}, respectively, such that

(i$_c$) $x^{*j} \in X^j$, $p^* \cdot x^{*j} \leqslant p^* \cdot \omega^j + d_j^*$, for every $j \in N$;

(i$_f$) $\sum_{i \in N} d_i^* \leqslant \sum_{T \in \mathcal{T}^*} p^* \cdot y^{*T}$, and $y^{*T} \in Y(T)$ for every $T \in \mathcal{T}^*$;

(ii$_c$) it is not true that there exist $j \in N$ and $x^j \in X^j$ satisfying $p^* \cdot x^j \leqslant p^* \cdot \omega^j + d_j^*$, such that $u^j(x^j) > u^j(x^{*j})$;

(ii$_f$) it is not true that there exist $S \in \mathcal{N}$ such that $\sum_{j \in S} d_j^* < v_{p^*}(S)$; and

(iii) $\sum_{j \in N} x^{*j} \leqslant \sum_{j \in N} \omega^j + \sum_{T \in \mathcal{T}^*} y^{*T}$.

The production-set correspondence $Y(\cdot)$ is not necessarily additive, so function $v_p(\cdot)$ may not be additive. Böhm's ingenuity lies in the fact that he introduced the core of game v_p instead of the Radon-Nikodym derivative, as the latter may not exist. Of course, the two coincide when the latter exists. Böhm (1973) established an existence theorem for market equilibria with a stable firm structure in the following way. He first observed that the core correspondence, $p \mapsto C(v_p, \mathscr{T})$, is lower semicontinuous in Δ^{l-1}, so there is its continuous selection, $p \mapsto d(p)$, due to Michael's (1956) theorem. The standard technique for establishing the existence of market equilibria then applies to the situation in which given each price vector p, every consumer demands his utility-maximizing commodity bundle subject to the budget constraint,

$$x^j \in X^j, \; p \cdot x^j \leqslant p \cdot \omega^j + d_j(p),$$

and every producer chooses a profit-maximizing input-output vector. Actually, the continuity property of the core correspondence (for the side-payment games) is a special case of a theorem due to Walkup and Wets (1969). See Delbaen (1974) for the non-continuity property of the core correspondence in the infinite-player case.

Böhm's (1973) economy is a hybrid of the neoclassical market economy and the side-payment games parameterized by price vectors, and his equilibrium concept (market equilibrium with a stable firm structure) is a hybrid of the competitive equilibrium and the core. Ichiishi (1977) pointed out difficulties in interpreting Böhm's model, and showed that the model of coalition production economy could describe an economy in which firms are managed by the laborers (human-resource holders) who work for it. The economy presented in Section 3.1 (Definition 3.1.4) is a hybrid of the neoclassical market economy and the non-side-payment games parameterized by strategy bundles and price vectors, and the equilibrium concept (Definition 3.1.5) is a hybrid of the competitive equilibrium and the core (the strong equilibria are the fixed-points of the core correspondence). Böhm's technique of applying a continuous selection of the core correspondence does not work for proving an equilibrium existence theorem here, since (1) the core of a non-side-payment game can be a disconnected set, and (2) the core correspondence for the non-side-payment games is not lower semicontinuous. In order to establish an equilibrium existence theorem for this economy (like Theorem 3.4.11), one has to look into the logic that underlies a core nonemptiness theorem for a non-side-payment game (like Theorem 2.2.1). Indeed, Theorem 3.4.11 was proved by unifying the technique (Debreu, 1952) for proving a competitive equilibrium existence theorem and the technique (Ichiishi, 1981a) for proving a core nonemptiness theorem.

3.6 Theorems on closed coverings of a simplex

Knaster, Kuratowski and Mazurkiewicz (1929) established a theorem on closed coverings of a simplex (called here the K-K-M theorem), and used it to provide a simple alternative proof of Brouwer's (1912) fixed-point theorem. Conversely, Kim C. Border and Edward J. Green (see Border (1985)), and Dugundji and Granas (1982) independently provided a simple proof of the K-K-M theorem using Brouwer's fixed-point theorem; the proof is based on Browder's (1968) technique which involves a partition of unity.

As was pointed out at the end of the last section, the social coalitional equilibrium existence theorem (Theorem 3.4.11) was proved largely based on a certain technique for proving Scarf's theorem for nonemptiness of the core (Theorem 2.2.1). It has appeared that virtually every available proof of the Scarf theorem boils down to a generalization of the K-K-M theorem. The purpose of this section is to review these theorems on closed coverings of a simplex, to clarify relationships among them, and to elucidate their positions in the fixed-point literature. Relationships with game theory will also be pointed out. The materials here are taken from Ichiishi and Idzik (1990).

Let N be a nonempty finite set, and let $\{e^i\}_{i\in N}$ be the unit vectors of the $(\#N)$-dimensional Euclidean space $\mathbf{R}^N$; $e^j_j=1$ and $e^j_i=0$ for every $i\neq j$. Denote by $\mathcal{N}$ the family of nonempty subsets of N (i.e., $\mathcal{N}:=2^N\backslash\{\phi\}$). The faces of the unit simplex are then given by $\Delta^S:=\mathrm{co}\{e^i \mid i\in S\}$ (the convex hull of $\{e^i \mid i\in S\}$), $S\in\mathcal{N}$. The simplex Δ^N is endowed with the relativized Euclidean topology. For each $S\in\mathcal{N}$, its characteristic vector is given by $\chi_S:=\sum_{i\in S} e^i$. It was more than sixty years ago that Sperner (1928) published the following result:

Theorem 3.6.1 (Sperner). *Let $\{C^i\}_{i\in N}$ be a closed covering of Δ^N such that $\Delta^{N\backslash\{i\}}\cap C^i=\phi$ for every $i\in N$. Then $\bigcap_{i\in N} C^i\neq\phi$.*

The closed covering given in Theorem 3.6.1 has the property that $\Delta^{N\backslash\{i\}}\subset \bigcup_{j\in N\backslash\{i\}} C^j$, so $\Delta^S\subset\bigcup_{j\in S} C^j$. A year later, Knaster, Kuratowski and Mazurkiewicz (1929) published the following generalization of Theorem 3.6.1, called here the K-K-M theorem:

Theorem 3.6.2 (Knaster, Kuratowski and Mazurkiewicz). *Let $\{C^i\}_{i\in N}$ be a family of closed subsets of Δ^N such that $\Delta^S\subset\bigcup_{i\in S} C^i$ for every $S\in\mathcal{N}$. Then $\bigcap_{i\in N} C^i\neq\phi$.*

Fan (1968) pointed out that Theorem 3.6.1 can be re-formulated as the following dual form to Theorem 3.6.2:

Theorem 3.6.3 (Sperner, as re-formulated by Fan). *Let $\{C^i\}_{i\in N}$ be a closed covering of Δ^N such that $\Delta^{N\backslash\{i\}}\subset C^i$ for every $i\in N$. Then $\bigcap_{i\in N} C^i\neq\phi$.*

(To show the equivalence of Theorems 3.6.1 and 3.6.3, use the Lebesgue number: For any open cover $\{U^i\}_{i\in I}$ of a compact metric space, there exists a positive number δ, called the *Lebesgue number*, such that any open ball of radius δ is contained in at least one of the U^i.) Theorems 3.6.1 and 3.6.3 each can also be shown to be equivalent to Brouwer's fixed-point theorem.

Let K be a finite set such that $K \supset N$, let $A := ((a_{ij}))_{i \in N, j \in K}$ be a $(\# N) \times (\# K)$ real matrix whose rows (columns, resp.) are indexed by $i \in N$ (by $j \in K$, resp.) and let $c := (c_i)_{i \in N}$ be a $(\# N) \times 1$ real matrix such that

$$a_{ij} = \begin{cases} 1 & \text{if } i = j \in N; \\ 0 & \text{if } i, j \in N \text{ but } i \neq j; \end{cases}$$
$$c_i > 0 \quad \text{for every } i \in N.$$

Notice that $\{x \in \mathbf{R}_+^K \mid Ax = c\} \neq \phi$. Theorem 3.6.3 is a special case of the following Scarf's (1967b) theorem:

Theorem 3.6.4 (Scarf). *Let $\{C^j\}_{j \in K}$ be a closed covering of Δ^N such that $\Delta^{N \setminus \{j\}} \subset C^j$ for every $j \in N$. Assume that the set $\{x \in \mathbf{R}_+^K \mid Ax = c\}$ is bounded. Then there exists $x \in \mathbf{R}_+^K$ such that $Ax = c$ and $\cap \{C^j \mid j \in K, x_j > 0\} \neq \phi$.*

Theorem 3.6.4 is still valid even when the assumption $[\forall i \in N: c_i > 0]$ is replaced by a weaker assumption $[\forall i \in N: c_i \geqslant 0]$, but the theorem is actually trivial if $c_i = 0$ for some $i \in N$. Scarf (1967a, 1967b) used the "path-following technique" of Lemke and Howson (1964) to establish a theorem on primitive sets (Theorem 3.6.11 below), and then used the latter theorem to prove Theorem 3.6.4. An alternative proof of Theorem 3.6.11 was made by Kannai (1970); he used Brouwer's fixed-point theorem only.

A generalization of Theorem 3.6.2 was made by Shapley (1973).

Theorem 3.6.5 (Shapley). *Let $\{C^S\}_{S \in \mathcal{N}}$ be a family of closed subsets of Δ^N such that $\Delta^T \subset \cup_{S \subset T} C^S$ for every $T \in \mathcal{N}$. Then there exists a balanced family $\mathcal{B}$ such that $\cap_{S \in \mathcal{B}} C^S \neq \phi$.*

To see that Theorem 3.6.5 includes Theorem 3.6.2, let $\{C^i\}_{i \in N}$ be a closed covering as given in Theorem 3.6.2. Define $\{C^S\}_{S \in \mathcal{N}}$ by: $C^{\{i\}} := C^i$ for every $i \in N$, and $C^S := \phi$ if $\# S \geqslant 2$, and then apply Theorem 3.6.5. Shapley (1973) established Theorem 3.6.5 by using the "path-following technique" of Lemke and Howson (1964). Todd (1978, 1979) has a proof of Theorem 3.6.5 which makes use of Brouwer's fixed-point theorem and a sequence of simplicial partitions. Shapley (1987) has a shorter proof of Theorem 3.6.5 using Kakutani's (1941) fixed-point theorem. Ichiishi (1981a) has a yet shorter proof of Theorem 3.6.5 using Fan's (1969) coincidence theorem; see also Ichiishi (1983). To see the relationship between the conclusions of Theorem 3.6.4 and Theorem 3.6.5, let $\tilde{A}$ be the $(\# N) \times (\# \mathcal{N})$ matrix such that column S is precisely χ_S, $S \in \mathcal{N}$. The set $\{x \in \mathbf{R}_+^{\mathcal{N}} \mid \tilde{A}x = \chi_N\}$ is nonempty and bounded. Then the conclusion of Theorem 3.6.5 is re-formulated as: There exists $x \in \mathbf{R}_+^{\mathcal{N}}$ such that

$\tilde{A}x = \chi_N$, and
$\cap \{C^S \mid S \in \mathcal{N}, x_S > 0\} \neq \phi$.

Ichiishi (1988b) established the following theorem, which is dual to Theorem 3.6.5 just as Theorem 3.6.3 is dual to Theorem 3.6.2, and which is also a generalization of Theorem 3.6.3.

Theorem 3.6.6. *Let* $\{C^S\}_{S \in \mathcal{N}}$ *be a family of closed subsets of* Δ^N *such that* $\Delta^T \subset \cup_{S \supset N \setminus T} C^S$ *for every* $T \in \mathcal{N}$. *Then there exists a balanced family* $\mathcal{B}$ *such that* $\cap_{S \in \mathcal{B}} C^S \neq \phi$.

David Schmeidler pointed out that Theorems 3.6.5 and 3.6.6 are equivalent; his argument is reproduced in Ichiishi (1988b). To see that Theorem 3.6.6 includes Theorem 3.6.3, let $\{C^i\}_{i \in N}$ be a closed covering as given in Theorem 3.6.3. Define $\{C^S\}_{S \in \mathcal{N}}$ by $C^S := \cap_{i \in S} C^i$ for every $S \in \mathcal{N}$, and then apply Theorem 3.6.6. Neither of Theorems 3.6.4 and 3.6.6 includes the other.

Let K, N be given as before, and define $M := K \setminus N$. Let $B := ((b_{ij}))_{i \in N, j \in \mathcal{N} \cup M}$ and $c := (c_i)_{i \in N}$ be a $(\# N) \times (\# \mathcal{N} + \# M)$ matrix and a $(\# N) \times 1$ matrix respectively such that

$$c_i > 0 \text{ for every } i \in N;$$
$$b_{ij} = \begin{cases} c_i & \text{if } i \in j \in \mathcal{N}; \\ 0 & \text{if } i \in N, j \in \mathcal{N} \text{ but } i \notin j. \end{cases}$$

The following theorem is a special case of Ichiishi and Idzik (1990, Theorem 2.2), but includes Theorem 3.6.5.

Theorem 3.6.7. *Let* $\{C^j\}_{j \in \mathcal{N} \cup M}$ *be a closed covering of* Δ^N *such that* $\Delta^T \subset \bigcup_{S \subset T} C^S$ *for every* $T \in \mathcal{N} \setminus \{N\}$. *Assume that the set* $\{x \in \mathbf{R}_+^{\mathcal{N} \cup M} \mid Bx = c\}$ *is bounded. Then there exists* $x \in \mathbf{R}_+^{\mathcal{N} \cup M}$ *such that* $Bx = c$ *and* $\cap \{C^j \mid j \in \mathcal{N} \cup M, x_j > 0\} \neq \phi$.

The proof of Theorem 3.6.7 uses the following claim:

Claim 3.6.8. *Let* $n \leqslant k$, *let* B *be an* $n \times k$ *matrix whose first* n *columns constitute the unit matrix, and let* c *be an* $n \times 1$ *nonnegative matrix. Then the following two conditions (i) and (ii) are equivalent:*
(i) *The set* $\{z \in \mathbf{R}_+^k \mid Bz = c\}$ *is bounded; and*
(ii) $\neg \exists z \in \mathbf{R}_+^k \setminus \{\mathbf{0}\}$: $Bz = \mathbf{0}$.
If, moreover, c *is nonzero, then any of the conditions (i) and (ii) implies the following condition (iii).*
(iii) $\neg \exists z \in \mathbf{R}_+^k$: $Bz = -c$.

Proof of Theorem 3.6.7. Without loss of generality, assume $c \in \Delta^N$. Denote by b^j column j of the matrix B, $j \in \mathcal{N} \cup M$, and define

$\forall S \in \mathcal{N}$: $m^S := b^S / \sum_{i \in S} c_i$; and
$\forall j \in M$: $m^j := b^j + (1 - \sum_{i \in N} b_{ij})\, c$.

Then, $m^S \in \Delta^S$ for every $S \in \mathcal{N}$, and $m^j \in \text{aff } \Delta^N$ (the affine hull of Δ^N) for every $j \in M$. Define for each $x \in \Delta^N$,

$$F(x) := \text{co}\{m^j \mid j \in \mathcal{N} \cup M.\ C^j \ni x\},$$
$$G(x) := \{m^N\}.$$

The correspondences F and G from Δ^N to aff Δ^N are upper semicontinuous, and nonempty-, closed-, convex-valued. Now, choose any $x \in \Delta^N$ and any $p \in \mathbf{R}^N$ such that $p \cdot x = \min p \cdot \Delta^N$.

If $x \notin \text{icr}\Delta^N$ (the relative interior of Δ^N), then there exists $T \in \mathcal{N} \backslash \{N\}$ such that $x \in \text{icr}\Delta^T$. Then, $p \cdot y = \min p \cdot \Delta^N$ for all $y \in \Delta^T$. By the assumption there exists $S \subset T$ such that $x \in C^S$, and for this S,

$$m^S \in F(x),\ p \cdot m^S = \min p \cdot \Delta^N.$$

There exist, therefore, $u \in F(x)$ and $v \in G(x)$ such that $p \cdot u \leqslant p \cdot v$.

If $x \in \text{icr}\Delta^N$, then $p \cdot y = p \cdot z$ for all $y, z \in \text{aff } \Delta^N$; in particular, for all $u \in F(x)$ and $v \in G(x)$, $p \cdot u = p \cdot v$.

Thus, all the assumptions of Fan's coincidence theorem (Theorem 3.4.12) are satisfied, so there exists $x^* \in \Delta^N$ such that $F(x^*) \cap G(x^*) \neq \phi$. Define $I_1 := \{S \in \mathcal{N} \mid C^S \ni x^*\}$ and $I_2 := \{j \in M \mid C^j \ni x^*\}$. Then there exists $\{z_j\}_{j \in I_1 \cup I_2} \subset \mathbf{R}_+$ such that $m^N = \sum_{j \in I_1 \cup I_2} z_j m^j$. By substituting the definition of m^j's and by setting $t_j := 1 - \sum_{i \in N} b_{ij}$, one obtains

$$c = \sum_{S \in I_1} z_S b^S / \sum_{i \in S} c_i + \sum_{j \in I_2} z_j (b^j + t_j c).$$

There exist, therefore, $z'_j \in \mathbf{R}_+$, $j \in I_1 \cup I_2$, not all zero, such that

$$(1 - \sum_{j \in I_2} z'_j t_j) c = \sum_{j \in I_2 \cup I_2} z'_j b^j.$$

By Claim 3.6.8,

$$1 - \sum_{j \in I_2} z'_j t_j > 0,$$

thus there exists $z^* \in \mathbf{R}_+^{\mathcal{N} \cup M}$ such that

$$Bz^* = c, \text{ and } \cap \{C^j \mid z^*_j > 0\} \supset \sum_{j \in I_1 \cup I_2} C^j \neq \phi. \ \square$$

The following theorem is a special case of Ichiishi and Idzik (1990, Theorem 2.6); it is dual to Theorem 3.6.7, and includes Theorems 3.6.4 and 3.6.6.

Theorem 3.6.9. *Let* $\{C^j\}_{j\in\mathcal{N}\cup M}$ *be a closed covering of* Δ^N *such that* $\Delta^T\subset\bigcup_{S\supset N\setminus T}C^S$ *for every* $T\in\mathcal{N}\setminus\{N\}$. *Assume that the set* $\{x\in\mathbf{R}_+^{\mathcal{N}\cup M}\mid Bx=c\}$ *is bounded. Then there exists* $x\in\mathbf{R}_+^{\mathcal{N}\cup M}$ *such that* $Bx=c$ *and* $\bigcap\{C^j\mid j\in\mathcal{N}\cup M,\ x_j>0\}\neq\phi$.

Proof. The proof is analogous to that of Theorem 3.6.7: Assume without loss of generality that $c\in\Delta^N$, and define $\{m^j\}_{j\in\mathcal{N}\cup M}$, F and G in the same way. Choose any $x\in\Delta^N$ and any $p\in\mathbf{R}^N$ such that $p\cdot x=\min\ p\cdot\Delta^N$. If $x\in\operatorname{icr}\Delta^N$, then there exists $T\in\mathcal{N}\setminus\{N\}$ such that $x\in\operatorname{icr}\Delta^T$. For this T, $p\cdot y=\min\ p\cdot\Delta^N$ for all $y\in\Delta^T$. By the assumption, there exists $S\supset N\setminus T$ such that $x\in C^S$, so $m^S\in F(x)$. By the definition of matrix B,

$$\exists\,\alpha\in[0,1]\colon m^N=\alpha m^S+(1-\alpha)m^{N\setminus S},$$

and moreover, $p\cdot m^{N\setminus S}=\min\ p\cdot\Delta^N$, in view of the fact $N\setminus S\subset T$. Thus $p\cdot m^N\leqslant p\cdot m^S$. There exist, therefore, $u\in F(x)$ and $v\in G(x)$ such that $p\cdot u\geqslant p\cdot v$. The rest of the proof is identical to the corresponding part of the proof of Theorem 3.6.7. □

Scarf (1967a) established the following Theorem 3.6.11, and then derived from it his theorem for nonemptiness of the core of a non-side-payment game (Theorem 2.2.1). Let K, A, c be given as in the paragraph that precedes the statement of Theorem 3.6.4. Choose vectors $P:=\{\pi^j\}_{j\in K}$ in $\mathbf{R}^N$ such that

$$\pi^i=(R_i,\ldots,R_i,\overset{i}{0},R_i,\ldots,R_i)\ \text{if}\ i\in N;$$
$$\pi^j\in(\Delta^N-\mathbf{R}_+^N)\cap\mathbf{R}_+^N\ \text{if}\ j\in K\setminus N,$$

where $R_i>1$ for each $i\in N$. The vectors π^j, $j\in K\setminus N$, can actually be chosen arbitrarily from $\mathbf{R}_+^N$, provided that the R_i, $i\in N$, are suitably re-defined.

Definition 3.6.10. A subset of P, $\{\pi^j\}_{j\in I}$, is called a *primitive set*, if there does not exist $\pi\in P$ such that

$$\forall\,i\in N\colon \pi_i>\min\{\pi_i^j\mid j\in I\}.$$

Theorem 3.6.11 (Scarf). *If the set* $\{x\in\mathbf{R}_+^K\mid Ax=c\}$ *is bounded, then there exists* $x\in\mathbf{R}_+^K$ *such that* $Ax=c$ *and* $\{\pi^j\mid j\in K,\ x_j>0\}$ *is a primitive set.*

Due to arbitrariness of the finite set K (provided that it contains N), and hence the generality of matrix A compared with $\tilde{A}$ (the matrix $\tilde{A}$ was introduced in a paragraph between the statements of Theorems 3.6.5 and 3.6.6), Theorem 3.6.11 together with a certain nondegeneracy assumption summarizes an analytical feature of Scarf's algorithm to compute a member of the core; indeed, this is Scarf's original proof of Theorem 2.2.1.

It was pointed out earlier that Scarf (1967b) derived Theorem 3.6.4 from Theorem 3.6.11. Conversely, Theorem 3.6.11 can be derived from Theorem 3.6.4.

Derivation of Theorem 3.6.11 from Theorem 3.6.4. Define $C_1^j := \{\pi^j\} - \mathbf{R}_+^N$. Denote by F the boundary of $\bigcap_{j \in K} C_1^j$, and define for each $j \in K$,

$$C^j := \{z \in \Delta^N \mid \exists y \in C_1^j \cap F\colon z = y/\textstyle\sum_{i \in N} y_i\}.$$

If $\pi \notin \mathring{\mathbf{R}}_+^N$ for any $\pi \in P$, then the assertion of Theorem 3.6.11 is trivial. Assume, therefore, that there exists $\pi \in P \cap \mathring{\mathbf{R}}_+^N$. Then $\mathbf{0}$ is in the interior of $\bigcup_{j \in K} C_1^j$, so $\{C^j\}_{j \in K}$ is a closed covering of Δ^N. Observe that $y \in F$, if $y \in \bigcup_{j \in K} C_1^j$ and $y_i \geqslant R_i$ for some $i \in N$. By this observation, it is easy to check $\Delta^{N \setminus \{j\}} \subset C^j$. Thus $\{C^j\}_{j \in K}$ satisfies the assumption of Theorem 3.6.4, so there exists $x \in \mathbf{R}_+^K$ such that $Ax^* = c$ and $\bigcap \{C_j \mid j \in K, x_j^* > 0\} \neq \phi$. Set $I := \{j \in K \mid x_j^* > 0\}$, choose $z^* \in \bigcap_{j \in I} C^j$, and consider $y^* \in F$ defined by $z^* = y^*/\sum_{i \in N} y_i^*$. Then $\pi^j \geqslant y^*$ for all $j \in I$, so $\{\pi^j\}_{j \in I}$ is the required primitive set. □

Many alternative proofs of Scarf's core nonemptiness theorem (Theorem 2.2.1) have appeared in the literature: Shapley (1973) derived Theorem 2.2.1 from Theorem 3.6.5. Keiding and Thorlund-Petersen (1987) and Vohra (1987) proved Theorem 2.2.1, using the K-K-M theorem (Theorem 3.6.2) and Kakutani's (1941) fixed-point theorem, respectively. Ichiishi (1988b) pointed out that the geometric insights of Keiding and Thorlund-Petersen and of Vohra boil down to Theorem 3.6.6 (dual of Theorem 3.6.5). It will be shown now that Theorem 2.2.1 follows simply from a theorem which is weaker than Theorem 3.6.4 and weaker than Theorem 3.6.6. The proof is based on Vohra's (1987) idea. It should be pointed out that Shapley (1973) applied Theorem 3.6.5 to a suitable simplex contained in the negative cone, $-\mathbf{R}_+^N$, and that the following proof applies Theorem 3.6.6 to a simplex contained in the positive cone, $\mathbf{R}_+^N$.

Proof of Theorem 2.2.1 either from Theorem 3.6.4 or from Theorem 3.6.6. The special case of Theorem 3.6.4 and of Theorem 3.6.6, in which $K = \mathcal{N}$, $A = \tilde{A}$ and $c = \chi_N$, will be used here. As in Step 1 of the proof of Theorem 2.2.1 (Section 3.4), one may assume without loss of generality that for all $S \in \mathcal{N}$, $\mathbf{0} \in \mathring{V}(S)$ and the set $\{u \in V(S) \mid u \geqslant \mathbf{0}, \forall j \in N \setminus S\colon u_j = 0\}$ is bounded. Choose two real numbers M_1 and M_2 such that $M_1 > M_2 > M$, and denote by F the boundary of the set,

$$\bigcup_{i \in N} \{u \in V(\{i\}) \mid \forall k \in N \setminus \{i\}\colon u_k \leqslant M_1\} \cup \bigcup_{S \in \mathcal{N}: \# S \geqslant 2} \{u \in V(S) \mid \forall k \in N \setminus S\colon u_k \leqslant M_2\}.$$

For each $\pi \in \Delta^N$, consider the unique point $f(\pi) \in F \cap \mathbf{R}_+^N$ defined by $\pi = f(\pi)/\sum_{i \in N} f_i(\pi)$. Define $C^S := \{\pi \in \Delta^N \mid f(\pi) \in V(S)\}$ for every $S \in \mathcal{N}$. The family

$\{C^S\}_{S\in\mathcal{N}}$ is a closed covering of Δ^N, and it is easy to check $\Delta^{N\setminus\{j\}}\subset C^{\{j\}}$ for every $j\in N$. All the assumptions of Theorem 3.6.4 or of Theorem 3.6.6 are satisfied, so there exist $x^*\in\mathbf{R}_+^{\mathcal{N}}$ and $\pi^*\in\Delta^N$ such that $\tilde{A}x^*=\chi_N$ and $\pi^*\in\bigcap\{C^S\mid S\in\mathcal{N}, x_S^*>0\}$. The point $f(\pi^*)$ will be shown to be a member of $C(V)$. The family $\mathcal{B}:=\{S\in\mathcal{N}\mid x_S^*>0\}$ is balanced and $f(\pi^*)\in\bigcap_{S\in\mathcal{B}}V(S)$. So by the balancedness assumption on V, $f(\pi^*)\in V(N)$. Consequently, $f(\pi^*)\in\{u\in F\mid\forall\, i\in N\colon u_i<M\}$, which implies that the utility allocation $f(\pi^*)$ cannot be improved upon by any coalition. □

The social coalitional equilibrium existence theorem (Theorem 3.4.11) was established by extending the technique of Ichiishi (1981a) to prove Theorem 3.6.5; this extended argument is outlined in Section 3.4. Zhou (1990) re-formulated Theorem 3.6.4 and established the role of the re-formulated version in unified treatment of the core, various kinds of bargaining sets, and a strong equilibrium. Ichiishi and Idzik (1991) extended Theorem 3.6.7 to a closed covering of a compact convex polyhedron, and derived from the extended theorem Gale's (1984) theorem on a family of n closed coverings of a simplex. Gale's theorem is basic to the existence of a competitive equilibrium of an assignment game.

Appendix to Chapter 3: Alternative model of the capitalistic economy

In the capitalistic economy as given in Definition 3.2.1, there are (2^n-1) stocks as part of the l commodities, so information on all the stock markets is complete. The model formulates, therefore, the idealized situation in the following sense: Stock prices of all possible firms are provided in the competitive market, and the stock prices of the firms that are not formed at present should be understood as *state-contingent* prices – prices of the stocks that will be delivered contingent upon formation of those firms. The purpose of this Appendix is, however, to sketch a variant of the capitalistic economy in which information on the stock market is incomplete. This variant is essentially the model of Ichiishi (1982b).

Let $\mathcal{E}$ be the basic economic model constructed in Section 3.1 (Definition 3.1.4). An alternative capitalistic version will be constructed by specifying $\mathcal{E}$, based on the view that stocks are issued and purchased not through the neoclassical market, but rather as a part of the cooperative game played by the n economic agents. One has to specify, therefore, the sets $E^j, j\in N$.

Space E^j has $\mathbf{R}\times\mathbf{R}$ as its subspace. The intended interpretation of $(s_{\mathrm{I}}^j, s_{\mathrm{II}}^j)\in\mathbf{R}\times\mathbf{R}$, $s_{\mathrm{I}}^j\geqslant 0$, $s_{\mathrm{II}}^j\leqslant 0$, is that agent j invests s_{I}^j (nominal value) in firms, and his firm S invests $-s_{\mathrm{II}}^j$ (nominal value) in the other firms. The model does not distinguish the content of the portfolio; it explains only the total value of investment by each economic agent.

If the only non-marketed commodities (other than stocks) are k types of labor, and if there are m commodities in the future (Example 3.1.2), then

$$E^j = \mathbf{R} \times \mathbf{R} \times \mathbf{R}^k \times \mathbf{R} \times \mathrm{ca}(\mathbf{R}^m),$$

and its generic element is denoted by $x^j_{\mathrm{III}} = (s^j_{\mathrm{I}}, s^j_{\mathrm{II}}, L^j, w^j, \mu^j)$.

Suppose $(\bar{x}, \bar{p}, \bar{\mathscr{T}}) \in X \times \Delta^{l-1} \times \mathscr{T}$ is given at the outset. Suppose firm S is to form in spite of the existing coalition structure $\bar{\mathscr{T}}$, and is to choose a strategy bundle x^S. Firm S monopolizes supply of its own stock. Recall that the output-demand function is a standard concept in the traditional partial equilibrium analysis of monopoly. It is postulated here, therefore, that all the members of S agree in expectation that $s_S(\bar{x}, \bar{p}, \bar{\mathscr{T}}, x^S)$ (nominal value) of its stock will be demanded. The feasible-strategy set $F^S(\bar{x}, \bar{p}, \bar{\mathscr{T}})$ $(\subset X^S)$ is readily defined: A strategy bundle x^S is in $F^S(\bar{x}, \bar{p}, \bar{\mathscr{T}})$ only if:

$$s^j_{\mathrm{II}} = s^j_{\mathrm{II}} =: s^{(S)}_{\mathrm{II}}, \text{ for all } i, j \in S, \text{ and}$$
$$\sum_{j \in S} (\bar{p} \cdot x^j_{\mathrm{I}} + s^j_{\mathrm{I}}) \leqslant \bar{p} \cdot x^{(S)}_{\mathrm{II}} + \bar{p} \cdot \sum_{j \in S} \omega^j + s^{(S)}_{\mathrm{II}} + s_S(\bar{x}, \bar{p}, \bar{\mathscr{T}}, x^S).$$

The equilibrium of the present capitalistic version is defined exactly as in Definition 3.1.5. Under the postulate on the functions $s_S(\cdot)$ that the expectations are static, i.e., for each $(\bar{x}, \bar{p}, \bar{\mathscr{T}})$,

$$\sum_{j \in N} \bar{s}^j_{\mathrm{I}} = \sum_{T \in \bar{\mathscr{T}}} \bar{s}^{(T)}_{\mathrm{II}} + \sum_{T \in \bar{\mathscr{T}}} s_T(\bar{x}, \bar{p}, \bar{\mathscr{T}}, \bar{x}^T),$$

one obtains Walras' law at the fixed-point, so the equilibrium existence theorem (Theorem 3.4.6) is now readily applicable.

4 Welfare implications of the nature of the firm

This chapter continues to study the general equilibrium model of an economy and the equilibrium concept proposed in Sections 3.1 and 3.2. Section 4.1 demonstrates by a simple example that neither of the two fundamental theorems of welfare economics holds true for this equilibrium. (The problem of achieving a Pareto optimum will be studied in Chapter 5 in the context of increasing returns to scale.) A different type of welfare problem is addressed in Section 4.2. The macro versions of the capitalistic economy and the associated socialistic economy are defined there, and in this macro context, the following theorem is established: If the socialistic economy can be decomposed into subeconomies, each satisfying increasing returns with respect to the firm size, then for each equilibrium of the capitalistic economy there exists an equilibrium of the socialistic economy such that the former is Pareto superior to the latter. Several examples are also provided. The comparative study of two systems is not new (see, e.g., Sertel (1982) for a modern treatment). What is new here is the comparison of two systems in terms of a new descriptive equilibrium concept which is based on *cooperative* behavior of the agents. Indeed, the above result in comparative economic systems is proved in Section 4.3 by applying a result in comparative cooperative non-side-payment game theory. Section 4.3 first establishes the property of an ordinal convex game that it has a large core, and then uses this property to make welfare comparison of the cores of two non-side-payment games. Also proved in this section is another property of an ordinal convex game, announced in Section 2.2, that its core contains all the marginal worth vectors. The comparative economic systems result of Section 4.2 is the only result one can hope for on a welfare comparison of two systems, given the generality of the models. This point is clarified in Section 4.4, in which the comparative cooperative game theory is systematically developed within the framework of side-payment games.

4.1 Pareto non-optimality of an equilibrium

The two fundamental theorems of welfare economics say that any competitive equilibrium of a private ownership economy (Definitions 3.3.3 and 3.3.4) is Pareto optimal, and conversely that for any Pareto optimum of a private ownership economy, one can re-allocate the income levels so that the resulting competitive equilibrium is the given Pareto optimum (see, e.g., Lange (1942), Arrow (1951) and Debreu (1951)). The theorems highlight performance of the competitive market mechanism from the welfare point of view. If another mechanism replaces the market mechanism, however, the final allocation of commodities may not be Pareto optimal. That is, an alternative mechanism may not possess the *invisible hand* which would transform individual egoism into social optimum.

In Section 3.1 a new model of economy was constructed, which features the neoclassical market mechanism for allocation of non-human resources and a cooperative game for allocation of human resources. With the available structure of the model (Definition 3.1.4), however, the Pareto optimality cannot be defined, because the feasible-strategy correspondence does not delineate the underlying production set, but rather, it essentially describes the derived budget-set correspondence. Moreover, it cannot be defined independent of any resource allocation mechanism (market mechanism or non-market mechanism) if the generality of Definition 3.1.4 has to be kept so that utility functions are price-dependent. The purpose of this section is to construct a simple example of a specific case of this model, for which the Pareto optimality is well-defined, but the equilibria of which are not Pareto optimal.

The example in this section is essentially a static economy with two agents, two types of labor, no other input, and one output; it is the socialistic economy (Definition 3.2.3) obtained by further specializing Example 3.1.3, $(\{X^j, \omega^j, u^j\}_{j\in N}, \{G^S(\cdot)\}_{S\in\mathcal{N}}, \mathscr{T})$, in which (1) $n=2$ (two-agent economy); (2) $\mathscr{T}=\{\{\{1\},\{2\}\},\{\{1,2\}\}\}$; (3) $m=1$ (so that one may set $M=\{c\}$, $p_c\equiv 1$); (4) $X^j_{\mathrm{I}}:=\{x^j_{\mathrm{I}}\in\mathbf{R}^l \mid x^j\in X^j\}=\{\mathbf{0}\}$ and $\omega^j=\mathbf{0}$ (so that there is no consumption of marketed commodity today, and commodity for future consumption is produced only from labor input today); (5) each agent supplies one type of labor, and the types of labor supplied by the two agents are different (so that $k=2$, $L^1=(L^1_1, 0)$, $L^2=(0, L^2_2)$); (6) there is no uncertainty in the future (so that the future consumption is completely determined as today's strategy, i.e., $[\mu^j\in\mathscr{M}(\mathbf{R})]$ is replaced by $[x^j_{\mathrm{III},c}\in\mathbf{R}]$); and (7) the technology of firm S is described by a production function g^S: $\mathbf{R}^2_+\to\mathbf{R}_+$ which assigns an output level to each labor bundle. Then, $G^S(\cdot)$ is the constant correspondence, $(\bar{x}, \bar{p}, \bar{\mathscr{T}})\mapsto G^S$, given by

$$G^S = \{x^S \in X^S \mid \sum_{j \in S} x^j_{\mathrm{III},c} \leqslant g^S(-\sum_{j \in S} L^j)\}.$$

In order to treat a non-degenerate case, define the strategy space X^j by: $(x^j_{\mathrm{I}}, x^j_{\mathrm{II}}, L^j, w^j, x^j_{\mathrm{III},c}) \in X^j$, iff

$$x^j_{\mathrm{I}} = x^j_{\mathrm{II}} = \mathbf{0},\ w^j = 0,\ x^j_{\mathrm{III},c} \geqslant 0, \text{ and}$$
$$L^j_i \in \begin{cases} [-1, 0] & \text{if } i = j, \\ \{0\} & \text{if } i \neq j. \end{cases}$$

The production functions are given by:

$$g^N(-L_1, -L_2) = 0 \text{ for all } (L_1, L_2),$$
$$g^{\{j\}}(-L_1, -L_2) = \begin{cases} -L_2 & \text{if } j = 1, \\ -L_1 & \text{if } j = 2, \end{cases}$$

which describes the situations that (1) the grand coalition is very inefficient, and (2) the labor of agent j is not useful in his own firm $\{j\}$, but is useful in the firm of the other agent. The utility functions are given by:

$$u^j(\mathbf{0}, L^j, x^j_{\mathrm{III},c}) = 2\, x^j_{\mathrm{III},c} + L^j_j.$$

Then, the only equilibrium utility allocation is

$$(u^\dagger_1, u^\dagger_2) = (0, 0).$$

A Pareto optimum is achieved only when the finest coalition structure $\{\{1\}, \{2\}\}$ is organized and firm $\{j\}$ uses the labor of the other agent in its production. The set of (strict) Pareto optimal utility allocations is

$$\{(u_1, u_2) \in \mathbf{R}^2 \mid u_1 + u_2 = 2,\ u_1, u_2 \geqslant -1\}.$$

None of the equilibria is, therefore, Pareto optimal.

The point of this example is that since there is no labor market, agent 1 cannot sell his labor to firm {2} which really needs 1's labor. If agent 2 tries to form a larger firm {1, 2}, say by merger, so that agent 1 as a member of the enlarged firm can supply the required labor, there arises the inefficiency of oversize of the firm, which kills the advantage of the merger.

In order to achieve a Pareto optimum in the economies of the class defined in Sections 3.1 and 3.2, therefore, one has to institute a mechanism other than those that would give rise to the equilibrium of Definition 3.1.5. This problem will be studied in Chapter 5 in the context of increasing returns to scale. A different kind of welfare problem on the economic mechanisms of Sections 3.1 and 3.2 will be addressed in the remaining sections of this chapter.

4.2 Comparative economic systems

Let $\mathscr{E}_c := (\{X^j, \omega^j\}_{j\in N}, \{F^S(\cdot)\}_{S\in\mathscr{N}}, \{u_S^j(\cdot)\}_{j\in S\in\mathscr{N}}, \mathscr{T})$ be a capitalistic economy, and let $\mathscr{E}_s := (\{X^j, \omega^j\}_{j\in N}, \{G^S(\cdot)\}_{S\in\mathscr{N}}, \{u_S^j(\cdot)\}_{j\in S\in\mathscr{N}}, \mathscr{T})$ be the socialistic economy associated with $\mathscr{E}_c$ (Definition 3.2.4). The crucial difference between the two economies $\mathscr{E}_c$ and $\mathscr{E}_s$ is that in the former the capital markets serve as a channel for re-distribution of the initial resources. This fact is a consequence of Definition 3.2.3 of $\mathscr{E}_s$, and is summarized by the following condition:

Condition 4.2.1.

$$\forall S\in\mathscr{N}: \forall(\bar{x}, \bar{p}, \bar{\mathscr{T}})\in X\times\Delta^{l-1}\times\mathscr{T}: G^S(\bar{x}, \bar{p}, \bar{\mathscr{T}})\subset F^S(\bar{x}, \bar{p}, \bar{\mathscr{T}}).$$

The purpose of this section is to establish that under certain economically meaningful conditions, Condition 4.2.1 results in a more efficient allocation of resources in $\mathscr{E}_c$ than in $\mathscr{E}_s$. The precise content of the phrase, "more efficient" will be specified as the assertion of Theorem 4.2.3 below. The materials here are taken from Ichiishi (1990b). In order to see clearly the implications of the nature of the firm as a cooperative resource allocation mechanism, the effects of a change in relative market prices of commodities are abstracted away; in this sense, the model of this section is macroeconomic. Recall that in the economies $\mathscr{E}_c$ and $\mathscr{E}_s$ of Section 3.2 there were m marketed physical commodities and services, so $l=m+(2^n-1)$, and the index set for these m commodities was denoted by M. The macroeconomic assumption imposed in this section is stated explicitly as $m=1$. Set, therefore, $M=\{c\}$.

In the macro model of socialistic economy $\mathscr{E}_s$, there are no "externalities" influencing the feasible-strategy sets (see the discussion of the cause for "externalities" in the fourth paragraph of Section 3.2), and $p_c\equiv 1$ (the unique point of Δ^{m-1}). Thus, one may make the following basic assumption:

Postulate 4.2.2. For each coalition S, the feasible-strategy set $G^S(\bar{x}, \bar{p}, \bar{\mathscr{T}})$ is independent of $(\bar{x}, \bar{p}, \bar{\mathscr{T}})$. For each member j of S, his utility function $u_S^j(\bar{x}, \bar{p}, \bar{\mathscr{T}}, x^S)$ is independent of $(\bar{x}, \bar{p}, \bar{\mathscr{T}})$ in $\mathrm{gr}G^S$.

This postulate justifies the notation, $G^S := G^S(\bar{x}, \bar{p}, \bar{\mathscr{T}})$, $u_S^j(x^S) := u_S^j(\bar{x}, \bar{p}, \bar{\mathscr{T}}, x^S)$. In the macro socialistic economy $\mathscr{E}_s$, the set of *attainable utility allocations* of each coalition S is given by:

$$W(S) := \left\{ u\in\mathbf{R}^N \,\middle|\, \begin{array}{l}\text{There exists } x^S\in G^S \text{ such that}\\ \text{for each } j\in S,\ u_j\leqslant u_S^j(x^S).\end{array} \right\}.$$

(Inclusion of the coordinates that correspond to $N\backslash S$ is made simply for notational convenience.) The *superadditivity* assumption on W says that

$$(\forall S, T \in \mathcal{N}: S \cap T = \phi): W(S) \cap W(T) \subset W(S \cup T).$$

This condition is satisfied in $\mathscr{E}_s$ if the integration of any two firms can be made without losing efficiency. Set $W(\phi) := \phi$. The *ordinal convexity* assumption on the non-side-payment game W (see Section 2.2),

$$\forall S, T \in \mathcal{N}: W(S) \cap W(T) \subset W(S \cap T) \cup W(S \cup T),$$

strengthens the superadditivity condition, and characterizes the increasing returns with respect to the coalition size. To see this meaning, choose any two coalitions S and T, and consider four firms $S \cap T$, S, T, and $S \cup T$. If the minimal firm $S \cap T$ cannot realize utility levels $\{u_j\}_{j \in S \cap T}$ to the members $S \cap T$ (i.e., $(\{u_j\}_{j \in S \cap T}, \{u_j\}_{j \in N \setminus (S \cap T)}) \notin W(S \cap T)$ for any $\{u_j\}_{j \in N \setminus (S \cap T)}$), but if each of two larger firms S and T can realize it (i.e., $(\{u_j\}_{j \in S \cap T}, \{v_j^S\}_{j \in N \setminus (S \cap T)}) \in W(S)$ for some $\{v_j^S\}_{j \in N \setminus (S \cap T)}$, and an analogous condition for $W(T)$), then the maximal firm $S \cup T$ can also realize it (i.e., $(\{u_j\}_{j \in S \cap T}, \{v_j\}_{j \in N \setminus (S \cap T)}) \in W(S \cup T)$ for some $\{v_j\}_{j \in N \setminus (S \cap T)}$ for which $v_j = v_j^S$ if $j \in S \setminus T$ and $v_j = v_j^T$ if $j \in T \setminus S$).

The increasing returns with respect to the coalition size is a questionable assumption, as was carefully argued by Williamson (1985, Ch. 6). Weaker assumptions are, therefore, now introduced. For each coalition S, define

$$\bar{W}(S) := \bigcup_{\mathscr{P}} \bigcap_{P \in \mathscr{P}} W(P),$$

where the union in the right-hand side is taken with respect to all the partitions $\mathscr{P}$ of S. A utility allocation u is in $\bar{W}(S)$ if there exists a way to divide the set S of agents into smaller sets $\{P_i\}_{i \in I}$ ($\bigcup_{i \in I} P_i = S$, and $P_i \cap P_j = \phi$ if $i \neq j$) so that each firm P_i can realize the utility allocation $\{u_j\}_{j \in P_i}$ for its members. By definition, $\bar{W}$ automatically satisfies the superadditivity assumption. The ordinal convexity assumption on $\bar{W}$,

$$\forall S, T \in \mathcal{N}: \bar{W}(S) \cap \bar{W}(T) \subset \bar{W}(S \cap T) \cup \bar{W}(S \cup T),$$

weakens the ordinal convexity assumption on W, and allows for the impact of eventual diminishing returns with respect to the coalition size (see Example 4.2.7 below).

Another way to allow for the impact of eventual diminishing returns is formulated as:

$$\begin{aligned}
&\exists \mathscr{T}^{\dagger} \in \mathscr{T}: \\
&\forall T \in \mathscr{T}^{\dagger}: \forall S, S' \subset T: W(S) \cap W(S') \subset W(S \cap S') \cup W(S \cup S'), \text{ and} \\
&(\forall \{T_i\}_{i \in I} \subset \mathscr{T}^{\dagger}: T_i \neq T_j \text{ if } i \neq j): \\
&(\forall \{S_i\}_{i \in I}: \phi \neq S_i \subset T_i \text{ for all } i): W(\bigcup_{i \in I} S_i) \subset \bigcup_{i \in I} W(S_i).
\end{aligned}$$

See Example 4.2.7 below.

A utility allocation u is in $\bar{W}(N)$ if there is a coalition structure $\mathscr{P}$ such that $\{u_j\}_{j \in S}$ is attainable in each coalition $S \in \mathscr{P}$, i.e., there exists $x^S \in G^S$ such that $u_j \leqslant u_S^j(x^S)$ for all $j \in S$. The final assumption discussed here is the efficiency of the admissible coalition structures: The above coalition structure $\mathscr{P}$ can be chosen to be admissible. Formally, this assumption is formulated as:

$$\bar{W}(N) = \bigcup_{\mathscr{T} \in \mathscr{T}} \bigcap_{T \in \mathscr{T}} W(T).$$

The main result of this section is the following theorem, which says that if the socialistic economy can be decomposed into several subeconomies, each satisfying increasing returns with respect to the firm size, then for each equilibrium of the capitalistic economy there exists an equilibrium of the socialistic economy such that the former is Pareto superior to the latter. The proof will be given in the next section.

Theorem 4.2.3. *Let $\mathscr{E}_c$ and $\mathscr{E}_s$ be the macro models of the capitalistic economy and the associated socialistic economy that satisfy Postulate 4.2.2. Suppose that $\mathscr{E}_s$ satisfies either*

(i) $\forall S, T \in \mathscr{N}$: $\bar{W}(S) \cap \bar{W}(T) \subset \bar{W}(S \cap T) \cup \bar{W}(S \cup T)$, *and*
$\bar{W}(N) = \bigcup_{\mathscr{T} \in \mathscr{T}} \bigcap_{T \in \mathscr{T}} W(T)$;

or

(ii) $\exists \mathscr{T}^\dagger \in \mathscr{T}$:
$\forall T \in \mathscr{T}^\dagger$: $\forall S, S' \subset T$: $W(S) \cap W(S') \subset W(S \cap S') \cup W(S \cup S')$, *and*
$(\forall \{T_i\}_{i \in I} \subset \mathscr{T}^\dagger$: $T_i \neq T_j$ if $i \neq j)$:
$(\forall \{S_i\}_{i \in I}$: $\phi \neq S_i \subset T_i$ *for all* $i)$: $W(\bigcup_{i \in I} S_i) \subset \bigcup_{i \in I} W(S_i)$.

Then, for each equilibrium $(x^*, p^*, \mathscr{T}^*)$ of $\mathscr{E}_c$ for which $p_c^* > 0$, there exists an equilibrium $(x^\dagger, \mathscr{T}^\dagger)$ of $\mathscr{E}_s$ such that

$$u_{T(j)}^j(x^*, p^*, \mathscr{T}^*, x^{*T(j)}) \geqslant u_{U(j)}^j(x^{\dagger U(j)}) \text{ for all } j \in N,$$

where $j \in T(j) \in \mathscr{T}^*$ and $j \in U(j) \in \mathscr{T}^\dagger$.

Section 4.4 shows why the assertion of Theorem 4.2.3 is the only result one can hope for on welfare comparison of the two systems, given Condition 4.2.1.

Example 4.2.4. Consider the simplest socialistic economy $\mathscr{E}_s$ of Example 3.2.5, and let W be the non-side-payment game derived from $\mathscr{E}_s$. Define

$$g^\phi(a) := \begin{cases} 0 \text{ if } a = 0, \\ \infty \text{ if } a > 0. \end{cases}$$

The following claim is an extension of a result of Moulin (1987, Appendix B); Moulin treated the case in which $g^S = g^T$ for all $S, T \in \mathscr{N}$. □

Claim 4.2.5. *Suppose the production functions g^S: $\mathbf{R}_+ \to \mathbf{R}_+$, $S \in \mathscr{N}$, satisfy that*

$$g^S(0) = 0,$$
$$g^S(a) + g^T(b) \leqslant g^{S \cap T}(c) + g^{S \cup T}(a + b - c),$$

for all $S, T \in \mathcal{N}$ and any $c \leqslant \min\{a, b\}$. Suppose also that each utility function u^j: $\mathbf{R} \times \mathbf{R}_+ \to \mathbf{R}$ is non-decreasing in $\mathbf{R} \times \mathbf{R}_+$, and that $\{N\} \in \mathcal{T}$. Then,

$$\forall\, S, T \in \mathcal{N}\text{: } W(S) \cap W(T) \subset W(S \cap T) \cup W(S \cup T), \text{ and}$$

$$W(N) = \bigcup_{\mathcal{T} \in \mathcal{T}} \bigcap_{T \in \mathcal{T}} W(T).$$

Proof. *Step 1.* For any $a, b, c, d, A, B, C, D \in \mathbf{R}_+$ and any $S, T \in \mathcal{N}$ such that $A + B \leqslant g^S(a + b)$ and $C + D \leqslant g^T(c + d)$, at least one of the following four inequalities holds true: $B \leqslant g^{S \cap T}(b)$, $C \leqslant g^{S \cap T}(c)$, $A + B + D \leqslant g^{S \cup T}(a + b + d)$, and $A + C + D \leqslant g^{S \cup T}(a + c + d)$. Indeed, suppose $B > g^{S \cap T}(b)$ and $C > g^{S \cap T}(c)$. If $b \leqslant c$, then $b \leqslant \min\{a + b, c + d\}$. By the present assumption on g^S's,

$$\begin{aligned}
&A + B + C + D \\
&\leqslant g^S(a + b) + g^T(c + d) \\
&\leqslant g^{S \cap T}(b) + g^{S \cup T}(a + b + c + d - b) \\
&< B + g^{S \cup T}(a + c + d).
\end{aligned}$$

Consequently, $A + C + D \leqslant g^{S \cup T}(a + c + d)$. Similarly, if $b \geqslant c$, then $A + B + D \leqslant g^{S \cup T}(a + b + d)$.

Step 2. One needs to show that the non-side-payment game W is ordinal convex. In view of the monotonicity of the utility functions u^j, it suffices to show that if $x^S \in G^S$ and $y^T \in G^T$, then $x^{S \cap T} \in G^{S \cap T}$, or $y^{S \cap T} \in G^{S \cap T}$, or $(x^S, y^{T \setminus S}) \in G^{S \cup T}$, or $(x^{S \setminus T}, y^T) \in G^{S \cup T}$. Now, $x^S \in G^S$ ($y^T \in G^T$, resp.) means that $\sum_{j \in S} x^j_{\mathrm{IIIc}} \leqslant g^S(\sum_{j \in S}(-x^j_{\mathrm{Ic}}))$ ($\sum_{j \in T} y^j_{\mathrm{IIIc}} \leqslant g^T(\sum_{j \in T}(-y^j_{\mathrm{Ic}}))$, resp.). Set $a := \sum_{j \in S \setminus T}(-x^j_{\mathrm{Ic}})$, $b := \sum_{j \in S \cap T}(-x^j_{\mathrm{Ic}})$, $c := \sum_{j \in S \cap T}(-y^j_{\mathrm{Ic}})$, $d := \sum_{j \in T \setminus S}(-y^j_{\mathrm{Ic}})$, $A := \sum_{j \in S \setminus T} x^j_{\mathrm{IIIc}}$, $B := \sum_{j \in S \cap T} x^j_{\mathrm{IIIc}}$, $C := \sum_{j \in S \cap T} y^j_{\mathrm{IIIc}}$, $D := \sum_{j \in T \setminus S} y^j_{\mathrm{IIIc}}$, and apply Step 1. □

Remark 4.2.6. The assumption on g^S's in Claim 4.2.5 implies *both* increasing marginal product with respect to scale for each firm S,

$$g^S(a + h) - g^S(a) \leqslant g^S(b + h) - g^S(b) \text{ for all } a \leqslant b \text{ and all } h \geqslant 0,$$

and increasing efficiency with respect to the coalition size (in terms of the production functions),

$$g^S(a) \leqslant g^T(a) \text{ for all } a \text{ and all } S \subset T. \ \square$$

Example 4.2.7. $N = \{1, 2, 3\}$,

$$W(\{j\}) = \{u \in \mathbf{R}^3 \mid u_j \leqslant 0\},\ j = 1, 2, 3,$$
$$W(\{1, 2\}) = \{u \in \mathbf{R}^3 \mid u_1 + u_2 \leqslant 1\},$$

$W(S)=\{u\in\mathbf{R}^3 \mid u_j\leqslant 0 \text{ for each } j\in S\}$, if $S\ni 3$.
$\{\{1, 2\}, \{3\}\}\in\mathscr{T}$.

This non-side-payment game does not satisfy ordinal convexity nor superadditivity. The subeconomy {1, 2} satisfies increasing returns, but the economy beyond {1, 2} does not. Notice that

$$\bar{W}(S)=W(S), \text{ if } S\neq N,$$
$$\bar{W}(N)=\{u\in\mathbf{R}^3 \mid u_1+u_2\leqslant 1, u_3\leqslant 0\},$$

so Assumptions (i) and (ii) of Theorem 4.2.3 are both satisfied. □

4.3 Comparative cooperative game theory

Sharkey (1982b) introduced the concept of large core for a side-payment game, and established that every convex game has a large core. In fact, the same result also says that each subgame of a convex game has a large core, because the subgames of a convex game are convex. Moulin (1990, Theorem 1) established the converse that given a side-payment game v, if each subgame of v has a large core, then v has to be convex. The first part of this section extends the large-core concept to a non-side-payment game, and establishes that every ordinal convex game has a large core (Theorem 4.3.2). The work of Peleg (1986) is essential in proving this theorem here. Two theorems in comparative cooperative game theory are then established as applications of Theorem 4.3.2. One of the two theorems, in turn, is used to prove the main theorem of the preceding section (Theorem 4.2.3). Also proved in this section is Theorem 2.2.3, which says that the core of an ordinal convex game contains all the marginal worth vectors. This section is based upon Ichiishi (1990a). Theorem 2.2.3 is new. For an alternative approach to the comparative cooperative game theory, see Ichiishi (1987d).

Let N be a finite set of players, *a priori* given and fixed throughout this section. Denote by $\mathscr{N}$ the family of nonempty coalitions $2^N\setminus\{\phi\}$. To emphasize the player-set of a game, denote by $C(N, W)$ the core of game W with player-set N.

Definition 4.3.1. Let $W\colon \mathscr{N}\to\mathbf{R}^N$ be a non-side-payment game. Game W is said to *have a large core*, if for every $x\in\mathbf{R}^N$ for which $x\notin \mathring{W}(S)$ for every $S\in\mathscr{N}$, there exists $y\in C(N, W)$ such that $y\leqslant x$.

To interpret a large core, suppose that the players N agree on an initial utility allocation x in which all coalitional objections are avoided; this allocation may not be feasible. When the core is large, however, the allocation x can always be taken as an upper bound for a final feasible utility allocation. That is, by reduction across the board of all utilities, a core element y ($\leqslant x$) can always be achieved.

Theorem 4.3.2. *Let* $W\colon \mathcal{N} \to \mathbf{R}^N$ *be a non-side-payment game, and define* $b \in \mathbf{R}^N$ *by* $b_j := \sup\{u_j \in \mathbf{R} \mid u \in V(\{j\})\}$ *for each* $j \in N$. *Game* W *has a large core, if*

(i) $W(S) - \mathbf{R}^N_+ = W(S)$ *for every* $S \in \mathcal{N}$;
(ii) *there exists* $M \in \mathbf{R}$ *such that for every* $S \in \mathcal{N}$, $[u \in W(S),\ u \geqslant b]$ *implies* $[u_i < M$ *for every* $i \in S]$;
(iii) $W(N)$ *is closed in* $\mathbf{R}^N$; *and*
(iv) W *is ordinal convex.*

In order to state two lemmas of Peleg (1986), two further concepts have to be introduced:

Definition 4.3.3. Let $W\colon \mathcal{N} \to \mathbf{R}^N$ be a non-side-payment game, and let $T \in \mathcal{N}$. The *subgame* W_T is the non-side-payment game with player set T defined by

$$W_T(S) := \{u^T \in \mathbf{R}^T \mid \exists\, u^{N \setminus T} \in \mathbf{R}^{N \setminus T}\colon (u^T, u^{N \setminus T}) \in W(S)\}, \text{ if } \phi \neq S \subsetneqq T,$$
$$W_T(T) := \text{closure of } \{u^T \in \mathbf{R}^T \mid \exists\, u^{N \setminus T} \in \mathbf{R}^{N \setminus T}\colon (u^T, u^{N \setminus T}) \in W(T)\}.$$

Definition 4.3.4. Let $W\colon \mathcal{N} \to \mathbf{R}^N$ be a non-side-payment game, let $T \in \mathcal{N} \setminus \{N\}$, and let $z^T := \{z_i\}_{i \in T} \in W_T(T)$. Define $T^c := N \setminus T$. The *reduced game* $W^*_{T^c}$ is the non-side-payment game with the player set T^c defined by

$$W^*_{T^c}(S) := \bigcup_{R \subset T} \left\{ u^{N \setminus T} \in \mathbf{R}^{N \setminus T} \,\middle|\, \begin{array}{l} \exists\, u^T \in \mathbf{R}^T\colon u^T \gg z^T, \\ \text{and } (u^{N \setminus T}, u^T) \in W(S \cup R) \end{array} \right\}, \text{ if } \phi \neq S \subsetneqq T^c,$$

$$W^*_{T^c}(T^c) := \{u^{N \setminus T} \in \mathbf{R}^{N \setminus T} \mid (u^{N \setminus T}, z^T) \in W(N)\}.$$

The meaning of the subgame is evident. In the reduced game $W^*_{T^c}$ a utility allocation $\{u_j\}_{j \in S}$ is attainable by coalition $S \subsetneqq T^c$, if coalition S can make it by its own effort in the original game W, or if S can give an incentive to coalition $R\,(\subset T)$ to cooperate with S in the original game W by giving each member i of R a higher utility level u_i than z_i, and still can provide the utility level u_j to each of its members $j \in S$.

Lemma 4.3.5 (Peleg). *Let* $W\colon \mathcal{N} \to \mathbf{R}^N$ *be an ordinal convex game satisfying assumptions (i) and (iii) of Theorem 4.3.2, let* $T \in \mathcal{N} \setminus \{N\}$, *and let* $z^T \in W_T(T)$. *Define* $T^c := N \setminus T$. *Suppose*

(v) $z^T \in C(T, W_T)$; *and*
(vi) $z^T \notin \overline{W_T(R)}$, *for any* $R \subsetneqq T$.

Then, $W^*_{T^c}$ *is an ordinal convex game.*

Proof. Choose any two nonempty coalitions $S_i \subsetneqq T^c$, $i = 1, 2$, and any $u^{T^c} \in W^*_{T^c}(S_1) \cap W^*_{T^c}(S_2)$. One needs to show $u^{T^c} \in W^*_{T^c}(S_1 \cap S_2) \cup W^*_{T^c}(S_1 \cup S_2)$. For each $i = 1, 2$, there exist $R_i \subset T$ and $u^{T,i} \gg z^T$ such that $(u^{T^c}, u^{T,i}) \in W(S_i \cup R_i)$. Define

$u^T := u^{T,1} \wedge u^{T,2}$ (i.e., $u_j^T := \min\{u_j^{T,1}, u_j^{T,2}\}$);
$u := (u^{T^c}, u^T)$.

Then by (i), $u \in W(S_1 \cup R_1) \cap W(S_2 \cup R_2)$, so by (iv),

$$u \in W((S_1 \cap S_2) \cup (R_1 \cap R_2)) \tag{1}$$

or else

$$u \in W(S_1 \cup S_2 \cup R_1 \cup R_2). \tag{2}$$

Suppose (1) is the case. Then, $S_1 \cap S_2 \neq \phi$, for otherwise the fact $[u \in W(R_1 \cap R_2),\ u^T \gg z^T]$ contradicts the hypothesis (v). By Definition 4.3.4, therefore, $u^{T^c} \in W^*_{T^c}(S_1 \cap S_2)$, which establishes the required result.

Suppose (2) is the case. If $S_1 \cup S_2 \neq T^c$, then $u^{T^c} \in W^*_{T^c}(S_1 \cup S_2)$, so assume $S_1 \cup S_2 = T^c$. If $R_1 \cup R_2 = T$, then by Definition 4.3.4, $u^{T^c} \in W^*_{T^c}(T^c)$. It remains to establish $u^{T^c} \in W^*_{T^c}(T^c)$ for the subcase $R_1 \cup R_2 \subsetneq T$. By assumptions (v) and (vi), and by (2) and assumption (i), there exists a sequence $\{z^{T,k}\}_k \subset \mathbf{R}^T$ such that

$z^{T,k} \to z^T$, as $k \to \infty$;
$(u^{T^c}, z^{T,k}) \in W(T)$,
$(u^{T^c}, z^{T,k}) \notin W(R_1 \cup R_2)$, and
$(u^{T^c}, z^{T,k}) \in W(T^c \cup (R_1 \cup R_2))$, for every k.

By the ordinal convexity of W,

$$W(T) \cap W(T^c \cup (R_1 \cup R_2)) \subset W(R_1 \cup R_2) \cup W(N),$$

so $(u^{T^c}, z^{T,k}) \in W(N)$ for every k. By assumption (iii), $(u^{T^c}, z^T) \in W(N)$, so $u^{T^c} \in W^*_{T^c}(T^c)$. □

Lemma 4.3.6 (Peleg). *Let W, T, z^T be chosen as in Lemma 4.3.5, and suppose assumptions (i)–(vi) of Theorem 4.3.2 and Lemma 4.3.5 are satisfied. Choose any $y^{T^c} \in C(N\backslash T, W^*_{T^c})$ and any $h \in \mathbf{R}_+^{N\backslash T}\backslash\{\mathbf{0}\}$. Define*

$\tau := \max\{r \in \mathbf{R} \mid (z^T, y^{T^c} + rh) \in W(N)\}$,
$u := (z^T, y^{T^c} + \tau h)$.

Then, $u \in C(N, W)$.

Proof. Since u is well-defined and $u \in W(N)$, it suffices to show that u is not improved upon by any coalition. Suppose the contrary, i.e.,

$$\exists S \in \mathcal{N}: \exists w \in W(S): \forall j \in S: w_j > u_j.$$

If $S \subset T$, then in the subgame W_T,

$$(\exists S: \phi \neq S \subset T): \exists w^T \in W_T(S): \forall j \in S: w_j^T > u_j = z_j,$$

which contradicts assumption (v). Therefore, $S\backslash T \neq \phi$. Clearly, $S\backslash T \subset T^c$. If $S\backslash T \subsetneqq T^c$, then in the reduced game $W^*_{T^c}$,

$$(\exists\, S\backslash T: \phi = S\backslash T \subset T^c): \exists\, w^{T^c} \in W^*_{T^c}(S\backslash T):$$
$$\forall j \in S\backslash T: w_j^{T^c} > u_j \geqslant y_j^{T^c},$$

which contradicts the choice of y^{T^c} as a member of $C(N\backslash T, W^*_{T^c})$. Therefore, $S\backslash T = T^c$. If $S = N$, then $w \in W(N)$ and $w > (z^T, w^{T^c})$. In view of assumption (i), $(z^T, w^{T^c}) \in W(N)$. But $w^{T^c} \gg y^{T^c} + \tau h$, which contradicts the definition of τ. Set $R := S \cap T$. It has been shown that

$$S = T^c \cup R,\ R \subsetneqq T. \tag{1}$$

Since $z^T \in W_T(T)$, there exists a sequence $\{z^{T,k}\} \subset \mathbf{R}^T$ converging to z^T such that

$$(z^{T,k}, w^{T^c}) \in W(T) \text{ for all } k. \tag{2}$$

By assumption (vi) one may assume without loss of generality,

$$z^{T,k} \notin \overline{W_T(R')} \text{ for all } k \text{ and all } R' \subsetneqq T. \tag{3}$$

Since $(z^{T,k}, w^{T^c}) \leqslant (z^{T\backslash S,k}, w^S)$ for all k sufficiently large in view of (1), and since $(z^{T\backslash S,k}, w^S) \in W(S)$, assumption (i) implies

$$(z^{T,k}, w^{T^c}) \in W(S) \text{ for all } k \text{ sufficiently large.} \tag{4}$$

By ordinal convexity of W and by (1),

$$W(T) \cap W(S) \subset W(R) \cup W(N),$$

so by (2) and (4),

$$(z^{T,k}, w^{T^c}) \in W(R) \cup W(N) \text{ for all } k \text{ sufficiently large,}$$

therefore by (1) and (3),

$$(z^{T,k}, w^{T^c}) \in W(N) \text{ for all } k \text{ sufficiently large.}$$

Thus,

$$(z^T, w^{T^c}) \in W(N),$$

which contradicts the definition of τ. □

Proof of Theorem 4.3.2. By induction on $\#N$. The theorem is trivial for a one-person game. Choose any integer $n \geqslant 2$. Assume that the theorem is true for all k-person games with $k \leqslant n-1$. Let N be a player set such that $\#N = n$, and let $W: 2^N \to \mathbf{R}^N$ be a game that satisfies assumptions (i)–(iv). Choose any $x \in \mathbf{R}^N \backslash \cup_{S \in \mathcal{N}} \mathring{W}(S)$. Then there exist $z \leqslant x$ and $T \in \mathcal{N}$ such that $z \notin \bigcup_{S \in \mathcal{N}} \mathring{W}(S)$, but $z \in \overline{W(T)}$. If $z \in \overline{W(N)}$ $(= W(N))$, then $z \in C(N, W)$, so there is nothing to prove. Assume, therefore,

$$z \notin W(N). \tag{1}$$

Without loss of generality, T can be assumed to be a minimal set having the property that $z \in \overline{W(T)}$. Then,

$$z^T \in C(T, W_T),$$
$$z^R \notin \overline{W(R)} \text{ for all } R \subset T, R \neq T, \text{ and}$$
$$\phi \neq T \neq N, \text{ in view of (1).}$$

Set $T^c := N \backslash T$. Consider the reduced game $W^*_{T^c}$ given z^T (Definition 4.3.4); it is ordinal convex by Lemma 4.3.5.

One now claims that $z^{T^c} \notin \mathring{W}^*_{T^c}(S)$ for any $S \subset T^c$. Indeed, suppose the contrary, i.e., $\exists\, S \subset T^c$: $z^{T^c} \in \mathring{W}^*_{T^c}(S)$. Then, there exists $y^{T^c} \in W^*_{T^c}(S)$ such that $y_i^{T^c} > z_i^{T^c}$ for all $i \in T^c$. If $S \neq T^c$, then there exist $R \subset T$ and y^T such that $(y^{T^c}, y^T) \in W(S \cup R)$ and $y_i^T > z_i^T$ for all $i \in T$, so that $(z^{T^c}, z^T) \in \mathring{W}(S \cup R)$ – a contradiction. If $S = T^c$, then $(y^{T^c}, z^T) \in W(N)$, so $(z^{T^c}, z^T) \in W(N)$ – a contradiction of (1). The claim is thus proved.

By the inductive hypothesis, there exists $y^{T^c} \in C(T^c, W^*_{T^c})$ such that $y^{T^c} \leqslant z^{T^c} \leqslant x^{T^c}$. If $y^{T^c} = x^{T^c}$, then $y^{T^c} = z^{T^c}$, so $(z^{T^c}, z^T) \in W(N)$ – a contradiction of (1). Therefore, $h := x^{T^c} - y^{T^c} \in \mathbf{R}_+^{T^c} \backslash \{\mathbf{0}\}$. Choose τ as in Lemma 4.3.6. Then $(z^T, y^{T^c} + \tau h) \in C(N, W)$. It remains to show that $y^{T^c} + \tau h \leqslant x^{T^c}$, or equivalently that $\tau \leqslant 1$. Suppose $\tau > 1$. Then $y^{T^c} + \tau h \geqslant x^{T^c}$. In view of $(z^T, y^{T^c} + \tau h) \in W(N)$, it follows that $(z^T, x^{T^c}) \in W(N)$. Then, $(z^T, z^{T^c}) \in W(N)$ – a contradiction of (1). □

Another proof of Theorem 4.3.2, which is constructive, is due to Moulin (1990, Remark 3).

Let V and W be non-side-payment games, both having the same player set N. The cores $C(N, V)$ and $C(N, W)$ are now compared. Perhaps the strongest welfare criterion is: for every $y \in C(N, W)$ and every $x \in C(N, V)$, $y \ll x$. This criterion would hardly be obtained, however, unless game V is "sufficiently" more efficient than game W. Weaker criteria are considered.

Definition 4.3.7. Let $V, W: \mathcal{N} \to \mathbf{R}^N$ be two non-side-payment games. The core of V is said to *dominate* the core of W, if for every $y \in C(N, W)$ there exists $x \in C(N, V)$ such that $y \leqslant x$.

Definition 4.3.8. Let $V, W: \mathcal{N} \to \mathbf{R}^N$ be two non-side-payment games. The core of V is said to *dominate* the core of W *in the dual sense*, if for every $x \in C(N, V)$ there exists $y \in C(N, W)$ such that $y \leqslant x$.

Definition 4.3.9. Let $V, W: \mathcal{N} \to \mathbf{R}^N$ be two non-side-payment games. The core of V is said to *weakly dominate* the core of W, if there exist $y \in C(N, W)$ and $x \in C(N, V)$ such that $y \leqslant x$.

Theorem 4.3.10. *Let V, W: $\mathcal{N} \to \mathbf{R}^N$ be two non-side-payment games, and define $b \in \mathbf{R}^N$ by $b_j := \sup \{u_j \in \mathbf{R} \mid u \in V(\{j\})\}$ for each $j \in N$. Suppose*
(i) *$W(S) - \mathbf{R}^N_+ = W(S)$ for every $S \in \mathcal{N}$;*
(ii) *there exists $M \in \mathbf{R}$ such that for every $S \in \mathcal{N}$, $[u \in W(S), u \geqslant b]$ implies $[u_i < M$ for every $i \in S]$;*
(iii) *$W(N)$ is closed in $\mathbf{R}^N$; and*
(iv) *W is ordinal convex.*
If, moreover, $W(S) \subset V(S)$ for every $S \in \mathcal{N}$, then the core of V dominates the core of W in the dual sense.

Proof. Choose any $x \in C(N, V)$. Then, $x \notin \mathring{V}(S)$ for any $S \in \mathcal{N}$, so $x \notin \mathring{W}(S)$ for any $S \in \mathcal{N}$ by the last assumption of the theorem. Since game W has a large core, there exists $y \in C(N, W)$ such that $y \leqslant x$. □

Theorem 4.3.11. *Let V, W: $\mathcal{N} \to \mathbf{R}^N$ be two non-side-payment games. Suppose both games V and W satisfy assumptions (i)–(iv) of Theorem 4.3.10. If, moreover, $W(N) \subset V(N)$, and for any S, $T \in \mathcal{N}$, $V(S) \cap W(T) \subset V(S \cap T) \cup W(S \cap T) \cup V(S \cup T) \cup W(S \cup T)$, then the core of V weakly dominates the core of W.*

Proof. Define the non-side-payment game U by: $U(S) := V(S) \cup W(S)$, for every $S \in \mathcal{N}$. Under assumption of the theorem, it is routine to verify that game U satisfies (i)–(iv) of Theorem 4.3.10, and that $U(N) = V(N)$. By Theorem 2.2.2, $C(N, U) \neq \phi$. Choose any $x \in C(N, U)$. On the one hand, $x \in C(N, V)$. On the other hand, $x \notin \mathring{U}(S)$ so that $x \notin \mathring{W}(S)$ for any $S \in \mathcal{N}$, which guarantees (by the large core property of W) the existence of $y \in C(N, W)$ such that $y \leqslant x$. □

Proof of Theorem 4.2.3. The same notation as in Section 4.2 is used here. Let $(x^*, p^*, \mathcal{T}^*)$ be an equilibrium of $\mathcal{E}_c$ for which $p^*_c > 0$. Define non-side-payment games V, $\bar{V}$: $\mathcal{N} \to \mathbf{R}^N$ by:

$$V(S) := \left\{ u \in \mathbf{R}^N \;\middle|\; \begin{array}{l} \exists\, x^S \in F^S(x^*, p^*, \mathcal{T}^*): \forall j \in S: \\ u_j \leqslant u^j_S(x^*, p^*, \mathcal{T}^*, x^S) \end{array} \right\}$$

$$\bar{V}(S) := \bigcup_{\mathcal{P}} \bigcap_{P \in \mathcal{P}} V(P),$$

where the union in the right-hand side is taken with respect to all the partitions $\mathcal{P}$ of S. Define also

$$H := \bigcup_{\mathcal{T} \in \mathcal{T}} \bigcap_{T \in \mathcal{T}} V(T).$$

Let u^* be the equilibrium utility allocation: $u_j^* := u_{T(j)}^j(x^*, p^*, \mathscr{T}^*, x^{*S})$, for every $j \in N$. The allocation u^* is in the core of game (V, H), $H \setminus \cup_S \mathring{V}(S)$. To see that it is also in the core of the game $(\bar{V}, H)$, suppose there exist $S \in \mathscr{N}$ and $u \in \bar{V}(S)$ such that $u_j^* < u_j$ for all $j \in S$. There exists a partition $\mathscr{P}$ of S such that $u \in V(P)$ for all $P \in \mathscr{P}$. Each P improves upon u^*, which contradicts the fact that u^* is in the core of game (V, H).

By Condition 4.2.1, $\bar{W}(S) \subset \bar{V}(S)$ for every S.

Assumption (i) says that by setting $K := \cup_{\mathscr{T} \in \mathscr{T}} \cap_{T \in \mathscr{T}} W(T)$, $(\bar{W}, K)$ is an ordinal convex game. Theorem 4.3.10 is now applicable, and there exists a core utility allocation $u^\dagger$ of game $(\bar{W}, K)$ such that $u^* \geqslant u^\dagger$.

The first condition of Assumption (ii) says that the subgame W_T is ordinal convex for each $T \in \mathscr{T}^\dagger$; its core is large by Theorem 4.3.2. By the second condition of Assumption (ii) and by the fact that the $W(S)$ are cylinders, for any $\{T_i\}_{i \in I} \subset \mathscr{T}^\dagger$ for which $T_i \neq T_j$ if $i \neq j$,

$$\mathring{W}(\bigcup_{i \in I} S_i) \subset \bigcup_{i \in I} \mathring{W}(S_i), \text{ for all } \{S_i\}_{i \in I} \text{ such that } \phi \neq S_i \subset T_i.$$

So, for any $P \in \mathscr{N}$,

$$\mathring{W}(P) \subset \cup \{\mathring{W}(S) \mid S \subset T, \text{ for some } T \in \mathscr{T}^\dagger\},$$

consequently,

$$\cup \{\mathring{W}(P) \mid P \in \mathscr{N}\} = \cup \{\mathring{W}(S) \mid S \subset T, \text{ for some } T \in \mathscr{T}^\dagger\}.$$

Thus, by setting $K^\dagger := \cap_{T \in \mathscr{T}^\dagger} W(T)$,

$$\begin{aligned}\text{Core of } (W, K) &= K \setminus \cup \{\mathring{W}(S) \mid S \in \mathscr{N}\} \\ &= K \setminus \cup \{\mathring{W}(S) \mid S \subset T, \text{ for some } T \in \mathscr{T}^\dagger\} \\ &\supset K^\dagger \cup \{\mathring{W}(S) \mid S \subset T, \text{ for some } T \in \mathscr{T}^\dagger\} \\ &= \text{the product of the cores of } W_T,\ T \in \mathscr{T}^\dagger.\end{aligned}$$

The core of (W, K) thus contains the product of the large cores of the subgames. It is large itself. Hence the assertion of the theorem. □

Proof of Theorem 2.2.3. The same notation as in Section 2.2 is used here. Choose any $\sigma \in G_n$, and define $i_h := \sigma^{-1}(h)$ for each $h \in \{1, 2, \ldots, n\}$. Define for simplicity, $a := a^\sigma(V)$. Proved here is a sharper result,

$$(a_{i_1}, \ldots, a_{i_j}) \in C(\{i_1, \ldots, i_j\}, \mathrm{V}_{\{i_1, \ldots, i_j\}}), \text{ for each } j = 1, 2, \ldots, n.$$

(Recall Definition 4.3.3 of the subgame.) Since n is arbitrary, one has to prove only for $j = n$, assuming that

$$(a_{i_1}, \ldots, a_{i_{n-1}}) \in C(\{i_1, \ldots, i_{n-1}\}, V_{\{i_1, \ldots, i_{n-1}\}}),$$

Define for simplicity, therefore, $N' := \{i_1, i_2, \ldots, i_{n-1}\}$. For any positive real number ϵ, define a non-side-payment game $V^\epsilon : \mathscr{N} \to \mathbf{R}^N$ inductively by:

$$V^\epsilon(S) := \begin{cases} V(S), \text{ if } \#S \leqslant n-2; \\ V(S) + \epsilon\{\chi_N\}, \text{ if } \#S = n-1; \\ V(N) \cup \left[\left\{ u \in V^\epsilon(Q) \cap V^\epsilon(R) \setminus V^\epsilon(Q \cap R) \,\middle|\, \begin{matrix} \exists Q, R \subsetneqq N \\ Q \cup R = N \end{matrix} \right\} - \mathbf{R}^N_+ \right], \text{ if } S = N, \end{cases}$$

where χ_N is the n-vector each of whose component is 1, and $V(\phi) := \phi$. Then,

$$(a_{i_1} + \epsilon, a_{i_2} + \epsilon, \ldots, a_{i_{n-1}} + \epsilon) \in C(N', V^\epsilon_{N'}) \setminus \bigcup_{R \subsetneqq N'} \overline{V^\epsilon_{N'}(R)},$$

and V^ϵ is ordinal convex. Define

$$a^\epsilon_{i_n} := \max \{t \in \mathbf{R} \mid (a_{i_1} + \epsilon, \ldots, a_{i_{n-1}} + \epsilon, t) \in V^\epsilon(N)\}.$$

Then, by Lemma 4.3.6,

$$(a_{i_1} + \epsilon, \ldots, a_{i_{n-1}} + \epsilon, a^\epsilon_{i_n}) \in C(N, V^\epsilon).$$

Let a_{i_n} be a limit point of $\{a^\epsilon_{i_n}\}_\epsilon$ as $\epsilon \downarrow 0$.
Then,

$$(a_{i_1}, \ldots, a_{i_{n-1}}, a_{i_n}) \in C(N, V),$$

and

$$a_{i_n} = \max \{t \in \mathbf{R} \mid (a_{i_1}, \ldots, a_{i_{n-1}}, t) \in V(N)\}. \ \square$$

Remark 4.3.12. For other types of comparative cooperative game theory problem, in which effects of a change in player-set are studied, see e.g., Mo (1988), Scotchmer and Wooders (1988), and Edward C. Rosenthal (1990). Among the related works are Young (1985b), Chun and Thomson (1988), Moulin and Thomson (1988), Moulin (1990), Alkan, Demange and Gale (1991), and Sprumont (1990). Milgrom and Shannon (1991) recently systematically studied the monotonicity properties of various solutions with respect to changes in parameters, by looking at super-modular functions defined on a general lattice. □

4.4 Extent of the implications

The purpose of this section is to systematically develop the comparative cooperative game theory within the framework of side-payment games. By doing so, the dominance result (in the dual sense) on the equilibria of the capitalistic economy over the equilibria of the associated socialistic economy (Theorem 4.2.3) is shown to be the only welfare result one can hope for, given the generality of the model. This section is taken from Ichiishi (1990a).

Let N denote a finite set of players, given throughout this section, and let $\mathcal{N}$ denote the family of nonempty coalitions $2^N \setminus \{\phi\}$. A side-payment game is called simply a *game* in this section. Denote by $C(v)$ the core of game v. The three welfare criteria introduced in the preceding section (Definitions 4.3.7, 4.3.8 and 4.3.9) are re-formulated in the present setup of side-payment games as

Definition 4.4.1. Let v, w: $\mathcal{N} \to \mathbf{R}$ be two side-payment games. The core of v is said to *dominate* the core of w, if for every $y \in C(w)$ there exists $x \in C(v)$ such that $y \leqslant x$.

Definition 4.4.2. Let v, w: $\mathcal{N} \to \mathbf{R}$ be two side-payment games. The core of v is said to *dominate* the core of w *in the dual sense*, if for every $x \in C(v)$ there exists $y \in C(w)$ such that $y \leqslant x$.

Definition 4.4.3. Let v, w: $\mathcal{N} \to \mathbf{R}$ be two side-payment games. The core of v is said to *weakly dominate* the core of w, if there exist $y \in C(w)$ and $x \in C(v)$ such that $y \leqslant x$.

Necessary and sufficient conditions for each criterion will be established. First, the dominance criterion is studied.

Definition 4.4.4. Let v be a side-payment game. The *efficiency cover of* v is the function v^*: $\mathcal{N} \to \mathbf{R}$ defined by $v^*(S) := \max \{\sum_{j \in S} x_j \mid x \in C(v)\}$. The *extended efficiency cover* of v is the function v^*: $\mathbf{R}^N_+ \to \mathbf{R}$ defined by $v^*(p) := \max \{p \cdot x \mid x \in C(v)\}$.

The efficient cover associates with each coalition S its payoff that is given by the most efficient core allocation from S's point of view. Since coalition $S \in \mathcal{N}$ is identified with its characteristic vector $\chi_S \in \mathbf{R}^N_+$, no confusion arises between the efficiency cover and the extended efficiency cover. These concepts play crucial roles in the present study, so it would be useful to note the following fact:

Proposition 4.4.5. *Let v be a side-payment game with a nonempty core, and let v^* be its extended efficiency cover. Then*:

(i) $v^*(p) = \min \left\{ \kappa v(N) - \sum_{S \in \mathcal{N}} \lambda_S v(S) \;\middle|\; \begin{array}{l} (\kappa, \lambda) \in \mathbf{R}_+ \times \mathbf{R}^{\mathcal{N}}_+ \\ \kappa \chi_N - \sum_{S \in \mathcal{N}} \lambda_S \chi_S = p \end{array} \right\}$;

(ii) *The function v^*: $\mathbf{R}^N_+ \to \mathbf{R}$ is sublinear, i.e., for any $p, q \in \mathbf{R}^N_+$ and any $r \in \mathbf{R}_+$, $v^*(rp) = rv^*(p)$ and $v^*(p+q) \leqslant v^*(p) + v^*(q)$.*

Proof. The number $v^*(p)$ is the optimal value of the linear programming problem,

$$\begin{aligned} &\max \quad p \cdot x, \\ &\text{subject to } \chi_S \cdot x \geqslant v(S) \text{ for every } S \in \mathcal{N}, \\ &\qquad \text{and } -\chi_N \cdot x \geqslant -v(N). \end{aligned}$$

So the duality theorem establishes assertion (i). Assertion (ii) is straightforward. □

The first result (Theorem 4.4.6) provides a general characterization of the *dominance* of the core of game v over the core of another game w.

Theorem 4.4.6. *Let v, w be side-payment games with a nonempty core, and let v^* and w^* be their extended efficiency covers respectively. Then, the following two conditions are equivalent:*
(i) *For every $y \in C(w)$ there exists $x \in C(v)$ such that $y \leqslant x$;*
(ii) *$w^*(p) \leqslant v^*(p)$, for every $p \in \mathbf{R}_+^N$.*

Proof. Define

$$A(v) := C(v) - \mathbf{R}_+^N.$$

Condition (i) is equivalent to: $C(w) \subset A(v)$. The latter condition in turn is shown to be equivalent to condition (ii), by applying an elementary version of the separation theorem (see, e.g., Ichiishi (1983, Theorem 1.5.1, p. 18)) to the closed, convex, comprehensive set $A(v)$. (Here, a subset A of $\mathbf{R}^N$ is called comprehensive if $A = A - \mathbf{R}_+^N$.) □

Corollary 4.4.7. *Let v, w be side-payment games with a nonempty core. Then, any of the two conditions (i) and (ii) of Theorem 4.4.6 is satisfied, if for every $\lambda \in \mathbf{R}_+^{\mathcal{N}}$ for which $\sum_{S \in \mathcal{N}} \lambda_S \chi_S \leqslant \chi_N$, it follows that $\sum_{S \in \mathcal{N}} \lambda_S (v(S) - w(S)) \leqslant v(N) - w(N)$.*

The set $A(v)$ that appeared in the proof of Theorem 4.4.6 will be used often in the rest of the section. Define also

$$B(v) := \{x \in \mathbf{R}^N \mid \forall S \in \mathcal{N}: \chi_S \cdot x \leqslant v^*(S)\}.$$

Notice that by the duality theorem for linear programming problems (see, e.g., Ichiishi (1983, Ch. 5, Exercise 4, p. 115)),

$$\forall p \geqslant \mathbf{0}: \quad \max\{p \cdot x \mid x \in B(v)\} = \min\{\textstyle\sum \lambda_S v^*(S) \mid \lambda \geqslant \mathbf{0}, \sum \lambda_S \chi_S = p\}. \tag{*}$$

In spite of the generality of Theorem 4.4.6, condition (ii) therein may not be practical, because one has to go through checking the *continuum* of inequalities parameterized by $p \in \mathbf{R}_+^N$. Of course, if the cores $C(v)$ and $C(w)$ are known, then condition (ii) can be checked in finitely many steps. Indeed, denote by ext $C(v)$ the set of extreme points of the convex polyhedron $C(v)$. Then, the negation of condition (ii) is equivalent to the existence of $\bar{p} \in \mathbf{R}_+^N$, $\bar{x} \in \text{ext } C(v)$ and $\bar{y} \in \text{ext } C(w)$, such that

$$\bar{p} \cdot \bar{x} \geqslant \bar{p} \cdot x \text{ for all } x \in \text{ext } C(v),$$
$$\bar{p} \cdot \bar{y} \geqslant \bar{p} \cdot y \text{ for all } y \in \text{ext } C(w), \text{ and}$$
$$\bar{p} \cdot \bar{y} > \bar{p} \cdot \bar{x},$$

which can be verified in finitely many steps. One would like to check condition (ii), however, not by looking at the endogenous variables $C(v)$

and $C(w)$, but by looking only at the exogenous data v and w (and v^* and w^*, in view of Proposition 4.4.5 (i)). For a certain class of games, the cardinality of the set of inequalities to check reduces down to $\#\mathcal{N}$ (*finite*). A game v is called *additive* if $v(S)=\sum_{j\in S} v(\{j\})$ for each $S\in\mathcal{N}$. The core of an additive game v is a singleton $\{x\}$, given by $x_j=v(\{j\})$. Additive games are convex, convex games are exact, and exact games have a nonempty core (Section 2.1).

A new class of exact games is now introduced: An exact game v is called a *no-gap game*, if for every $p\in\mathbf{R}^N_+$ there exists $\lambda\in\mathbf{R}^{\mathcal{N}}_+$ such that $\sum_{S\in\mathcal{N}}\lambda_S\chi_S=p$ and $\sum_{S\in\mathcal{N}}\lambda_S v^*(S)\leqslant v^*(p)$. (The last inequality may be replaced by an equality, due to Proposition 4.4.5 (ii). A *gap game* v has a "gap" at some $p\in\mathbf{R}^N_+$, i.e., for any $\lambda\in\mathbf{R}^{\mathcal{N}}_+$ for which $\sum_{S\in\mathcal{N}}\lambda_S\chi_S=p$, it follows that $v^*(p)<\sum_{S\in\mathcal{N}}\lambda_S v^*(S)$.)

Proposition 4.4.8. *Let v be an exact game, and let v^* be its efficiency cover. Then, the following two conditions are equivalent:*
(i) *Game v is a no-gap game;*
(ii) *For every $x\in\mathbf{R}^N$ for which $\sum_{j\in S}x_j\leqslant v^*(S)$ for every $S\in\mathcal{N}$, there exists $y\in C(v)$ such that $x\leqslant y$.*

Proof. The no-gap condition (i) means:

$$\forall p\geqslant\mathbf{0}\text{: }\min\{\textstyle\sum\lambda_S v^*(S)\mid\lambda\geqslant\mathbf{0},\ \sum\lambda_S\chi_S=p\}\leqslant v^*(p).$$

By identity (*), this condition becomes:

$$\forall p\geqslant\mathbf{0}\text{: }\max\{p\cdot x\mid x\in B(v)\}\leqslant\max\{p\cdot x\mid x\in A(v)\},$$

which in turn is equivalent to: $B(v)\subset A(v)$, by a separation theorem. This last condition is precisely condition (ii). □

Proposition 4.4.9. *Convex games are no-gap exact games.*

Proof. Let v be a convex game. Choose any $p\in\mathbf{R}^N_+$, and let $\{\mu_i, T_i\}_{i=1}^s$ be the canonical form of p, i.e.,

$$T_1\supsetneqq T_2\supsetneqq\cdots\supsetneqq T_s,$$
$$\mu_i>0,\ i=1,\ldots,s,\text{ and}$$
$$\sum_{i=1}^s\mu_i\chi_{T_i}=p.$$

By Corollary 2.1.4, there exists $x\in C(v)$ such that $\sum_{j\in N\setminus T_i}x_j=v(N\setminus T_i)$ for all i, or equivalently such that

$$\sum_{j\in T_i}x_j=v(N)-v(N\setminus T_i)=v^*(T_i),\ i=1,\ldots,s.$$

Then,

$$\sum_{i=1}^{s} \mu_i v^*(T_i) = \sum_{i=1}^{s} \mu_i \sum_{j \in T_i} x_j = p \cdot x \leqslant v^*(p). \ \square$$

Theorem 4.4.10. *Let v be an exact game, and let v^* be its efficiency cover. Suppose on the one hand that v is a no-gap game. Let w be any side-payment game with a nonempty core and let w^* be its efficiency cover. Then, the following two conditions (i) and (ii) are equivalent:*

(i) *For every $y \in C(w)$ there exists $x \in C(v)$ such that $y \leqslant x$;*

(ii) *$w^*(S) \leqslant v^*(S)$, for every $S \in \mathcal{N}$.*

Conditions (i) and (ii) are implied by the following condition (iii). If, moreover, game w is exact, then any of conditions (i) and (ii) implies condition (iii):

(iii) $v(S) - w(S) \leqslant v(N) - w(N)$, for every $S \in 2^N \backslash \{N\}$.

Suppose on the other hand, v is not a no-gap game. Then, there exists an additive game w (say, $w(S) = \sum_{j \in S} y_j$, so that $C(w) = \{y\}$) such that $w^*(S) \leqslant v^*(S)$ for every $S \in \mathcal{N}$, yet $y \nleqslant x$ for any $x \in C(v)$.

Proof. Suppose v is a no-gap exact game. Due to Theorem 4.4.6, one needs to show only that (ii) implies (i). Suppose there exists $y \in C(w)$ such that $y \nleqslant x$ for any $x \in C(v)$. Then, $y \notin A(v)$, so (by Proposition 4.4.8 (ii)) $y \notin B(v)$. Consequently, there exists $S \in \mathcal{N}$ such that $w^*(S) \geqslant \sum_{j \in S} y_j > v^*(S)$, which contradicts (ii). Assertions about condition (iii) follow from the identities, $w^*(S) = w(N) - \bar{\bar{w}}(N \backslash S)$ (here, $\bar{\bar{w}}$ is the exact envelope of w), and $v^*(S) = v(N) - v(N \backslash S)$ (here, v is exact).

Suppose v is not a no-gap game. Then (by Proposition 4.4.8 (ii)) there exists $y \in B(v) \backslash A(v)$. Define an additive game w by $w(\{j\}) = y_j$. Game w satisfies all the required properties. $\square$

Example 4.4.11. An exact game which is not a no-gap game: Let $N = \{1, 2, 3, 4, 5\}$. Let μ, υ, π be payoff vectors given as: $\mu = (0, 5, 3, 2, 2)$, $\upsilon = (5, 0, 5, 0, 2)$, and $\pi = (5, 2, 4, 1, 0)$. Define game v by $v(S) := \min \{\mu(S), \upsilon(S), \pi(S)\}$ for every $S \in \mathcal{N}$.

It is routine to verify general facts: Game w is exact, iff there exists a family of additive games $\{\mu^i \mid i \in I\}$ satisfying $\mu^i(N) = \mu^j(N)$ for all $i, j \in I$, such that $w(S) = \min \{\mu^i(S) \mid i \in I\}$ for every $S \in \mathcal{N}$. In this case, $\mu^i \in C(w)$ for all $i \in I$, and $w^*(S) = \max \{\mu^i(S) \mid i \in I\}$ for all $S \in \mathcal{N}$.

By these general facts, the present example v is exact, and for vector $x := (2, 5, 3, 1, 0) \in \mathbf{R}^N$, $\sum_{j \in S} x_j \leqslant v^*(S)$ for every $S \in \mathcal{N}$, so $x \in B(v)$. Notice:

$$\begin{aligned}
x_2 + x_3 \qquad\qquad &= 8 = v^*(\{2, 3\}) \\
x_1 + x_2 \qquad + x_4 \qquad &= 8 = v^*(\{1, 2, 4\}) \\
x_1 + x_2 \qquad\qquad + x_5 &= 7 = v^*(\{1, 2, 5\}) \\
x_1 + x_2 + x_3 + x_4 + x_5 &= 11 < v^*(\{1, 2, 3, 4, 5\}).
\end{aligned}$$

Therefore, there exists no $y \geqslant x$ satisfying $\sum_{j \in S} y_j \leqslant v^*(S)$ for $S = \{2, 3\}, \{1, 2, 4\}, \{1, 2, 5\}$ and $\sum_{j \in N} y_j = v^*(N)$. So, $x \notin A(v)$. □

Example 4.4.12. A no-gap exact game which is not convex: Let $N = \{1, 2, 3, 4\}$. Let $\mu = (4, 2, 4, 2)$, and $\upsilon = (3, 4, 1, 4)$, and define an exact game v by $v(S) := \min\{\mu(S), \upsilon(S)\}$ for every $S \in \mathcal{N}$. This example is due to Schmeidler (1972), who showed that it is not convex. In order to show that this is a no-gap game, it suffices to show:

$$\forall p \geqslant \mathbf{0}: \exists \lambda^p \in \mathbf{R}_+^N: \exists x^p \in C(v): \textstyle\sum \lambda_S^p \chi_S = p, \text{ and } \sum \lambda_S^p v^*(S) = p \cdot x^p. \quad (1)$$

Due to the symmetry in players 2 and 4 in this example, one may assume without loss of generality $p_2 \leqslant p_4$. One may also assume $p_m := \min\{p_j \mid j \in N\} = 0$. Indeed, suppose $p_m > 0$. Then, define $q \in \mathbf{R}_+^N$ by: $q_j := p_j - p_m$ for every j. Since $q_m = 0$, there exist $\lambda^q \in \mathbf{R}_+^{\mathcal{N}}$ and $x^q \in C(v)$ satisfying condition (1) for q. Notice $\lambda_N^q = 0$. Define $\lambda^p \in \mathbf{R}_+^{\mathcal{N}}$ by: $\lambda_S^p := \lambda_S^q$ if $S \neq N$; and $\lambda_N^p := p_m$. Then, (λ^p, x^q) satisfies condition (1) for the given p. Now, condition (1) is verified for various cases according to the order among $\{p_1, p_2, p_3, p_4\}$. If $0 = p_1 \leqslant p_2 \leqslant p_3 \leqslant p_4$, for example, define λ^p and x^p by: $\lambda_{\{4\}}^p := p_4 - p_3$; $\lambda_{\{3,4\}}^p := p_3 - p_2$; $\lambda_{\{2,3,4\}}^p := p_2$; $\lambda_S^p := 0$ for all other S; $x^p := (3, 3, 2, 4)$. It is routine to verify that λ^p, x^p are the vectors required for (1). One can verify (1) analogously for the other cases, although it is tedious. □

Remark 4.4.13. There are two factors which cause the dominance of $C(v)$ over $C(w)$; they are the best captured when game v is no-gap exact and w is exact. One factor requires that the grand coalition is more efficient in game v than in game w, i.e., $v(N) - w(N)$ (the right-hand side of the inequality of condition (iii) of Theorem 4.4.10) is suitably big to guarantee the inequality. The other factor requires that the blocking power of each coalition S in game v is not overly big compared with that in game w, i.e., $v(S) - w(S)$ (the left-hand side of condition (iii)) is suitably small to guarantee the inequality. This insightful observation is due to Shmuel Zamir. □

The next welfare criterion is the dominance criterion in the dual sense. Let v be a game with a nonempty core. The *extended exact envelope* of v is the function $\bar{\bar{v}}: \mathbf{R}_+^N \to \mathbf{R}$ defined by $\bar{\bar{v}}(p) := \min\{p \cdot x \mid x \in C(v)\}$. Notice that:

$$\bar{\bar{v}}(p) = v(N) - v^*(\chi_N - p), \text{ for every } p \in \mathbf{R}^N \text{ such that } \mathbf{0} \leqslant p \leqslant \chi_N.$$

(This identity is false for a non-balanced game.) The following two results, Theorems 4.4.14 and 4.4.15, are dual to Theorems 4.4.6 and 4.4.10. The proofs are also dual, so are omitted.

Theorem 4.4.14. *Let v, w be side-payment games with a nonempty core, and let $\bar{\bar{v}}$ and $\bar{\bar{w}}$ be their extended exact envelopes respectively. Then, the following two conditions are equivalent:*

(i) *For every* $x \in C(v)$ *there exists* $y \in C(w)$ *such that* $y \leqslant x$;
(ii) $\bar{\bar{w}}(p) \leqslant \bar{\bar{v}}(p)$ *for every* $p \in \mathbf{R}^N_+$.

Sharkey (1982b) defined a game with a large core; a game v *has a large core*, if for every $z \in \mathbf{R}^N$ for which $v(S) \leqslant \sum_{j \in S} z_j$ for every $S \in \mathcal{N}$, there exists $x \in C(v)$ such that $x \leqslant z$. Sharkey showed that convex games have large cores, but not conversely. In view of Proposition 4.4.8, the exact games with a large core play precisely the same role in the result dual to Theorem 4.4.10 (as the no-gap exact games do in Theorem 4.4.10):

Theorem 4.4.15. *Let* v *be an exact game, and* w *be an exact game with a large core. Then, the following two conditions are equivalent:*
(i) *For every* $x \in C(v)$ *there exists* $y \in C(w)$ *such that* $y \leqslant x$;
(ii) $w(S) \leqslant v(S)$ *for every* $S \in \mathcal{N}$.

The third criterion is the *weak dominance* of $C(v)$ over $C(w)$.

Theorem 4.4.16. *Let* v *be a side-payment game with a nonempty core, and let* w *be an exact game. Then, the following two conditions are equivalent:*
(i) *There exist* $y \in C(w)$ *and* $x \in C(v)$ *such that* $y \leqslant x$;
(ii) $\bar{\bar{w}}(p) \leqslant v^*(p)$ *for every* $p \in \mathbf{R}^N_+$.

Proof. The negation of condition (i) says $A(v) \cap C(w) = \phi$, which is equivalent to: $\exists p \in \mathbf{R}^N_+ \backslash \{\mathbf{0}\}$: $\max p \cdot A(v) < \min p \cdot C(w)$. This last condition is the negation of condition (ii), since w is exact. □

Corollary 4.4.17. *Let* v, w *be two side-payment games. Then, the following two conditions are equivalent:*
(i) *There exist* $y \in C(w)$ *and* $x \in C(v)$ *such that* $y \leqslant x$;
(ii) *For any* $\lambda, \mu \in \mathbf{R}^{\mathcal{N}}_+$ *for which* $\sum_{S \in \mathcal{N}} (\lambda_S + \mu_S) \chi_S = \chi_N$, *and for any* $\alpha \in \mathbf{R}$ *for which* $\max_{j \in N} \sum_{S \ni j} \lambda_S \leqslant \alpha \leqslant 1$, *it follows that*

$$\sum_{S \in \mathcal{N}} (\lambda_S v(S) + \mu_S w(S)) \leqslant \alpha v(N) + (1 - \alpha) w(N).$$

Proof. Notice first that condition (ii) implies that both w and v are balanced. By substituting the exact envelope formula for $w(p)$ and the extended efficiency cover formula for $v^*(p)$ in condition (ii) of Theorem 4.4.16, the present condition (i) is equivalent to:

$$\begin{aligned}
&(\forall p \in \mathbf{R}^N_+):\\
&(\forall (\lambda, \alpha) \in \mathbf{R}^{\mathcal{N}}_+ \times \mathbf{R}_+ : -\textstyle\sum \lambda_S \chi_S + \alpha \chi_N = p):\\
&(\forall (\mu, \beta) \in \mathbf{R}^{\mathcal{N}}_+ \times \mathbf{R}_+ : \textstyle\sum \mu_S \chi_S - \beta \chi_N = p):\\
&\qquad \textstyle\sum \mu_S w(S) - \beta w(N) \leqslant -\sum \lambda_S v(S) + \alpha v(N).
\end{aligned}$$

It is routine to verify that this last condition is equivalent to the present condition (ii). □

Corollary 4.4.18. *Let v, w be two convex games. Then, the following two conditions are equivalent:*
(i) *There exist $y \in C(w)$ and $x \in C(v)$ such that $y \leqslant x$;*
(ii) $w(S) + v(N \backslash S) \leqslant v(N)$, *for every $S \in \mathcal{N}$.*

Proof. It suffices to show that the present condition (ii) implies condition (ii) of Theorem 4.4.16. The former is equivalent to:

$$w(S) \leqslant v^*(S), \text{ for every } S \in \mathcal{N}.$$

Choose any $p \geqslant \mathbf{0}$, and let $\{\mu_i, T_i\}_{i=1}^{s}$ be the canonical form of p (see the proof of Proposition 4.4.9 for the definition). Then,

$$w(p) = \sum \mu_i w(T_i), \text{ and}$$
$$v^*(p) = \sum \mu_i v^*(T_i).$$

Condition (ii) of Theorem 4.4.16 now follows. □

Remark 4.4.19. Game v is said to *dominate* game w, if $w(S) \leqslant v(S)$ for all $S \in \mathcal{N}$. Dominance of game v over game w may not result in weak dominance of the core $C(v)$ over $C(w)$; there is an abundance of such examples. Shift of a social system from w to a dominating system v may, therefore, result in "exploitation" of somebody in the society in the sense that for any $y \in C(w)$ and any $x \in C(v)$ there exists $j \in N$ such that $y_j > x_j$. If both game w and a dominating game v satisfy increasing returns (so that condition (ii) of Corollary 4.4.18 is obviously satisfied), however, shift from w to v always retains the possibility of "no exploitation." □

The comparative economic systems result of Section 4.2 (Theorem 4.2.3) is based on the inclusion,

$$W(S) \subset V_{\bar{x}, \bar{p}, \bar{\mathcal{F}}}(S) \text{ for every } S \in \mathcal{N},$$

which is a direct consequence of Condition 4.2.1. This inclusion corresponds to the inequalities,

$$w(S) \leqslant v(S) \text{ for every } S \in \mathcal{N},$$

in the side-payment case. In view of Theorem 4.4.15, this inequality system *characterizes* the dominance of $C(v)$ over $C(w)$ in the dual sense if v is exact and w is convex.

5 Normative theory of a production economy with increasing returns to scale

The works of Chapters 3 and 4 are descriptive. The resource allocation mechanism formulated there realizes as its social outcome the phenomena observed in the present-day economy, capitalistic or market-cooperative socialistic, and it turns out that this social outcome may not be Pareto optimal. The work of this chapter is, on the other hand, normative. Proposed here is a new allocation mechanism whose social outcome is Pareto optimal. The new mechanism works in many of the situations that exhibit increasing returns to scale. To see the role of increasing returns to scale, one has to make explicit use of the production-set concept, or its derivative concept such as the cost function. The model used in this chapter is, therefore, a coalition production economy $\mathscr{E}_{cp}$ (Definition 3.5.1). In order to use the cost-function concept, the commodities are classified into primary and final goods. Section 5.1 presents the new resource allocation mechanism and equilibrium concept. The basic framework for the mechanism may be summarized as follows: Two market systems are introduced, one for the exchange of primary goods with primary goods, and the other for the exchange of final goods with final goods. The two systems are disconnected, however, in the sense that the exchange of primary goods with final goods is prohibited. Thus, for example, the value of primary goods is measured in terms of dollars, the value of final goods is measured in terms of coupons, and it is prohibited by the constitution to exchange dollars with coupons. There are concepts of cost (in terms of dollars) and revenue (in terms of coupons), but there is no concept of profit. A coalition as a production unit cooperatively determines the dollar value and coupon value for each member as his income levels, and an activity compatible to these dollar/coupon payments. Each member in turn determines noncooperatively his consumption bundle given the two budget constraints. The two price vectors are determined to clear markets. Section 5.2 establishes sufficient conditions under which an equilibrium exists; the underlying postulate is non-decreasing returns to scale. Section 5.3 briefly discusses the literature.

5.1 General equilibrium model

The models of Sections 3.1, 3.2 and 4.2 are descriptive: The resource allocation mechanism formulated in these models is the mechanism of the present-day economy, capitalistic or market-cooperative socialistic, which realizes the observed phenomena as its social outcome. It was shown in Section 4.1 that this social outcome may not be Pareto optimal. Given the institutional framework of the present-day economy, one has to accept this non-optimality as a fact of life, regardless of whether or not one likes it.

The work of this chapter is, on the other hand, normative: A new allocation mechanism whose social outcome is Pareto optimal is proposed here. If a country institutes a new constitution so that this mechanism is embodied in its economy, and if the economic agents follow this constitutional rule while pursuing their self-interest, then a social optimum will be achieved at the social outcome.

Recall that the second fundamental theorem of welfare economics fails to be true for the private ownership economy $\mathscr{E}_{po}$ (Definition 3.3.3) if the production sets Y^j are non-convex (in particular, if the technologies satisfy increasing returns to scale). The new resource allocation mechanism, on the other hand, is based explicitly on the assumption of non-decreasing returns to scale. To formulate this assumption, the commodities are classified into two categories. One category consists of l types of commodities called *primary goods*; they are used in production as inputs. There are m types of commodities in the other category, called *final goods*; they are produced as outputs.

Like the models of Sections 3.1, 3.2 and 4.2, the model of this chapter formulates the view that a firm is an organization (Section 1.1). Unlike the models of Sections 3.1, 3.2 and 4.2, the present model has to make explicit use of the production-set concept, or its derivative concept such as the cost function, in order to see the role of increasing returns to scale. Thus, one is led to use the model of coalition production economy $\mathscr{E}_{cp}$ (Definition 3.5.1), in which there are $(l+m)$ commodities rather than l commodities. The usual sign convention for demand and supply is adopted. Labor is one of the l primary goods. *Throughout this section and Section 5.2, it is postulated that there exists no positive amount of any final good as an initial endowment of the economy.* Much of the analysis of a coalition production economy with increasing returns to scale which has some positive final goods as initial endowments will be left as an open problem. The definition of the model is reproduced below, where new notation is adopted to take into account the distinction between the primary and the final goods:

Definition 5.1.1. Let N be a finite set of economic agents, and let $\mathscr{N}$ be the family of nonempty coalitions, $2^N \backslash \{\phi\}$. Set $n := \# N$. A *coalition production* *economy* is a list of specified data $\mathscr{E}_{cp} := (\{C^j, u^j, \omega^j\}_{j \in N}, \{T(S)\}_{S \in \mathscr{N}})$ of agent j's consumption set $C^j (\subset \mathbf{R}^l \times \mathbf{R}^m)$, utility function u^j: $C^j \rightarrow \mathbf{R}$ and initial endowment $\omega^j (\in \mathbf{R}^l)$, and coalition S's production set $T(S) (\subset (-\mathbf{R}^l_+) \times \mathbf{R}^m_+)$.

A generic element of C^j will be denoted by (x^j, y^j), with $x^j \in \mathbf{R}^l$ and $y^j \in \mathbf{R}^m$, and a generic element of $T(S)$ will be denoted by (z, y), with $z \in -\mathbf{R}^l_+$ and $y \in \mathbf{R}^m_+$. One way to formulate the non-decreasing returns to scale for production set $T(S)$ would be to impose the condition,

$$[(z, y) \in T(S), \lambda \geqslant 1] \Rightarrow [(\lambda z, \lambda y) \in T(S)].$$

Instead of this condition, however, a weaker condition will be adopted (Postulate 5.1.4) taking advantage of the distinction between the primary and the final goods.

A *core allocation* of economy $\mathscr{E}_{cp}$ can be defined as in Definition 3.5.2. Here, the strategy space of each coalition S is the space $\prod_{j \in S} C^j \times T(S)$, a subset of the $(l+m) \cdot (\#S+1)$-dimensional space.

It was emphasized earlier that the cooperative *behavior* is consistent both with "cooperative" decision-making *rules* and with the top-down decision-making *rule* (Remark 3.1.8). The new resource allocation mechanism proposed here is also based on the cooperative behavior and is consistent with any of these rules, but it stipulates (1) that the strategy space of coalition S is a particular subset of the $2 \cdot (\#S)$-dimensional space, and (2) that given a newly defined strategy bundle of coalition S, the noncooperative behavior of the members of S results in the choice of commodity bundles in $C^j, j \in S$. The mechanism is thus based in part on a decentralized noncooperative behavior. This is made possible by introducing two "disconnected" market systems, which are now defined.

Given a positive integer k, denote by Δ^{k-1} the $(k-1)$-dimensional unit simplex, $\{x \in \mathbf{R}^k \mid x \geqslant \mathbf{0}, \sum_{i=1}^k x_i = 1\}$. Two types of price vectors are introduced: $p \in \Delta^{l-1}$ and $q \in \Delta^{m-1}$. Here, primary goods are exchanged with primary goods under the price vector p, and final goods are exchanged with final goods under the price vector q, but the two systems of prices are disconnected in the sense that any exchange of primary goods with final goods is prohibited. Thus, for example, the value of primary goods is measured in terms of dollars, the value of final goods is measured in terms of coupons, and it is prohibited by the constitution to exchange dollars with coupons.

The *generalized cost function* of firm S is the function c^S: $\Delta^{l-1} \times \Delta^{m-1} \times \mathbf{R}_+ \rightarrow \mathbf{R}_+$, defined by:

$$c^S(p, q, \eta) := \inf\{-p \cdot z \mid (z, y) \in T(S), q \cdot y \geqslant \eta\}.$$

There are concepts of revenue (say, in terms of coupons) and cost (say, in terms of dollars). There is no concept of profit definable here. The value

$c^S(p, q, \eta)$ is the minimal cost (in terms of dollars) that firm S incurs in order to produce value η (in terms of coupons) when price vectors (p, q) prevail. The *indirect utility function* of agent j is the function v^j: $\Delta^{l-1} \times \Delta^{m-1} \times \mathbf{R}^2 \to \mathbf{R}$, defined by:

$$v^j(p, q, \xi^j, \eta^j)$$
$$:= \sup \{u^j(x^j, y^j) \mid (x^j, y^j) \in C^j, p \cdot x^j \leqslant \xi^j, q \cdot y^j \leqslant \eta^j\}.$$

This indirect utility function presupposes the following noncooperative behavior of agent j as a consumer: He is given value ξ^j (in terms of dollars) and value η^j (in terms of coupons) as two types of his income. He will spend ξ^j and η^j for the purchase of primary goods and final goods, respectively. Under the prevailing price vectors (p, q), he has two budget constraints, $p \cdot x^j \leqslant \xi^j$ and $q \cdot y^j \leqslant \eta^j$. He demands primary and final goods, both for consumption purposes, to maximize his utility subject to the two budget constraints.

In the coalition production economy $\mathscr{E}_{cp}$ the proposed resource allocation mechanism works in the following way: Each agent is a price-taker. Suppose price vectors $(\bar{p}, \bar{q})$ prevail. The economic agents play the cooperative game, in which a strategy of agent j is his two income levels (ξ^j, η^j), his utility function is given as $v^j(\bar{p}, \bar{q}, \cdot, \cdot)$: $\mathbf{R}^2 \to \mathbf{R}$, and strategy bundle $\{\xi^j, \eta^j\}_{j \in S}$ of coalition S is feasible if

$$\sum_{j \in S} \xi^j + c^S(\bar{p}, \bar{q}, \sum_{j \in S} \eta^j) \leqslant \bar{p} \cdot \sum_{j \in S} \omega^j.$$

that is, if the coalition's total income in terms of dollars $(\bar{p} \cdot \sum_{j \in S} \omega^j)$ is distributed to the total primary-good-consumption value $(\sum_{j \in S} \xi^j)$ and the investment (c^S), and this investment yields the total final-good-consumption value in terms of coupons $(\sum_{j \in S} \eta^j)$. The attainability of each coalition is summarized, therefore, by the non-side-payment game $V_{\bar{p},\bar{q}}$: $\mathscr{N} \to \mathbf{R}^N$, defined by:

$$V_{\bar{p},\bar{q}}(S) := \left\{ u \in \mathbf{R}^N \;\middle|\; \begin{array}{l} \exists \{\xi^j, \eta^j\}_{j \in S} \in (\mathbf{R}^2)^S: \\ \sum_{j \in S} \xi^j + c^S(\bar{p}, \bar{q}, \sum_{j \in S} \eta^j) \leqslant \bar{p} \cdot \sum_{j \in S} \omega^j, \\ \forall j \in S: u_j \leqslant v^j(\bar{p}, \bar{q}, \xi^j, \eta^j) \end{array} \right\}.$$

The cooperative game realizes a core utility allocation $\{u^{*j}(\bar{p}, \bar{q})\}_{j \in N} \in C(V_{\bar{p},\bar{q}})$, and the associated core strategy bundle $\{\xi^{*j}(\bar{p}, \bar{q}), \eta^{*j}(\bar{p}, \bar{q})\}_{j \in N}$. While playing the above cooperative game on the one hand, each agent also behaves noncooperatively on the other to determine a commodity bundle for his consumption. If coalition S chooses a feasible joint strategy $\{\xi^j, \eta^j\}_{j \in S}$, then each member j chooses his best commodity bundle $(x^j, y^j) \in C^j$ subject to his two budget constraints, so that

$$u^j(x^j, y^j) = v^j(\bar{p}, \bar{q}, \xi^j, \eta^j),$$

and the coalition also chooses the cost-minimizing activity $(z, y) \in T(S)$, so that

$$-\bar{p}\cdot z \leqslant c^S(\bar{p}, \bar{q}, \bar{q}\cdot y), \text{ and } \sum_{j\in S} \eta^j \leqslant \bar{q}\cdot y.$$

Thus, associated with the core strategy bundle $\{\xi^{*j}(\bar{p}, \bar{q}), \eta^{*j}(\bar{p}, \bar{q})\}_{j\in N}$, the individuals choose the commodity bundles $\{x^{*j}(\bar{p}, \bar{q}), y^{*j}(\bar{p}, \bar{q})\}_{j\in N}$, and the realized firm (the grand coalition) chooses the activity $(z^*(\bar{p}, \bar{q}), y^*(\bar{p}, \bar{q}))$. The total excess demands in the $(l+m)$ markets are:

$$\sum_{j\in N} x^{*j}(\bar{p}, \bar{q}) - z^*(\bar{p}, \bar{q}) - \sum_{j\in N} \omega^j$$

$$\sum_{j\in N} y^{*j}(\bar{p}, \bar{q}) - y^*(\bar{p}, \bar{q}).$$

Notice that the two Walras' laws hold true: For every $(\bar{p}, \bar{q}) \in \Delta^{l-1} \times \Delta^{m-1}$,

$$\bar{p}\cdot \sum_{j\in N} x^{*j}(\bar{p}, \bar{q}) \leqslant \bar{p}\cdot z^*(\bar{p}, \bar{q}) + \bar{p}\cdot \sum_{j\in N} \omega^j,$$

$$\bar{q}\cdot \sum_{j\in N} y^{*j}(\bar{p}, \bar{q}) \leqslant \bar{q}\cdot y^*(\bar{p}, \bar{q}).$$

Price of commodity h then rises (falls, resp.), if its total excess demand is positive (negative, resp.). An equilibrium price vector (p^*, q^*) is eventually established, at which all the total excess demands are non-positive. The resource allocation mechanism just presented and the following equilibrium concept were introduced by Ichiishi and Quinzii (1983).

Definition 5.1.2. An *equilibrium* of coalition production economy $\mathscr{E}_{cp}$ is a quadruple $(\{x^{*j}, y^{*j}\}_{j\in N}, (z^*, y^*), \{\xi^{*j}, \eta^{*j}\}_{j\in N}, (p^*, q^*))$ of members of $\prod_{j\in N} C^j$, $T(N)$, $(\mathbf{R}^2)^N$, $\Delta^{l-1} \times \Delta^{m-1}$, respectively, such that

(i) for every $j \in N$, (x^{*j}, y^{*j}) maximizes $u^j(x^j, y^j)$ subject to the constraints,

$$p^*\cdot x^j \leqslant \xi^{*j}, \; q^*\cdot y^j \leqslant \eta^{*j}, \; (x^j, y^j) \in C^j;$$

(ii) (z^*, y^*) minimizes $-p^*\cdot z$ subject to the constraints,

$$(z, y) \in T(N), \; \sum_{j\in N} \eta^{*j} \leqslant q^*\cdot y;$$

(iii) it is not true that there exist S and $\{\xi^j, \eta^j\}_{j\in S}$ such that

$$\sum_{j\in S} \xi^j + c^S(p^*, q^*, \sum_{j\in S} \eta^j) \leqslant p^*\cdot \sum_{j\in S} \omega^j,$$

$$v^j(p^*, q^*, \xi^j, \eta^j) > v^j(p^*, q^*, \xi^{*j}, \eta^{*j}) \text{ for all } j \in S; \text{ and}$$

(iv) $\sum_{j\in N} x^{*j} \leqslant z^* + \sum_{j\in N} \omega^j,$

$$\sum_{j\in N} y^{*j} \leqslant y^*.$$

Observe that the stability condition (iii) of Definition 5.1.2 is stronger than the stability condition (ii) of Definition 3.5.2. The following property of the equilibrium is, therefore, immediate.

Proposition 5.1.3. *Let* $\mathscr{E}_{cp}$ *be a coalition production economy (Definition 5.1.1), and let* $(\{x^{*j}, y^{*j}\}_{j\in N}, (z^*, y^*), \{\xi^{*j}, \eta^{*j}\}_{j\in N}, (p^*, q^*))$ *be its equilibrium (Definition 5.1.2). Then,* $(\{x^{*j}, y^{*j}\}_{j\in N}, (z^*, y^*))$ *is a core allocation of* $\mathscr{E}_{cp}$ *(Definition 3.5.2).*

To enable this resource allocation mechanism to work for the normative purpose, two kinds of governmental involvement are called for. The first kind is to guarantee by means of governmentally enforced transfer of resources among firms that a core allocation of $\mathscr{E}_{cp}$, and in particular an equilibrium of $\mathscr{E}_{cp}$, are Pareto optimal. It was pointed out in Section 4.1 that there exists a coalition production economy whose core allocation is not Pareto optimal. This point can be rephrased as follows: There are two economic agents, 1 and 2. To utilize the technology $T(\{j\})$ of singleton-coalition $\{j\}$ productively, the resources held by the other agent $i\,(\neq j)$ are needed. But if the two agents form the grand coalition in an attempt to supply i's resources to j's production, their joint technology becomes inefficient, possibly reflecting oversize of the firm, i.e., the set $T(\{1, 2\})$ is too small. In order to overcome this difficulty with the grand coalition, the government keeps the two singleton-coalitions running their own production activities, but enforces appropriate transfer of resources among them. Thus, the finest coalition structure $\{\{1\}, \{2\}\}$ is realized, each coalition $\{j\}$ uses its technology $T(\{j\})$ which is more efficient than $T(\{1, 2\})$, and there is appropriate transfer of resources between the two coalitions. One may view this as Chandler's (1962) firm in multidivisional form, in which the grand coalition is realized as a firm, but it actually consists of two divisions $\{1\}$ and $\{2\}$. The production set of the grand coalition is then re-defined as

$$T(\{1, 2\}) \cup (T(\{1\}) + T(\{2\})).$$

Let $\mathscr{E}_{cp}$ be a coalition production economy defined in its full generality (Definition 5.1.1). Given the governmental enforcement of resource transfer, or given the possibility of multidivisional form firms, the production sets of $\mathscr{E}_{cp}$ are re-defined so that they are *superadditive*:

$$\sum_{i\in I} T(S_i) \subset T(\bigcup_{i\in I} S_i),$$

for any family $\{S_i\}_{i\in I}$ of mutually disjoint coalitions.

It is easy to check that under this superadditivity condition, any core allocation of $\mathscr{E}_{cp}$ is Pareto optimal. Radner (1992) was the first to emphasize the need for the resource-transfer concept and superadditivity of a production-set correspondence within the framework of a multidivisional form firm; he computed core resource-transfers for several interesting examples.

In the definitions of variants of the core of a coalition production economy (Definitions 5.1.2, 3.5.2 and 5.2.7), the feasibility condition was given with respect to the grand coalition rather than to a coalition structure, because transferability of resources and superadditivity of a production-set correspondence are implicitly postulated.

The second kind of governmental involvement is to facilitate the workings of the two market mechanisms. In particular, it provides information on the labor market. One might then ask: If perfectly competitive markets are to be instituted, then why not institute the private ownership economy (Definition 3.3.3), in which primary goods can be traded with final goods? The point here is that the resource allocation mechanism presented in this section works in many of the situations that exhibit increasing returns to scale, while the private ownership economy in those situations does not. Indeed, the present mechanism is explicitly based on the following postulate of non-decreasing returns to scale:

Postulate 5.1.4. Let $\mathscr{E}_{cp}$ be a coalition production economy (Definition 5.1.1), and let $c^N\colon \Delta^{l-1}\times\Delta^{m-1}\times\mathbf{R}_+\to\mathbf{R}_+$ be the generalized cost function derived from $T(N)$. Then for every (p, q), the average generalized cost is non-decreasing in η, that is,

$$\frac{c^N(p, q, \eta)}{\eta} \geqslant \frac{c^N(p, q, \eta')}{\eta'} \text{ if } 0<\eta\leqslant\eta'.$$

Section 5.2 will clarify those situations in which the present mechanism does work.

5.2 Equilibrium existence theorem

Let $\mathscr{E}_{cp}$ be a coalition production economy (Definition 5.1.1). The following simplifying assumption will be made throughout this section: There exists $b^j_L\in\mathbf{R}^l$ such that

$$C^j=\{(b^j_L, \mathbf{0})\}+\mathbf{R}^{l+m}_+.$$

By re-defining x^j and ω^j if necessary, one may assume without loss of generality that $b^j_L=\mathbf{0}$. Thus, $C^j=\mathbf{R}^{l+m}_+$.

In this section, sufficient conditions for the existence of equilibria (Definition 5.1.2) are provided for two cases: one case in which consumption/supply of primary goods does not affect consumers' utility levels, and the other case in which both consumption of primary goods and consumption of final goods affect consumers' utility levels. To formulate these two cases, call commodity h *non-desirable* to consumer j if $[a, a' \in C^j, a_k = a'_k$ for all $k \neq h]$ implies $[u^j(a) = u^j(a')]$, and define

$$C^j_d := \{a \in C^j \mid a_h = 0 \text{ if commodity } h \text{ is non-desirable to } j\}.$$

The intended interpretation of $[(z^j, y^j) \in C^j_d]$ is that at commodity bundle (z^j, y^j) consumer j demands the minimal amount of each non-desirable commodity, or supplies the maximal amount of labor if his leisure time is non-desirable. The first case in which the primary goods are non-desirable is then defined as $C^j_d = \{\mathbf{0}\} \times \mathbf{R}^m_+$ for all $j \in N$, and the second case in which all goods are desirable is defined as $C^j_d = \mathbf{R}^{l+m}_+$ for all $j \in N$.

Roughly stated, for the case in which the primary goods are non-desirable, the postulate of non-decreasing returns to scale (Postulate 5.1.4) and the assumption of diminishing marginal rate of technical substitution (Assumption 5.2.3) together ensure the existence of equilibria. For the case in which all goods are desirable, these two conditions (Postulate 5.1.4 and Assumption 5.2.3) and the elasticity condition (Condition 5.2.8) together ensure the existence of equilibria. The elasticity condition clarifies a relationship between the consumption sector and the production sector of the economy; it was introduced by Quinzii (1982). Needless to say, one also needs some assumptions that are standard in the existence literature, and some boundary conditions.

First, assumptions on the production sector of $\mathscr{E}_{cp}$ will be presented. To simplify notation, define

$$T := T(N), \text{ and } c(\cdot, \cdot, \cdot) := c^N(\cdot, \cdot, \cdot).$$

For each output bundle y $(\in \mathbf{R}^m_+)$, let $S_T(y)$ denote the *input requirement set*,

$$S_T(y) := \{z \in -\mathbf{R}^l_+ \mid (z, y) \in T\}.$$

The customarily defined *cost function* g: $\Delta^{l-1} \times \mathbf{R}^m_+ \to \mathbf{R}_+$ will also be used:

$$g(p, y) := \inf\{p \cdot (-z) \mid z \in S_T(y)\}.$$

Assumption 5.2.1. Let $\mathscr{E}_{cp}$ be a coalition production economy (Definition 5.1.1), and set $T := T(N)$:

(i) T is a closed subset of $(-\mathbf{R}^l_+) \times \mathbf{R}^m_+$;
(ii) $(\mathbf{0}, \mathbf{0}) \in T$;
(iii) $[(z, y) \in T, z' \in -\mathbf{R}^l_+, y' \in \mathbf{R}^m_+, (z', y') \leqslant (z, y)] \Rightarrow [(z', y') \in T]$;
(iv) $[y, y' \in \mathbf{R}^m_+, y > y'] \Rightarrow [S_T(y) \subset \mathring{S}_T(y')]$;
(v) For every $p \in \Delta^{l-1}$, if $\|y\| \to \infty$, then $g(p, y) \to \infty$;
(vi) $\beta := \sup\{\eta \in \mathbf{R}_+ \mid \exists (p, q) \in \Delta^{l-1} \times \Delta^{m-1}: c(p, q, \eta) \leqslant p \cdot \sum_{j \in N} \omega^j\} \in \mathbf{R}$; and
(vii) $T(S) \subset T$ for every $S \in \mathscr{N}$.

Here, $\|y\|$ denotes the Euclidean norm of vector y. All the seven conditions in Assumption 5.2.1 are standard: Condition (i) is technical, but is made in virtually all the literature on production technology. Condition (ii) means that inaction is possible. Condition (iii) is the free disposal. Condition (iv) is a strong form of monotonicity; it implies in particular that all inputs are needed to produce an output. Conditions (v) and (vi) say that with limited cost one cannot obtain unlimited outputs. Condition (vii) means that the grand coalition possesses the most efficient technology; it is satisfied if inaction is possible in every coalition and if the production-set correspondence is superadditive (recall the discussion in the paragraph that follows the statement of Proposition 5.1.3).

Let $(\bar{p}, \bar{q}) \gg (\mathbf{0}, \mathbf{0})$. Under Assumption 5.2.1, it is easy to check that there exists a neighborhood $U \times V$ of $(\bar{p}, \bar{q})$ in $\Delta^{l-1} \times \Delta^{m-1}$ such that (i) function g is well-defined and continuous in $U \times \mathbf{R}^m_+$; (ii) for each $p \in U$, the function $y \mapsto g(p, y)$ is strictly increasing, i.e., $[y, y' \in \mathbf{R}^m_+, y > y'] \Rightarrow [g(p, y) > g(p, y')]$; (iii) function c is well-defined and continuous in $U \times V \times \mathbf{R}_+$; and (iv) for each $(p, q) \in U \times V$, the function $\eta \mapsto c(p, q, \eta)$ is strictly increasing. The next assumption says that these conditions hold true even on the relative boundary of $\Delta^{l-1} \times \Delta^{m-1}$.

Assumption 5.2.2. Let $\mathscr{E}_{cp}$ be a coalition production economy (Definition 5.1.1), and set $c(\cdot, \cdot, \cdot) := c^N(\cdot, \cdot, \cdot)$:

(i) Function g is well-defined and continuous in $\Delta^{l-1} \times \mathbf{R}^m_+$;
(ii) For each $p \in \Delta^{l-1}$, the function $y \mapsto g(p, y)$ is strictly increasing, i.e., $[y, y' \in \mathbf{R}^m_+, y > y'] \Rightarrow [g(p, y) > g(p, y')]$;
(iii) Function c is well-defined and continuous in $\Delta^{l-1} \times \Delta^{m-1} \times \mathbf{R}_+$; and
(iv) For each $(p, q) \in \Delta^{l-1} \times \Delta^{m-1}$, the function $\eta \mapsto c(p, q, \eta)$ is strictly increasing.

The next assumption is essentially the postulate of diminishing marginal rate of technical substitution. Thus, all the possible convexity assumptions are made here provided that they are compatible with the postulate of non-decreasing returns to scale.

Assumption 5.2.3. Let $\mathscr{E}_{cp}$ be a coalition production economy (Definition 5.1.1):

(i) For every $y > \mathbf{0}$, $S_T(y)$ is nonempty and strictly convex; and
(ii) For every $p \in \Delta^{l-1}$, the function $y \mapsto g(p, y)$ is strictly quasi-convex.

As the concept dual to the input requirement set, define for each input bundle z $(\in -\mathbf{R}^l_+)$ the *output possibility set*,

$$S'_T(z) := \{y \in \mathbf{R}^m_+ \mid (z, y) \in T\}.$$

An easy application of the separation theorem on convex sets establishes that Assumption 5.2.1 (i) (ii) and Assumption 5.2.3 (ii) imply closedness, nonemptiness and strict convexity of $S'_T(z)$. See Figures 5.1 and 5.2 for a typical production set T.

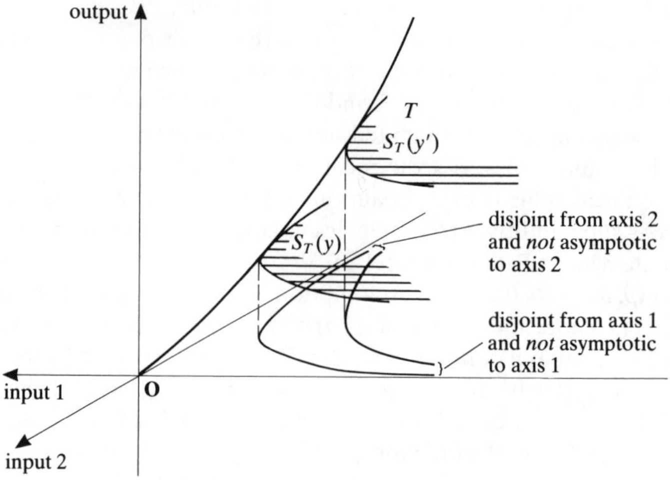

5.1 Production set which satisfies increasing returns to scale

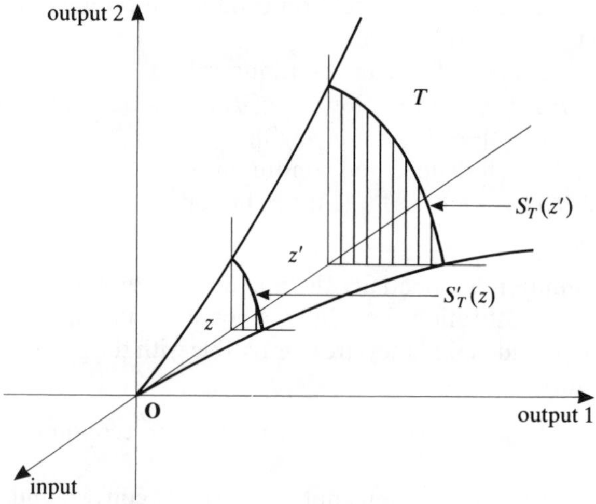

5.2 Production set which satisfies increasing returns to scale

One now turns to assumptions on the consumption sector of $\mathscr{E}_{cp}$. The following assumption is standard. The first condition characterizes completeness, transitivity, closedness and weak monotonicity of the preference relations, and the diminishing marginal rate of substitution:

Assumption 5.2.4. Let $\mathscr{E}_{cp}$ be a coalition production economy (Definition 5.1.1). For every $j \in N$,

(i) u^j is continuous, non-decreasing in C_d^j, and strictly quasi-concave in icr C_d^j;
(ii) $\omega^j \gg \mathbf{0}$.

Let $(\bar{p}, \bar{q}) \gg (\mathbf{0}, \mathbf{0})$ and $(\bar{\xi}^j, \bar{\eta}^j) \geqslant \mathbf{0}$, and denote by $(x^{*j}(\bar{p}, \bar{q}, \bar{\xi}^j, \bar{\eta}^j), y^{*j}(\bar{p}, \bar{q}, \bar{\xi}^j, \bar{\eta}^j))$ the solution of:

$$\begin{array}{ll} \max & u^j(x^j, y^j), \\ \text{subject to} & (x^j, y^j) \in C_d^j, \\ & \bar{p} \cdot x^j \leqslant \bar{\xi}^j,\ \bar{q} \cdot y^j \leqslant \bar{\eta}^j. \end{array}$$

This solution uniquely exists, due to Assumption 5.2.4. Needless to say,

$$v^j(\bar{p}, \bar{q}, \bar{\xi}^j, \bar{\eta}^j) = u^j(x^{*j}(\bar{p}, \bar{q}, \bar{\xi}^j, \bar{\eta}^j), y^{*j}(\bar{p}, \bar{q}, \bar{\xi}^j, \bar{\eta}^j)).$$

Moreover, it is easy to check that for the case $C_d^j = \{\mathbf{0}\} \times \mathbf{R}_+^m$, the functions v^j, x^{*j}, y^{*j} are continuous in $\Delta^{l-1} \times (\text{icr } \Delta^{m-1}) \times \mathbf{R}_+^2$ (v^j and y^{*j} do not depend on p or ξ^j, and $x^{*j}(p, q, \xi^j, \eta^j) \equiv \mathbf{0}$), and that for the case $C_d^j = \mathbf{R}_+^{l+m}$, the functions v^j, x^{*j}, y^{*j} are continuous in $(\text{icr } \Delta^{l-1}) \times (\text{icr } \Delta^{m-1}) \times \mathbf{R}_+^2$. The next assumption concerns the behavior of these functions on the relative boundary of the domain.

Assumption 5.2.5. Let $\mathscr{E}_{cp}$ be a coalition production economy (Definition 5.1.1). For every $j \in N$,

(i) v^j is continuous in $\Delta^{l-1} \times \Delta^{m-1} \times \mathbf{R}_+^2$;
(ii) for the case $C_d^j = \{\mathbf{0}\} \times \mathbf{R}_+^m$, if $\{(p^k, q^k, \xi^{j,k}, \eta^{j,k})\}_k$ is a sequence in $\Delta^{l-1} \times (\text{icr } \Delta^{m-1}) \times \mathbf{R}_+^2$ converging to $(p^0, q^0, \xi^{j,0}, \eta^{j,0})$ with $q^0 \in \Delta^{m-1} \setminus \text{icr } \Delta^{m-1}$, $\eta^{j,0} > 0$, then $\|y^{*j}(p^k, q^k, \xi^{j,k}, \eta^{j,k})\| \to \infty$ when $k \to \infty$;
(iii) for the case $C_d^j = \mathbf{R}_+^{l+m}$, x^{*j} (y^{*j}, resp.) can be extended continuously to $(\text{icr } \Delta^{l-1}) \times \Delta^{m-1} \times \mathring{\mathbf{R}}_+^2$ (to $\Delta^{l-1} \times (\text{icr } \Delta^{m-1}) \times \mathring{\mathbf{R}}_+^2$, resp.). If $\{(p^k, q^k, \xi^{j,k}, \eta^{j,k})\}_k$ is a sequence in $(\text{icr } \Delta^{l-1}) \times \Delta^{m-1} \times \mathring{\mathbf{R}}_+^2$ (in $\Delta^{l-1} \times (\text{icr } \Delta^{m-1}) \times \mathring{\mathbf{R}}_+^2$, resp.) converging to (p, q, ξ^j, η^j) with $p \in \Delta^{l-1} \setminus \text{icr } \Delta^{l-1}$, $\xi^j > 0$, and $\eta^j > 0$ (with $q \in \Delta^{m-1} \setminus \text{icr } \Delta^{m-1}$, $\xi^j > 0$, and $\eta^j > 0$ resp.), then $\|x^{*j}(p^k, q^k, \xi^{j,k}, \eta^{j,k})\| \to \infty$ when $k \to \infty$ ($\|y^{*j}(p^k, q^k, \xi^{j,k}, \eta^{j,k})\| \to \infty$ when $k \to \infty$, resp.).

The last two assumptions will be made only for the case $C_d^j = \mathbf{R}_+^{l+m}$. The first assumption is made on the hypothetical situation in which agent j, acting alone as the production unit $\{j\}$, has the best technology T.

Assumption 5.2.6. Let $\mathscr{E}_{cp}$ be a coalition production economy (Definition 5.1.1), and suppose $C_d^j = \mathbf{R}_+^{l+m}$. Set $a_L^j := \omega^j/2$. Choose any $(\bar{p}, \bar{q}) \in \Delta^{l-1} \times \Delta^{m-1}$. If $(\xi^j, \eta^j) \geqslant \mathbf{0}$ satisfies

$$v^j(\bar{p}, \bar{q}, \xi^j, \eta^j) \geqslant v^j(\bar{p}, \bar{q}, \bar{p} \cdot a_L^j, \sup \{\bar{q} \cdot y \mid (-a_L^j, y) \in T\}),$$

then $(\xi^j, \eta^j) \gg \mathbf{0}$.

To understand this assumption, suppose that agent j divides his initial endowment into two parts. He keeps one part (say, $a_L^j := \omega^j/2$) with him, and uses the other part (a_L^j) for production by himself (i.e., within the coalition $\{j\}$). This way, he obtains two numbers $(\bar{\xi}^j, \bar{\eta}^j) := (\bar{p}\cdot a_L^j, \sup\{\bar{q}\cdot y \mid (-a_L^j, y) \in T\})$ as a pair of input and output values, and subject to the budget constraints determined by these values, attains his utility level $v^j(\bar{p}, \bar{q}, \bar{\xi}^j, \bar{\eta}^j)$. Now, Assumption 5.2.6 says that any pair (ξ^j, η^j) of input and output values which gives rise to this utility level should be strictly greater than **0**. It excludes a corner equilibrium of the agent.

In order to formulate the second assumption, consider a fictitious situation in which the primary good value (in terms of dollars) and the final good value (in terms of coupons) can be exchanged under the "price vector" $(1, \theta) \in \mathbf{R}_+^2$, where the primary good value is taken as a numéraire. Then, the *compensated demand* for the primary good value and for the final good value, given the utility level v_j, is the solution $(\xi^{*j}(p, q, \theta, v_j), \eta^{*j}(p, q, \theta, v_j))$ of:

$$\begin{aligned}&\text{Min} \quad \xi^j + \theta\eta^j,\\ &\text{subject to } (\xi^j, \eta^j) \geqslant (p\cdot b_L^j, 0),\\ &\qquad\qquad v^j(p, q, \xi^j, \eta^j) \geqslant v_j.\end{aligned}$$

The strict quasi-concavity of function u^j (Assumption 5.2.4 (i)) implies the strict quasi-concavity of the indirect utility function $v^j(p, q, \cdot)$, so the program has a unique solution. Define

$$\eta^*(p, q, \theta, v) := \textstyle\sum_{j\in N} \eta^{*j}(p, q, \theta, v_j).$$

Of particular interest is a utility allocation which is Pareto optimal relative to (p, q).

Definition 5.2.7. Let $\mathscr{E}_{cp}$ be a coalition production economy (Definition 5.1.1), and let $(p, q) \in \Delta^{l-1} \times \Delta^{m-1}$. Set $c(\cdot, \cdot, \cdot) := c^N(\cdot, \cdot, \cdot)$. A utility allocation $\bar{v} \in \mathbf{R}^N$ is called *Pareto optimal relative to* (p, q), if

(i) there exists $\{\bar{\xi}^j, \bar{\eta}^j\}_{j\in N} \in (\mathbf{R}_+^2)^N$ such that $\sum_{j\in N} \bar{\xi}^j + c(p, q, \sum_{j\in N} \bar{\eta}^j) \leqslant p\cdot\sum_{j\in N} \omega^j$, and $v^j(p, q, \bar{\xi}^j, \bar{\eta}^j) \geqslant \bar{v}^j$ for every $j \in N$; and

(ii) it is not true that there exists $\{(\xi^j, \eta^j)\}_{j\in N} \in (\mathbf{R}_+^2)^N$ such that $\sum_{j\in N} \xi^j + c(p, q, \sum_{j\in N} \eta^j) \leqslant p\cdot\sum_{j\in N} \omega^j$, and $v^j(p, q, \xi^j, \eta^j) > \bar{v}^j$ for every $j \in N$.

Condition 5.2.8. Let $\mathscr{E}_{cp}$ be a coalition production economy (Definition 5.1.1), and set $c(\cdot, \cdot, \cdot) := c^N(\cdot, \cdot, \cdot)$. The economy $\mathscr{E}_{cp}$ satisfies the *elasticity condition* (i) (*elasticity condition* (ii), resp.), if for each price-vector pair $(\bar{p}, \bar{q})$ and each utility allocation $\bar{v}$ which is Pareto optimal relative to $(\bar{p}, \bar{q})$, the following condition (i) (condition (ii), resp.) is satisfied for all $\bar{\theta} > 0$:

(i) $\left.\dfrac{\partial}{\partial\theta}\eta^*(\bar{p}, \bar{q}, \theta, \bar{v})\right|_{\theta=\bar{\theta}} \cdot \left.\dfrac{\partial^2}{\partial\eta^2}c(\bar{p}, \bar{q}, \eta)\right|_{\eta=\eta^*(\bar{p},\bar{q},\bar{\theta},\bar{v})} < 1;$

(ii) [θ-elasticity of $\eta^*(\bar{p}, \bar{q}, \cdot, \bar{v})$ at $\bar{\theta}$]

$\times$ [η-elasticity of $\dfrac{\partial}{\partial\eta}c(\bar{p}, \bar{q}, \cdot)$ at $\eta^*(\bar{p}, \bar{q}, \bar{\theta}, \bar{v})$] < 1.

Of course,

$$\theta\text{-elasticity of } \eta^*(\bar{p}, \bar{q}, \cdot\ \bar{v}) \text{ at } \bar{\theta} = \frac{\bar{\theta} \cdot \frac{\partial}{\partial \theta} \eta^*(\bar{p}, \bar{q}, \theta, \bar{v}) \Big|_{\theta = \bar{\theta}}}{\eta^*(\bar{p}, \bar{q}, \bar{\theta}, \bar{v})},$$

$$\eta\text{-elasticity of } \frac{\partial}{\partial \eta} c(\bar{p}, \bar{q}, \cdot) \text{ at } \eta^*(\bar{p}, \bar{q}, \bar{\theta}, \bar{v})$$

$$= \frac{\eta^*(\bar{p}, \bar{q}, \bar{\theta}, \bar{v}) \cdot \frac{\partial^2}{\partial \eta^2} c(\bar{p}, \bar{q}, \eta) \Big|_{\eta = \eta^*(\bar{p}, \bar{q}, \bar{\theta}, \bar{v})}}{\frac{\partial}{\partial \eta} c(\bar{p}, \bar{q}, \eta) \Big|_{\eta = \eta^*(\bar{p}, \bar{q}, \bar{\theta}, \bar{v})}}.$$

The two elasticity conditions are equivalent at an equilibrium point, since at such a point

$$\bar{\theta} = \frac{\partial}{\partial \eta} c(\bar{p}, \bar{q}, \eta) \Big|_{\eta = \eta^*(\bar{p}, \bar{q}, \bar{\theta}, \bar{v})}$$

(see Step 7 of the proof of Theorem 5.2.9). The elasticity conditions are automatically satisfied under constant returns to scale, because under this condition, $\partial^2 c / \partial \eta^2 = 0$. Quinzii (1982, pp. 46–47) has a non-trivial example which satisfies the elasticity condition (ii).

The main result of this section is the following existence theorem, which is due to Ichiishi and Quinzii (1983):

Theorem 5.2.9. *Let $\mathscr{E}_{cp}$ be a coalition production economy (Definition 5.1.1) which satisfies non-decreasing returns to scale (Postulate 5.1.4) and Assumptions 5.2.1–5.2.5:*

(i) *If $C_d^j = \{\mathbf{0}\} \times \mathbf{R}_+^m$ for every $j \in N$, then there exists an equilibrium of $\mathscr{E}_{cp}$ (Definition 5.1.2);*

(ii) *If $C_d^j = \mathbf{R}_+^{l+m}$ for every $j \in N$, and if the economy $\mathscr{E}_{cp}$ further satisfies Assumption 5.2.6 and one of the two elasticity conditions (Condition 5.2.8), then there exists an equilibrium of $\mathscr{E}_{cp}$ (Definition 5.1.2).*

Intuitively, if the utilities of the agents do not depend upon consumption of primary goods (the case $C_d^j = \{\mathbf{0}\} \times \mathbf{R}_+^m$) the agents are willing to supply all their primary goods for production; the economy fully enjoys the effect of increasing returns, so has an equilibrium (a particular core allocation) in this case. If the utilities of the agents *do* depend upon consumption of primary goods (the case $C_d^j = \mathbf{R}_+^{l+m}$), however, the economy cannot fully enjoy the effect of increasing returns, because supply of primary goods for production sacrifices the utility that comes from consumption of those primary goods. The existence of equilibrium in this case is true only under a specific relationship between the production sector and the consumption sector, as summarized by a specific condition on the marginal cost function

$\eta \mapsto \frac{\partial}{\partial \eta} c(p, q, \eta)$ and the compensated total demand function $\theta \mapsto \eta^*(p, q, \theta, v)$. The elasticity condition turns out to be the required relationship.

The proof of Theorem 5.2.9 is partly based on Scarf's (1973) result on the one-primary-good one-final-good case ($l=m=1$). In this case, a core allocation (Definition 3.5.2) and an equilibrium (Definition 5.1.2) coincide, and the generalized cost function,

$$\eta \mapsto c^S(1, 1, \eta) =: c^S(\eta)$$

is the inverse of the production function.

Theorem 5.2.10 (Scarf). *Let $\mathscr{E}_{cp}$ be a coalition production economy (Definition 5.1.1), in which there are one primary good and one final good ($l=m=1$), and in which the cost functions*

$$c^S(y) := \min\{-z \in \mathbf{R}_+ \mid (z, y) \in T(S)\}$$

are well-defined. Assume that $\mathscr{E}_{cp}$ satisfies non-decreasing returns to scale (Postulate 5.1.4). Assume further that the grand coalition possesses the most efficient technology (Assumption 5.2.1 (vii)), and that u^j is non-decreasing in C^j for every $j \in N$. Then, the associated non-side-payment game $V: \mathscr{N} \to \mathbf{R}^N$ defined by

$$V(S) := \left\{ u \in \mathbf{R}^N \;\middle|\; \begin{array}{l} \exists \{x^j, y^j\}_{j \in S} \in \prod_{j \in S} C^j: \\ \sum_{j \in S} x^j + c^S(\sum_{j \in S} y^j) \leqslant \sum_{j \in S} \omega^j, \\ \forall j \in S: u_j \leqslant u^j(x^j, y^j) \end{array} \right\}$$

is balanced.

The essential idea of the proof of Theorem 5.2.9 may be outlined as follows: Define $\alpha := \max\{p \cdot \sum_{j \in N} \omega^j \mid p \in \Delta^{l-1}\}$, and recall the definition of β (Assumption 5.2.1 (vi)). The abstract model of a society $\mathscr{S}_0$ (Definition 3.4.9) will be constructed from coalition production economy $\mathscr{E}_{cp}$. The player set consists of the given agent set N and a fictitious "market participant" called the $(n+1)$st player, $N_0 := N \cup \{n+1\}$. Define $\mathscr{N}_0 := \{S \mid \phi = S \subset N_0\}$. The strategy space of player j is:

$$\Sigma^j := \begin{cases} \{(\xi^j, \eta^j) \in \mathbf{R}^2 \mid 0 \leqslant \xi^j \leqslant \alpha, 0 \leqslant \eta^j \leqslant \beta\} & \text{if } j \in N, \\ \Delta^{l-1} \times \Delta^{m-1} & \text{if } j = n+1. \end{cases}$$

A pair (ξ^j, η^j) will sometimes be denoted by σ^j. Define $\Sigma^S := \prod_{j \in S} \Sigma^j$ for each $S \in \mathscr{N}_0$, and set $\Sigma_0 := \Sigma^{N_0}$. A generic element of Σ_0 is denoted by (σ, σ^{n+1}), with $\sigma \in \Sigma^N$ and $\sigma^{n+1} = (p, q) \in \Delta^{l-1} \times \Delta^{m-1}$. The feasible-strategy correspondences $F^S: \Sigma_0 \to \Sigma^S$ are defined by:

$$F^S(\bar{\sigma}, \bar{\sigma}^{n+1}) := \left\{ \sigma^S \in \Sigma^S \;\middle|\; \begin{array}{l} (\xi^j, \eta^j) \geqslant \mathbf{0} \text{ for every } j \in S, \\ \sum_{j \in S} \xi^j + c(\bar{p}, \bar{q}, \sum_{j \in S} \eta^j) \leqslant \bar{p} \cdot \sum_{j \in S} \omega^j \end{array} \right\} \text{ if } S \subset N;$$

$$F^{\{n+1\}}(\bar{\sigma}, \bar{\sigma}^{n+1}) := \Delta^{l-1} \times \Delta^{m-1};$$
$$F^{S}(\bar{\sigma}, \bar{\sigma}^{n+1}) := F^{S\setminus\{n+1\}}(\bar{\sigma}, \bar{\sigma}^{n+1}) \times F^{\{n+1\}}(\bar{\sigma}, \bar{\sigma}^{n+1}) \text{ if } S \ni n+1.$$

The utility functions v^j: $\Sigma_0 \times \Sigma^j \to \mathbf{R}$ are defined by:

$$v^j(\bar{\sigma}, \bar{\sigma}^{n+1}, \sigma^j) := v^j(\bar{p}, \bar{q}, \xi^j, \eta^j), \text{ if } j \in N;$$
$$v^{n+1}(\bar{\sigma}, \bar{\sigma}^{n+1}, p, q)$$
$$:= p\cdot[\text{the total excess demand for primary goods, given } (\bar{\sigma}, \bar{p}, \bar{q})]$$
$$+ q\cdot[\text{the total excess demand for final goods, given } (\bar{\sigma}, \bar{p}, \bar{q})].$$

The only admissible coalition structure is the partition of N_0 into N and $\{n+1\}$, $\{N, \{n+1\}\}$. The society associated with $\mathscr{E}_{cp}$ is thus given as $\mathscr{S}_0 := (\{\Sigma^j\}_{j \in N_0}, \{F^S\}_{S \in \mathscr{N}_0}, \{v^j\}_{j \in N_0}, \{\{N, \{n+1\}\}\})$. Using the two Walras' laws, one on the primary-good markets and the other on the final-good markets, one can show that a social coalitional equilibrium of $\mathscr{S}_0$ (Definition 3.4.10) gives rise to the required equilibrium of $\mathscr{E}_{cp}$. One needs to show, therefore, that all the assumptions of the social coalitional equilibrium existence theorem (Theorem 3.4.11) are satisfied. The crucial assumptions are balancedness (assumption (iv) of Theorem 3.4.11) and convexity (assumption (v) of Theorem 3.4.11). Once $(\bar{\sigma}, \bar{\sigma}_{n+1})$ is fixed, the present model in which player j's strategy space is $\Sigma^j (\subset \mathbf{R}^2)$ can be considered as Scarf's (1973) model of one primary good and one final good; the value ξ^j of primary goods here is considered as Scarf's primary good, and the value η^j of final goods here is considered as Scarf's final good. By Theorem 5.2.10, the balancedness assumption is satisfied. It will turn out that for the case $C^j_d = \{\mathbf{0}\} \times \mathbf{R}^m_+$ the convexity assumption is automatically satisfied. For the case $C^j_d = \mathbf{R}^{l+m}_+$, the elasticity condition will ensure the convexity. Actually, v^{n+1} is not well-defined on the relative boundary of Σ_0, so a little elaborate argument is necessary.

Proof of Theorem 5.2.10. *Step 1.* Observe first that due to the assumption that the grand coalition possesses the most efficient technology, one may assume without loss of generality that $c^S = c^N =: c$ for all $S \in \mathscr{N}$; for if $\mathscr{E}'_{cp}$ is the economy which differs from $\mathscr{E}_{cp}$ in that $T'(S) = T(N) =: T$ for all S, and if the game associated with $\mathscr{E}'_{cp}$ is balanced, then game V is also balanced. Choose any balanced subfamily $\mathscr{B}$ of $\mathscr{N}$ with the associated coefficients $\{\lambda_S\}_{S \in \mathscr{B}}$, and any $u \in \bigcap_{S \in \mathscr{B}} V(S)$. Without loss of generality, $\lambda_S > 0$ for all $S \in \mathscr{B}$. If $N \in \mathscr{B}$, then $u \in V(N)$; there is nothing to prove in this case. Assume, therefore, $N \notin \mathscr{B}$. Then $\sum_{S \in \mathscr{B}} \lambda_S > 1$. For each $S \in \mathscr{B}$ there exists $\{x^{S,j}, y^{S,j}\}_{j \in S} \in \prod_{j \in S} C^j$ such that

$$\sum_{j \in S} x^{S,j} + c\Big(\sum_{j \in S} y^{S,j}\Big) \leqslant \sum_{j \in S} \omega^j, \text{ and}$$
$$u_j \leqslant u^j(x^{S,j}, y^{S,j}) \text{ for every } j \in S.$$

Define the average cost $ac(S) := c(\sum_{j\in S} y^{S,j})/\sum_{j\in S} y^{S,j}$; set $ac(S) := \infty$ if $\sum_{j\in S} y^{S,j} = 0$. Introduce any linear order on $\mathscr{B}$, and write

$$\mathscr{B} = \{S_1, S_2, \cdots, S_m\},\ \lambda_i := \lambda_{S_i}.$$

One may assume without loss of generality that there exists $k < m$, such that $\lambda_1 + \lambda_2 + \cdots + \lambda_k = 1$. Indeed, if there is no such k, let k be the integer such that $\sum_{i=1}^{k-1}\lambda_i < 1$ and $\sum_{i=1}^{k}\lambda_i > 1$, and consider the balanced family $\{S'_1, S'_2, \cdots, S'_{m+1}\}$ and the associated coefficients $\{\lambda'_1, \lambda'_2, \cdots, \lambda'_{m+1}\}$ defined by: $S'_i := S_i$ and $\lambda'_i := \lambda_i$, if $i \leqslant k-1$; $S'_k := S_k$ and $\lambda'_k := 1 - \sum_{i=1}^{k-1}\lambda_i$; $S'_{k+1} := S_k$ and $\lambda'_{k+1} := \lambda_k - \lambda'_k$; and $S'_i := S_{i-1}$ and $\lambda'_i := \lambda_{i-1}$, if $i > k+1$.

Step 2. If $u \notin V(N)$, then there exist $\alpha_1, \alpha_2, \cdots, \alpha_k, \beta_{k+1}, \beta_{k+2}, \cdots, \beta_m \in \mathbf{R}_+$ such that

$$\sum_{i=1}^{k}\alpha_i = 1,\ \sum_{i=k+1}^{m}\beta_i = 1,$$

$$\sum_{i=1}^{k}\alpha_i ac(S_i) > \sum_{i=k+1}^{m}\beta_i ac(S_i).$$

In order to prove this, notice first that for any $S \in \mathscr{B}$ and any selection $(x^{T(j),j}, y^{T(j),j})$ for each $j \in N\backslash S$, where $j \in T(j) \in \mathscr{B}$, the hypothesis $[u \notin V(N)]$ implies

$$\sum_{j\in S} x^{S,j} + \sum_{j\notin S} x^{T(j),j} + c(\sum_{j\in S} y^{S,j} + \sum_{j\notin S} y^{T(j),j}) > \sum_{j\in N}\omega^j,$$

so in view of the non-decreasing returns to scale,

$$\begin{aligned} & ac(S)\cdot\sum_{j\notin S} y^{T(j),j} \\ & \geqslant c(\sum_{j\in S} y^{S,j} + \sum_{j\notin S} y^{T(j),j}) - c(\sum_{j\in S} y^{S,j}) \\ & \geqslant c(\sum_{j\in S} y^{S,j} + \sum_{j\notin S} y^{T(j),j}) - \sum_{j\in S}(\omega^j - x^{S,j}) \\ & > \sum_{j\notin S}(\omega^j - x^{T(j),j}). \end{aligned} \tag{1}$$

Now, choose any S_i, $1 \leqslant i \leqslant k$, and define

$$\mathscr{J}_i := \{\{T(j), j\}_{j\in N\backslash S_i} \mid j \in T(j) \in \{S_{k+1}, \ldots, S_m\}\}.$$

By the assumption that $N \notin \mathscr{B}$ and by the choice of k, $\mathscr{J}_i \neq \phi$. By (1),

$$\begin{aligned} & ac(S_i)\cdot \sum_{\{T(j),j\}_j\in\mathscr{J}_i}\Big(\prod_{j\notin S_i}\frac{\lambda_{T(j)}}{\sum_{\substack{g\geqslant k+1\\ S_g\ni j}}\lambda_g}\Big)\cdot\sum_{j\notin S_i} y^{T(j),j} \\ & > \sum_{\{T(j),j\}_j\in\mathscr{J}_j}\Big(\prod_{j\notin S_i}\frac{\lambda_{T(j)}}{\sum_{\substack{g\geqslant k+1\\ S_g\ni j}}\lambda_g}\Big)\cdot\sum_{j\notin S_i}(\omega^j - x^{T(j),j}). \end{aligned} \tag{2}$$

The left-hand side (the right-hand side, resp.) of (2) is a nonnegative linear combination of the $y^{T,j}$s (of the $(\omega^j - x^{T,j})$s, resp.), $j \in N \backslash S_i$, $T \in \{S_h \mid h \geqslant k+1, S_h \ni j\}$. The coefficient of $y^{T,j}$ (of $(\omega^j - x^{T,j})$, resp.) is:

$$ac(S_i)\cdot\frac{\lambda_T}{\sum_{\substack{g\geqslant k+1\\ S_g\ni j}}\lambda_g} \qquad \left(\frac{\lambda_T}{\sum_{\substack{g\geqslant k+1\\ S_g\ni j}}\lambda_g}, \text{ resp.}\right).$$

Therefore, inequality (2) becomes:

$$ac(S_i)\cdot\sum_{j\notin S_i}\sum_{\substack{h\geqslant k+1\\ S_h\ni j}}\frac{\lambda_h}{\sum_{\substack{g\geqslant k+1\\ S_g\ni j}}\lambda_g}\cdot y^{S_h,j}$$
$$>\sum_{j\notin S_i}\sum_{\substack{h\geqslant k+1\\ S_h\ni j}}\frac{\lambda_h}{\sum_{\substack{g\geqslant k+1\\ S_g\ni j}}\lambda_g}\cdot(\omega^j - x^{S_h,j}).$$

By multiplying both hand sides by λ_i and adding the resulting inequalities with respect to $i = 1, 2, \cdots, k$, one obtains:

$$\sum_{i\leqslant k}\sum_{j\notin S_i}\sum_{\substack{h\geqslant k+1\\ S_h\ni j}}\lambda_i\cdot ac(S_i)\cdot\frac{\lambda_h}{\sum_{\substack{g\geqslant k+1\\ S_g\ni j}}\lambda_g}\cdot y^{S_h,j}$$
$$>\sum_{h\geqslant k+1}\sum_{j\in S_h}\sum_{\substack{i\leqslant k\\ S_i\not\ni j}}\lambda_i\cdot\frac{\lambda_h}{\sum_{\substack{g\geqslant k+1\\ S_g\ni j}}\lambda_g}\cdot(\omega^j - x^{S_h,j}). \tag{3}$$

Notice that

$$\sum_{\substack{i\leqslant k\\ S_i\not\ni j}}\lambda_i = 1 - \sum_{\substack{i\leqslant k\\ S_i\ni j}}\lambda_i, \text{ by definition of } k,$$
$$= \sum_{\substack{i\geqslant k+1\\ S_i\ni j}}\lambda_i, \text{ by definition of } \mathscr{B},$$

so

$$\sum_{\substack{i\leqslant k\\ S_i\not\ni j}}\lambda_i\cdot\frac{\lambda_h}{\sum_{\substack{g\geqslant k+1\\ S_g\ni j}}\lambda_g} = \lambda_h. \tag{4}$$

Thus, the right-hand side of (3)

$$= \sum_{h\geqslant k+1}\sum_{j\in S_h}\lambda_h\cdot(\omega^j - x^{S_h,j})$$
$$\geqslant \sum_{h\geqslant k+1}\lambda_h\cdot c\Big(\sum_{j\in S_h}y^{S_h,j}\Big)$$
$$= \sum_{h\geqslant k+1}\Big(\lambda_h\cdot\sum_{j\in S_h}y^{S_h,j}\Big)\cdot ac(S_h).$$

By (3) and this last inequality,

$$\sum_{i \leqslant k}[\sum_{j \notin S_i} \sum_{\substack{h \geqslant k+1 \\ S_h \ni j}} \lambda_i \cdot \frac{\lambda_h}{\sum_{\substack{g \geqslant k+1 \\ S_g \ni j}} \lambda_g} \cdot y^{S_h, j}] \cdot ac(S_i)$$

$$> \sum_{h \geqslant k+1} [\lambda_h \cdot \sum_{j \in S_h} y^{S_h, j}] \cdot ac(S_h). \tag{5}$$

The left-hand side (the right-hand side, resp.) of (5) is a nonnegative linear combination of $ac(S_1), \cdots, ac(S_k)$ (of $ac(S_{k+1}), \cdots, ac(S_m)$, resp.). It suffices to show that the sum of the coefficients in the left-hand side is equal to the sum of the coefficients in the right-hand side; for then by normalizing both sides, one obtains the required result.

the sum of the coefficients in the left-hand side

$$= \sum_{i \leqslant k} \sum_{j \notin S_i} \sum_{\substack{h \geqslant k+1 \\ S_h \ni j}} \lambda_i \cdot \frac{\lambda_h}{\sum_{\substack{g \geqslant k+1 \\ S_g \ni j}} \lambda_g} \cdot y^{S_h, j}$$

$$= \sum_{h \geqslant k+1} \sum_{j \in S_h} (\sum_{\substack{i \leqslant k \\ S_i \not\ni j}} \lambda_i \cdot \frac{\lambda_h}{\sum_{\substack{g \geqslant k+1 \\ S_g \ni j}} \lambda_g}) \cdot y^{S_h, j}$$

$$= \sum_{h \geqslant k+1} \sum_{j \in S_h} \lambda_h \cdot y^{S_h, j}, \text{ by (4)}$$

= the sum of the coefficients in the right-hand side.

Step 3. Consider the specific order on $\mathscr{B}$ so that

$$ac(S_1) \leqslant ac(S_2) \leqslant \ldots \leqslant ac(S_m).$$

This yields a contradiction to Step 2. □

Remark 5.2.11. Under the same assumptions as in Theorem 5.2.10, except that the assumption of non-decreasing returns to scale (Postulate 5.1.4) is replaced by:

$$c^{\phi}(y) := \begin{cases} \infty & \text{if } y = 0. \\ 0 & \text{if } y > 0, \end{cases}$$

$$c^S(0) = \infty,$$

$$c^S(y) + c^T(y') \geqslant c^{S \cap T}(y'') + c^{S \cup T}(y + y' - y'')$$

for all $S, T \in \mathscr{N}$ and any $y'' \leqslant \min\{y, y'\}$, the non-side-payment game V associated with $\mathscr{E}_{cp}$ is ordinal convex. This is due to Claim 4.2.5. See also Remark 4.2.6. □

Proof of Theorem 5.2.9. *Step 1*. In view of Assumption 5.2.1 (vii), one may assume that $T(S) = T$ for all $S \in \mathscr{N}$, because an equilibrium of the economy that is constructed from $\mathscr{E}_{cp}$ by substituting T for $T(S)$ for every S is also an equilibrium of $\mathscr{E}_{cp}$. Define α, N_0, $\mathscr{N}_0$, $\{\Sigma^j\}_{j\in N_0}$, Σ^S, Σ_0, and $\{F^S\}_{S\in\mathscr{N}}$ as in the paragraph that follows the statement of Theorem 5.2.10. Actually, each F^S depends only upon Σ^{n+1}.

Step 2. For every $S\in\mathscr{N}$ the correspondence F^S is nonempty-valued and both upper and lower semicontinuous (u.s.c. and l.s.c.) in Σ^{n+1}. Indeed, nonempty-valuedness and upper semicontinuity of F^S are straightforward. To show lower semicontinuity of F^S, choose any sequence $\{\bar{p}^k, \bar{q}^k\}_k$ in Σ^{n+1} which converges to $(\bar{p}, \bar{q})$ and any strategy bundle $\sigma^S=\{\xi^i, \eta^j\}_{j\in S}$ in $F^S(\bar{p}, \bar{q})$. Set $\bar{w}^k:=\bar{p}^k\cdot\sum_{j\in S}\omega^j$, and $\bar{w}:=\bar{p}\cdot\sum_{j\in S}\omega^j$. Then

$$\sum_{j\in S}\xi^j+c(\bar{p}, \bar{q}, \sum_{j\in S}\eta^j)\leqslant\bar{w}. \tag{1}$$

If the strict inequality "$<$" holds true in (1), then for all k large enough, the constant sequence $\sigma^{S,k}:=\sigma^S$ satisfies $\sigma^{S,k}\in F(\bar{p}^k, \bar{q}^k)$, and of course converges to σ^S. Suppose the equality "$=$" holds true in (1). For each k, let t^k be the smallest $t\geqslant 0$ such that

$$\sum_{j\in S}(1-t)\xi^j+c(\bar{p}^k, \bar{q}^k, \sum_{j\in S}(1-t)\eta^j)\leqslant\bar{w}^k,$$

and set $\sigma^{S,k}:=(1-t^k)\sigma^S$. It suffices to show that $\{\sigma^{S,k}\}_k$ converges to σ^S, or equivalently that t^k converges to 0. Fix any real number ϵ, $0<\epsilon\leqslant 1$. Observe that if $\xi^j=0$ for all $j\in S$, then $\sum_{j\in S}\eta^j>0$. Then, regardless whether $\xi^j=0$ or $\xi^j>0$, it follows from Assumptions 5.2.2 (iv) and 5.2.4 (ii) that

$$\sum_{j\in S}(1-\epsilon)\xi^j+c(\bar{p}, \bar{q}, \sum_{j\in S}(1-\epsilon)\eta^j)<\bar{w}.$$

By continuity (Assumption 5.2.2 (iii)), there exists k_ϵ such that for all $k>k_\epsilon$,

$$\sum_{j\in S}(1-\epsilon)\xi^j+c(\bar{p}^k, \bar{q}^k, \sum_{j\in S}(1-\epsilon)\eta^j)<\bar{w}^k.$$

Therefore, for all $k>k_\epsilon$, $t^k\leqslant\epsilon$.

Step 3. There exist continuous functions

$$y^*: \Delta^{l-1}\times\Delta^{m-1}\times\mathbf{R}_+\to\mathbf{R}^m_+ \text{ and } z^*: (\operatorname{icr}\Delta^{l-1})\times\Delta^{m-1}\times\mathbf{R}_+\to-\mathbf{R}^l_+,$$

such that

$$\begin{aligned}&\forall (p, q, \eta)\in\Delta^{l-1}\times\Delta^{m-1}\times\mathbf{R}_+:\\ &q\cdot y^*(p, q, \eta)=\eta \text{ and } g(p, y^*(p, q, \eta))=c(p, q, \eta); \text{ and} \qquad (2)\\ &\forall (p, q, \eta)\in(\operatorname{icr}\Delta^{l-1})\times\Delta^{m-1}\times\mathbf{R}_+:\\ &(z^*(p, q, \eta), y^*(p, q, \eta))\in T \text{ and } p\cdot z^*(p, q, \eta)=c(p, q, \eta). \qquad (3)\end{aligned}$$

Moreover, if $\{p^k, q^k, \eta^k\}_k$ is a sequence in $(\operatorname{icr}\Delta^{l-1})\times\Delta^{m-1}\times\mathbf{R}_+$ converging to (p, q, η) with $p\in\Delta^{l-1}\backslash(\operatorname{icr}\Delta^{l-1})$ and $\eta>0$, then $\|z^*(p^k, q^k, \eta^k)\|\to\infty$ as

$k \to \infty$. Indeed, in order to show the existence of the required function y^*, observe first that $c(p, q, \eta)$ is the optimal value of the problem,

$$\begin{aligned} &\min && g(p, y), \\ &\text{subject to} && q \cdot y \geqslant \eta \text{ and } y \in \mathbf{R}^m_+. \end{aligned}$$

By Assumption 5.2.2 (ii), the constraint set of this minimization problem can be written as $\{y \in \mathbf{R}^m_+ \mid q \cdot y = \eta,\ y_h = 0 \text{ if } q_h = 0\}$, which is a compact set. The strict quasi-concavity of $g(p, \cdot)$ implies the unique existence of the solution $y^*(p, q, \eta)$. This establishes (2). In order to prove continuity of the function y^*, consider a sequence $\{p^k, q^k, \eta^k\}_k$ in $\Delta^{l-1} \times \Delta^{m-1} \times \mathbf{R}_+$ converging to (p, q, η). One needs to show that $y^*(p^k, q^k, \eta^k) \to y^*(p, q, \eta)$ as $k \to \infty$. Suppose that the sequence $\{y^*(p^k, q^k, \eta^k)\}_k$ is not bounded. Then, by Assumption 5.2.1 (v), the sequence $\{g(p^k, y^*(p^k, q^k, \eta^k))\}_k$ is not bounded. But $g(p^k, y^*(p^k, q^k, \eta^k)) = c(p^k, q^k, \eta^k)$, and by continuity of function c, this converges to $c(p, q, \eta)$, hence a contradiction. The sequence $\{y^*(p^k, q^k, \eta^k)\}_k$ has thus at least one cluster point $\bar{y}$. By passing through the sequence converging to $\bar{y}$, one obtains: $q \cdot \bar{y} = \eta$, and $g(p, \bar{y}) = c(p, q, \eta)$. The uniqueness of the solution of the minimization problem implies that $\bar{y} = y^*(p, q, \eta)$. This is true for all cluster points of $\{y^*(p^k, q^k, \eta^k)\}_k$. Thus the sequence $\{y^*(p^k, q^k, \eta^k)\}_k$ converges to $y^*(p, q, \eta)$.

Since y^* is well-defined in $\Delta^{l-1} \times \Delta^{m-1} \times \mathbf{R}_+$, $c(p, q, \eta)$ can be defined as the optimal value of the problem,

$$\begin{aligned} &\min && -p \cdot z, \\ &\text{subject to} && (z, y^*(p, q, \eta)) \in T. \end{aligned}$$

This problem has a solution if $p \gg \mathbf{0}$, since the constraint set can be chosen to be compact. (Fix any $\bar{z} \in S_T(y^*(p, q, \eta))$. Then, the required compact constraint set is $\{z \in -\mathbf{R}^l_+ \mid z \in S_T(y^*(p, q, \eta)), p \cdot \bar{z} \leqslant p \cdot z\}$.) Assumption 5.2.3 (i) implies that this solution is unique, so that the function $z^*(p, q, \eta)$ is well-defined on $(\text{icr}\,\Delta^{l-1}) \times \Delta^{m-1} \times \mathbf{R}_+$. By the maximum theorem, it is continuous. To prove the last assertion of this step, choose any sequence $\{p^k, q^k, \eta^k\}_k$ in $(\text{icr}\,\Delta^{l-1}) \times \Delta^{m-1} \times \mathbf{R}_+$ converging to (p, q, η) with $p \in \Delta^{l-1} \backslash (\text{icr}\,\Delta^{l-1})$ and $\eta > 0$. Suppose that the sequence $\{z^*(p^k, q^k, \eta^k)\}_k$ were bounded. Then there would exist a cluster point $\bar{z}$ such that $(\bar{z}, y^*(p, q, \eta)) \in T$ and $p \cdot \bar{z} = g(p, y^*(p, q, \eta)) = c(p, q, \eta)$. The condition $[\eta > 0]$ implies $y^*(p, q, \eta) > \mathbf{0}$ and, by Assumption 5.2.1 (iv), $\bar{z} \ll \mathbf{0}$. Let i be a component such that $p_i = 0$ and j be a component such that $p_j > 0$. Assumptions 5.2.1 (iii), 5.2.3 (i) and the strict negativity of $\bar{z}$ imply that there exist $\alpha_i > 0$ and $\alpha_j > 0$ such that $\bar{z} - \alpha_i e^i + \alpha_j e^j \in S_T(y^*(p, q, \eta))$ (where e^i and e^j denote the ith and the jth unit vectors of $\mathbf{R}^l$ respectively). But $p \cdot (\bar{z} - \alpha_i e^i + \alpha_j e^j) > p \cdot \bar{z} = -g(p, y^*(p, q, \eta))$, which contradicts the definition of $g(p, y^*(p, q, \eta))$. Thus, $\|z^*(p^k, q^k, \eta^k)\| \to \infty$ as $k \to \infty$.

Notice that if $p_j > 0$, $\{z_j^*(p^k, q^k, \eta^k)\}_k$ stays bounded, since $\lim_k p^k \cdot z^*(p^k, q^k, \eta^k) = c(p, q, \eta)$.

Step 4. Define:

$$\Sigma_0' := \{(\sigma, p, q) \in \Sigma_0 \mid \forall j \in N: \eta^j > 0\},$$
$$\Sigma_0'' := \{(\sigma, p, q) \in \Sigma_0 \mid \forall j \in N: (\xi^j, \eta^j) \gg \mathbf{0}\},$$
$$\Sigma_{0+} := \{(\sigma, p, q) \in \Sigma_0 \mid p \in \operatorname{icr} \Delta^{l-1}, q \in \operatorname{icr} \Delta^{m-1}\},$$
$$\Sigma_{0L} := \{(\sigma, p, q) \in \Sigma_0 \mid p \in \Delta^{l-1} \backslash (\operatorname{icr} \Delta^{l-1}), q \in \operatorname{icr} \Delta^{m-1}\},$$
$$\Sigma_{0M} := \{(\sigma, p, q) \in \Sigma_0 \mid p \in \operatorname{icr} \Delta^{l-1}, q \in \Delta^{m-1} \backslash (\operatorname{icr} \Delta^{m-1})\},$$
$$\Sigma_{0LM} := \{(\sigma, p, q) \in \Sigma_0 \mid p \in \Delta^{l-1} \backslash (\operatorname{icr} \Delta^{l-1}), q \in \Delta^{m-1} \backslash (\operatorname{icr} \Delta^{m-1})\},$$
$$\Sigma_{0+}' := \Sigma_0' \cap \Sigma_{0+}, \Sigma_{0L}' := \Sigma_0' \cap \Sigma_{0L},$$
$$\Sigma_{0M}' := \Sigma_0' \cap \Sigma_{0M}, \Sigma_{0LM}' := \Sigma_0' \cap \Sigma_{0LM},$$
$$\Sigma_{0+}'' := \Sigma_0'' \cap \Sigma_{0+}, \Sigma_{0L}'' := \Sigma_0'' \cap \Sigma_{0L},$$
$$\Sigma_{0M}'' := \Sigma_0'' \cap \Sigma_{0M}, \Sigma_{0LM}'' := \Sigma_0'' \cap \Sigma_{0LM}.$$

Notice that $\{\Sigma_{0+}', \Sigma_{0L}', \Sigma_{0M}', \Sigma_{0LM}', \Sigma_0 \backslash \Sigma_0'\}$ and $\{\Sigma_{0+}'', \Sigma_{0L}'', \Sigma_{0M}'', \Sigma_{0LM}'', \Sigma_0 \backslash \Sigma_0''\}$ are partitions of Σ_0.

Step 5. Definitions of correspondences G_l: $\Sigma_0 \to \Delta^{l-1}$, G_m: $\Sigma_0 \to \Delta^{m-1}$, and G: $\Sigma_0 \to \Sigma^{n+1}$. Given the definitions of G_l and G_m, G will be defined as $G(\sigma, p, q) := G_l(\sigma, p, q) \times G_m(\sigma, p, q)$. Recall the notation $z^*(p, q, \eta)$, $y^*(p, q, \eta)$, $x^{*j}(p, q, \sigma^j)$ and $y^{*j}(p, q, \sigma^j)$ (Step 3 of the present proof and the paragraph that follows the statement of Assumption 5.2.4).

For the case $C_d^j = \{\mathbf{0}\} \times \mathbf{R}_+^m$, the correspondences are defined as follows:

- if $(\bar\sigma, \bar p, \bar q) \in \Sigma_{0+}' \cup \Sigma_{0M}'$, $G_l(\bar\sigma, \bar p, \bar q)$ is the set of solutions of the problem: Max $p \cdot (-z^*(\bar p, \bar q, \sum_{j \in N} \bar\eta^j) - \sum_{j \in N} \omega^j)$ subject to $p \in \Delta^{l-1}$;
- if $(\bar\sigma, \bar p, \bar q) \in \Sigma_{0L}' \cup \Sigma_{0LM}'$, $G_l(\bar\sigma, \bar p, \bar q) := \{p \in \Delta^{l-1} \mid p \cdot \bar p = 0\}$;
- if $(\bar\sigma, \bar p, \bar q) \in \Sigma_0 \backslash \Sigma_0'$, $G_l(\bar\sigma, \bar p, \bar q) := \Delta^{l-1}$;
- if $(\bar\sigma, \bar p, \bar q) \in \Sigma_{0+}' \cup \Sigma_{0L}'$, $G_m(\bar\sigma, \bar p, \bar q)$ is the set of solutions of the problem: Max $q \cdot (\sum_{j \in N} y^{*j}(\bar p, \bar q, \bar\sigma^j) - y^*(\bar p, \bar q, \sum_{j \in N} \bar\eta^j))$ subject to $q \in \Delta^{m-1}$;
- if $(\bar\sigma, \bar p, \bar q) \in \Sigma_{0M}' \cup \Sigma_{0LM}'$, $G_m(\bar\sigma, \bar p, \bar q) := \{q \in \Delta^{m-1} \mid q \cdot \bar q = 0\}$;
- if $(\bar\sigma, \bar p, \bar q) \in \Sigma_0 \backslash \Sigma_0'$, $G_m(\bar\sigma, \bar p, \bar q) := \Delta^{m-1}$.

For the case $C_d^j = \mathbf{R}_+^{l+m}$, the correspondences are defined as follows:

- if $(\bar\sigma, \bar p, \bar q) \in \Sigma_{0+}'' \backslash \Sigma_{0M}''$, $G_l(\bar\sigma, \bar p, \bar q)$ is the set of solutions of the problem: Max $p \cdot (\sum_{j \in N} x^{*j}(\bar p, \bar q, \bar\sigma^j) - z^*(\bar p, \bar q, \sum_{j \in N} \bar\eta^j) - \sum_{j \in N} \omega^j)$ subject to $p \in \Delta^{l-1}$;
- if $(\bar\sigma, \bar p, \bar q) \in \Sigma_{0L}'' \cup \Sigma_{0LM}''$, $G_l(\bar\sigma, \bar p, \bar q) := \{p \in \Delta^{l-1} \mid p \cdot \bar p = 0\}$;
- if $(\bar\sigma, \bar p, \bar q) \in \Sigma_0 \backslash \Sigma_0''$, $G_l(\bar\sigma, \bar p, \bar q) := \Delta^{l-1}$;
- if $(\bar\sigma, \bar p, \bar q) \in \Sigma_{0+}'' \cup \Sigma_{0L}''$, $G_m(\bar\sigma, \bar p, \bar q)$ is the set of solutions of the problem: Max $q \cdot (\sum_{j \in N} y^{*j}(\bar p, \bar q, \bar\sigma^j) - y^*(\bar p, \bar q, \sum_{j \in N} \bar\eta^j))$ subject to $q \in \Delta^{m-1}$;
- if $(\bar\sigma, \bar p, \bar q) \in \Sigma_{0M}'' \cup \Sigma_{0LM}''$, $G_m(\bar\sigma, \bar p, \bar q) := \{q \in \Delta^{m-1} \mid q \cdot \bar q = 0\}$;
- if $(\bar\sigma, \bar p, \bar q) \in \Sigma_0 \backslash \Sigma_0''$, $G_m(\bar\sigma, \bar p, \bar q) := \Delta^{m-1}$.

Step 6. The data $(\{\Sigma^j\}_{j \in N}, \{F^S\}_{S \in \mathcal{N}}, \{v^j\}_{j \in N}, \Sigma^{n+1}, G)$ may be considered a family of societies with player set N, parameterized by $(p, q) \in \Sigma^{n+1}$. A *social coalitional equilibrium* is a pair of a strategy bundle and a parameter value $(\sigma^*, p^*, q^*) \in \Sigma_0$ such that $\sigma^* \in F^N(p^*, q^*)$, $(p^*, q^*) \in G(\sigma^*, p^*, q^*)$, and it is not true that there exist $S \in \mathcal{N}$ and $\sigma^S \in F^S(p^*, q^*)$ for which $v^j(p^*, q^*, \sigma^j) > v^j(p^*, q^*, \sigma^{*j})$ for every $j \in S$. As in the proof of Theorem 3.4.11, one can prove the following existence theorem for the parameterized societies: *There exists a social coalitional equilibrium if*

(i) *for every $j \in N_0$, Σ^j is a nonempty, convex, compact subset of a Euclidean space;*
(ii) *for every $S \in \mathcal{N}$, F^S is both u.s.c. and l.s.c. in Σ^{n+1}, and is nonempty-valued;*
(iii) *for every $j \in N$, v^j is continuous in $\Sigma^{n+1} \times \Sigma^j$;*
(iv) *for every $(\bar{p}, \bar{q}) \in \Sigma^{n+1}$, the non-side-payment game $V_{\bar{p},\bar{q}}: \mathcal{N} \to \mathbf{R}^N$ defined by*

$$V_{\bar{p},\bar{q}}(S) := \left\{ u \in \mathbf{R}^N \,\middle|\, \begin{array}{l} \exists\, \sigma^S \in F^S(\bar{p}, \bar{q}): \\ \forall j \in S: u_j \leqslant v^j(\bar{p}, \bar{q}, \sigma^j) \end{array} \right\}$$

is balanced;
(v) *for every $(\bar{p}, \bar{q}) \in \Sigma^{n+1}$ and for every utility allocation u in the core of $V_{\bar{p},\bar{q}}$, the set $\{\sigma \in F^N(\bar{p}, \bar{q}) \mid \forall j \in N: u_j \leqslant v^j(\bar{p}, \bar{q}, \sigma^j)\}$ is convex; and*
(vi) *G is u.s.c. in Σ_0, and is nonempty- and convex-valued.*

Let $(\sigma^*, p^*, q^*) \in \Sigma_0$ be a social coalitional equilibrium in the present context. Then, $(\{x^{*j}(p^*, q^*, \sigma^{*j}), y^{*j}(p^*, q^*, \sigma^{*j})\}_{j \in N}, (z^*(p^*, q^*, \sum_{j \in N} \eta^{*j}), y^*(p^*, q^*, \sum_{j \in N} \eta^{*j})), \{\xi^{*j}, \eta^{*j}\}_{j \in N}, (p^*, q^*))$ is well-defined, and is an equilibrium of $\mathscr{E}_{cp}$. In order to check this fact for the case $C_d^j = \{\mathbf{0}\} \times \mathbf{R}_+^m$, it will be first shown that $(\sigma^*, p^*, q^*) \in \Sigma'_{0+}$ in this case. Since the utility allocation $\{v^j(p^*, q^*, \sigma^{*j})\}_{j \in N}$ is in the core of V_{p^*,q^*}, it is in particular individually rational. Then,

$$\eta^{*j} \geqslant \max \{q^* \cdot y \mid (-\omega^j, y) \in T\}.$$

The assumptions of free disposal (5.2.1 (iii)) and of continuity of the cost function g in $\Delta^{l-1} \times \mathbf{R}_+^m$ (5.2.2 (i)) imply that if $z \ll \mathbf{0}$, there exists $y \gg \mathbf{0}$ such that $(z, y) \in T$. Indeed, choose any $p \in \text{icr}\, \Delta^{l-1}$ and any $y \gg \mathbf{0}$. Then, by the continuity assumption, $g(p, \epsilon y) \downarrow 0$ as $\epsilon \downarrow 0$. For the output vector ϵy, denote by $z(\epsilon)$ the cost-minimizing input vector, i.e., $(z(\epsilon), \epsilon y) \in T$ and $p \cdot (-z(\epsilon)) = g(p, \epsilon y)$. But $p \cdot (-z(\epsilon)) \geqslant (\min_h p_h) \sum_h (-z_h(\epsilon))$, so there exists $\epsilon_0 > 0$ such that $\sum_h (-z_h(\epsilon_0)) < -z_i$ for all $i = 1, \cdots, l$. By the free disposal assumption, $(z, \epsilon_0 y) \in T$. Therefore, in view of Assumption 5.2.4 (ii), $\eta^{*j} > 0$, that is, $(\sigma^*, p^*, q^*) \in \Sigma'_0$. Since $(p^*, q^*) \in G(\sigma^*, p^*, q^*)$, (σ^*, p^*, q^*) cannot be in $\Sigma'_{0L} \cup \Sigma'_{0M} \cup \Sigma'_{0LM}$ due to the definition of G. Therefore, $(\sigma^*, p^*, q^*) \in \Sigma'_{0+}$. Then, $y^{*j} := y^{*j}(p^*, q^*, \sigma^{*j})$, $z^* := z^*(p^*, q^*, \sum_{j \in N} \eta^{*j})$, $y^* := y^*(p^*, q^*, \sum_{j \in N} \eta^{*j})$ are all well-defined. It remains to show the market clearance condition. For every $p \in \Delta^{l-1}$,

$$p\cdot(-z^* - \sum_{j\in N}\omega^j)$$
$$\leqslant p^*\cdot(-z^* - \sum_{j\in N}\omega^j)$$
$$= c(p^*, q^*, \sum_{j\in N}\eta^{*j}) - p^*\cdot\sum_{j\in N}\omega^j$$
$$\leqslant 0.$$

Therefore,

$$-z^* - \sum_{j\in N}\omega^j \leqslant \mathbf{0}.$$

A similar reasoning shows that

$$\sum_{j\in N} y^{*j} - y^* \leqslant \mathbf{0}.$$

In order to prove the fact for the case $C_d^j = \mathbf{R}_+^{l+m}$ that $(\{x^{*j}(p^*, q^*, \sigma^{*j}), y^{*j}(p^*, q^*, \sigma^{*j})\}_{j\in N}, (z^*(p^*, q^*, \sum_{j\in N}\eta^{*j}), y^*(p^*, q^*, \sum_{j\in N}\eta^{*j})), \{\xi^{*j}, \eta^{*j}\}_{j\in N}, (p^*, q^*))$ is well-defined, and is an equilibrium of $\mathscr{E}_{cp}$, observe first that $(\sigma^*, p^*, q^*) \in \Sigma_0''$ in the light of Assumption 5.2.6, and conclude that $(\sigma^*, p^*, q^*) \in \Sigma_{0+}''$. The rest of the proof is the same as in the case $C_d^j = \{\mathbf{0}\} \times \mathbf{R}_+^m$.

Thus, it remains to establish that all the conditions (i)–(vi) of the above social coalitional equilibrium existence theorem are satisfied. Conditions (i) and (iii) are trivially satisfied. Condition (ii) has already been checked in Step 2. Condition (iv) is satisfied due to Theorem 5.2.10 (Scarf). Condition (vi) is satisfied due to Assumption 5.2.5 and Step 3.

Step 7. Condition (v) of the social coalitional equilibrium existence theorem (Step 6) is satisfied. Indeed, choose any $(\bar{p}, \bar{q}) \in \Sigma^{n+1}$, any utility allocation $\bar{u}$ in the core of $V_{\bar{p},\bar{q}}$, and any two members σ^0, σ^1 of $F^N(\bar{p}, \bar{q})$ such that

$$\forall j \in N\colon \bar{u}_j \leqslant \min\{v^j(\bar{p}, \bar{q}, \sigma^0), v^j(\bar{p}, \bar{q}, \sigma^1)\}.$$

Choose any $t \in [0, 1]$, and set $\sigma^t := \{\sigma^{t,j}\}_{j\in N} := t\sigma^1 + (1-t)\sigma^0$. In view of the quasi-concavity of $v^j(\bar{p}, \bar{q}, \cdot)$ (Assumption 5.2.4 (i)), one needs to show only $\sigma^t \in F^N(\bar{p}, \bar{q})$.

For the case $C_d^j = \{\mathbf{0}\} \times \mathbf{R}_+^m$, $\xi^{t,j} = \xi^{0,j} = \xi^{1,j} = 0$ for every j. By monotonicity of $c(\bar{p}, \bar{q}, \cdot)$,

$$c(\bar{p}, \bar{q}, \sum_{j\in N}\eta^{t,j})$$
$$\leqslant c(\bar{p}, \bar{q}, \max\{\sum_{j\in N}\eta^{0,j}, \sum_{j\in N}\eta^{1,j}\})$$
$$\leqslant p\cdot\sum_{j\in N}\omega^j.$$

Hence $\sigma^t \in F^N(\bar{p}, \bar{q})$.

For the case $C_d^j = \mathbf{R}_+^{l+m}$, it suffices to show that σ^0 and σ^1 are necessarily identical. Notice first that $\bar{u}$ is Pareto optimal relative to $(\bar{p}, \bar{q})$. Then, σ belongs to $F^N(\bar{p}, \bar{q})$ and satisfies $v^j(\bar{p}, \bar{q}, \sigma^j) \geqslant \bar{u}_j$ for all $j \in N$, iff σ is a solution of the program,

$$\begin{aligned} \min \quad & \sum_{j\in N} \xi^j + c(\bar{p}, \bar{q}, \sum_{j\in N} \eta^j), \\ \text{subject to} \quad & v^j(\bar{p}, \bar{q}, \xi^j, \eta^j) \geqslant \bar{u}_j \text{ for all } j \in N. \end{aligned}$$

The first-order conditions imply that the vectors

$$\left(\frac{\partial v^j}{\partial \xi^j}, \frac{\partial v^j}{\partial \eta^j}\right), j \in N,$$

$$(1, \frac{\partial}{\partial \eta} c(\bar{p}, \bar{q}, \sum_{j\in N} \eta^j)),$$

are proportional. The only vector σ which satisfies these conditions and the condition,

$$v^j(\bar{p}, \bar{q}, \xi^j, \eta^j) \geqslant \bar{u}_j \text{ for all } j \in N,$$

is the compensated-demand bundle taken at the points $(\bar{p}, \bar{q}, \frac{\partial}{\partial \eta} c(\bar{p}, \bar{q}, \sum_{j\in N} \eta^i), \bar{u}_j), j \in N$. Therefore, a solution of the minimization problem must be of the form,

$$(\xi^{*j}(\bar{p}, \bar{q}, \frac{\partial}{\partial \eta} c(\bar{p}, \bar{q}, \eta), \bar{u}_j), \eta^{*j}(\bar{p}, \bar{q}, \frac{\partial}{\partial \eta} c(\bar{p}, \bar{q}, \eta), \bar{u}_j)),$$

and must satisfy:

$$\eta = \sum_{j\in N} \eta^{*j}(\bar{p}, \bar{q}, \frac{\partial}{\partial \eta} c(\bar{p}, \bar{q}, \eta), \bar{u}_j).$$

If the function $\eta \mapsto \sum_{j\in N} \eta^{*j}(\bar{p}, \bar{q}, \frac{\partial}{\partial \eta} c(\bar{p}, \bar{q}, \eta), \bar{u}_j)$ has at most one fixed-point, the minimization problem must have a unique solution. This is guaranteed if the function has a slope less than 1 for all η. This last condition is precisely the elasticity condition (i). □

5.3 Discussion of the literature

Let $\mathscr{E}_{cp} := (\{C^j, u^j, \omega^j\}_{j\in N}, \{T(S)\}_{S\in\mathscr{N}})$ be a coalition production economy, as given in Definition 5.1.1 except that $\omega^j = (\omega_L^j, \omega_M^j)$, $\omega_L^j \in \mathbf{R}^l$ and $\omega_M^j \in \mathbf{R}^m$, and $T(S) \subset (-\mathbf{R}_+^l) \times \mathbf{R}^m$. (Definition 5.1.1, and hence Sections 5.1 and 5.2, treated the specific case where $\omega_M^j = \mathbf{0}$, which justified the notation ω^j for ω_L^j there, and $T(S) \subset (-\mathbf{R}_+^l) \times \mathbf{R}_+^m$.) Since some final goods (some of the m commodities) may be used as inputs in production in the present general

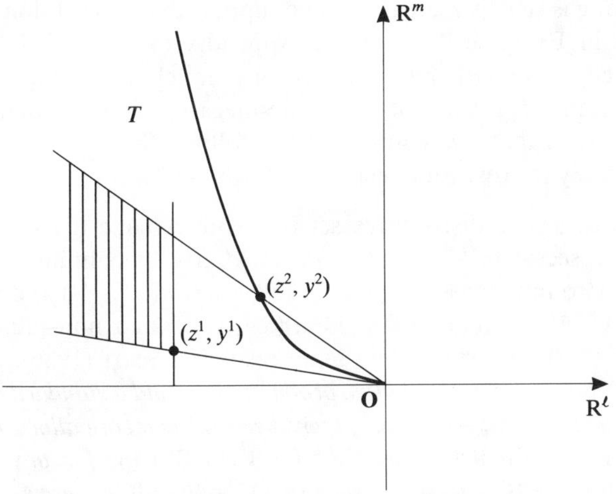

5.3 Distributive set

setup, the term "final good" may not be appropriate. This terminology will nevertheless continue to be adopted here; no confusion arises.

As in Section 5.2, assume that $C^j = \mathbf{R}_+^{l+m}$. The focus of this section is the core allocations of $\mathscr{E}_{cp}$ (Definition 3.5.2). The grand coalition is assumed to have the most efficient technology (Assumption 5.2.1 (vii)). One may assume without loss of generality, therefore, that

$$T(S) = T, \text{ for all } S \in \mathscr{N}.$$

Also as in Section 5.2, two cases are considered here: one case in which consumption/supply of primary goods does not affect consumers' utility levels ($C_d^j = \{\mathbf{0}\} \times \mathbf{R}_+^m$ for every j), and the other case in which both consumption of primary goods and consumption of final goods affect consumers' utility levels ($C_d^j = \mathbf{R}_+^{l+m}$ for every j).

Study of the economy $\mathscr{E}_{cp}$ which exhibits increasing returns to scale was initiated by Scarf (1963, 1986); the first draft of Scarf (1986) had been circulated as a working paper since 1963. In this latter paper, he proposed the following class of production sets:

Definition 5.3.1. A production set $T (\subset (\mathbf{R}_+^l) \times \mathbf{R}^m)$ is called a *distributive set*, if for any finitely many feasible activities $\{(z^i, y^i)\}_{i \in I}$ and any of their nonnegative linear combinations (z, y) such that $z \leqslant z^i$ for all $i \in I$, it follows that $(z, y) \in T$ (see Figure 5.3).

Remark 5.3.2. For the case $m = 1$, a production set T is represented by the associated production function $g: \mathbf{R}_+^l \to \mathbf{R}_+$, so that $(z, y) \in T$ iff $y \leqslant g(-z)$.

Assume that g is strictly increasing. The supportability condition on g was introduced in Example 2A.1 of the Appendix to Chapter 2, and was characterized in Remark 2A.2 as: For any finitely many input bundles $\{x^i\}_{i\in I}\subset\mathbf{R}^l_+$ and for any of their nonnegative linear combinations $\bar{x}=\sum_{i\in I}\lambda_i x^i$ such that $x^i\leqslant\bar{x}$ for all $i\in I$, it follows that $\sum_{i\in I}\lambda_i g(x^i)\leqslant g(\bar{x})$. This is precisely the distributiveness condition on T. □

Needless to say, a distributive set is a convex cone if $l=0$. Call the consumption sector $\{C^j, u^j, \omega^j\}_{j\in N}$ *standard*, if u^j is continuous, weakly monotone, strongly quasi-concave ($[u^j(x^j, y^j)<u^j(x'^j, y'^j)$ and $0<\alpha<1]$ implies $u^j(x^j, y^j)<u^j(\alpha(x^j, y^j)+(1-\alpha)(x'^j, y'^j)))$ and non-satiated, and $(\omega^j_L, \omega^j_M)\gg(\mathbf{0}, \mathbf{0})$. There are two main results in Scarf (1986): (1) *If the economy $\mathscr{E}_{cp}$ possesses a distributive production set and a standard consumption sector such that $C^j_d=\{\mathbf{0}\}\times\mathbf{R}^m_+$, then there exists a core allocation of $\mathscr{E}_{cp}$* and (2) *Given a production set $T(\subset(-\mathbf{R}^l_+)\times\mathbf{R}^m)$, if, for any standard consumption sector $\{C^j, u^j, \omega^j\}_{j\in N}$ such that $C^j_d=\{\mathbf{0}\}\times\mathbf{R}^m_+$, there exists a core allocation in the resulting economy $(\{C^j, u^j, \omega^j\}_{j\in N}, T)$, then the set T has to be distributive.* (Actually, Scarf defined a new concept of social equilibrium for $\mathscr{E}_{cp}$, which gives rise to a member of the core of $\mathscr{E}_{cp}$, and proved a stronger result than (1), i.e., the existence of a social equilibrium.) Result (2) specifically implies the following negative result on the core in the presence of increasing returns: (3) *Given a production set $T(\subset(-\mathbf{R}^l_+)\times\mathbf{R}^m)$, if, for any standard consumption sector $\{C^j, u^j, \omega^j\}_{j\in N}$ such that $C^j_d=\mathbf{R}^{l+m}_+$, there exists a core allocation in the resulting economy $(\{C^j, u^j, \omega^j\}_{j\in N}, T)$, then the set T has to be a convex cone.* Indeed, result (3) can be obtained from result (2), by setting $l=0$ in (2) and by re-naming the number of commodities. Scarf (1963) also has a negative result analogous to (3), in which $T\subset(-\mathbf{R}^l_+)\times\mathbf{R}^m_+$, $\omega^j_L\gg\mathbf{0}$ and $\omega^j_M=\mathbf{0}$.

Throughout the rest of this section, it will be assumed that $T\subset(-\mathbf{R}^l_+)\times\mathbf{R}^m_+$

One notable work which dispenses with the distributiveness assumption on a production set, yet obtains a positive result on the core in the presence of increasing returns is due to Scarf (1973), for the case $l=m=1$ and $\omega^j_M=0$. His theorem and proof are reproduced in the previous section (Theorem 5.2.10).

Subsequent works are all based on the distributiveness assumption, at least implicitly. Sharkey (1979) and Quinzii (1982) are the first to introduce the cost function to study the core of the economy $\mathscr{E}_{cp}$. Since the cost function presupposes availability of a factor price vector, the equilibrium concept they independently came up with is a hybrid of a primary-good market equilibrium and a cooperative solution. This new equilibrium concept is different from Scarf's (1986) concept of social equilibrium, but it also gives rise to a utility allocation in the core. Sharkey (1979) studied the

Table 5.1. *Tabulations summarizing the literature on increasing returns to scale (coalition production economy)*

(a) Results for the case $C_d^j = \{\mathbf{0}\} \times \mathbf{R}_+^m$

l \ m	$m=1$	$m=$ arbitrary
$l=1$		Sharkey's (1979) equilibrium existence theorem
$l=$ arbitrary		Scarf's (1986) theorems on a distributive production set Ichiishi's (1980) generalization of Sharkey's theorem

(b) Results for the case $C_d^j = \mathbf{R}_+^{l+m}$ and $\omega_M^j \gg \mathbf{0}$

l \ m	$m=$ arbitrary
$l=$ arbitrary	Scarf's (1986) negative result on nonemptiness of the core

(c) Results for the case $C_d^j = \mathbf{R}_+^{l+m}$ and $\omega_M^j = \mathbf{0}$

l \ m	$m=1$	$m=$ arbitrary
$l=1$	Scarf's (1973) positive result on nonemptiness of the core	
$l=$ arbitrary	Quinzii's (1982) equilibrium existence theorem	Scarf's (1963) negative results on nonemptiness of the core for $l \geqslant 2$ Ichiishi and Quinzii's (1983) equilibrium existence theorem

case $l=1$ and $C_d^j=\{0\}\times \mathbf{R}_+^m$, and established an equilibrium existence theorem; his result turned out to be included, however, in Scarf's (1986) theorem for nonemptiness of the core. Ichiishi (1980) extended Sharkey's existence theorem, by allowing for an arbitrary l. As for the case $C_d^j=\mathbf{R}_+^{l+m}$, one cannot hope for the nonemptiness of the core in the presence of increasing returns without imposing a condition on the relationship between the production sector and the consumption sector, in the light of Scarf's (1963, 1986) negative results. Quinzii (1982) introduced the elasticity condition (Condition 5.2.8) as the required relationship, and established an equilibrium existence theorem for the case $C_d^j=\mathbf{R}_+^{l+m}$, $m=1$ and $\omega_M^j=0$. Ichiishi and Quinzii (1983) unified the works of Sharkey (1979), Ichiishi (1980) and Quinzii (1982); in particular they extended Quinzii's (1982) work by allowing for an arbitrary m.

The above discussion of the literature is summarized in Table 5.1. Sharkey (1989) contains an excellent survey on the cooperative game-theoretical approach to increasing returns to scale. Quinzii (1991) contains an excellent treatment of the general equilibrium analysis of increasing returns to scale, both the marginal cost pricing equilibrium analysis and the core analysis.

The theme of this chapter may be considered a specific issue of the general cost allocation problem. The papers in Young (1985a) present various approaches to the cost allocation problem, in particular, (1) application of cooperative game theory in the design of normative formulas; (2) application of noncooperative game theory in the design of normative cost allocation mechanism; and (3) actual practices of cost allocation methods. The present chapter concerns application of cooperative game theory in the design of a normative cost allocation mechanism.

6 Stable hierarchical structures

Unlike Chapters 3–5, which present general equilibrium theory of the firm, this chapter presents partial equilibrium theory. The study object is *one* firm; the set of its members is denoted by N. A hierarchical structure is defined as an extensive game form (K, P, U, C) for N, where K is a game tree, P is a player partition, U is an information partition, and C is a choice partition. There are no chance moves. Let Z be the set of endpoints of the tree K, interpreted as the outcome set of the firm. A preference profile is a function $h: Z \to \mathbf{R}^N$. A hierarchical structure (K, P, U, C) is called α-stable if for any preference profile h the extensive game (K, P, U, C, h) has a nonempty α-core. The class of α-stable hierarchical structures is characterized here as follows: There exist vertices $x_1, x_2, \cdots, x_H$ and at most two agents i and j such that (1) x_1 is the origin, x_{h+1} is an immediate successor of x_h, $h=1, 2, \cdots, H-1$; (2) the move x_H and all the moves that come after x_H are controlled by i or j; and (3) for each $h=1, 2, \cdots, H-1$, all the moves that come after x_h without passing through the edge $\overline{x_h x_{h+1}}$ are controlled by the same agent as the one who controls x_h. See Figures 6.3 and 6.7 below. Section 6.1 provides the definition of an extensive game with or without perfect information, and the definition of a hierarchical structure. Section 6.2 presents the above characterization result for the authoritative case, i.e., the case with perfect information. Section 6.3 presents the characterization result for the general case.

6.1 Hierarchical structure formulated as an extensive game form

Consider a firm as an organization of a finite set N of laborers (including managers). A hierarchical structure of the firm is a part of its institutional framework, within which a series of choices, successive or simultaneous, lead to realization of an outcome. An outcome is a complete specification of the firm activities, e.g., a specification of an input-output bundle, wage structure and dividend policy, etc. This section formulates a hierarchical structure as a particular component of a game in extensive form; the latter is defined first.

Let N be a finite set of players, fixed throughout this chapter. The first ingredient is a *tree* K which has its unique *origin* 0. The vertices of K are partitioned into the *endpoints* Z and its complement (the *moves*) X. The second ingredient is a *player partition* $P:=\{P^j\}_{j\in N}$ of the moves X into sets P^js. For each $x\in X$, denote by E_x the set of edges that originate at x. If $x\in P^j$, player j controls choice of an edge from E_x. The third ingredient is a *preference profile* $h:=\{h^j\}_{j\in N}$, where $h^j\colon Z\to\mathbf{R}$ is a utility function of player j.

Definition 6.1.1. A *game in extensive form with perfect information* (or an *extensive game with perfect information*) is a list of specified data (K, P, h) of a tree K, a player partition P of the moves of K, and a preference profile h defined on the endpoints of K. The pair (K, P) is called an *extensive game form with perfect information.*

Let (K, P) be an extensive game form with perfect information. Associated with it is the game form $(\{\Sigma^j\}_{j\in N}, Z, g)$ (see the first paragraph of Section 2.4) defined as follows: The space of outcomes Z is the set of endpoints of tree K. For each player j, his strategy σ^j specifies his choice from E_x at every move x that he controls. Formally it is a function

$$\sigma^j\colon P^j\to \bigcup_{x\in X} E_x \text{ such that } \forall x\in P^j\colon \sigma^j(x)\in E_x.$$

The set of all strategies of player j is denoted by Σ^j. Define $\Sigma:=\prod_{j\in N}\Sigma^j$. The outcome function $g\colon \Sigma\to Z$ is defined as follows: Let any $\sigma\in\Sigma$ be given. First, determine $i_1, i_2, \ldots, i_{M-1}\in N$ and $x_1, x_2, \ldots, x_M\in X\cup Z$ inductively by

$$\begin{aligned}
&x_1:=\text{the origin } 0;\\
&\forall m=1,\ldots, M-1\colon P^{i_m}\ni x_m, \text{ and}\\
&x_{m+1}:=\text{the endpoint (other than } x_m) \text{ of } \sigma^{i_m}(x_m);\\
&x_M\in Z.
\end{aligned}$$

Second, set

$$g(\sigma):=x_M.$$

An extensive game with perfect information (K, P, h) is thus reduced to the associated game in strategic form $(\{\Sigma^j\}_{j\in N}, Z, g, h)$.

Definition 6.1.2. Given a firm with its laborer set N, an *authoritative hierarchical structure* is an extensive game form with perfect information (K, P).

Example 6.1.3. An authoritative hierarchical structure in a firm with three laborers $N=\{1, 2, 3\}$ is given in Figure 6.1. Here, $Z=\{a, b, c, d, e, f, g\}$. According to this structure, laborer 1 is the President, laborer 2 is the

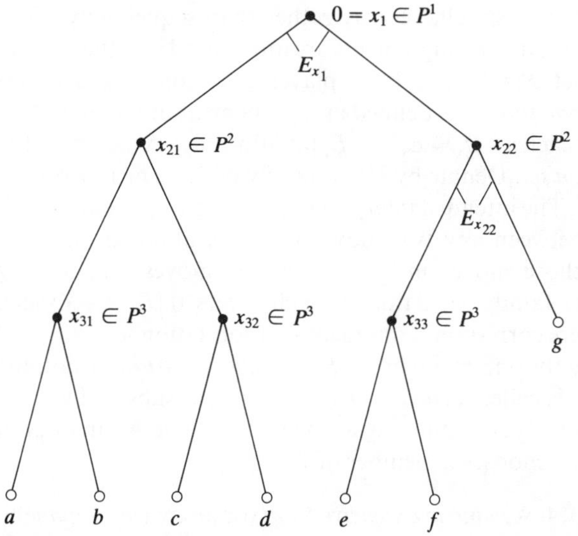

6.1 Authoritative hierarchical structure

middle-level manager, and laborer 3 is a worker. Move x_1 is controlled by the President ($P_1=\{x_1\}$), moves x_{21} and x_{22} are controlled by the middle-level manager ($P_2=\{x_{21}, x_{22}\}$), and moves x_{31}, x_{32}, x_{33} are controlled by the worker ($P_3=\{x_{31}, x_{32}, x_{33}\}$). Notice that $X=P_1 \cup P_2 \cup P_3$. A strategy of the President is an edge from x_1. A strategy of the middle-level manager is a function σ^2: $\{x_{21}, x_{22}\}\to$ {the edges} such that $\sigma^2(x) \in E_x$. The President is the Stackelberg leader, the middle-level manager is a Stackelberg follower, and a strategy σ^2 is a reaction function.[1] There is a further follower, the worker. An extensive game with perfect information is, therefore, a generalization of Stackelberg's model of duopoly. Unlike Stackelberg's treatment, however, the noncooperative behavioral principle is not postulated in this monograph because the treatment here allows for coordination of strategies. □

In many situations a superior may not explicitly reveal his choice to his followers. In the same firm as in Example 6.1.3, the President may not inform his followers which edge in E_{x_1} he has chosen, so the middle-level manager may not know which move he is at, x_{21} or x_{22}. In other situations, laborer 1 and laborer 2 may have the same authoritative power, so that the

[1] (Ignoring player 3 for the time being), a Stackelberg equilibrium is a subgame perfect Nash equilibrium, that is, a Nash equilibrium (σ^1, σ^2) such that $\sigma^2(x)$ is player 2's best response to *every* $x \in P^2$, regardless of whether or not x lies in the equilibrium path.

two make choices simultaneously rather than sequentially. To allow for these situations, further ingredients are introduced into the model. Let K be a tree and let $P:=\{P^j\}_{j\in N}$ be a player partition of the moves X. An *information partition* U is defined as a refinement of the player partition P such that for each $u\in U$, $\# E_x = \# E_y$ for all $x, y \in u$. A member of U is called an *information set*. Denote by U^j the family of those members of U that are subsets of P^j. The intended interpretation of $[u\in U^j]$ is that player j can not distinguish between any two moves inside u, although he can certainly distinguish those moves inside u from the moves outside u. A *choice partition* C is a family of partitions which covers $\cup\{E_x \mid x\in X\}$ such that for each $c\in C$ there corresponds uniquely an information set $u\in \cup_{j\in N} U^j$, and c contains exactly one member of E_x for every $x\in u$ and nothing else. A member of C is called a *choice*. Denote by C_u the subset of all choices in C that consist of edges originating at the vertices in u. At an information set $u\in U^j$, player j chooses a member of C_u.

Definition 6.1.4. A *game in extensive form* (or an *extensive game*) is a list of specified data (K, P, U, C, h) of a tree K, a player partition P, an information partition U, a choice partition C, and a preference profile h. The quadruple (K, P, U, C) is called an *extensive game form.*

An extensive game with perfect information is an extensive game whose information partition is the finest partition of the moves; in this case one may write C_x for $C_{\{x\}}$.

One can also reduce an extensive game form (K, P, U, C) to the associated game form $(\{\Sigma^j\}_{j\in N}, Z, g)$: The space of outcomes Z is the set of endpoints of tree K. For each player j, his strategy specifies his choice from C_u at every information set u that he controls. Formally it is a function

$$\sigma^j\colon U^j \to C \text{ such that } \forall\, u\in U^j\colon \sigma^j(u)\in C_u.$$

The set of all strategies of player j is denoted by Σ^j. The outcome function g: $\prod_{j\in N}\Sigma^j \to Z$ can be defined as in the case of perfect information.

Definition 6.1.5. Given a firm with its laborer set N, a *hierarchical structure* is an extensive game form (K, P, U, C).

Example 6.1.6. A hierarchical structure in a firm with three laborers $N=\{1, 2, 3\}$ is given in Figure 6.2. Here, $Z=\{a, b, c, d, e, f, g\}$. According to this structure, laborer 2 cannot distinguish between the two moves x_{21} and x_{22}, that is, he cannot see which choice laborer 1 has made, so laborer 2 and laborer 1 are in effect making simultaneous choice. Laborer 2's information set is $u_2=\{x_{21}, x_{22}\}$. Let l be the edges $\{\overline{x_{21}x_{31}}, \overline{x_{22}x_{33}}\}$ and let r be the edges $\{\overline{x_{21}x_{32}}, \overline{x_{22}g}\}$. Then, $C_{u_2}=\{l, r\}$. If the two laborers, 1 and 2, behave non-

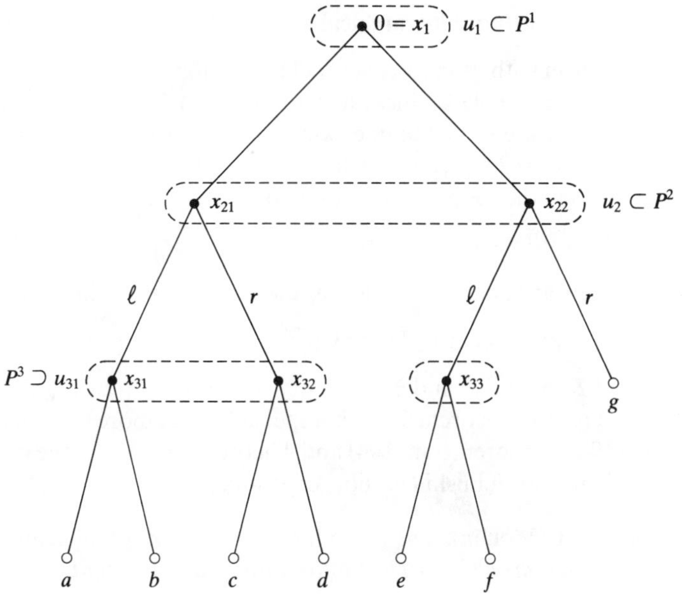

6.2 Hierarchical structure

cooperatively and passively, each having C_{u_j} as his strategy space, $j = 1, 2$, then the model becomes Cournot's model of duopoly (ignoring player 3 at this moment). Of course, the noncooperative behavioral principle is not postulated in this monograph because the treatment here allows for coordination of strategies. □

Given a vertex x, the succession of the vertices and edges that connects the origin 0 and x is called a *path to x*, and is denoted by $\overline{0x}$. The following claim is straightforward:

Claim 6.1.7. *Let (K, P, U, C) be an extensive game form, and let $(\{\Sigma^j\}_{j\in N}, Z, g)$ be the associated game form. Assume that $\# E_x \geqslant 2$ for every $x \in X$. Then, the outcome function g is surjective, if and only if for each endpoint $z \in Z$ and each information set $u \in U$, it follows that $\#(\overline{0z} \cap u) \leqslant 1$.*

The α-stability and β-stability concepts for a game form (Section 2.4) are applicable to the present reduced game forms $(\{\Sigma^j\}_{j\in N}, Z, g)$, with or without complete information. The purpose of this chapter is to characterize these stability conditions in terms of the given data of hierarchical structure (K, P, U, C).

6.2 Stable authoritative hierarchical structures

Consider a firm with its laborer set N. This section characterizes the class of stable authoritative hierarchical structures (K, P). The game form $(\{\Sigma^j\}_{j\in N}, Z, g)$ is understood to be the one associated with (K, P). Set $\Sigma^S := \prod_{j\in S}\Sigma^j$ for each $S\in\mathcal{N} := 2^N\setminus\{\phi\}$, and define $\Sigma := \Sigma^N$. For any move x of tree K, denote by $D(x)$ the set of vertices that come after x:

$$D(x) := \{y\in X\cup Z \mid x\in\overline{0y},\ y\neq x\}.$$

For an edge e at x, denote by $D(x, e)$ the set of vertices that come after e:

$$D(x, e) := \{y\in X\cup Z \mid e\subset\overline{0y}\}.$$

Let E_α and E_β be the α- and β-effectivity functions of $(\{\Sigma^j\}_{j\in N}, Z, g)$.

The first result (Theorem 6.2.1) is a special case of more general results by Moulin (1983, Theorem 3 (p. 104) and Theorem 2 (p. 174)); the proof given here is taken from Ichiishi (1986b, Appendix 1).

Theorem 6.2.1 (Moulin). *The game form* $(\{\Sigma^j\}_{j\in N}, Z, g)$ *associated with an extensive game form with perfect information* (K, P) *is tight.*

Proof. Since $E_\alpha(S)\subset E_\beta(S)$ by definition, it suffices to show that $E_\beta(S)\subset E_\alpha(S)$. This will be done by induction on $\#X$.

If $\#X = 1$, say $X = \{x\} = P^k$, then for every $S\in\mathcal{N}$,

$$E_\alpha(S) = E_\beta(S) = \begin{cases} 2^Z\setminus\{\phi\}, & \text{if } S\ni k;\\ \{Z\}, & \text{if } S\not\ni k.\end{cases}$$

Let $\#X$ be an arbitrary integer greater than 1, and suppose that the assertion of the theorem is true for all extensive game forms with perfect information the number of whose moves is less than $\#X$. Choose any $S\in\mathcal{N}$ and $B\in E_\beta(S)$. Since K is a finite tree, one may choose $\bar{x}\in X$ such that $D(\bar{x})\subset Z$. Let k be the player such that $\bar{x}\in P^k$. Construct a new extensive game form $(\tilde{K}, \tilde{P})$ with the same player set N as follows:

$$\tilde{X} := X\setminus\{\bar{x}\};\qquad \tilde{C}_x := C_x \text{ for every } x\in\tilde{X};$$
$$\tilde{Z} := (Z\cup\{\bar{x}\})\setminus D(\bar{x});$$
$$\tilde{P}^j := \begin{cases} P^k\setminus\{\bar{x}\}, & \text{if } j = k;\\ P^j, & \text{if } j\in N\setminus\{k\}.\end{cases}$$

By the inductive hypothesis, the α-effectivity function $\tilde{E}_\alpha$ of $(\tilde{K}, \tilde{P})$ and the β-effectivity function $\tilde{E}_\beta$ of $(\tilde{K}, \tilde{P})$ are the same. There are two mutually exclusive and exhaustive cases: (1) $\forall\,\sigma^{N\setminus S}: \exists\,\sigma^S: g(\sigma^S, \sigma^{N\setminus S})\in B\setminus D(\bar{x}) =: B'$; and (2) $\exists\,\bar{\sigma}^{N\setminus S}: \forall\,\sigma^S: g(\sigma^S, \bar{\sigma}^{N\setminus S})\notin B'$.

Case (1): In this case, $B'\in E_\beta(S)$. Since $B'\cap D(\bar{x}) = \phi$, choice at $\bar{x}$ does not affect whether $g(\sigma)\in B'$ or not. So, $B'\in\tilde{E}_\beta(S) = \tilde{E}_\alpha(S)$. Consequently

$B' \in E_\alpha(S)$ by the same reason that choice at $\bar{x}$ does not affect whether $g(\sigma) \in B'$ or not. By monotonicity, $B \in E_\alpha(S)$.

Case (2): In this case, let $\bar{\sigma}^S$ denote any strategy bundle such that $\bar{z} := g(\bar{\sigma}^S, \bar{\sigma}^{N\setminus S}) \in B$; such a $\bar{\sigma}^S$ exists. Then, necessarily $\bar{z} \in B \cap D(\bar{x})$. Define $\tilde{B} := (B \cup \{\bar{x}\}) \setminus D(\bar{x})$. Then $\tilde{B} \in \tilde{E}_\beta(S) = \tilde{E}_\alpha(S)$. Let $\tilde{\bar{\sigma}}^S$ be the strategy of S in $(\tilde{K}, \tilde{P})$ such that $\tilde{g}(\tilde{\bar{\sigma}}^S, \tilde{\sigma}^{N\setminus S}) \in \tilde{B}$ for every $\tilde{\sigma}^{N\setminus S}$. Now, if $k \in S$, define $\bar{\sigma}^S$ by

$$\bar{\sigma}^j(x) := \begin{cases} \tilde{\bar{\sigma}}^j(x), \text{ if } j \in S\setminus\{k\} \text{ or } x \in \tilde{P}^k; \\ \text{the edge that connects } \bar{x} \text{ and } \bar{z}, \text{ if } j = k \text{ and } x = \bar{x}. \end{cases}$$

Then $g(\bar{\sigma}^S, \sigma^{N\setminus S}) \in B$ for all $\sigma^{N\setminus S}$, proving that $B \in E_\alpha(S)$. If on the other hand $k \notin S$, then $D(\bar{x}) \subset B$. So $g(\tilde{\bar{\sigma}}^S, \sigma^{N\setminus S}) \in B$ for all $\sigma^{N\setminus S}$, proving that $B \in E_\alpha(S)$. □

In the light of Theorem 6.2.1, one may write $E(S) := E_\alpha(S) = E_\beta(S)$, and call the function E *the effectivity function* of $(\{\Sigma^j\}_{j\in N}, Z, g)$.

To avoid messy arguments on trivial matters, one may postulate without loss of generality,

Assumption 6.2.2. For each $x \in X$, $\# C_x \geqslant 2$.

Assumption 6.2.3. For each $j \in N$ and each $x \in P^j$, if $y \in D(x)$ satisfies $[\overline{0y} \setminus \overline{0x}] \cap X = \{y\}$ then $y \notin P^j$.

Assumption 6.2.3 says that no player has consecutive moves. The following theorem is the main result of this section. The result [(i)⇔(ii)] is a consequence of Theorems 2.4.3, 2.4.5 and 6.2.1, and Lemma 2.4.8. The result [(i)⇔(iii)] is due to Ichiishi (1986b).

Theorem 6.2.4. *Let (K, P) be an authoritative hierarchical structure that satisfies Assumptions 6.2.2 and 6.2.3, and let E be the effectivity function of the associated game form. Then, the following three conditions are equivalent*:

(i) *The effectivity function E is convex*;
(ii) *The authoritative hierarchical structure (K, P) is stable and*;
(iii) *It is not true that there exist three distinct agents $i, j, k \in N$, a vertex $x^\circ \in P^k$, two distinct edges e and e' at x° such that $D(x^\circ, e) \cap P^i \neq \phi$ and $D(x^\circ, e') \cap P^j \neq \phi$.*

Theorem 6.2.4 is a special case of Theorem 6.3.3; the latter theorem will be proved in Section 6.3 below.

It would be useful to visualize the class of all authoritative hierarchical structures that satisfy condition (iii) of Theorem 6.2.4. It is straightforward to verify that under Assumptions 6.2.2 and 6.2.3 condition (iii) is equivalent to:

$$\exists\, i, j \in N\colon \exists\, x^\circ \in P^i\colon X \setminus D(x^\circ) \subset \overline{0x^\circ}, \text{ and } D(x^\circ) \setminus Z \subset P^i \cup P^j.$$

See Figure 6.3, in which the members of X are depicted by solid dots, and the members of Z are depicted by small circles. The inclusion

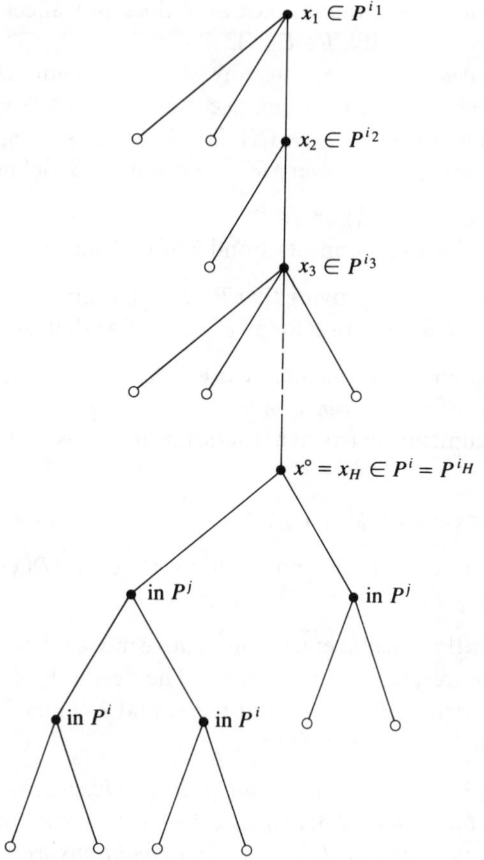

6.3 Stable authoritative hierarchical structure

$[X \backslash D(x^\circ) \subset \overline{0x^\circ}]$ means that all the vertices in $X \backslash D(x^\circ)$ are lined up on one path $\overline{0x^\circ}$. The inclusion $[D(x^\circ) \backslash Z \subset P^i \cup P^j]$ means that the subgame with the origin at x° is an at-most-two-person game.

Example 6.2.5. A canonical "bad" tree with specific payoffs with respect to which no endpoint is a core outcome is illustrated in Figure 6.4: Here $Z = \{a, b, c, d\}$. Let $E'(S)$ be the minimal elements (with respect to the set-theoretic inclusion) of $E(S)$; in particular,

$$E'(\{1, 2\}) = \{\{a\}, \{b\}, \{c, d\}\},$$
$$E'(\{1, 3\}) = \{\{c\}, \{d\}, \{a, b\}\},$$
$$E'(\{2, 3\}) = \{\{a, c\}, \{a, d\}, \{b, c\}, \{b, d\}\}.$$

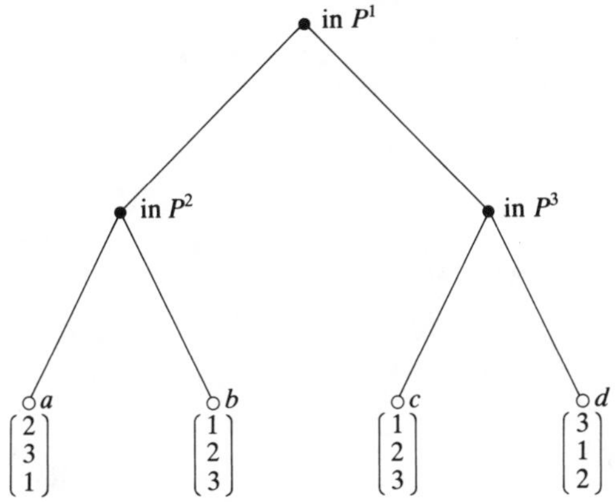

6.4 Unstable hierarchical structure

Outcome a is blocked by coalition {1, 3} who would effectively choose d; outcome d is blocked by coalition {2, 3} who is effective on $\{b, c\}$; both outcomes b and c are blocked by coalition {1, 2} who would effectively choose a. This example is a specific case of the situation of Peleg (1984a, Lemma 6.3.12, p. 132) in which the subadditive cover of E is not well-behaved. □

Remark 6.2.6. Let (K, P) be a stable extensive game form with perfect information characterized as in Figure 6.3. At the moves $x_1, \cdots, x_{H-1}$ (i.e., at the moves that precede the at-most-two-person subgame with the origin at $x°(=x_H)$), the players function more than choosing whether to end the game or to leave it with the successors. This point is illustrated in Figure 6.5: Here $Z=\{a, b, c, d\}$. The outcomes $\{b, c\}$ are the Nash equilibrium outcomes of the subgame (with the origin at x_H), and outcome c is the unique core outcome of the subgame. Outcome a is the unique Nash equilibrium outcome of the game. The unique core outcome of the game is, however, d. □

Remark 6.2.7. The extensive game form of Figure 6.5 is stable, yet has no strong equilibrium outcome with respect to the payoffs given in Figure 6.5. Indeed, one can establish: *An extensive game form with perfect information which satisfies Assumptions 6.2.2 and 6.2.3 is strongly consistent, iff it is a one-person game form.* Sufficiency of this assertion is straightforward. In order to prove necessity, let (K, P) be an at-least-two-person extensive game form with perfect information which satisfies Assumptions 6.2.2 and 6.2.3. Then there exist x_1 and $x_2 \in X$ such that (1) x_2 is an immediate successor of x_1 (i.e., $x_2 \in D(x_1)$ and $[\overline{0x_2} \backslash \overline{0x_1}] \cap X = \{x_2\}$), and (2) the successors of x_2 are all

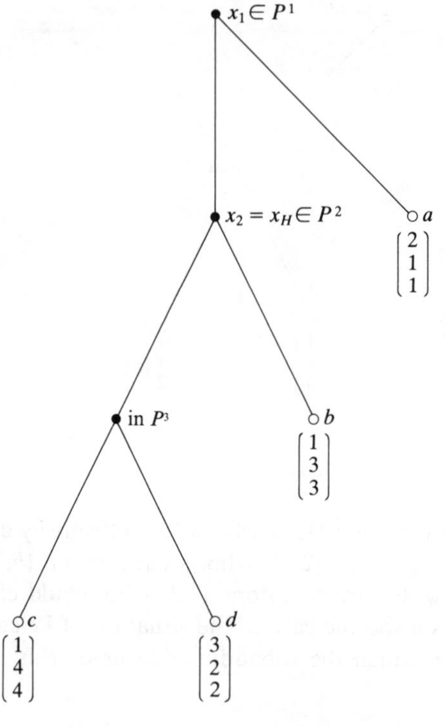

6.5 Effect on a subgame

endpoints (i.e., $D(x_2) \subset Z$). Without loss of generality, suppose $x_i \in P^i$, $i=1$, 2. Let e_1 be the edge that connects x_1 and x_2, and choose any $e_2 \in C_{x_2}$. Now define a payoff function $h: Z \rightarrow \mathbf{R}^N$ by: If $e \in C_{x_1} \backslash \{e_1\}$ and $z \in D(x_1, e) \cap Z$, then $h^1(z)=2$, $h^2(z)=1$, and $h^j(z)=0$ for all $j \in N \backslash \{1, 2\}$. If $\{z\}=D(x_2, e_2)$, then $h^1(z)=3$, $h^2(z)=2$, and $h^j(z)=0$ for all $j \in N \backslash \{1, 2\}$. If $e \in C_{x_2} \backslash \{e_2\}$ and $\{z\}=D(x_2, e)$, then $h^1(z)=1$, $h^2(z)=4$, and $h^j(z)=0$ for all $j \in N \backslash \{1, 2\}$. For all other $z \in Z$, $h^j(z)=-1$ for all $j \in N$. It is easy to verify that the game (K, P, h) possesses no strong equilibrium outcome. □

Remark 6.2.8. An effectivity function E is called *balanced* if for every balanced family $\mathscr{B}$ and every $\{B_S\}_{S \in \mathscr{B}} \in \prod_{S \in \mathscr{B}} E(S)$, it follows that $\bigcap_{j \in N} \bigcup_{S \in \mathscr{B}: S \ni j} B_S \neq \phi$. E is balanced iff for any payoff function h the non-side-payment game associated with (E, h) is balanced. Therefore, one can establish a proposition: *Every balanced effectivity function is stable.* In spite of this proposition, the balancedness condition on an effectivity function is not so useful for study of extensive game forms. Indeed, there is a stable extensive game form with perfect information whose effectivity function is

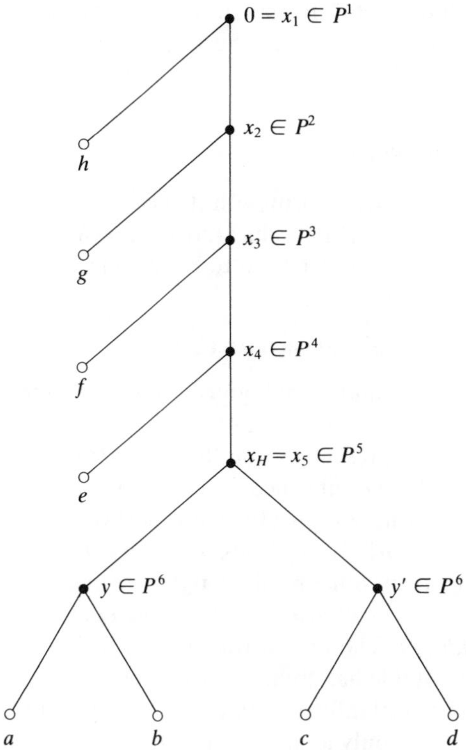

6.6 Non-balanced, convex effectivity function

not balanced. Consider, for example, the extensive game form of Figure 6.6. Here, $N=\{1, 2, 3, 4, 5, 6\}$, $Z=\{a, b, c, d, e, f, g, h\}$. Define a balanced family $\mathscr{B}:=\{S_1, S_2, S_3, S_4)\subset\mathscr{N}$ by: $S_1=\{2, 4, 6\}$, $S_2=\{1, 3, 6\}$, $S_3=\{1, 4, 5\}$, and $S_4=\{2, 3, 5\}$. Define $B_i:=B_{S_i}\in E_\alpha(S_i)$, $i=1, 2, 3, 4$, by: $B_1=\{a, c, f, h\}$, $B_2=\{b, d, e, g\}$, $B_3=\{a, b, f, g\}$, $B_4=\{c, d, e, h\}$. It is straightforward to verify that $\bigcap_{j=1}^{6}\bigcup_{S\in\mathscr{B}:S\ni j} B_S=\phi$. Combining this example with Theorem 6.2.4 and stability of a balanced effectivity function, one concludes: *Within the context of the effectivity function theory for the extensive game forms with perfect information, the balancedness assumption is strictly stronger than the convexity assumption.* □

The result of this section is in sharp contrast to the results of cooperative voting theory (see, e.g., Moulin (1983), in which the positive result (i.e., stability) has been obtained for many extensive game forms. This is the case because payoff functions in voting theory are defined *not* on Z but on the quotient $Z/\sim$, given a certain equivalence relation $\sim$. That is, the outcome space is no longer the endpoint set Z. Rather, it is the set of candidates. The equivalence relation $\sim$ on Z means that the same candidate has to be assigned to endpoints z and z', if $z \sim z'$.

6.3 α-stable hierarchical structures

The section continues to consider a firm with its laborer set N. Stability questions are addressed on general hierarchical structures (K, P, U, C) here. The game form $(\{\Sigma^j\}_{j \in N}, Z, g)$ is understood to be the one associated with (K, P, U, C). The basic assumption is:

Assumption 6.3.1. For each $z \in Z$ and each $u \in U$, $\#(\overline{0z} \cap u) \leqslant 1$.

(Recall Claim 6.1.7). Define Σ^S and Σ analogously, and let E_α and E_β be the α- and β-effectivity functions of $(\{\Sigma^j\}_{j \in N}, Z, g)$.

Given the generality of the present section, the game form is no longer tight. Recall that Dalkey (1953) established a characterization of the Nash consistent extensive game forms. Kolpin (1988) established that *the Dalkey condition is also a characterization of tightness of an extensive game form.* Due to this Kolpin result and his other result on tightness of a β-stable game form (Lemma 2.4.9), *a hierarchical structure is β-stable iff it is α-stable and satisfies the Dalkey condition.* The rest of this section will be devoted to characterizations of the α-stable hierarchical structures.

Upon introducing non-trivial information partitions, Assumption 6.2.3 becomes non-innocuous. The only assumption made in this section apart from Assumption 6.3.1 is, therefore,

Assumption 6.3.2. For each $u \in U$, $\# C_u \geqslant 2$.

The main result of this section is the following Theorem 6.3.3. The result [(i)⇒(ii)] is a consequence of Theorem 2.4.3. The remaining implications are due to Ichiishi (1987a). There is a natural partial order $\leqslant$ on the vertices: For $x, y \in X \cup Z$, $x \leqslant y$ iff y comes after x or $y = x$, i.e., iff $x \in \overline{0y}$.

Theorem 6.3.3. *Let (K, P, U, C) be a hierarchical structure that satisfies Assumptions 6.3.1 and 6.3.2, and let E_α be the α-effectivity function of the associated game form. Then, the following four conditions are equivalent:*

(i) *The α-effectivity function E_α is convex;*
(ii) *The α-effectivity function E_α is stable;*
(iii) *It is not true that there exist three distinct agents $i, j, k \in N$, a vertex $x_k \in P^k$, two distinct edges e and e' at x_k such that $D(x_k, e) \cap P^i \neq \phi$ and $D(x_k, e') \cap P^j \neq \phi$; and*
(iv) *There exist a vertex $x_H \in X$ and at most two agents $i, j \in N$ such that $(D(x_H) \cup \{x_H\}) \cap X \subset P^i \cup P^j$ and such that by denoting*

$$\overline{0x_H} \cap X = \{x_1, x_2, \cdots, x_H\},\ x_t \in P^{i_t},\ x_s \leqslant x_t \textit{ iff } s \leqslant t,$$

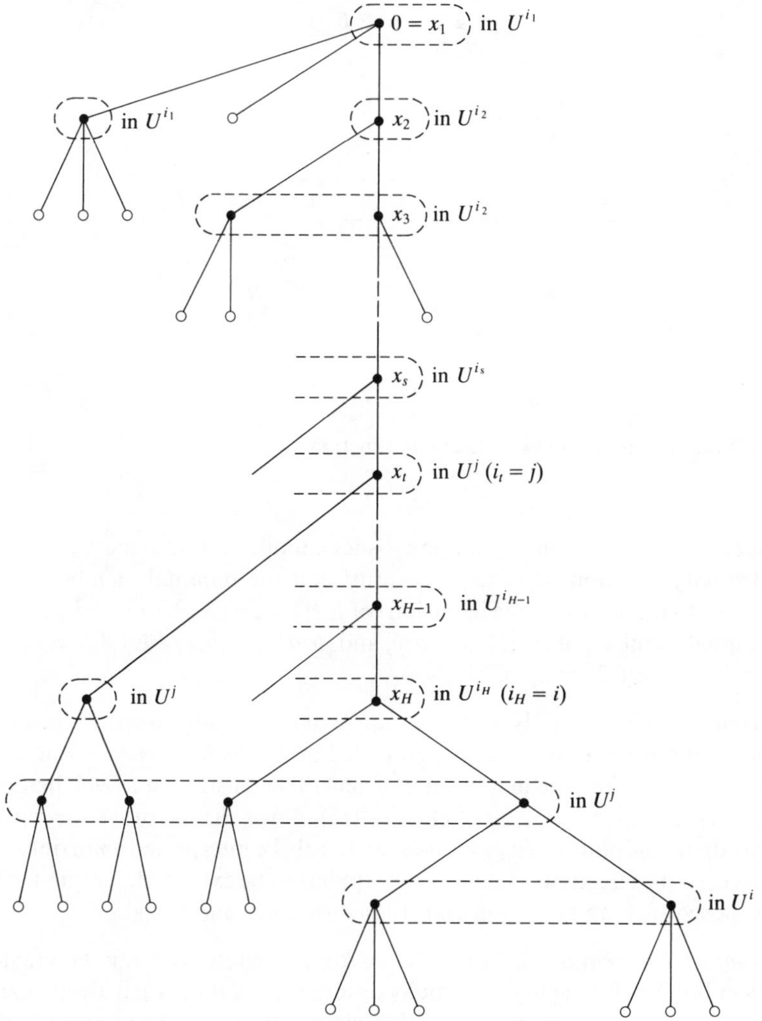

6.7 Stable hierarchical structure

it follows that $D(x_t)\backslash(D(x_{t+1}) \cup \{x_{t+1}\}) \subset P^{i_t} \cup Z$ *for every* $t = 1, 2, \cdots, H-1$.

Condition (iv) of Theorem 6.3.3 is illustrated in Figure 6.7.

Remark 6.3.4. The implication [(ii)⇒(i)] of Theorem 6.3.3 is not included in Theorem 2.4.5. To show this fact, it suffices to construct an example of an extensive game form whose α-effectivity function is convex but not maximal. Consider the extensive game form of Figure 6.8. Here, $N = \{1, 2\}$

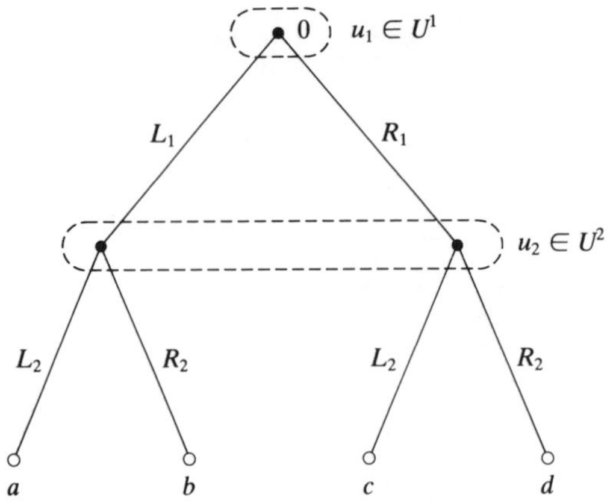

6.8 Non-maximal, convex α-effectivity function

and $Z=\{a, b, c, d\}$. This example satisfies condition (iv), so has a convex α-effectivity function. It is easy to verify that the minimal members (with respect to the set-theoretic inclusion) of $E_\alpha(\{1\})$ are $\{a, b\}$ and $\{c, d\}$, and the minimal members of $E_\alpha(\{2\})$ are $\{a, c\}$ and $\{b, d\}$. So, $\{b, c\} \notin E_\alpha(\{1\})$, yet $Z\backslash\{b, c\}=\{a, d\} \notin E_\alpha(\{2\})=E_\alpha(N\backslash\{1\})$. □

Remark 6.3.5. Precisely speaking, an extensive game form as given in Definition 6.1.4 should have been called an *extensive game form without chance moves*. For the definition of a general extensive game which allows for chance moves, see, e.g., Selten (1975). Once chance moves are introduced, the endpoints of a game tree can hardly be interpreted as an outcome space, so the effectivity function concept has to be extended. Kolpin (1989) proposed such an extension and studied stability questions. □

Proof of Theorem 6.3.3. For all $x, y \in X \cup Z$, denote by $x \wedge y$ the greatest lower bound of $\{x, y\}$ in the partially ordered set $(X \cup Z, \leqslant)$; it always exists uniquely due to the uniqueness of the origin of the tree K. For any $u \in U$, any $c \in C_u$ and any vertex x in u, denote by $c[x]$ the unique member of c that is an edge at x. Define also $D(x, c) := D(x, c[x])$.

(ii)⇒(iii). Suppose there exist three distinct agents 1, 2, $3 \in N$, a vertex $x_j \in P^j$, $j=1, 2, 3$, two distinct edges e, e' at x_3 such that $x_1 \in D(x_3, e)$ and $x_2 \in D(x_3, e')$. One needs to construct a preference profile $h\colon Z \to \mathbf{R}^N$ with respect to which an α-core outcome of the present game form Γ cannot exist.

Step 1. Let $u_j \in U^j$ be such that $x_j \in u_j$, $j=1, 2, 3$. One may assume without loss of generality that for all $i \in N\backslash\{1, 2, 3\}$

$$[\overline{0x_1}\backslash\overline{0x_3}] \cap P^i = \phi \text{ and } [\overline{0x_2}\backslash\overline{0x_3}] \cap P^i = \phi. \tag{1}$$

Set

$$S_1 := \{1, 3\},\ S_2 := \{2, 3\},\ N' := N\backslash\{1, 2, 3\},$$
$$T := N\backslash\{3\} = \{1, 2\} \cup N'.$$

For each $i = 1, 2$ choose any $\sigma_i := (\sigma_i^i\ \sigma_i^3) \in \Sigma^i \times \Sigma^3$, satisfying:

$$\forall\, x \in \overline{0x_i} \cap P^i\backslash\{x_i\}:\ \sigma_i^i(u)[x] \subset \overline{0x_i} \text{ where } x \in u \in U^i; \tag{2}$$
$$\forall \in \overline{0x_i} \cap P^3:\ \sigma_i^3(u)[x] \subset \overline{0x_i} \text{ where } x \in u \in U^3; \text{ and} \tag{3}$$
$$\text{If } \exists\, x_i' \in [\overline{0x_j}\backslash\overline{0x_3}] \cap u_i, \text{ then } \sigma_i^i(u_i)[x_i'] \not\subset \overline{0x_j} \text{ where } j \in \{1, 2\}\backslash\{i\}. \tag{4}$$

The choice of σ_i is possible due to Assumption 6.3.1. Let B_i be the set of outcomes generated by σ_i, $g(\sigma_i, \prod_{m \neq i,3}\Sigma^m)$. Then $B_i \in E_\alpha(S_i)$, $i = 1, 2$.

Choose any $\sigma_t := (\sigma_t^m)_{m \in T} \in \prod_{m \in T} \Sigma^m$ satisfying

$$\forall\, i, j = 1, 2:\ \forall\, x \in \overline{0x_i} \cap P^j\backslash\{x_i\}:\ \sigma_t^j(u)[x] \subset \overline{0x_i}, \text{ where } x \in u \in U^j; \tag{5}$$
$$\sigma_t^1(u_1) \neq \sigma_1^1(u_1); \tag{6}$$
$$\sigma_t^2(u_2) \neq \sigma_2^2(u_2); \text{ and} \tag{7}$$
$$\forall\, i \in N':\ \forall\, x \in \overline{0x_3} \cap P^i:\ \sigma_t^i(u)[x] \subset \overline{0x_3}, \text{ where } x \in U^i. \tag{8}$$

Given conditions (4) and (5), condition (6), ((7), resp.) is redundant (but consistent) if $\overline{0x_2} \cap u_1 \neq \phi$ (if $\overline{0x_1} \cap u_2 \neq \phi$, resp.). In regard to condition (8), recall condition (1). Let C be the set of outcomes generated by σ_t, $g(\sigma_t, \Sigma^3)$. Then $C \in E_\alpha(T)$.

Step 2. The three sets, $B_1 \cap D(x_3)$, $B_2 \cap D(x_3)$ and $C \cap D(x_3)$ are mutually disjoint. Indeed, $B_1 \cap B_2 \cap D(x_3) = \phi$, because of (3) and $[e \neq e']$.

To prove $B_i \cap C \cap D(x_3) = \phi$, for $i = 1, 2$, let $C_i := \{z \in C \mid x_3 \leqslant z \wedge x_i \neq x_i,\ z \wedge x_i \in P^3\}$. Then the required condition is straightforward by:

$$[B_i \cap D(x_3)] \cap [D(x_i, \sigma_t^i(u_i)) \cup C_i] = \phi,$$
$$[B_i \cap D(x_3)] \subset D(x_3, \sigma_i^3(u_3)), \text{ and}$$
$$[C \cap D(x_3)] \cap D(x_3, \sigma_i^3(u_3)) \subset D(x_i, \sigma_t^i(u_i)) \cup C_i.$$

Step 3. By the definitions given in Step 1,

$$(\forall\, z \in Z\backslash D(x_3):\ z \wedge x_3 \in P^1):\ z \notin B_1 \cup C.$$
$$(\forall\, z \in Z\backslash D(x_3):\ z \wedge x_3 \in P^2):\ z \notin B_2 \cup C.$$
$$(\forall\, z \in Z\backslash D(x_3):\ z \wedge x_3 \in P^3):\ z \notin B_1 \cup B_2.$$
$$(\forall\, z \in Z\backslash D(x_3):\ z \wedge x_3 \in P^i,\ i \in N'):\ z \notin C.$$

Step 4. Define subsets of Z by

$$Z_1 := [B_1 \cap D(x_3)] \cup \{z \in Z\backslash D(x_3) \mid z \wedge x_3 \in P^2\},$$
$$Z_2 := [B_2 \cap D(x_3)] \cup \{z \in Z\backslash D(x_3) \mid z \wedge x_3 \in P^1\},$$
$$Z_3 := [C \cap D(x_3)] \cup \{z \in Z\backslash D(x_3) \mid z \wedge x_3 \in P^3\},$$
$$Z_i := \{z \in Z\backslash D(x_3) \mid z \wedge x_3 \in P^i\},\ i \in N'.$$

Table 6.1. *Proof of Theorem 6.3.3, (ii)⇒(iii)*

j \ z	$z \in Z_1$	$z \in Z_2$	$z \in Z_3$	$z \in D(x_3) \cap Z$, $z \notin B_1 \cup B_2 \cup C$	$z \in Z_i$, $i \in N'$
$j=1$	2	0	1	0	2
$j=2$	0	1	2	0	2
$j=3$	1	2	0	0	2
$j \in N'$	1	1	2	1	0 if $j=i$ 1 if $j \neq i$

Then, in view of Step 2, these subsets and the set $D(x_3) \cap Z \backslash (B_1 \cup B_2 \cup C)$ constitute a partition of Z. Now, define h: $Z \to \mathbf{R}^N$ by Table 6.1. The (j, z)-element of the table represents the value of $h^j(z)$.

Then (a) each $z \in Z_1$ is improved upon by coalition S_2; (b) each $z \in Z_2$ is improved upon by coalition T; (c) each $z \in Z_3$ is improved upon by coalition S_1; (d) each $z \in D(x_3) \cap Z \backslash (B_1 \cup B_2 \cup C)$ is improved upon by any of the coalitions S_1, S_2 and T; and (e) each $z \in Z_i$ for some $i \in N'$ is improved upon by coalition $\{i\}$. Assertion (a) is straightforward, since $[\zeta \in B_2 \backslash D(x_3)]$ implies $[\zeta \wedge x_3 \in P^1 \cup \bigcup_{i \in N'} P^i]$ and consequently

$$\forall \zeta \in B_2\text{: } h^j(\zeta) \begin{cases} \geq 1 \text{ if } j=2, \\ =2 \text{ if } j=3. \end{cases}$$

Assertions (b)–(d) are similarly proved. To prove assertion (e), just notice that for each $i \in N'$ coalition $\{i\}$ can choose σ^i satisfying

$$(\forall \zeta \in Z \backslash D(x_3)\text{: } \zeta \wedge x_3 \in P_i)\text{: } \sigma^i(u)[\zeta \wedge x_3] \subset \overline{0x_3}$$

where $\zeta \wedge x_3 \in u \in U^i$, so

$$g(\sigma^i, \prod_{j \neq i} \Sigma^j) \subset \{\zeta \in Z \backslash D(x_3) \mid \zeta \wedge x_3 \notin P^i\} \cup D(x_3).$$

Step 4 establishes that Γ does not possess an α-core outcome with respect to h.

(iii)⇒(iv). Consider $x_1 = 0 \in P^{i_1}$. If $D(x_1) \backslash Z \subset P^{i_1}$, there is nothing to prove, so assume $\exists j_1 \in N \backslash \{i_1\}$ and $\exists e_1$ edge at x_1 such that $D(x_1, e_1) \cap P^{j_1} \neq \phi$. By (iii), $D(x_1, e) \backslash Z \subset P^{i_1} \cup P^{j_1}$ for all edges e at x_1 other than e_1. If $\forall k \in N \backslash \{i_1, j_1\}$: $D(x_1, e_1) \cap P^k = \phi$, then $D(x_1) \backslash Z \subset P^{i_1} \cup P^{j_1}$ and there is nothing to prove, so assume $\exists k_1 \in N \backslash \{i_1, j_1\}$: $D(x_1, e_1) \cap P^{k_1} \neq \phi$. Then, again by (iii), $D(x_1, e) \backslash Z \subset P^{i_1}$ for all edges e at x_1 other than e_1.

Let x_2 be the endpoint of edge e_1 other than x_1, and let $x_2 \in P^{i_2}$. Repeat the same argument on x_2 as in the preceding paragraph.

Continue this procedure until the required point x_H is reached.

(iv)⇒(i). Choose any $S, T \in \mathcal{N}$, $B \in E_\alpha(S)$ and $C \in E_\alpha(T)$. One has to show that $B \cap C \in E_\alpha(S \cup T)$ or $B \cup C \in E_\alpha(S \cap T)$. Since the α-effectivity function is superadditive, one may assume without loss of generality that $S \cap T \neq \phi$. One may also assume without loss of generality that B and C are minimal sets, i.e., B (C, resp.) are the outcomes generated by σ_B^S (by σ_C^T, resp.). There are four mutually exclusive, exhaustive cases: (1) $B \cap D(x_H) = \phi$ and $C \cap D(x_H) = \phi$; (2) $B \cap D(x_H) \neq \phi$ and $C \cap D(x_H) \neq \phi$; (3) $B \cap D(x_H) \neq \phi$ and $C \cap D(x_H) = \phi$; and (4) $B \cap D(x_H) = \phi$ and $C \cap D(x_H) \neq \phi$. By symmetry, one needs to consider only cases (1)–(3).

Case (1): The specific vertices $x_1, x_2, \cdots, x_H$ are given in condition (iv). Let $x_h \in u_h \in U^{i_h}$, for all $h = 1, 2, \cdots, H$. There exists h: $1 \leqslant h < H$, such that $i_h \in S$ and the edge $\sigma_B^{i_h}(u_h)[x_h]$ leads to the unique outcome $z_{i_h} \in B$ after x_h. Choose h as the smallest such number. Then,

$$B = \bigcup \{Z \cap D(x_j) \backslash (D(x_{j+1}) \cup \{x_{j+1}\}) \mid j < h,\ i_j \notin S\} \cup \{z_{i_h}\}.$$

One may also choose k as the smallest number such that $1 \leqslant k < H$, $i_k \in T$, and the edge $\sigma_C^{i_k}(u_k)[x_k]$ leads to the unique outcome $z'_{i_k} \in C$ after x_k. Without loss of generality, assume $h \leqslant k$. Then,

$$C = \bigcup \{Z \cap D(x_j) \backslash (D(x_{j+1}) \cup \{x_{j+1}\}) \mid j < k,\ i_j \notin T\} \cup \{z'_{i_k}\}.$$

$$B \cap C = \begin{cases} \bigcup \{Z \cap D(x_j) \backslash (D(x_{j+1}) \cup \{x_{j+1}\}) \mid j < h,\ i_j \notin S \cup T\} \cup \{z_{i_h}\}, \\ \qquad \text{if } [h = k,\ z_{i_h} = z'_{i_k}] \text{ or } [h < k,\ i_h \notin T]; \\ \bigcup \{Z \cap D(x_j) \backslash (D(x_{j+1}) \cup \{x_{j+1}\}) \mid j < h,\ i_j \notin S \cup T\}, \\ \qquad \text{if } [h = k,\ z_{i_h} \neq z'_{i_k}] \text{ or } [h < k,\ i_h \in T]. \end{cases}$$

$$\begin{aligned} B \cup C = {} & \bigcup \{Z \cap D(x_j) \backslash (D(x_{j+1}) \cup \{x_{j+1}\}) \mid j < h,\ i_j \notin S \cap T\} \cup \{z_{i_h}\} \\ & \cup \bigcup \{Z \cap D(x_j) \backslash (D(x_{j+1}) \cup \{x_{j+1}\}) \mid h \leqslant j < k,\ i_j \notin T\} \cup \{z'_{i_k}\}. \end{aligned}$$

If $h = k$, then $i_h \in S \cap T$. By having i_j choose $\sigma_B^{i_j}(u_j)$ for all $j \leqslant h$ for which $i_j \in S \cap T$, one concludes $B \cup C \in E_\alpha(S \cap T)$. Suppose, therefore, $h < k$. If $i_h \notin T$, then $z_{i_h} \in B \cap C$. By having i_j choose either $\sigma_B^{i_j}(u_j)$ or $\sigma_C^{i_j}(u_j)$ for all $j \leqslant h$ for which $i_j \in S \cup T$, one concludes $B \cap C \in E_\alpha(S \cup T)$. If $i_h \in T$, then by having i_j choose $\sigma_B^{i_j}(u_j)$ for all $j \leqslant h$ for which $i_j \in S \cap T$, one concludes $B \cup C \in E_\alpha(S \cap T)$.

Case (2): By symmetry in S and T, it suffices to consider only the following ten subcases:

(a) $[i, j \notin S]$ and $[i, j \notin T]$;
(b) $[i \in S, j \notin S]$ and $[i, j \notin T]$;
(c) $[i \in S, j \notin S]$ and $[i \in T, j \notin T]$;

(d) $[i \notin S, j \in S]$ and $[i, j \notin T]$;
(e) $[i \notin S, j \in S]$ and $[i \in T, j \notin T]$;
(f) $[i \notin S, j \in S]$ and $[i \notin T, j \in T]$;
(g) $[i, j \in S]$ and $[i, j \notin T]$;
(h) $[i, j \in S]$ and $[i \in T, j \notin T]$;
(i) $[i, j \in S]$ and $[i \notin T, j \in T]$;
(j) $[i, j \in S]$ and $[i, j \in T]$.

Now clearly,

$$B \backslash D(x_H) = \bigcup \{Z \cap D(x_j) \backslash (D(x_{j+1}) \cup \{x_{j+1}\}) \mid 1 \leqslant j < H,\ i_j \notin S\},$$
$$C \backslash D(x_H) = \bigcup \{Z \cap D(x_j) \backslash (D(x_{j+1}) \cup \{x_{j+1}\}) \mid 1 \leqslant j < H,\ i_j \notin T\},$$

so

$$(B \cap C) \backslash D(x_H) = \bigcup \{Z \cap D(x_j) \backslash (D(x_{j+1}) \cup \{x_{j+1}\}) \mid 1 \leqslant j < H,\ i_j \notin S \cup T\},$$
$$(B \cup C) \backslash D(x_H) = \bigcup \{Z \cap D(x_j) \backslash (D(x_{j+1}) \cup \{x_{j+1}\}) \mid 1 \leqslant j < H,\ i_j \notin S \cap T\}.$$

Also,

$$B \cap D(x_H) = \{g(\sigma^S, \sigma^{N \backslash S}) \mid \sigma^{N \backslash S} \in \Sigma^{N \backslash S}\} \cap D(x_H),$$

for some σ^S such that $\sigma^{i_h}(u_h) \subset \overline{0x_H}$ for all h: $1 \leqslant h < H$ for which $i_h \in S$. This set would be $D(x_H) \cap Z$ if $i, j \notin S$; and would be a point in $D(x_H) \cap Z$ if $i, j \in S$. An analogous characterization is valid for $C \cap D(x_H)$. Therefore, it is straightforward to check $B \cap C \in E_\alpha(S \cup T)$ for subcases (a), (b), (d), (e) and (g); and $B \cup C \in E_\alpha(S \cap T)$ for subcases (a), (b), (c), (d), (f), (g), (h), (i) and (j).

Case (3): Here, B (C, resp.) is characterized as in Case (2) (as in Case (1), resp.). So

$$B \cap C = (B \cap C) \backslash D(x_H)$$
$$= \begin{cases} \bigcup \{Z \cap D(x_j) \backslash (D(x_{j+1}) \cup \{x_{j+1}\}) \mid j < k,\ i_j \notin S \cup T\} \cup \{z'_{i_k}\}, & \text{if } i_k \notin S; \\ \bigcup \{Z \cap D(x_j) \backslash (D(x_{j+1}) \cup \{x_{j+1}\}) \mid j < k,\ i_j \notin S \cup T\}, & \text{if } i_k \in S. \end{cases}$$

If $i_k \in S$, then $i_k \in S \cap T$. By having i_j choose $\sigma_C^{i_j}(u_j)$ for all $j \leqslant k$ for which $i_j \in S \cap T$, one concludes $B \cup C \in E_\alpha(S \cap T)$. If $i_k \notin S$, then $z'_{i_k} \in B \cap C$. By having i_j choose the edge that lies on $\overline{0x_H}$ for all $j < k$ for which $i_j \in S \cup T$, and by having i_k choose $\sigma_C^{i_k}(u_k)$, one concludes $B \cap C \in E_\alpha(S \cup T)$. □

Notation

For statements P and Q:

$P \Rightarrow Q$. If statement P holds true, then statement Q holds true.
$P \Leftrightarrow Q$. Statement P holds true if and only if statement Q holds true.
P iff Q. Statement P holds true if and only if statement Q holds true.
$\neg P$. The negation of statement P.

For sets A and B:

$\# A :=$ the cardinality of A.
$2^A :=$ the power set of A; the family $\{C \mid C \subset A\}$.
$x \in A$. Point x is a member of set A.
$A \subset B$. Set A is included in set B; that is, $[x \in A \Rightarrow x \in B]$.
$A \cup B$. The union of A and B; the set $\{x \mid x \in A \text{ or } x \in B\}$.
$A \cap B$. The intersection of A and B; the set $\{x \mid x \in A \text{ and } x \in B\}$.
$A \backslash B$. The set-theoretical difference, $\{x \mid x \in A \text{ and } x \notin B\}$.
$A + B$. The set-theoretical sum; identified with the set of those (i, x) for which $(1, x) \in \{1\} \times A$ or $(2, x) \in \{2\} \times B$.
$A \times B$. The Cartesian product of A and B.
$\exists x \in X$: $P(x)$. There exists x in X such that statement $P(x)$ holds true.
$\forall x \in X$: $P(x)$. For any x in X, statement $P(x)$ holds true.
$\phi :=$ the empty set.
$A/\sim :=$ The partition of A into the equivalence classes determined by an equivalence relation $\sim$ in A, namely, the quotient set of A over $\sim$.
f: $A \rightarrow B$. Function f from A to B, which assigns point $f(x)$ in B to each point $x \in A$, or correspondence f from A to the subsets of B, which assigns subset $f(x)$ of B to each point x in A. In either case, the mapping may also be written as $x \mapsto f(x)$.

For functions $f: A \to B$ and $g: B \to C$, and for correspondence $F: A \to B$:

$g \circ f :=$ the composite of f and g, defined by $(g \circ f)(x) := g(f(x))$.
gr $F :=$ the graph of F; the set $\{(x, y) \in A \times B \mid y \in F(x)\}$.

For a finite set N:

$\mathbf{R} :=$ the set of real numbers, endowed with the usual metric.
$\mathbf{R}_+ :=$ the set of nonnegative real numbers.
$\mathbf{R}^N :=$ the Euclidean space[1] whose coordinates are indexed by set N.
$\mathbf{R}^n :=$ the n-dimensional Euclidean space.[2]
$\mathbf{R}_+^N :=$ the nonnegative orthant of $\mathbf{R}^N$.
$\Delta^N :=$ the unit simplex[3] in $\mathbf{R}^N$; the set $\{x \in \mathbf{R}_+^N \mid \sum_{j \in N} x_j = 1\}$.
$\Delta^{n-1} :=$ the $(n-1)$-dimensional unit simplex.

For $x \in \mathbf{R}$,

$\lceil x \rceil :=$ the smallest integer z such that $z \geqslant x$.

For $x, y \in \mathbf{R}^N$, and for $S \subset N$:

$x \geqslant y$ means $x_j \geqslant y_j$ for all $j \in N$.
$x > y$ means $[x \geqslant y$ and $x \neq y]$.
$x \gg y$ means $x_j > y_j$ for all $j \in N$.
$\|x\|_1 := \sum_{j \in N} |x_j|$.
$\|x\| :=$ the Euclidean norm, $(\sum_{j \in N} (x_j)^2)^{\frac{1}{2}}$.
$\|x\|_\infty := \max_{j \in N} |x_j|$.
$x \cdot y :=$ the Euclidean inner product, $\sum_{j \in N} x_j y_j$.
$\chi_S :=$ the characteristic vector of S; the vector in $\mathbf{R}^N$ defined by $(\chi_S)_j := 1$ if $j \in S$, $(\chi_S)_j := 0$ if $j \notin S$.

For sets X and Y in a vector space E:

aff $X :=$ the affine hull of X.
co $X :=$ the convex hull of X.
ext $X :=$ the set of extreme points of X.
icr $X :=$ the algebraic relative interior[4] of X.
span $X :=$ the linear subspace spanned by X.
$X + Y :=$ the vector sum of X and Y; the set $\{x + y \mid x \in X$ and $y \in Y\}$.
$\mathbf{0} :=$ the origin of E.

[1] For $S \subset N$, $\mathbf{R}^S$ is sometimes identified with the subspace $\{x \in \mathbf{R}^N \mid \forall j \notin S: x_j = 0\}$.
[2] For $n := \# N$, $\mathbf{R}^N$ and $\mathbf{R}^n$ are identified.
[3] For $S \subset N$, Δ^S is sometimes identified with the subface $\{x \in \Delta^N \mid \forall j \notin S: x_j = 0\}$.
[4] Whenever this concept appears in the text, space E is assumed finite dimensional and set X is assumed convex. In this case, the algebraic concept icr X coincides with the concept of relative interior, which involves the Euclidean topology on E.

For a square matrix A,

$\det A :=$ the determinant of A.

For a set X:

$\oplus_X \mathbf{R} :=$ the set of all functions from X to $\mathbf{R}$ with a finite support; the set $\{f\colon X \to \mathbf{R} \mid f(x) = 0$ for all but finitely many $x\}$.

For a set X in a topological space E:

$\mathring{X} :=$ the topological interior of X in E.
$\bar{X} =$ the topological closure of X in E.
$\mathrm{ca}(E) :=$ the space of all countably additive measures on the Borel σ-algebra of subsets of E, endowed with the weak* topology.
$\mathcal{M}(E) :=$ the space of all probability measures on the Borel σ-algebra of subsets of E, endowed with the weak* topology.

References

Abdou, J. (1982). Stabilité de la fonction veto cas du veto maximal. *Mathématiques et Sciences Humaines* **80**, 39–63.

(1987). Stable effectivity functions with an infinity of players and alternatives. *Journal of Mathematical Economics* **16**, 291–295.

(1988). Neutral veto correspondences with a continuum of alternatives. *International Journal of Game Theory* **17**, 135–164.

Abdou, J. and J.-F. Mertens (1988). Correlated effectivity functions. CORE Discussion Paper, No. 8823, CORE, Université Catholique de Louvain.

Alchian, A. A. and H. Demsetz (1972). Production, information costs, and economic organization. *American Economic Review* **62**, 777–795.

Alkan, A., G. Demange and D. Gale (1991). Fair allocation of indivisible goods and criteria of justice. *Econometrica* **59**, 1023–1039.

Arrow, K. J. (1951). An extension of the basic theorems of classical welfare economics. In J. Neyman (ed.), *Proceedings of the Second Berkeley Symposium on Mathematical Statistics and Probability*, pp. 507–532. Berkeley: Univ. of California Press.

(1969). The organization of economic activity: Issues pertinent to the choice of market versus nonmarket allocation. In U.S. Joint Economic Committee, 91st Congress, 1st Session, *The Analysis and Evaluation of Public Expenditures: The PPB System*, pp. 47–64. Washington, DC: U.S. Government Printing Office. (Reproduced as: Arrow, K. J., Political and economic evaluation of social effects and externalities. In J. Margolis (ed.), *The Analysis of Public Output*, pp. 1–23. New York: National Bureau of Economic Research, 1970.)

(1974). *The Limits of Organization*. New York: Norton.

Arrow, K. J. and G. Debreu (1954). Existence of an equilibrium for a competitive economy. *Econometrica* **22**, 265–290.

Arrow, K. J. and F. Hahn (1971). *General Competitive Analysis*. San Francisco: Holden-Day.

Aubin, J.-P. (1979). *Mathematical Methods of Game and Economic Theory*. Amsterdam: North-Holland.

Aumann, R. J. (1959). Acceptable points in general cooperative n-person games. In A. W. Tucker and R. D. Luce (eds.), *Contributions to the Theory of Games, Vol. IV*, pp. 287–324. Princeton: Princeton Univ. Press.

(1961). The core of a cooperative game without side payments. *Transactions of the American Mathematical Society* **98**, 539–552.

(1967). A survey of cooperative games without side payments. In M. Shubik (ed.), *Essays in Mathematical Economics (in Honor of Oskar Morgenstern)*, pp. 3–27. Princeton: Princeton Univ. Press.

(1974). Subjectivity and correlation in randomized strategies. *Journal of Mathematical Economics* **1**, 67–96.

Aumann, R. J. and B. Peleg (1960). Von Neumann-Morgenstern solutions to cooperative games without side payments. *Bulletin of the American Mathematical Society* **66**, 173–179.

Barnard, C. I. (1938). *The Functions of the Executive*. Cambridge, MA: Harvard Univ. Press.

Barro, R. and H. Grossman (1976). *Money, Employment and Inflation*. Cambridge, U.K.: Cambridge Univ. Press.

Baumol, W. J. (1959). *Business Behavior, Value and Growth*. New York: Macmillan.

Baumol, W. J., E. E. Bailey and R. D. Willig (1977). Weak invisible hand theorems on the sustainability of multiproduct natural monopoly. *American Economic Review* **67**, 350–365.

Benassy, J.-P. (1975). Neo-Keynesian disequilibrium theory in a monetary economy. *Review of Economic Studies* **42**, 503–523.

Berle, Jr., A. A. and G. C. Means (1932). *The Modern Corporation and Private Property*. New York: Macmillan.

Bernheim, B. D., B. Peleg and M. D. Whinston (1987). Coalition-proof Nash equilibria I: Concepts. *Journal of Economic Theory* **42**, 1–12.

Bernheim, B. D. and M. D. Whinston (1987). Coalition-proof Nash equilibria II: Applications. *Journal of Economic Theory* **42**, 13–29.

Billera, L. J. (1970). Some theorems on the core of an *n*-person game without side-payments. *SIAM Journal on Applied Mathematics* **18**, 567–579.

(1974). On games without side payments arising from a general class of markets. *Journal of Mathematical Economics* **1**, 129–139.

Böhm, V. (1973). Firms and market equilibria in a private ownership economy. *Zeitschrift für Nationalökonomie* **33**, 87–102.

(1974). The core of an economy with production. *Review of Economic Studies* **41**, 429–436.

Bondareva, O. N. (1962). Teoriia iadra v igre *n* lits. *Vestnik Leningrad University Math.* **13**, 141–142 (in Russian).

(1963). Nekotorye primeneniia metodov linejnogo programmirovaniia k teorii kooperativnykh igr. *Problemy Kibernet* **10**, 119–139.

Border, K. C. (1984). A core existence theorem for games without ordered preferences. *Econometrica* **52**, 1537–1542.

(1985). *Fixed Point Theorems with Applications to Economics and Game Theory*. Cambridge, U.K.: Cambridge Univ. Press.

Brouwer, L. E. J. (1912). Invarianz des *n*-dimensionalen Gebiets. *Mathematische Annalen* **71**, 305–313.

Browder, F. E. (1968). The fixed point theory of multi-valued mappings in topological vector spaces. *Mathematische Annalen* **177**, 283–301.

Brus, W. (1981). Political pluralism and markets in communist systems. Paper presented at the Sixth Bosphorus Workshop on Industrial Democracy, Boğaziçi Universitesi, Istanbul, June 22–26.

Cain, G. G. (1976). The challenge of segmented labor market theories to orthodox theory: A survey. *Journal of Economic Literature* **14**, 1215–1257.

Chakrabarti, S. K. (1985). Refinements of some core-like solution concept and an application to oligopolies. Ph.D. Dissertation. Univ. of Iowa.

(1988). Refinements of the β-core and the strong equilibrium and the Aumann proposition. *International Journal of Game Theory* **17**, 205–224.

(1990). Characterizations of the equilibrium payoffs of inertia supergames. *Journal of Economic Theory* **51**, 171–183.

Champsaur, P. (1975). How to share the cost of a public good? *International Journal of Game Theory* **4**, 113–129.

Chandler, Jr., A. D. (1962). *Strategy and Structure*. Cambridge, MA: MIT Press.

Chun, Y. and W. Thomson (1988). Monotonicity properties of bargaining solutions when applied to economics. *Mathematical Social Sciences* **15**, 11–27.

Clower, R. (1966). The Keynesian counterrevolution: A theoretical appraisal. In F. P. R. Brechling and F. H. Hahn (eds.), *The Theory of Interest Rates*, pp. 103–125. London: Macmillan.

Coase, R. H. (1937). The nature of the firm. *Economica* **4**, 386–405. Reprinted in K. E. Boulding and G. J. Stigler (eds.), *Readings in Price Theory*, pp. 331–351. Chicago: Irwin, 1952. Reprinted also in Coase (1988), pp. 33–55.

(1960). The problem of social cost. *Journal of Law and Economics* **3**, 1–44. Reprinted in Coase (1988), pp. 95–156.

(1988). *The Firm, the Market, and the Law*. Chicago: Univ. of Chicago Press.

Cournot, A. A. (1838). *Recherches sur les principes mathématiques de la théorie des richesses*. Paris: Libraire des sciences politiques et sociales, M. Rivière et cie. (English transl.: *Researches into the Mathematical Principles of the Theory of Wealth*. New York: Macmillan, 1897.)

Dalkey, N. (1953). Equivalence of information patterns and essentially determinate games. In H. W. Kuhn and A. W. Tucker (eds.), *Contributions to the Theory of Games, Vol. II*, pp. 217–243. Princeton: Princeton Univ. Press.

Debreu, G. (1951). The coefficient of resource utilization. *Econometrica* **19**, 273–292.

(1952). A social equilibrium existence theorem. *Proceedings of the National Academy of Sciences of the U.S.A.* **38**, 886–893.

(1959). *Theory of Value*. New York: Wiley.

Debreu, G. and H. Scarf (1963). A limit theorem on the core of an economy. *International Economic Review* **4**, 235–246.

Delbaen, F. (1974). Convex games and extreme points. *Journal of Mathematical Analysis and Applications* **45**, 210–233.

Demange, G. (1987). Nonmanipulable cores. *Econometrica* **55**, 1057–1074.

Doeringer, P. B. and M. J. Piore (1971). *Internal Labor Markets and Manpower Analysis*. Lexington: Heath.

Domar, E. (1966). The Soviet collective farm. *American Economic Review* **56**, Part 1, 734–757. Reprinted in Vanek (1975), pp. 369–393.

Dubey, P. (1980). Nash equilibria of market games: Finiteness and inefficiency. *Journal of Economic Theory* **22**, 363–376.
(1982). Price-quantity strategic market games. *Econometrica* **50**, 111–126.
(1986). Inefficiency of Nash equilibria. *Mathematics of Operations Research* **11**, 1–8.
Dugundji, J. and A. Granas (1982). *Fixed Point Theory, Vol.I.* Warszawa: PWN-Polish Scientific Publishers.
Dutta, B. (1984). Effectivity functions and acceptable game forms. *Econometrica* **52**, 1151–1166.
Edgeworth, F. Y. (1881). *Mathematical Psychics.* London: Kegan Paul.
Fan, K. (1952). Fixed-point and minimax theorems in locally convex topological linear spaces. *Proceedings of the National Academy of Sciences of the U.S.A.* **38**, 121–126.
(1956). On systems of linear inequalities. In H. W. Kuhn and A. W. Tucker (eds.), *Linear Inequalities and Related Systems*, pp. 99–156. Princeton: Princeton Univ. Press.
(1968). A covering property of simplexes. *Mathematica Scandinavica* **22**, 17–20.
(1969). Extensions of two fixed point theorems of F. E. Browder. *Mathematische Zeitschrift* **112**, 234–240.
(1970). A combinatorial property of pseudo-manifolds and covering properties of simplexes. *Journal of Mathematical Analysis and Applications* **31**, 68–80.
(1972). A minimax inequality and applications. In O. Shisha (ed.), *Inequalities III*, pp. 103–113. New York: Academic Press.
(1984). Some properties of convex sets related to fixed point theorems. *Mathematische Annalen* **266**, 519–537.
(1990). A survey of some results closely related to the Knaster-Kuratowski-Mazurkiewicz theorem. In T. Ichiishi, A. Neyman and Y. Tauman (eds.), *Game Theory and Applications*, pp. 358–370. New York: Academic Press.
Ferfila, B. (1991). *The Economics and Politics of the Socialist Debacle: The Yugoslav Case.* Lanham: University Press of America.
Florenzano, M. (1989). On the non-emptiness of the core of a coalitional production economy without ordered preferences. *Journal of Mathematical Analysis and Applications* **141**, 484–490.
Friedman, J. W. (1986). *Game Theory with Applications to Economics.* Oxford: Oxford Univ. Press.
Gale, D. (1955). The law of supply and demand. *Mathematica Scandinavica* **3**, 155–169.
(1984). Equilibrium in a discrete exchange economy with money. *International Journal of Game Theory* **13**, 61–64.
Gillies, D. B. (1959). Solutions to general non-zero-sum games. In A. W. Tucker and R. D. Luce (eds.), *Contributions to the Theory of Games, Vol. IV*, pp. 47–85. Princeton: Princeton Univ. Press.
Glicksberg, I. L. (1952). A further generalization of the Kakutani fixed point theorem, with application to Nash equilibrium points. *Proceedings of the American Mathematical Society* **3**, 170–174.
Grandmont, J.-M. (1974). On the short-run equilibrium in a monetary economy. In

J. H. Drèze (ed.), *Allocation under Uncertainty: Equilibrium and Optimality*, pp. 213–228. London: Macmillan.

(1977). Temporary general equilibrium theory. *Econometrica* **45**, 535–572.

(1983). *Money and Value: A Reconsideration of Classical and Neoclassical Monetary Theories*. Cambridge, U.K.: Cambridge Univ. Press.

Gurvič, V. A. (1982). On the normal form of positional games. *Soviet Math. Dokl.* **25**, 572–575.

Hammond, P. (1975). Charity: Altruism or cooperative egoism? In E. S. Phelps (ed.), *Altruism, Morality, and Economic Theory*, pp. 115–131. New York: Russell Sage Foundation.

Hart, O. (1988). The nature and extent of the firm. Fisher-Schultz lecture, the European Meeting of the Econometric Society, Bologna, Italy, August 29–September 2.

Hayek, F. A. von (1935). *Collectivist Economic Planning*. London: Routledge.

Hicks, J. R. (1939). *Value and Capital*. 2nd ed. Oxford: Clarendon Press.

Hildenbrand, W. (1968). The core of an economy with a measure space of economic agents. *Review of Economic Studies* **35**, 443–452.

(1970). Existence of equilibria for economies with production and a measure space of consumers. *Econometrica* **38**, 608–623.

Hunnius, G., G. D. Garson and J. Case (eds.) (1973). *Workers' Control: A Reader on Labor and Social Change*. New York: Random House.

Ichiishi, T. (1975). Towards the general equilibrium theory of the labor-managed market economy. Discussion Paper No. 172, Center for Mathematical Studies in Economics and Management Science, Northwestern Univ. Revised as: T. Ichiishi, Labor-managed market economy: A general equilibrium approach. Mimeo., 1976.

(1977). Coalition structure in a labor-managed market economy. *Econometrica* **45**, 341–360.

(1980). A note on 'Existence of a core in a production economy with increasing returns to scale'. GSIA Working Paper No. 65–79–80, Carnegie-Mellon Univ.

(1981a). On the Knaster-Kuratowski-Mazurkiewicz-Shapley theorem. *Journal of Mathematical Analysis and Applications* **81**, 297–299.

(1981b). A social coalitional equilibrium existence lemma. *Econometrica* **49**, 369–377.

(1981c). Super-modularity: Applications to convex games and to the greedy algorithm for LP. *Journal of Economic Theory* **25**, 283–286.

(1982a). Non-cooperation and cooperation. In M. Deistler, E. Fürst and G. Schwödiauer (eds.), *Games, Economic Dynamics, and Time Series Analysis (A Symposium in Memorial Oskar Morgenstern)*, pp. 14–48. Vienna/Würzburg: Physica-Verlag.

(1982b). Management versus ownership, I. *International Economic Review* **23**, 323–336.

(1983). *Game Theory for Economic Analysis*. New York: Academic Press.

(1985). Management versus ownership, II. *European Economic Review* **27**, 115–138.

(1986a). The effectivity function approach to the core. In W. Hildenbrand, *et al.*

(eds.), *Contributions to Mathematical Economics (in Honor of Gerard Debreu)*, pp. 269–293. Amsterdam/New York: North-Holland.

(1986b). Stable extensive game forms with perfect information. *International Journal of Game Theory* **15**, 163–174.

(1987a). α-stable extensive game forms. *Mathematics of Operations Research* **12**, 626–633.

(1987b). Strong equilibria. In B.-L. Lin and S. Simons (eds.), *Nonlinear and Convex Analysis (Proceedings in Honor of Ky Fan)*, pp. 107–125. New York: Marcel Dekker.

(1987c). Strong equilibria of a repeated game with randomized strategies. *Mathematical Social Sciences* **14**, 201–224.

(1987d). Weak dominance of cores. Working Paper No. 87–05, Department of Economics, Ohio State Univ.

(1988a). Core-like solutions for games with probabilistic choice of strategies. *Mathematical Social Sciences* **15**, 51–60.

(1988b). Alternative version of Shapley's theorem on closed coverings of a simplex. *Proceedings of the American Mathematical Society* **104**, 759–763.

(1989). On Peleg's theorem for stability of convex effectivity functions: An alternative proof and applications to authority structures. *European Journal of Political Economy* **5**, Special Issue edited by M. R. Sertel and A. Steinherr on Economic Design, 149–160.

(1990a). Comparative cooperative game theory. *International Journal of Game Theory* **19**, 139–152.

(1990b). A contribution to the macro theory of comparative economic systems. *Journal of Comparative Economics* **14**, 15–32.

(forthcoming). Cooperative nature of the firm: Narrative. *Managerial and Decision Economics*. Special Issue edited by Koji Okuguchi on Labor-managed economy and its related problems.

Ichiishi, T. and A. Idzik (1990). Theorems on closed coverings of a simplex and their applications to cooperative game theory. *Journal of Mathematical Analysis and Applications* **146**, 259–270.

(1991). Closed covers of compact convex polyhedra. *International Journal of Game Theory* **20**, 161–169.

Ichiishi, T. and M. Quinzii (1983). Decentralization for the core of a production economy with increasing returns. *International Economic Review* **24**, 397–412.

Ichiishi, T. and J. J. Schäffer (1983). The topological core of a game without sidepayments. *Economic Studies Quarterly* **34**, 1–8.

Ichiishi, T. and S. Weber (1978). Some theorems on the core of a non-sidepayment game with a measure space of players. *International Journal of Game Theory* **7**, 95–112.

Kahn, C. and D. Mookherjee (1992). The good, the bad, and the ugly: Coalition proof Nash equilibrium in infinite games. *Games and Economic Behavior* **4**, 101–121.

Kakutani, S. (1941). A generalization of Brouwer's fixed-point theorem. *Duke Mathematical Journal* **8**, 457–459.

Kannai, Y. (1969). Countably additive measures in cores of games. *Journal of*

Mathematical Analysis and Applications **27**, 227–240.

(1970). On closed coverings of simplexes. *SIAM Journal on Applied Mathematics* **19**, 459–461.

Keiding, H. (1985). Necessary and sufficient conditions for stability of effectivity functions. *International Journal of Game Theory* **14**, 93–101.

Keiding, H. and L. Thorlund-Petersen (1987). The core of a cooperative game without side payments. *Journal of Optimization Theory and Applications* **54**, 273–288.

Kern, R. (1985). The Shapley transfer value without zero weights. *International Journal of Game Theory* **14**, 73–92.

Kerr, C. (1954). The Balkanization of labor markets. In E. W. Bakke (ed.), *Labor Mobility and Economic Opportunity*, pp. 92–110. Cambridge/New York: The Technology Press of MIT/Wiley.

Keynes, J. M. (1936). *The General Theory of Employment, Interest and Money*. London: Macmillan.

Klein, L. R. (1947). *The Keynesian Revolution*. New York: Macmillan.

Kleindorfer, P. R. and M. R. Sertel (1979). Profit-maximizing design of enterprises through incentives. *Journal of Economic Theory* **20**, 318–339.

Knaster, B., C. Kuratowski and S. Mazurkiewicz (1929). Ein Beweis des Fixpunktsatzes für *n*-dimensionale Simplexe. *Fundumenta Mathematicae* **14**, 132–137.

Knight, F. H. (1921). *Risk, Uncertainty and Profits*. Boston: Hart, Schaffner and Marx.

Kolpin, V. W. (1986). Extensions and applications of effectivity function theory. Ph.D. Dissertation. Univ. of Iowa.

(1988). A note on tight extensive game forms. *International Journal of Game Theory* **17**, 187–191.

(1989). Core implementation via dynamic game forms. *Social Choice and Welfare* **6**, 205–225.

Kotz, D. M. (1978). *Bank Control of Modern Corporations*. Berkeley: Univ. of California Press.

Kuhn, H. W. (1953). Extensive games and the problem of information. In H. W. Kuhn and A. W. Tucker (eds.), *Contributions to the Theory of Games, Vol. II*, pp. 193–216. Princeton: Princeton Univ. Press.

Kurz, M. (1977). Altruistic equilibrium. In B. Balassa and R. Nelson (eds.), *Economic Progress, Private Values, and Policy (Essays in Honor of William Fellner)*, pp. 177–200. Amsterdam: North-Holland.

Lange, O. (1942). The foundations of welfare economics. *Econometrica* **10**, 215–228.

Larner, R. J. (1966). Ownership and control in the 200 largest nonfinancial corporations, 1929 and 1963. *American Economic Review* **56**, 777–787.

Leijonhufvud, A. (1968). *On Keynesian Economics and the Economics of Keynes*. New York: Oxford Univ. Press.

Lemke, C. E. and J. T. Howson, Jr. (1964). Equilibrium points of bi-matrix games. *SIAM Journal on Applied Mathematics* **12**, 413–423.

Lippman, S. A. and J. J. McCall (1976a). The economics of job search: A survey,

Part I: Optimal job search policies. *Economic Inquiry* **14,** 155–189.
(1976b). The economics of job search: A survey, Part II: Empirical and policy implications of job search. *Economic Inquiry* **14**, 347–368.
Malmgren, H. B. (1961). Information, expectations, and the theory of the firm. *Quarterly Journal of Economics* **75**, 399–421.
March, J. G. and H. A. Simon (1958). *Organization*. New York: Wiley.
Marris, R. (1964). *The Economic Theory of 'Managerial' Capitalism*. New York: Macmillan.
McKenzie, L. W. (1954). On equilibrium in Graham's model of world trade and other competitive systems. *Econometrica* **22**, 147–161.
(1959). On the existence of general equilibrium for a competitive market. *Econometrica* **27**, 54–71. (*See also*: Some corrections. *Econometrica* **29** (1961), 247–248.)
Meade, J. (1972). The theory of labour-managed firms and of profit sharing. *Economic Journal* **82**, 402–428. Reprinted in Vanek (1975), pp. 394–422.
Mertens, J.-F. (1980). A note on the characteristic function of supergames. *International Journal of Game Theory* **9**, 189–190.
(1987). Repeated games. In A. Gleason (ed.), *Proceedings of the International Congress of Mathematicians, Berkeley, California, 1986, Vol. II*, pp. 1528–1577. Providence: American Mathematical Society. Reprinted in T. Ichiishi, A. Neyman and Y. Tauman (eds.), *Game Theory and Applications*, pp. 77–130. New York: Academic Press, 1990.
Michael, E. (1956). Continuous selection I. *Annals of Mathematics* **63**, 361–382.
Milgrom, P. and C. Shannon (1991). Monotone comparative statics. Technical Report No. 11, Stanford Institute for Theoretical Economics, Stanford Univ.
Mo, J.-P. (1988). Entry and structures of interest groups in assignment games. *Journal of Economic Theory* **46**, 66–96.
Modigliani, F. (1944). Liquidity preference and the theory of interest and money. *Econometrica* **12**, 45–88.
Morishima, M. (1947). Shohi-sha katsudo to kigyo-sha katsudo, Jo (Consumer behavior and firm behavior, Part I). *Keizai Ronso* **61**, 84–115 (in Japanese).
(1948). Shohi-sha katsudo to kigyo-sha katsudo, Ge (Consumer behavior and firm behavior, Part II). *Keizai Ronso* **62**, 224–258 (in Japanese).
Moulin, H. (1981a). *Théorie des jeux pour l'économie et la politique*. Paris: Hermann. (English transl.: *Game Theory for the Social Sciences*. Irvington: New York Univ. Press, 1982.)
(1981b). The proportional veto principle. *Review of Economic Studies* **48**, 407–416.
(1982). Voting with proportional veto power. *Econometrica* **50**, 145–162.
(1983). *The Strategy of Social Choice*. Amsterdam: North-Holland,
(1987). A core selection for regulating a single-output monopoly. *Rand Journal of Economics* **18**, 397–407.
(1990). Cores and large cores when population varies. *International Journal of Game Theory* **19**, 219–232.
Moulin, H. and B. Peleg (1982). Cores of effectivity functions and implementation

theory. *Journal of Mathematical Economics* **10**, 115–145.

Moulin, H. and W. Thomson (1988). Can everyone benefit from growth? *Journal of Mathematical Economics* **17**, 339–345.

Mueller, D. C. (1978). Voting by veto. *Journal of Public Economics* **10**, 57–75.

Nash, Jr., J. F. (1950). Equilibrium points in *n*-person games. *Proceedings of the National Academy of Sciences of the U.S.A.* **36**, 48–49.

(1951). Non-cooperative games. *Annals of Mathematics* **54**, 286–295.

Negishi, T. (1960). Welfare economics and existence of an equilibrium for a competitive economy. *Metroeconomica* **12**, 92–97.

Nikaido, H. (1956). On the classical multilateral exchange problem. *Metroeconomica* **8**, 135–145.

(1968). *Convex Structures and Economic Theory*. New York: Academic Press.

Oddou, C. (1976). Théorèmes d'existence et d'equivalence pour des économies avec production. *Econometrica* **44**, 265–281.

Owen, G. (1982). *Game Theory*, 2nd ed. New York: Academic Press.

Oxtoby, J. C. (1971). *Measure and Category*. New York/Heidelberg/Berlin: Springer-Verlag.

Papandreou, A. G. (1952). Some basic problems in the theory of the firm. In B. F. Haley (ed.), *A Survey of Contemporary Economics. Vol. II*, pp. 183–219. Homewood: Irwin.

Peleg, B. (1978). Consistent voting systems. *Econometrica* **46**, 153–161.

(1982). Convex effectivity functions. Research Memorandum No. 46, Center for Research in Mathematical Economics and Game Theory, The Hebrew Univ. of Jerusalem.

(1984a). *Game Theoretic Analysis of Voting in Committees*. Cambridge, U.K.: Cambridge Univ. Press.

(1984b). Core stability and duality of effectivity functions. In G. Hammer and D. Pallaschke (eds.), *Selected Topics in Operations Research and Mathematical Economics*, pp 272–287. New York: Springer-Verlag.

(1985). An axiomatization of the core of cooperative games without side payments. *Journal of Mathematical Economics* **14**, 203–214.

(1986). A proof that the core of an ordinal convex game is a von Neumann-Morgenstern solution. *Mathematical Social Sciences* **11**, 83–87.

(1987). On perfectly coalition-proof Nash equilibria. Research Memorandum No. 79, Center for Research in Mathematical Economics and Game Theory, The Hebrew Univ. of Jerusalem.

(1988/89). *Introduction to the Theory of Cooperative Games*, mimeo., Department of Mathematics, The Hebrew Univ. of Jerusalem.

Prakash, P. and M. R. Sertel (1974). On the existence of noncooperative equilibria in social systems. Discussion Paper No. 92, Center for Mathematical Studies in Economics and Management Science, Northwestern Univ.

Prasnikar, J. and J. Svejnar (1988). Economic behavior of Yugoslav enterprises. In Derek C. Jones and Jan Svejnar (eds.), *Advances in the Economic Analysis of Participatory and Labor Managed Firms, Vol. 3*, pp. 237–311. Greenwich: JAI Press.

Quinzii, M. (1982). An existence theorem for the core of a productive economy with increasing returns. *Journal of Economic Theory* **28**, 32–50.

(1991). *Increasing Returns and Economic Efficiency*. Oxford: Oxford Univ. Press.

Rabie, M. A. (1981). A note on the exact games. *International Journal of Game Theory* **10**, 131–132.

Radner, R. (1968). Competitive equilibrium under uncertainty. *Econometrica* **36**, 31–58.

(1975). Satisficing. *Journal of Mathematical Economics* **2**, 253–262.

(1985). Can bounded rationality resolve the prisoners' dilemma? In W. Hildenbrand, *et al.* (eds.), *Contributions to Mathematical Economics (in Honor of Gerard Debreu)*, pp. 387–399. Amsterdam/New York: North-Holland.

(1986). The large economy of large firms. *Economic Journal* **96**, Supplement, 1–22.

(1992). Transfer payments and the core of a profit-center game. In P. Dasgupta, D. Gale, O. Hart and E. Maskin (eds.). *Economic Analysis of Markets and Games (Essays in Honor of Frank Hahn)*, pp. 316–339. Cambridge, MA: MIT Press.

Rosenmüller, J. (1971). On core and value. *Operations Research Verfahren* **9**, 84–101.

(1975). Large games without side payments. *Operations Research Verfahren* **20**, 107–128.

(1981). *The Theory of Games and Markets*. Amsterdam/New York: North-Holland.

Rosenthal, E. C. (1990). Monotonicity of the core and value in dynamic cooperative games. *International Journal of Game Theory* **19**, 45–57.

Rosenthal, R. W. (1972). Cooperative games in effectiveness form. *Journal of Economic Theory* **5**, 88–101.

Rubinstein, A. (1980). Strong perfect equilibrium in supergames. *International Journal of Game Theory* **9**, 1–12.

Sappington, D. E. M. (1991). Incentives in principal-agent relationships. *Journal of Economic Perspectives* **5**, 45–66.

Scarf, H. (1963). An outline of some results on production and core. Mimeo.

(1967a). The core of an *n*-person game. *Econometrica* **35**, 50–69.

(1967b). The approximation of fixed points of a continuous mapping. *SIAM Journal on Applied Mathematics* **15**, 1328–1342.

(1971). On the existence of a cooperative solution for a general class of *n*-person games. *Journal of Economic Theory* **3**, 169–181.

(1973). *The Computation of Economic Equilibria*. New Haven: Yale Univ. Press.

(1986). Notes on the core of a productive economy. In W. Hildenbrand, *et al.* (eds.), *Contributions to Mathematical Economics (in Honor of Gerard Debreu)*, pp. 401–429. Amsterdam/New York: North-Holland.

Scherer, F. M. (1970). *Industrial Market Structure and Economic Performance*. Chicago: Rand McNally.

Schmeidler, D. (1967). On balanced games with infinitely many players. Research Program in Game Theory and Mathematical Economics, Research Memoran-

dum No. 28, Department of Mathematics, The Hebrew Univ. of Jerusalem.
(1972). Cores of exact games, I. *Journal of Mathematical Analysis and Applications* **40**, 214–225.
(1980). Walrasian analysis via strategic outcome functions. *Econometrica* **48**, 1585–1593.
Schumpeter, J. A. (1911). *Theorie der wirtschaftlichen Entwicklung*. (English transl.: *The Theory of Economic Development*. Cambridge, MA: Harvard Univ. Press, 1934.)
Scotchmer, S. and M. H. Wooders (1988). Monotonicity in games that exhaust gains to scale. Mimeo.
Selten, R. (1975). Reexamination of the perfectness concepts for equilibrium points in extensive games. *International Journal of Game Theory* **4**, 25–55.
Sertel, M. R. (1982). *Workers and Incentives*. Amsterdam/New York: North-Holland.
Shapley, L. S. (1953). A value for *n*-person games. In H. W. Kuhn and A. W. Tucker (eds.), *Contributions to the Theory of Games, Vol. II*, pp. 307–317. Princeton: Princeton Univ. Press.
(1967). On balanced sets and cores. *Naval Research Logistics Quarterly* **14**, 453–460.
(1969). Utility comparison and the theory of games. In *La Décision*, pp. 251–263. Paris: Edition du Centre National de la Recherche Scientifique.
(1971). Cores of convex games. *International Journal of Game Theory* **1**, 11–26.
(1973). On balanced games without side payments. In T. C. Hu and S. M. Robinson (eds.), *Mathematical Programming*, pp. 261–290. New York: Academic Press.
(1987). Lecture Notes. Univ. of California, Los Angeles. Included in Shapley and Vohra (1991).
Shapley, L. S. and M. Shubik (1967). Ownership and production function. *Quarterly Journal of Economics* **81**, 88–111.
Shapley, L. S. and R. Vohra (1991). On Kakutani's fixed point theorem, the K-K-M-S theorem and the core of a balanced game. *Economic Theory* **1**, 108–116.
Sharkey, W. W. (1979). Existence of a core when there are increasing returns. *Econometrica* **47**, 869–876.
(1981). Convex games without side payments. *International Journal of Game Theory* **10**, 101–106.
(1982a). *The Theory of Natural Monopoly*. Cambridge, U.K.: Cambridge Univ. Press.
(1982b). Cooperative games with large cores. *International Journal of Game Theory* **11**, 175–182.
(1989). Game theoretic modeling of increasing returns to scale. *Games and Economic Behavior* **1**, 370–431.
Sharkey, W. W. and L. G. Telser (1978). Supportable cost functions for the multiproduct firm. *Journal of Economic Theory* **18**, 23–37.
Shih, M.-H. and K.-K. Tan (1987a). Covering theorems on convex sets related to fixed-point theorems. In B.-L. Lin and S. Simons (eds.), *Nonlinear and Convex*

Analysis (Proceedings in Honor of Ky Fan), pp. 235–244. New York: Marcel Dekker.

(1987b). Shapley selections and covering theorems of simplexes. In B.-L. Lin and S. Simons (eds.), *Nonlinear and Convex Analysis (Proceedings in Honor of Ky Fan)*, pp. 245–251. New York: Marcel Dekker.

Shubik, M. (1982). *Game Theory in the Social Sciences: Concepts and Solution*. Cambridge, MA: MIT Press.

(1984). *A Game-Theoretic Approach to Political Economy*. Cambridge, MA: MIT Press.

Silver, M. and R. Auster (1969). Entrepreneurship, profit and limits on firm size. *Journal of Business* **42**, 277–281.

Simon, H. A. (1955). A behavioral model of rational choice. *Quarterly Journal of Economics* **69**, 99–118. Reprinted in H. A. Simon, *Models of Man*, pp. 241–260. New York: Wiley.

Sondermann, D. (1974a). Temporary competitive equilibrium under uncertainty. In J. H. Drèze (ed.), *Allocation under Uncertainty: Equilibrium and Optimality*, pp. 229–253. London: Macmillan.

(1974b). Economies of scale and equilibria in coalition production economies. *Journal of Economic Theory* **8**, 259–291.

Sperner, E. (1928). Neuer Beweis für die Invarianz der Dimensionszhal und des Gebietes. *Abhandlungen ans dem Mathematischen Seminar der Universität Hamburg* **6**, 265–272.

Sprumont, Y. (1990). Population monotonic allocation schemes for cooperative games with transferable utility. *Games and Economic Behavior* **2**, 378–394.

Stauss, J. H. (1944). The entrepreneur: The firm. *Journal of Political Economy* **52**, 112–127.

Stigum, B. P. (1969). Competitive equilibria under uncertainty. *Quarterly Journal of Economics* **83**, 533–561.

Suzuki, M. and S. Muto (1985). *Kyoryoku Game no Riron* (*Theory of Cooperative Games*). Tokyo: Univ. of Tokyo Press (in Japanese).

Thomas, H. and C. Logan (1982). *Mondragon: An Economic Analysis*. London: Allen and Unwin.

Tobin, J. (1972). Inflation and unemployment. *American Economic Review* **62**, 1–18.

Todd, M. (1978). Lecture Notes. School of Operations Research and Industrial Engineering, Cornell Univ.

(1979). Private communication.

Topkis, D. M. (1987). Activity optimization games with complementarity. *European Journal of Operations Research* **28**, 358–368.

Tychonoff, A. (1935). Ein Fixpunktsatz. *Mathematische Annalen* **111**, 767–776.

Vanek, Jan (1972). *The Economics of Workers' Management: A Yugoslav Case Study*. London: Allen and Unwin.

Vanek, Jaroslav (1970). *The General Theory of Labor-Managed Market Economies*. Ithaca: Cornell Univ. Press.

(1975). *Self-Management: Economic Liberation of Man*. Harmondsworth: Penguin.

Vilkov, V. B. (1977). Convex games without side payments. *Vestnik Leningradskiva University* **7**, 21–24 (in Russian).

Vohra, R. (1987). On Scarf's theorem on non-emptiness of the core: A direct proof through Kakutani's fixed-point theorem. Working Paper No. 87–2, Department of Economics, Brown Univ. Included in Shapley and Vohra (1991).

Von Neumann, J. and Morgenstern, O. (1947). *Theory of Games and Economic Behavior*. 2nd ed. Princeton: Princeton Univ. Press.

Walkup, D. W. and R. J.-B. Wets (1969). Lifting projections of convex polyhedra. *Pacific Journal of Mathematics* **28**, 465–475.

Ward, B. (1958). The firm in Illyria: Market syndicalism. *American Economic Review* **48**, 566–589.

Weber, M. (1922). *Wirtschaft und Gesellschaft. Grundriss der verstehenden Soziologie*, Tübingen: J. C. B. Mohr. (English transl.: *Economy and Society: An Outline of Interpretive Sociology*. New York: Bedminster Press, 1968.)

Weber, R. J. (1988). Probabilistic values for games. In A. E. Roth (ed.), *The Shapley Value (Essays in Honor of Lloyd S. Shapley)*, pp. 101–119. Cambridge, U.K.: Cambridge Univ. Press.

Weber, S. (1981). Some results on the weak core of a non-side-payment game with infinitely many players. *Journal of Mathematical Economics* **8**, 101–111.

Williamson, O. E. (1964). *The Economics of Discretionary Behavior*. Englewood Cliffs: Prentice-Hall.

(1975). *Markets and Hierarchies: Analysis and Antitrust Implications*. New York: Free Press.

(1985). *The Economic Institutions of Capitalism: Firms, Markets, Relational Contracting*. New York: Free Press.

Winter, Jr., S. G. (1971). Satisficing selection, and the innovating remnant. *Quarterly Journal of Economics* **85**, 237–261.

Yano, M. (1990). A local theory of cooperative games. *International Journal of Game Theory* **19**, 301–324.

Yanovskaya, E. B. (1971/72). Cores of noncooperative games. *International Journal of Game Theory* **1**, 209–215.

Young, H. P. (1985a). *Cost Allocation: Methods, Principles, Applications*. Amsterdam: North-Holland.

(1985b). Monotonic solutions of cooperative games. *International Journal of Game Theory* **14**, 65–72.

Zermelo, E. (1913). Über eine Anwendung der Mengenlehre auf die Theorie des Schachspiels. In E. W. Hobson and A. E. H. Love (eds.), *Proceedings of the Fifth International Congress of Mathematicians, Cambridge, England, 1912, Vol. II*, pp. 501–504. Cambridge, U.K.: Cambridge Univ. Press.

Zhao, J. (1992). The hybrid solutions of an n-person game. *Games and Economic Behavior* **4**, 145–160.

Zhou, L. (1990). An equilibrium existence lemma for n-person games and its applications. Mimeo.

Author Index

Subject index